BEEN COMING THROUGH
SOME HARD TIMES

Race, History, and Memory
in Western Kentucky

JACK GLAZIER

THE UNIVERSITY OF TENNESSEE PRESS / KNOXVILLE

Library of Congress Cataloging-in-Publication Data

Glazier, Jack.
Been coming through some hard times: race, history, and memory in western Kentucky / Jack
Glazier. — 1st ed.
      p. cm.
Includes bibliographical references and index.
ISBN 978-1-57233-915-6 (hardcover) — ISBN 1-57233-915-2 (hardcover)

    1. Hopkinsville (Ky.)—Race relations—History.
    2. Racism—Kentucky—Hopkinsville—History.
    3. Collective memory—Kentucky—Hopkinsville.
    4. African Americans—Kentucky—Hopkinsville—History.
    5. Whites—Kentucky—Hopkinsville—History.
    6. Christian County (Ky.)—Race relations—History.
    7. Racism—Kentucky—Christian County—History.
    8. Collective memory—Kentucky—Christian County.
    9. African Americans—Kentucky—Christian County—History.
   10. Whites—Kentucky—Christian County—History.
    I. Title.

F459.H8G63 2012
305.896'073076978—dc23
                    2012028808

In loving memory of

IDELLA BASS RICHARDSON

CONTENTS

ILLUSTRATIONS

FIGURES

Howard and Ammie McCray Weaver, 2002

Francis Eugene Whitney at his real estate office, Hopkinsville, 2002

MAP

PREFACE

This story has several beginnings. The most recent occurred in the summer of 2001. I had just completed my thirtieth year of teaching anthropology at Oberlin College, where much of what I taught was shaped by my research experiences, first in East Africa, and then from the 1980s forward, the United States, particularly in regard to immigrants and immigration. I had taken something of a break from writing and research following the publication at the end of the 1990s of a book that was several years in the making. Following my completion of an earlier book and related articles on East Africa in the mid-1980s, I asked myself, "What next?" and in 2001 asked the same question.

Among the social sciences and humanities, anthropology is a peculiar kind of discipline, both vocation and avocation, as the great savant Claude Levi-Strauss has told us. Its style of research, participant-observation, over a long term within a community is deeply personal. Eschewing questionnaires and other mediating devices of the social sciences, cultural anthropologists prefer instead to make themselves the primary data-gathering instrument and in so doing are apt to learn as much about themselves as about the people with whom they live and build relationships. The best anthropology gains its substance from these two very different but related levels of understanding. As a veteran producer and reader of anthropology, I am much more interested in the story the anthropologist has to tell about other people than about himself. The excesses of narcissism in the United States, brilliantly identified by Christopher Lasch in the 1970s, regrettably remain very much with us, and anthropology particularly, among the human sciences, has indulged itself in a sometimes unseemly exhibitionism. Still, the anthropologist remains a presence in his text, especially given the personal nature of the research, and some reasonable acknowledgment is desirable, which this preface intends. The aim of this book, however, is to illuminate the lives of others, not to trade on reflexivity, personal discovery, or other self-absorbed conceits of the postmodern world.

My research in East Africa centered on a rural community of small farmers and herders whose practices and beliefs challenged my abilities to understand and to live in an utterly unfamiliar place, which after all is what anthropologists do. After many months, my friendships across a vast cultural divide enabled me to comprehend the dramatic changes and human issues facing the community. Yet documenting and interpreting that way of life as objectively as possible left little room or relevance for including anything personal beyond my detached narrator's voice. Even my identification with generous and welcoming informants and neighbors was the kind of fiction deeply embedded in my profession, for I would ultimately take my leave from these relationships in order to return to the familiar cultural patterns of home.

In a very different vein, following my last field trip to Kenya, I began research and writing on the early twentieth century immigration to the United States and the ensuing dilemmas of belongingness and alienation faced by the newcomers and especially their children. I was as spare in my use of the first person as I had been in my earlier ethnographic research in a Kenyan community.

Yet my identification with the subject matter of immigration was nearly complete. My Russian-born parents had settled in Indianapolis, a relentlessly "all American city," predominantly white and Protestant, with relatively few immigrants. Their seven children felt the recurrent sting of second-generation marginality and the continuing pressure to negotiate a life in two worlds. We succumbed to the nearly irresistible pressures to assimilate as much as possible into a mainstream that at the same time lost few opportunities to tell us who we really were—Jews from the other, alien side of Europe with shallow roots in the new country. The elder Glazier sons, entering World War II combat in Europe, encountered in those particularly ironic circumstances, menacing reminders from other American servicemen that Jews were nothing but "Clorox niggers." Nonetheless, in fits and starts, we were on our way to becoming "white."

Another person in my family was neither Jewish nor European. Her roots in American soil could not have been deeper. Neither white nor on her way to becoming so, she exercised a formative and enduring influence on the lives of the younger Glazier siblings. Idella Bass was born in 1891 in southwestern Kentucky in Hopkinsville, some twenty miles from the Tennessee border. Her father was James Walter Bass, born into slavery on the eve of the Civil War in neighboring Todd County. Ambitious and entrepreneurial, he founded his own business, the City Laundry, in Princeton, Indiana, in 1881, and again facing down the odds he attended Oberlin College for two years in the mid-1880s. After Oberlin, James Bass returned to Princeton and reopened his laundry, at which point Oberlin College lost contact with him. Newly hired by Oberlin College in 1971, I spent my first day on the campus in the Archives and in the Office of Alumni Records trying to uncover James Bass's footprints, which once again I was crossing.

The Bass family began in Hopkinsville when James Bass settled there following his marriage to Johnnie Fiser of Springfield, Tennessee, in 1890. Her very light complexion embodied the mix of white, Cherokee, and African American ancestry that her formerly enslaved parents bequeathed to their children. Johnnie Fiser in turn passed to some of her children, including Idella Bass, the visibility of mixed ancestry that skin color records. James and Johnnie Bass remained in Hopkinsville, where they set for themselves and their children a determined course "up from slavery."

The Basses' eldest child, Idella, joined the great migration north in 1910, the first of her seven brothers and sisters to do so. She left for Chicago to enroll in secondary school because her hometown of Hopkinsville refused for another half decade to build a black high school. Idella Bass informed her father of her desire to become a nurse in order to help children and old people, and as she told us many times, her father encouraged her to aim higher and become a doctor. Embarking on this formidable course, she had to attend high school and therefore would have to leave Hopkinsville. The historical and cultural significance of James Bass's attendance at Oberlin, the extraordinary encouragement a former slave gave his young daughter in apartheid America of the early twentieth century, and the indomitable confidence and courage that underlay it all were utterly lost on me as a young person. Now half a lifetime later, I hope to recover the value and significance of these events in the pages that follow, for this small example of a father's advice to his daughter a century ago demands attention. While his advice was certainly exceptional, his goal of self-improvement for himself and his children was emblematic of a powerful drive toward accomplishment that marked so many African American lives in those first decades after slavery. Even now, popular representations of the black past still play on stereotypic images that ignore the reality of highly motivated black educational achievement.

Idella Bass's move to Chicago occurred five years after my father arrived in Indianapolis from what is now Belarus and three years prior to the settlement there of my mother and her family following their steerage voyage from little Ostroleke in Russia-Poland, by way of Hamburg. My parents married in 1922 and by 1929 had three little boys and a daughter on the way. They managed to earn a very modest living with only the rudiments of education and little in the way of useful skills. By the late 1920s, my mother had to spend more time working—purchasing fruits and vegetables from farmers and wholesalers in the early morning and selling the produce at the downtown city market. To care for the children, Idella Bass joined the household, entering into our lives and we into hers.

Prior to her move to Indianapolis, she had completed high school in Chicago as planned, but a dreadful accident in 1920 in the commercial laundry where she worked dashed her dreams of a medical or nursing career, though not her spirit. She lost through amputation the lower portion of her badly damaged right forearm, which she had caught in a large steam press. In 2001, twenty-eight years after her death, I found the answer to my question, "What next?" With this research project, personal factors once again helped to shape my research interests. That Hopkinsville ultimately yielded a particularly rich history was all the more gratifying.

In earliest childhood, I learned of Hopkinsville, Kentucky, and the lives of its black population. I intended, long before becoming an anthropologist, to visit the town, to walk about, to see the places important in Idella Bass's early life—the Freeman Chapel of the Christian Methodist Episcopal (C. M. E) Church, the Bass family property, "billy goat hill" on the East Side not far from Hays Street where Mr. Bass purchased the family's first house in 1890— and to find, if possible, any people who might have remembered the Basses. That anyone in Hopkinsville would recall the family was unlikely. No Bass relatives remained in town, and James and Johnnie Bass had both died in the middle 1920s, about a decade after their last child crossed the Ohio River. I found time to visit Hopkinsville in August 2001 and to pose some of the questions a less callow youth might have asked Idella Bass directly. Fortuitously, F. E. Whitney, about whom I write, was the sole person to recall Mr. Bass.

Research for this book was thus initially motivated by a desire to recover a personally meaningful part of the American past and to craft a biography of the Bass family. Many small, scattered pieces, however, proved insufficient to the task. Still, I can limn a picture of one black family a century ago. Although the sketch exists only in dim outline, it takes on a depth and clarity when considered in relation to the larger racial history of Hopkinsville and the experiences of other black families revealed in the research. They too survived within the tight strictures of a severely segregated society when every domain of social life was sorted by race and graded by color.

Writing of local "racial history" is really a redundancy, for the hierarchy of race has underpinned the economic, political, and social arrangements that have sustained the town since its founding at the end of the eighteenth century. More than forty years after the momentous changes of the 1960s, a local white official confided to me on condition of anonymity and with some embarrassment that in Hopkinsville every decision made by city government is, in one way or another, about race. He was not referring to affirmative action. For black people, this is a simple truism, manifested in many ways, including the differential distribution of city services and the deterioration through neglect of old neighborhoods. There are also the subtle indignities that express old racial attitudes, less menacing and obvious than in the past but nonetheless persistent. Matters of race are at the least implicit in the public discourse, and, while the latter can no longer remain deaf to the voices of black people, many individuals are indifferent. Historically, representations of black people have cast them as stereotypic figures in a southern tableau rather than as actors and narrators in their own right on the stages of their own setting, including churches, lodges, family circles and reunions, friendship groups, and the like. The echoes of the past continue to reverberate in the black conversations of the present. It is to those active voices, past and present, and the experiences they record, that this book attends.

ACKNOWLEDGMENTS

I acknowledge with thanks the Office of the President and the Research and Development Committee of Oberlin College and the American Philosophical Society for grants in support of my research in its several phases. I am also grateful for the assistance of the following research institutions and libraries: the University of Chicago Library (Special Collections), the National Archives, the Filson Historical Society, the Kentucky Historical Society, the Disciples of Christ Historical Society, the Duke University Library (Special Collections), the Kentucky State University Archives, Western Kentucky University (Kentucky Library), the Kentucky Wesleyan College Archives, the Kentucky Department for Libraries and Archives, the Tennessee State Library and Archives, and the Amistad Research Center. I am grateful, as always, for the assistance of the Oberlin College Library and Archives. Thanks are also due in Hopkinsville to the Hopkinsville-Christian County Public Library, the Christian County Historical Society, and the Pennyroyal Area Museum.

Any cultural anthropologist engaged in fieldwork inevitably incurs many debts to his host community for cooperation, assistance, and all around forbearance, and I may have sustained more than my share of obligations. I especially want to thank the congregants of Freeman Chapel in Hopkinsville, where I first became acquainted with the African American community. I initially met Reverend Carsten Shanklin and Betty Shanklin, who kindly invited me to join the church community. I appreciate the generous reception accorded me by many people. Particular thanks are due Pat Rogers, Dorothy Howell, Jacob White, Jessie Morgan, Ed Owens, Gerald Reed, Sam Adams III, Dorothy Bibb, Emma and James Jordan, and Trevor Hooks for their warm welcome. I also became well acquainted with many other people, black and white, in Hopkinsville who in ways that may not always be obvious contributed to my understandings of local history and culture. I am particularly indebted to Jim Killebrew for his generosity in sharing insights from his own research on local history, especially through his transcription of the Ellen Kenton McGaughey Wallace journal, available to researchers at the Kentucky Historical Society. With gratitude,

I want to acknowledge the help of Wynn Radford, Jessie Quarles, Patricia Bell, Wally Bryan, Daryll Lynch, Linda Wood, Fred Atkins, Marby Schlegel, Walter Shamble, Jennifer Brown, Sarah Nance, Thelma and Edward Moore, Paulette and Anthony Robinson, and Shirley Shelton. Special thanks to Martha Thomas of Evansville, Indiana, for introducing me to the McCray kindred and to the Nances, who brought me into the Bingham family circle. The late Margaret Bass Wilkerson of Evansville generously shared Bass family photos with me as well as stories about her grandfather, James Walter Bass.

The interest and support of friends and colleagues in Oberlin and elsewhere were very valuable. I'm grateful to Bob Soucy, Marly Merrill, Guneli Gun, and Renee Romano for reading and commenting on portions of the manuscript. I benefited from conversations with Roland Bauman and Gary Kornblith on our shared interests in black history. I deepened my understanding of African American religion in discussions with A. G. Miller. Ehrai Adams, a native of Hopkinsville, provided much insight on the process of school desegregation. I want to thank Kathy McCardwell, Elia Gilbert, Will Griscom, Daniel Klepacz, Sarvnaz Lotfi, Nina Moffitt, Emma Gormley, and Adam Beaudoin, outstanding Oberlin graduates who at various times were my research assistants. I also benefited from discussions with colleagues in anthropology, including Baron Pineda and, beyond Oberlin, Rubie Watson, Harriet Ottenheimer, Alice Kehoe, and Claude Jacobs. I also want to acknowledge the interest and early help of the late Kathleen A. Hauke, an independent scholar devoted to understanding Hopkinsville's African American community, and the Poston family in particular. I deeply regret that she died before the completion of this book.

My companion and colleague, Heidi Thomann Tewarson briefly shared the fieldwork experience with me. Her keen reading of the manuscript brought to bear a thoughtful and fresh view of race in America from a European vantage point. Her scholarship on Toni Morrison gave me new insights into a very old problem. I am also deeply grateful for her continuing encouragement over the long course of research and writing.

Finally, thanks are due to Scot Danforth, Director of the University of Tennessee Press, for his strong support and his assistance and advice in bringing the manuscript to publication.

Jack Glazier
Oberlin, Ohio
November 7, 2011

INTRODUCTION

This book represents a sustained effort to understand race relations over time in Hopkinsville and Christian County, Kentucky. Part contemporary ethnography and part history, it examines how black people and white people construe in very different ways their experience, both shared and separate, in the social universe of the town. There, the past weighs heavily, even amid the continuing transitions to a new racial landscape, including an expanding black middle class and increasing political empowerment over the past four and a half decades. Hopkinsville lends itself remarkably well to a study of continuity and change in race relations and attitudes because from the Civil War to the present the descendants of slaves and the descendants of slave owners have continued to inhabit the same social and historic space. The town, in other words, is unusually amenable to an examination of history, memory, and the cultural present as they pertain to race, which remains the most fraught issue in the American experience.

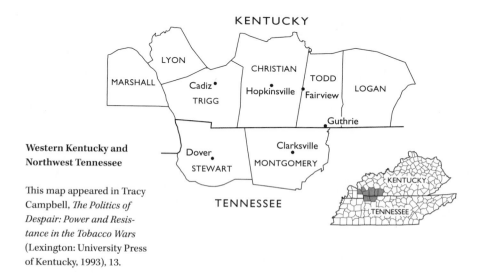

Western Kentucky and Northwest Tennessee

This map appeared in Tracy Campbell, *The Politics of Despair: Power and Resistance in the Tobacco Wars* (Lexington: University Press of Kentucky, 1993), 13.

As an anthropologist, I conducted fieldwork in Hopkinsville for some ten months, comprising several summers and a continuous residence of five months in 2005. I concentrated on heretofore largely neglected black perspectives and the black experience in the town and county. On my first visit, I attended a worship service at Freeman Chapel of the Christian Methodist Episcopal Church (CME). The pastor, with whom I had spoken in advance about attending the service, called on me to introduce myself and to tell the congregants what had brought me to the town and to the church. I explained that I wanted to trace the history of a family that had lived in Hopkinsville long ago and belonged to the Freeman Chapel. I described some of the major events in James Bass's life, including his origins in slavery; his education at Oberlin College; and his determined move toward economic independence, first as a businessman in Princeton, Indiana, and eventually as a householder, small farmer, and landowner in Hopkinsville. Many congregants recognized that the Bass family exemplified values and life goals widely distributed among Hopkinsville's African Americans in the early decades of the last century.

My reception at Freeman Chapel was very welcoming. Of course, I am well aware of a particular southern style of politeness and graceful civility that cuts across the racial divide and might well have come my way regardless of what I had said. Later, I was invited to join the church, and on each of my stays in town I was a regular at the Sunday service. Early on, I began to work outward from a familiar network of informants at the church, who in many cases became good friends over the course of my field visits and beyond the research. I became a fixture at community events, including city council meetings and forums at the Virginia Street Baptist Church next door to Freeman Chapel. These forums addressed issues such as education and the state of the schools, as well as relations between the police and the black community. They attracted large, interested audiences of African American and white citizens. I was invited to church suppers and family reunions, as well as to dinners with Freeman Chapel congregants, all the while appreciating their interest in my many questions. The continuing cooperation and engagement in my research was quite obviously something more than simple politeness. My relationships were not restricted to African Americans; I met a number of white townspeople as a result of my attendance at numerous community-wide meetings. I spoke extensively with white genealogists and local historians associated with the Christian County Historical Society who kindly made available to me some results of their own investigations. They in turn introduced me to their friends and colleagues. I also got well acquainted with several white and black members of the city council.

Ethnographic research strategies in this study remained informal, depending only on participant-observation and minimally directed informant interviews, which resembled low intensity conversations more than the stuff of strict social science procedure. A formal method based on a schedule of prefabricated questions would have failed to achieve my purpose—to understand local viewpoints about matters that community members, rather than the anthropologist, define as important. An anthropologist, in other words, tends to follow his informants in discerning from them what the relevant questions are. In the related matter of "sampling," or "informant selection," the canons of sociological method are not well suited to much of what occurs in ethnographic research. That is, members of a community, to a greater extent than is conventionally acknowledged, select the anthropologist, rather than vice versa. People do not cooperate unless they are so inclined. Moreover, informants quickly understood that I had nothing to teach or to impart and everything to learn, a largely novel experience for African Americans speaking with someone who, at least by appearance, was part of the racial majority.

As an anthropologist builds rapport with people in a community, he or she also begins to discover its particular qualities. That is, "place" is fundamental to anthropology because a field worker seeks to understand the defining characteristics of the community where research proceeds. "Place" thus implies much more than locale or a point on a map. It is where a discernible history, social and political relations, and a particular economic infrastructure combine to set a community, town, or region apart from others. The art of anthropological research is well suited to tracing distinct social contours of a place, for it enables the participant-observer to comprehend highly localized social arrangements and perspectives, staying in close touch with the concerns of people day by day through close listening and careful observation. Those understandings help the anthropologist draw an ethnographic portrait of a community. Simultaneously, because any question about local culture, or place, is perforce an inquiry into history, this study is acutely attuned to how contemporary Hopkinsville has taken shape. Accordingly, the historiography of the South, of race, of memory, and of civil rights apprehended through documentary and archival research and oral history is central to this study.

Race remains an abiding and divisive feature of the social, political, and economic landscape of Hopkinsville and environs, as it does in so many other places. In this regard, the town is not unique but rather may be taken as an American microcosm, for black people and white people throughout the United States have long inhabited separate domains. Those distinct social worlds, to be sure, intersected at various points, predominantly in a racially skewed labor market. But in the main, a deeply entrenched segregation both by law and by custom severely restricted the kinds of interactions that might permit people of different races to know each other in truly human terms. They still do not for the most part, a bleak reminder that integration mandated by law has yet to realize its loftier promises. Mitigated in recent decades and no longer sanctioned by law, racial separation in space and in mind continues to bedevil social and political life in Hopkinsville, as elsewhere. Separation, residentially and socially, can nurture "quiet racism." In Christian County and in Kentucky generally, where immigration has not had a major demographic or social impact, the polarity of black and white appears all the more stark and has been characterized as "biracial balkanization."[1] Since the 1960s, penetrating understandings of race and the violent, exclusionary underpinnings of the American past have made their way into a public discourse that would hardly admit them prior to that time. Yet that discourse remains contentious, as the fetters of our deeply racialized history continue to grip the present.

Understanding the dynamics of race in this corner of western Kentucky, then, requires a tacking back and forth between the particularities of place and the broader historical and social processes of which they are a part. Each place lives with the burden of its own history, and antecedent practices and beliefs accordingly constrain future possibilities. In this regard, historians and anthropologists walk in the footsteps of Karl Marx and Franz Boas, two very different social theorists for whom this profound insight was fundamental. Faulkner, too, in an artistic rather than social science vein, offered a similar interpretation of the force of established custom when he observed that the so-called dead past was neither dead nor past.

The weight of tradition thus exercises considerable influence on institutional arrangements, the organization of social life, and the design of memory. Yet, paradoxically perhaps, the present also determines the past, or rather the way the past is remembered. What historians and anthropologists call historical memory—the popular or vernacular portrayals of history—is inevitably filtered by present-day interests, values, and conventional understandings. This book, then, joins anthropology to history for several purposes. It aims to depict a contemporary community in the Upper South; the ways in which the past bears on a racially divided communal present; and the manner in which the present is projected backward by racially segmented historical memories. At the same time, the union of anthropology and history demonstrates how western Kentucky represents one revealing chapter of a much larger American story. The chapters that follow do not provide a comprehensive history of the town, county, or region from the Civil War period until the present, nor has that been my intent. Accordingly, some years within that century and a half receive light treatment. Instead, I focus on particular events and people at various points in time in order to describe and analyze the interplay of race and power, the leitmotif of the area for its entire history.

For reasons of ecology, economy, and history, Hopkinsville and Christian County are much more closely akin to the Deep South than to the Upper South of which they are geographically a part. The transportation networks and the nearby Tennessee and Cumberland Rivers oriented the economy southward rather than toward Louisville and Lexington, the distant population centers to the northeast. A political economy weighted toward plantation agriculture in the southern portion of the county bordering Tennessee depended on large slave populations to raise tobacco, a remarkably successful cultigen demanding highly intensive labor at each stage of its development. On the eve of the Civil War, slaves numbered nearly 50 percent of the total county population. In 1860, Christian County had the highest ratio of slaves to slave owners of all Kentucky counties, exceeding some of the state ratios of the old Confederacy. Plantation agriculture, uncommon in Kentucky outside of Christian and other western counties, resembled patterns of production more characteristic of the cotton growing regions of the Deep South.

With the end of the Civil War and the emancipation of Kentucky slaves, a small number of Christian County freedmen managed to secure their own land, but the vast majority worked as agricultural field hands, sharecroppers, or tenant farmers, and, in the town, as laborers or domestic servants. While slavery ended, the supremacy of white people and their economic and political domination continued, adapted to postbellum circumstances. This of course was not unique to Christian County; it characterized the South in general and much of the North for another century, until significant legal change began to dismantle the institutions of American apartheid. But it is the "rich history," alluded to in the Preface, that yields the distinctive story I hope to tell of race and power in one place from the Civil War era until the present. Even amid transformative change, the course of black-white relations taken up in the pages that follow exposes a remarkable continuity of beliefs and practices forged long ago.

White residents of Hopkinsville and Christian County were decidedly sympathetic to the preservation of slavery, even if they were Unionists. In this light, the unpublished journal of Ellen McGaughey Wallace, written between 1849 and 1865, reveals the world of a Hopkinsville slave owner, including her attitudes toward slaves and slavery as an institution. Her journal provides considerable insight into the most profound fear of the slave owner—insurrection. Hopkinsville lay close to the epicenter of white panic in 1856, which resonated through much of the South due to a rumor of a slave rebellion set for Christmas Day. What I term the "terror of imagination" resulted in horrific reprisals against the alleged plotters. To this day, historic markers, as well as popular knowledge, continue to accept as unchallenged fact the chimera of a slave insurrection in 1856.[2]

Wallace and others committed to slavery as an institution found the idea of black freedom nearly inconceivable, despite the presence in Hopkinsville of a few manumitted slaves, some of whom had purchased their freedom from money their masters permitted them to earn. These free blacks lived highly restricted lives—"slaves without masters" in the apt words of Ira Berlin.[3] White people regarded the mere presence of manumitted blacks as dangerous, for they were proximate, living examples to the slave majority of black freedom. Defenders of slavery for the most part saw only two possibilities for bondsmen in their midst. The vast majority would remain slaves; those manumitted would gain only exiled freedom in Liberia. When Wallace was ruminating in the 1850s about slave loyalty and resistance, a small number of slave owners in the county emancipated some bondsmen prior to consigning them to the Kentucky branch of the American Colonization Society for resettlement in Liberia. The missionary motives behind the manumission of Hopkinsville's most notable emigrant to Liberia, Alexander Cross, and the laudatory terms by which his passivity and pliability are described provide an unusually clear contrast to Wallace's anxious descriptions of what she feared most in her slaves—the conscious, active resistance to their condition.

The Wallace journal and other historical sources concerning slave insurrection, or even less extreme forms of active resistance to the master's will, lay bare a fundamental contradiction in the worldview of the slave owning elite. On the one hand, they described slaves living in happy passivity and their own paternalistic feelings, exemplified by their portrayal of Alexander Cross; on the other hand, they feared slave rebellion, which assumed an active, violent, and conspiratorial potential latent within every bondsman. Hence the ubiquity of security patrols around Christian County and indeed throughout the South. "The slave," in the words of John Hope Franklin "was never so completely subjugated as to allay all fears that he would make a desperate, bloody attempt to destroy the institution to which he was bound."[4]

This contradiction is part of a much larger issue affecting the understanding of African American life in the century after the Civil War. That issue centers on "agency," or the self-determined, active shaping of individual and communal lives, as opposed to reactive responses to white design and paternalism. The evidence from Hopkinsville points to a continuing effort by black people to shape their collective present and futures at each point in history, although their room for maneuver was severely limited by white political and economic control. In the immediate aftermath of the Civil War, newly freed bondsmen strived to build an African American community, starting with schools, churches, cemeteries, and later other institutions. They did so in the face of wholesale terror instigated against them by enraged supporters of the defeated Confederacy. In regard to religion, for example, they might have continued one of the worship patterns established during slavery, when they could attend white churches under the strictest rules of segregation. White churches were supportive of the idea, but newly free men and women chose to strike out on their own and form black congregations under black control. They had developed in slavery their own versions of Christianity that could only reach their fullest expression in churches they had designed. Moreover, the black church was vital in asserting common purpose, dignity, and meaning in the collective lives of freedmen and in providing sanctuary from the pervasive antagonism and denigration of the racial majority. Indeed, African American culture is built on the foundation of the black church.[5]

While freedom led directly to an emergent civil status for black people after 1865, the demise of slavery enraged many whites. Persistent antebellum racial custom, local and state laws, and violence combined to suppress the aspirations of black people. The records of the Kentucky Freedmen's Bureau document the earliest efforts to terrorize freedmen in Christian County and statewide. Black fear of raw white racial power took root early on in black historic memory through the bloody suppression of the imagined slave rebellion of 1856 and in post–Civil War reprisals against freedmen for being free, or for serving in the federal army, or for seeking an independent living. Yet white representations of race relations throughout the history of the town and county depict a harmonious, cooperative racial order. The idea of a friendly accord extending over the black-white divide is in part a fictive legacy of the Old South, now purged of its more overt racism. Nonetheless, the outlook associated with white southern heritage remains present, along with resistance to it, a reminder that the sensibility of Civil War memory continues to be palpable in and around Hopkinsville.

It is a matter of no small significance, historic and contemporary, that Jefferson Davis was born in Fairview, a small hamlet just nine miles from Hopkinsville. Of the many physical markers commemorating the Civil War, ranging from cemetery headstones to historic plaques scattered throughout Christian County and western Kentucky, none is more dramatic than the Davis Monument, a towering obelisk two-thirds the size of the Washington Monument. An enduring symbol of the Lost Cause, it is the site of the annual celebration of Davis's birthday each June 3rd, also known in Kentucky as Confederate Memorial Day. The commemoration was unusually large in 2008, when the Davis bicentennial was observed. The physical symbols of Civil War memory in western Kentucky, such as the Davis Monument and historic site, are predominantly paeans to the Confederacy and southern heritage. Erected with public and private money and completed in 1924, the Davis Monument is the most visible of many sites that recall a highly racialized southern past that in its sharpest contrasts now polarizes a small but vocal neo-Confederate movement and equally vociferous African Americans. Many locales of commemoration serve a dual purpose; they encode prevailing attitudes at their creation while also symbolizing contemporary political viewpoints that update and sanitize old beliefs about valor, heritage, states' rights, and loyal slaves.

The interplay of race and power underlies the historic lack of resources or public support for preserving or objectifying through monuments an African American rendering of the past from the Civil War to the present. Black people in western Kentucky and elsewhere have instead relied on other mnemonics, particularly rituals and narratives, to represent very different versions of southern heritage, race, and exclusion. The absence of monumental commemoration of African American history came into sharp focus in 2006, when the Toni Morrison Society inaugurated the "Bench by the Road Project." The society plans to put up benches at places important in African American history to prompt remembrance of slavery as well as critical events over the next century and a half. In 1989, Morrison described the lack of historical markers recalling the lives of slaves, saying, "There is no place you or I can go, to think about or not think about, to summon the presences of, or recollect the absences of slaves . . . There is no suitable memorial, or plaque, or wreath, or wall, or park, or skyscraper lobby. There's no 300-foot tower, there's no small bench by the road. There is not even a tree scored, an initial that I can visit or you can visit in Charleston or Savannah or New York or Providence or better still on the banks of the Mississippi. And because such a place doesn't exist . . . the book [*Beloved*] had to."[6]

The dynamics of race and power also explain not only historical amnesia, but also African American disappointments in the living memory of many people in Hopkinsville. As the story of town and county unfolds from the Civil War–era through a century of Jim Crow, of freedom without equality, to the modern movement for African American inclusion and freedom with equality, the more immediate events shaping contemporary thinking are also important. Included here is the retrospective criticism by black people of a number of features of school integration, the 1972 city council vote preventing the black mayor pro tem from becoming mayor when the office was vacated, the rejection by a racially divided city council in 1996 of a proposal to rename a street after Martin Luther King Jr., and the inequities of the justice system. The critique of a plan for inner city improvement in housing and infrastructure, particularly, brings into focus the import of class difference in inhibiting movement toward an American multiculture. In each instance, different "readings" of events vary, although not absolutely, along the lines of race, still the most salient identity among African Americans. Beyond turning the cold light of analysis onto the relationship between historical memory and historical facts, the contest over truth telling presents a grimly ironic index of the current state of race relations so many decades after the great legal triumphs on behalf of civic participation and civil rights.

COUNTY AND TOWN:
RACE AND A USABLE PAST

This chapter pursues the theme of "place" taken up in the Introduction. The story of the county and the town begins with the interrelationship between slavery and tobacco, an association accounting for the area's very large black population on the eve of the Civil War and continuing to the present. The discussion considers the characteristic features of the town, and the domination of economic and political life by the racial majority that, toward the end of the nineteenth century, began to assimilate a small European immigrant population into the white category. That domination also included access to and public representation of the past. A formidable challenge in overcoming historical amnesia has thus confronted anyone trying to enlarge the record of African American life and to hear black voices within it. Moreover, for black people in particular, locating a usable past has been vital in promoting self-esteem, mutual respect across the divide of race, and inclusion, both in civic affairs and in the public discourse. Here, "usable past" refers to a confident cultural self-awareness, making possible communal engagement and self-representation—a process that continues. Hardly unique to Hopkinsville, where it took on locally distinct contours, indifference to the highly constricted historical record of a disparaged minority was national in scope; moreover, the very possibility of a distinctly black usable past was widely doubted. Consequently, this discussion will continue to tack between local versions of black exclusion from history and broader patterns of which they were a part. These are fundamentally issues of authority and power, for knowledge and cultural-historical representation of one's community are surely as implicated in politics as are voting and civil rights.

AGRICULTURE, DEMOGRAPHY, ECOLOGY

Agriculture has been a dominant feature in Christian County history, and the county remains a center of extensive farming. Each growing season one sees across the rolling plains vast expanses of wheat, corn, and soybeans. The county has consistently ranked near the top in the production of these crops, as well as dark tobacco. Although the importance of the latter crop has diminished in recent decades, reminders of its once prominent place in the local economy are still evident. Particularly striking are the barns that belch out smoke as if the entire structure were about to go up in flames. Dark tobacco is cured by burning hardwoods within an enclosed shed, and what appears to be an impending conflagration is the highly controlled burning process before the cured dark leaf tobacco can be taken to market.

The number of farms raising tobacco has diminished, a trend reproduced in every tobacco-growing state since the mid-1950s, mainly because the market for tobacco has changed drastically in recent decades.[1] Historically, tobacco was a very attractive crop, since per acre earnings far exceeded the return on other crops. However, tobacco production has resisted mechanization, and the labor required usually exceeds the number of local people willing to do that difficult work. Increasingly, Latin American farm workers make up the difference. While fewer farmers are cultivating ever larger farms, tobacco acreage constitutes only a small portion of the total.

Given the labor intensity and the extent of tobacco production in Christian County up to the Civil War, the demography of slavery differed significantly from the statewide norm. Conventionally, Kentucky slavery has been portrayed as a modest enterprise ultimately determined by a rural economy not given to the kind of large-scale agricultural production characteristic of the cotton regions of the Deep South. In 1860, Kentucky slave owners across the state held on average 5.83 slaves, a number compatible with small to mid-level farming and domestic or service work, either on farms or in towns. Among slave states on the eve of the Civil War, only Delaware, Maryland, and Missouri—all Border States like Kentucky—had smaller ratios of slaves to owners.

By contrast, the ratio of slaves to slave owners in Christian County in 1860 was 10.16, the highest county ratio in Kentucky. That figure surpassed the 1860 statewide numbers for Arkansas (9.67), North Carolina (9.55), Tennessee (7.48), and Virginia (9.41) and approached the ratios for some states in the Deep South. The promise of wealth built on labor-intensive tobacco production led directly to a very large slave population, which in Christian County reached 9,951 in 1860, the third highest slave total among Kentucky counties. In that year, slaves constituted 46 percent of the county's total population of 21,627.[2]

Historical demography points to a steady expansion of slavery as the tobacco economy in the county intensified. Although Kentucky disallowed the importation of slaves for sale in 1833, the county's slave population grew as a result of natural increase, the in-migration of owners and slaves from elsewhere, or purchase within the state. In each of the three decades between 1830 and 1860, the growth of the slave population far outpaced that of the free population, with increases of 38.3, 35.7, and 22.2 percent, compared to a free population increase of 14.8, 19.2, and 2.0 percent.[3] Concomitantly, the Christian County tobacco yield in 1850 reached over 6.25 million pounds, the largest production in the state.[4] By 1860 the tobacco crop in Christian County nearly doubled, totaling 11.5 million pounds, more than 10 percent of the state total of 108 million pounds. Kentucky produced one quarter of all the tobacco marketed in the United States in 1860, with Christian County accounting for nearly 3 percent of the national total.[5]

Local ecological conditions were optimal for dark tobacco production. The Pennyroyal region, of which Christian County is a part, is named for a prolific variety of wild mint and encompasses a geological zone of rich soils lying above limestone bedrock. The pioneering cultural geographer, Carl Sauer observed that Christian County was situated in the most productive area of the Pennyroyal. Hopkinsville, in Sauer's words, "lies centrally to the richest body of land in western Kentucky, especially to the best tobacco country, the smooth limestone plain south of town."[6] The town consequently became the historic center of dark leaf production and marketing. The plains, or barrens as the early farmers called them, south of the town are rarely interrupted by rocky formations. Under these favorable environmental circumstances, tobacco production in Christian County could occur on a scale resembling plantation agriculture in the Deep South. By contrast the northern portions of the county, a marginal area in Sauer's terms, are markedly different from the southern Pennyroyal plains. Rocky outcrops militated against the kind of extensive agriculture characteristic of the land south of Hopkinsville. The northern soils cannot be penetrated more than a few inches without hitting a limestone barrier. Even today, the nature of the land limits the use of heavy farm machinery designed for cultivation in unobstructed fields.

Thus, within Christian County, a sharp ecological and demographic cline occurs between north and south. It is demarcated along the east-west axis of state road 68, once widely known as the Jefferson Davis highway, where the Davis obelisk surveys the north-south division. A larger population, both black and white, a greater scale and intensity of agriculture, and the fluorescence of the tobacco economy and slaveholding distinguished the southern area from the northern half of the county. While people in the northern portion of Christian County held many fewer slaves than those in the southern reaches, no evidence suggests less commitment in the northern areas to slavery as an institution. At the same time, people supporting slavery throughout the county did not ipso facto support secession. On the contrary, among the slaveholders were numbers of unionists.

Early on, the Pennyroyal became the world capital of dark tobacco production. While burley tobacco is grown in this part of the state, dark tobacco was dominant, giving the county and adjoining areas its distinct character and identity. Dark leaf tobacco is grown only in few places beyond this region of Kentucky and adjacent areas of Tennessee. The heavy tobacco leaf is a very deep, dark green that appears almost black in color, and indeed the counties of southwestern Kentucky and northwest Tennessee, where it is produced, have been known as the "Black Patch." That term, particularly among African Americans, has also referred to the hands that tended it from seedbed to curing. Dark tobacco was used primarily for cigars, snuff, and chewing tobacco, much more popular than cigarettes in the nineteenth century.

THE TOWN

Hopkinsville lies some twenty miles from the Tennessee state line and the city of Clarksville on the Cumberland River. Both communities are within the powerful economic orbit of Fort Campbell, with its thousands of soldiers and their dependents. By all accounts, the Tennessee town has been more hospitable to Fort Campbell's soldiers and families and consequently has benefited through much greater growth and prosperity than its close Kentucky neighbor. An old distinction, still resonant in Hopkinsville, divides white insiders—people who belong by virtue of their "old family" status—from others. The divide between old families and new families did little in the 1950s and 1960s to nurture the kind of welcome Clarksville extended to the fort, and some have claimed that the old families of Hopkinsville resisted any changes in the status quo. Road signs within Clarksville proclaim the town, "gateway to the New South," which codes a new attitude about black-white relations essential to building an economically congenial relationship with a modern army base.[7]

To the first-time visitor who has observed other midsize American communities, Hopkinsville seems familiar. Vacant spaces and parking lots dot the downtown where buildings once stood. Remnants of an earlier time include two old theaters adapted to new uses, the county court house, a family owned pharmacy, and a hamburger joint that started up many years ago for white patrons only. One retail space was home to three different restaurants over a recent five-year period. The surviving retail outlets in the central city attract little foot traffic, and the empty storerooms or partially rented spaces in large buildings along Main Street or Ninth Street likewise are silent reminders of a more vibrant time for downtown businesses. Where Ninth and Main streets intersect, local artists have painted a series of panels on the side of a building overlooking a parking lot where another building stood on this once prime real estate. The panels depict businesses, schools, an opera house, and other vanished institutions in old Hopkinsville, including, in multicultural acknowledgment, a black-owned tailoring business from the early twentieth century and the shuttered black high school, Crispus Attucks, a lamented 1967 casualty of school integration.

Much of the commercial life of the town has migrated to Fort Campbell Boulevard, which replaced the old Clarksville Pike, a name appropriate to the quaint country road once joining Hopkinsville to its close Tennessee neighbor. The drive southward into Tennessee starts on "the Boulevard." Hardly quaint, the road leading out of Hopkinsville reflects the troubled state of many American towns that have grown outward with little planning. It is a busy thoroughfare lined with fast food places, pawn shops, check cashing services, loan companies, off-brand filling stations, motels belonging to familiar chains as well as several individually owned by Indian immigrants, automobile dealerships, Chinese restaurants, a shopping mall, and all the rest of what has come to signify the slow death of American downtowns. The well-appointed offices of the Chamber of Commerce are located on Fort Campbell Boulevard, indicating that the business establishment has effectively ratified the process of sprawl, suburbanization, and central city abandonment, with all its implications. Trees and pedestrians are equally alien to the ironically named boulevard. A visitor has seen all of this before, and thus for the tangible uniqueness of the town—the defining features of the place—one must look elsewhere, in physical space and in memory.

Hopkinsville's historic district along south Main Street, beginning a few blocks past downtown, is very much about the distinctiveness of the town. It is defined by the commodious homes of the antebellum and postbellum eras, each an emplacement of a story about a family belonging to old Hopkinsville's white elite whose values and perspectives looked southward. A particularly telling example of the area's southern orientation is a portrait of Robert E. Lee, which until very recently was displayed in the office of the county treasurer. It was inscribed, "Compliments of Noble Jones Gregory." Gregory was the First District congressman from 1937–59. As described by a particularly keen local observer, "seventy-two years after the Civil War Western Kentucky political candidates continued to seek political support by distributing pictures of Lee . . . in an area that Lee never visited and in a state that never seceded from the Union [where] a Congressman's values were best summarized in such a picture, and thus his constituency."[8]

Hopkinsville's identification with the South was also summed up in a 1958 newspaper editorial congratulating the town on "its calm acceptance of token desegregation [which] only those familiar with its history and background can fully appreciate." The editorial continued, "This is the most Southern community in Kentucky. In their thinking, much of Hopkinsville and Christian County have always been more like a chunk out of Mississippi or Georgia than a part of Kentucky. It's safe to say that at least 90 per cent of the white residents of Hopkinsville are opposed to any form of race mixing."[9]

Accounts of its southern past and the privileged inhabitants of these stately homes provide in considerable detail the most well-known features of the town's historic profile and identity. The associated stories of black people who participated in the building of the historic homes, or who later worked in them as house servants, are much less accessible. Their recovery is also problematic, owing to the neglect of archivists and historians in the post–Civil War decades. Severely skewed, the dominant historic representation of the town reproduces and reflects the world of the white elite, not necessarily wrong or distorted, but seriously incomplete.

Black neighborhoods in and proximate to the central city contain a mix of owner occupied houses and rental properties. Absentee landlords have faced some of the least demanding real estate codes and enforcement procedures in western Kentucky. Likewise, abandoned or neglected properties have also rankled homeowners and community activists in these areas; they object on aesthetic as well as safety grounds, associating neighborhood deterioration with criminal activity, particularly related to drugs. They have regularly protested the lack of investment or upkeep in central city infrastructure, especially in discussions begun in 2005 after the contested city council passage of an ordinance known as the Inner City Residential Enterprise Zone. The neighborhoods still contain a few black-owned businesses that have not joined the out-migration to newer areas of the city. There are also lingering reminders of the earlier vitality of black institutions, some paradoxically the victims of integration. Included here are the Booker T. Washington primary school, Crispus Attucks high school, and the Episcopal Church school opened by a black Episcopal minister in the 1890s.

Beyond the central narrative of the town, black people constitute a separate but little attended to part of Hopkinsville, yet a very important one because of their historically substantial numbers. Since the era of slavery, Christian County and Hopkinsville as centers of black life have ranked, respectively, among the most populous counties and towns in the state. The 2000 census records a city population of 30,089 with the large black population numbering 30.9 percent of the total, although some residents believe that undercounting due to noncompliance and other factors may have missed as much as 8 percent of the black population at that time.[10] In most respects, black life has constituted a distinct social universe, parallel to but largely separate from that inhabited by white people. The constellation of black experience has assuredly been different from that of the racial majority by cultural content and especially by access to power and wealth. It is also remembered differently.

Despite African Americans from all over the South moving northward to Chicago, Detroit, Indianapolis, and other cities during the Great Migration beginning in the early twentieth century, descendants of Hopkinsville natives recreate and reaffirm their connections by returning to the town in order to participate in family reunions. At such events, the black view of the racial past is made manifest through ritual and narrative, with the experience of slavery at least implicit. Through family lore and history recitation, participants fill the spaces in the dominant discourse about Hopkinsville that often dismisses slavery or the subsequent racial caste system as features of a distant past irrelevant to the present. Black historical memory is suffused with themes of triumph over adversity to which family groups bear witness, in a deeply religious sense, as they find continuing inspiration in endurance and achievement.[11] One cannot attend a black family reunion in Christian County without feeling that the past is a living legacy, an unbroken chain linking the earliest known forbears to their contemporary descendants, thus giving historical memory a particularly sharp focus. Without public memorials or commemorative plaques recalling black historical figures, places, or occurrences, black people in Hopkinsville enact historical memory through events, rituals, and religious exhortation, all of which are on ample display at reunions.

HISTORICAL AMNESIA AND PARTIAL RECOVERY

Until recent decades, the racial biases of the keepers of archival collections and records in historical societies inevitably constricted the traditional writing of southern history, a pattern also evident in Hopkinsville. As W. Fitzhugh Brundage suggests, representations of the southern past reflected white domination of the economic, political, and cultural life of the region. White historians and archivists were at best indifferent to the black past, effectively banning black people as active figures in history just as they were banned from libraries and from the civic life of their towns and communities.[12] Anyone interested in recovering African American history thus contends with the consequences of a willful disregard of documents and other artifacts "speaking" in a black voice. In Hopkinsville, for example, eight black newspapers were published at various times, yet no copies can be found either at the public library or the museum archive of the Pennyroyal Area Museum.[13] The collections of the Christian County Historical Society are nearly as deficient, and black citizens seeking glimpses into local black history express frustration at the dearth of information in the town's historical repositories. In sum, the writing of black history in Hopkinsville and western Kentucky has been severely hampered but not foreclosed by the neglect of primary sources reflecting the black experience. Instead, a cosseted history and memory of the white south has long dominated popular and scholarly views of the past.

In reviewing various histories of Kentucky, historian George C. Wright sought background information for his own research on African Americans in Louisville. He came away disappointed, finding almost nothing useful for understanding the black past in Kentucky and concluded that African Americans "have either been ignored by scholars of Kentucky history or . . . not taken seriously by them." Black people throughout the histories of the state "have no control over their lives and merely react to what the larger white society does to them." In his view, oral history therefore is an essential component in research on the black past, often providing the only access to black voices in counterpoint to traditional historical views of writers expressing the paternalistic biases of the racial majority.[14] But oral history has also struggled for legitimacy as a research tool in a discipline traditionally defined by the investigation of written documents.

Historians of Kentucky and the South did much to establish and reinforce a southern perspective. E. Merton Coulter and J. Winston Coleman, writing primarily between the 1930s and 1950s and very much of their time and place, attributed little personal agency to African Americans. Coulter, for example, represents southern history from the perspective of a white apologist steeped in the values of race supremacy and the Lost Cause. He argued that slavery had not been an "unmixed evil" for black people because "it had brought them from barbarism . . . in Africa . . . and subjected them to the white man's civilization, the product of a thousand years of freedom." He espoused the pervasive southern view of Reconstruction, regarding black office holders as a sham, woefully unprepared for governing.[15] Moreover, writing of Kentucky, he argued that newly enfranchised African Americans were merely a tool of Republicans in the "decisive battle between Democracy and Radicalism."[16] Writing in 1940, Coleman saw slavery in Kentucky, compared to the Deep South, as an essentially benign institution defined by bonds of affection between master and bondsmen. He declared, "the yoke of bondage rested lightly."[17] While this conceit no longer enjoys currency among serious students of history, it still informs much popular understanding.[18] The renowned Kentucky writer, Wendell Berry, refers to this view as the "self-defensive myth of benevolence."[19] The most influential historian of slavery in the first half of the twentieth century, Ulrich Phillips, also betrays the regnant racial sentiments of the era in seeing slavery as a civilizing force of uplift for benighted Africans.[20]

The southern perspective on matters of race defined the work not only of historians native to the South but also of American historians more generally. For example, the interpretation of Reconstruction presented by Henry Steele Commager and Allan Nevins does not differ substantially in tone or content from what Coulter,

Coleman, or Phillips wrote. Nevins and Commager assert that the law creating the Freedmen's Bureau and the Civil Rights Act following the Civil War "unduly invaded the authority of Southern States." The fifteenth amendment, for example, conferred the right to vote on "densely ignorant colored men." Some of their grandfathers "had perhaps been African savages." Nevins and Commager explain that "self-respecting whites" using intimidation and violence came to rule themselves after establishing the Ku Klux Klan; blacks in their view grew tired of being used by northern politicians and "quietly gave up voting."[21]

Until the 1960s, the distortions or outright eclipse of the black past among historians was nearly complete and extended to the condition of African peoples prior to their enslavement in the New World. Black Africa in historical consciousness was little more than a footnote to the imperial struggles of the European powers. The diaspora of African peoples in the New World with a discernible history linked to their continent of origin was, with the notable exceptions of W. E. B. Du Bois and Melville Herskovits, regarded as unworthy of scholarly attention.[22] But even Du Bois very early in his career did not challenge majority views that the Negro had no past. Du Bois's outlook shifted following his "sudden awakening from the paralysis of this judgment," when, "too astonished to speak," he heard Franz Boas address the 1906 graduating class of Atlanta University. A signal event both for Du Bois and his students, Boas's speech examined the achievements of African kingdoms over a millennium. He told the graduates that the African past was cause for pride rather than shame. Yet his lesson in the substance and reality of African history would not take hold among white scholars for another six decades.[23] The small number of young African Americans in his audience, however, could legitimately internalize an esteemed rather than a degraded racial self, a continuing quest among many black Americans through the twentieth century.

W. E. B. Du Bois was also influenced by Boas's delineation of the culture concept, which underlay his inspiring speech of 1906. The development of a theory of culture ranks among Boas's most far-reaching and radical contributions to anthropology and to the emergence of a modern liberal consciousness. Culture, or learned tradition, not fictive biological race, or a putative inherited temperament, or a fixed racial nature, was the true wellspring of human action in the world. With customary incisiveness, Du Bois alluded to this pivotal insight in 1935, when he characterized the audience for his book, *Black Reconstruction in America*. Du Bois told the reader that "if he believes that the Negro in America and in general . . . is an average and ordinary human being, who under given environment develops like other human beings, then he will read this story and judge it by the facts adduced." If, on the other hand, the reader saw the Negro as inferior, unequipped for all time to participate in civilized endeavors, and whose "emancipation and enfranchisement were gestures against nature," then he would remain unpersuaded by facts.[24] Still a novel idea in 1935, the influence of environment, or culture in Boas's terms, in explaining human behavior was for the most part absent from southern history, unless the latter was written by black scholars.

The near-exclusion of African Americans from historical writing and their depiction by others in broad, stereotypic brush strokes was substantially a one-sided problem of race prejudice. Yet historical amnesia could afflict black people as well, for very different reasons, thus further inhibiting the quest for a usable past, as David Blight has suggested. This was particularly true of the period between the Civil War and the turn of the twentieth century. The racial majority regarded African Americans as a people lacking any record or evidence of achievement owing to an assumed racial inferiority "proven" by the scientific authorities of the late nineteenth century. If civil war and federal law had ended their enslavement, the rationales in popular thinking about why African peoples had been enslaved at all remained in place. In other words, freedmen faced an array of cultural attitudes that once rationalized slavery but then served new purposes, supporting the caste-like position of a despised minority believed to be a lesser race lacking any serviceable history or even the capacity to create one. Under these conditions, they could find precious little on which to build a sense of collective efficacy, pride, or belonging to an American civic order. The shame of slavery lingered on.[25]

Servitude and its indignities were, accordingly, best forgotten or suppressed. Toni Morrison observes that people wanted to escape the burden of historical memory and to move forward as quickly as they could.[26] My own experience confirms this powerful tendency toward silence about the past. Except for the occasional highly truncated anecdote, I found among my informants none who could sustain even a brief narrative of slavery handed down from a forbear, such was the historical sweep of forgetting across the generations. For example, when I asked Ammie Weaver, a Hopkinsville nonagenarian, what she had heard of slavery and its immediate aftermath from her grandparents and parents, the latter born in the 1870s, she said they did not speak of those experiences. Then, reflecting on the pain of remembrance, she said quietly, "They'd been coming through some hard times and didn't want to talk about it."[27] Edward Ball, a descendant of South Carolina slaveholders, who sought out the descendants of those held in bondage by his ancestors, found that they too wanted to turn away, as expressed by a granddaughter of slaves: "The older parents come up under such strain, with slavery, until they didn't tell the children things they should have told them. They didn't talk about it."[28]

There were certainly important exceptions in the form of slave narratives told outside of the kinship circle, including of course the most significant indictment of slavery and the slaveholder, Frederick Douglass's autobiography.[29] Marion Wilson

Starling's landmark study, *The Slave Narrative: Its Place in American History,* published long after its 1946 completion, meticulously searched out first person accounts by slaves, legitimating them as historical and literary sources rejected by historians and others since their first appearance.[30] Slave narratives and autobiographies provided the sharpest rebuke to the dismissive judgments of historians, such as Phillips, who spurned the autobiographies as propaganda in support of abolitionism.[31]

Early attention to the black voices of slave narratives cannot be separated from the assertion of personal and communal dignity. Amid the reigning indifference of white scholars to African Americans as historical actors, black writers and historians beginning in the late nineteenth century laid claim to the African and African American past. The study of black history, in effect, began as "a Jim Crow specialty."[32] Taking their cue particularly from Carter Woodson, founder in 1915 of the Association for the Study of African American Life and History, black historians focused on what white historians had devalued to the point of denigration. *The Journal of Negro History,* established by Woodson in 1916, became an important outlet for the publication of articles focused directly on an African American past populated by people, in slavery and freedom, with a distinct voice. By the 1920s and 1930s, black high schools and colleges, taking inspiration from Woodson's efforts, began offering courses on Negro history as a badly needed palliative to the racist views propounded in standard American textbooks of the period.[33]

Writing in *The Journal of Negro History* in 1935, John Cade argues that black writers "may interpret their people to the world more faithfully than white authors [and] can set forth the real black man as he was, is, and hopes to be." Six years before while teaching university courses in Louisiana, Cade supervised eighty-two student interviews of former slaves; their narratives touch on topics including clothing, food, work, family life, entertainment, religion, physical abuse, and sexual exploitation of black women by slave owners. The narratives are candid, and while a very few speak of positive experiences in slavery and a high regard for owners, most comments about slavery are unsparing about the cruelty of the institution. There is also condemnation of the postbellum pattern of exploitation of black labor, particularly in the sharecropping system. One of Cade's student interviewers observed that "even though slavery has been abolished, it still exists in parts of our country . . . where Negroes toil day after day . . . till the end of the year when they are told by the owners that they are yet in debt—which means that they must toil yet another year, only to find themselves where they started."[34]

The most extensive and best known collection of narratives told by former slaves appears in the multivolume series *The American Slave: A Composite Auto-biography* (1972), part of the Depression-era Federal Writers' Project of the Works Progress Administration (WPA). Since their publication after long delay, these narratives, along with nineteenth-century slave autobiographies, have figured prominently in uncovering agency, thought, and motivation among slaves, although most historians continued to describe them as silently compliant, passive bondsmen. Those scholars, as summed up in 1972 by George P. Rawick, the general editor of the WPA collection, conceived of the slave "as the victim who never enters his own history as its subject, but only as the object over which abstract forces and glorious armies fought."[35] The slave narratives have in effect played a central role in the transformation of the historical interpretation of slavery. Despite recurrent doubts about the reliability of the WPA narratives, scholars, including those who have raised questions about their trustworthiness, have made extensive use of the WPA collection.[36]

The Federal Writers' Project, a liberal New Deal program when Jim Crow was very much the order of the day, sought the inclusion of black people as researchers in the slave narrative project, as well as in the WPA state guides. Although black people participated in the collection of narratives of former slaves, the precise number of black interviewers is unknown.[37] Long after the completion of the project, racial identities of researchers were tabulated; black people constituted 25 percent of those who could be identified by race. This of course had numerous methodological implications, particularly regarding the elicitation of frank and honest testimony by white researchers. Obviously, aged former slaves, steeped in the deferential racial etiquette of the antebellum years and of the Jim Crow era, were accustomed to telling white people what they wanted to hear.[38] White collectors had a mixed record of eliciting candid testimonies about slavery. The Federal Writers' Project also sponsored research for a series of state guides. Unlike the collection of slave narratives, the research for the guides was directed toward publication, such as the *WPA Guide to Kentucky*. The project director pressed for inclusion of black writers who might have created in each book a much greater space for black people as subjects. But the established pattern of local Jim Crow custom remained in force, as "southern editors often resisted in accordance with the region's prevailing social mores."[39]

Attention on various levels—scholarly and popular—has thus turned more than ever before to comprehending a past populated by people whose active role on the American stage, even in slavery, remained largely hidden, except in religious institutions or other segments of their own restricted communities of color. The museum in Hopkinsville in recent years has joined these efforts by featuring exhibits of photos and artifacts on local black history, and by maintaining files of newspaper clippings, pictures, and other documents concerning notable black people from the area, such as the contemporary writer Gloria Watkins, known to her reading public as bell hooks.[40] Also represented from an earlier generation is the journalist Ted

Poston, whose biographer has shown the value of oral history in reconstructing his early life in Hopkinsville.[41] As published writers, hooks and Poston have of course told their own personal or professional stories, and hooks periodically has given public presentations in the town. Still, the museum collection on African Americans represents a very late start in preserving a neglected part of the past and must rely heavily on newspaper articles and other secondary sources, particularly to preserve a record of local African Americans.

This effort at recovery is consistent with what has been called the "contributionist" approach to African American history, focusing on the productive endeavors of black people not only on their own behalf but also for the country at large. Inspired by Carter Woodson and like-minded black scholars at the end of the nineteenth century, "contributionism" placed black people within the narrative of American nation building and achievement. Black history month each February is a continuing reminder that the contributionist view remains popular, lauding as it does admirable black figures in the American past. In Hopkinsville, Crispus Attucks, the black patriot slain in the Boston Massacre and for whom the renowned black high school was named in 1916, is a well-known local example of the contributionist worldview. As the centrality of black people in the American narrative has gained considerable recognition since the 1960s, contributionism no longer provides the same motivation it once did for the writing of black history. Nonetheless, contributionism is likely to remain vital in many black communities. This is particularly true when concerns about the education and aspirations of children are prompted by troubled educational systems and diminishing opportunities.[42] History and memory, in this view, help to establish the identity and self-esteem requisite to achievement against great odds. This is evident in the Hopkinsville museum's documentary holdings, which highlight local African Americans who serve as models of educational and professional success.

HOPKINSVILLE AND MULTICULTURALISM: RHETORIC AND SILENCE

"Multiculturalism" became a familiar term in the 1980s, following the civil rights movement and the onset of large-scale immigration of Asians, Latin Americans, and Caribbean peoples to the United States. Like many terms in the social sciences, the word has both a popular connotation and a more precise conceptual value for anthropologists and sociologists. The latter meanings will be taken up in Chapter 6.

In popular usage, multiculturalism suggests a form of cultural association in which tolerance, respect, and mutual acceptance between ethnic and racial groups are high values. The term is opposed to the more obvious and chauvinistic forms of ethnocentrism of an ethnic or racial majority and suggests an alternative vision of coexistent and diverse ethnic communities within a plural society. Likewise, the multicultural perspective is a reaction to a social policy promoting assimilation of diverse groups into the culture of the dominant group. Often, multiculturalism in popular usage embraces a bland celebration of cuisine, dress, musical styles, and the like, without considering the hard reality of class difference and privilege within and among cultural, ethnic, or racial groups. Nonetheless, multiculturalism in common parlance acknowledges multiple traditions within a community and an implied value on mutual respect among diverse cultural groups. Like other places across the country, Hopkinsville and Christian County are caught up in the discourse of multiculturalism, if not a social policy motivated by those values.

As in the rest of the country, diversity issues are more acknowledged than acted on in many venues, from the city council to churches to schools. Of course, the town has always been "multicultural" owing to its large black population and, at one time, a small Jewish community and a smattering of other European-derived immigrants. Hopkinsville encouraged the settlement of immigrants as early as 1879 through the Land and Immigration Office of the State of Kentucky. Praising the wholesomeness, economic opportunities, healthful environment, and the welcome that settlers from the North and East, as well as "Europeans of the better class," would encounter, the South Kentucky Immigration Society prepared a promotional booklet directed toward a decidedly white audience. Except for the notation that Christian County had free schools divided along racial lines, the advertisement was silent about race, but implied that European settlers would be categorized as white and that black people, not immigrants, were the true outsiders.[43]

What was implicit in the 1879 booklet became overt and racially hostile in a Hopkinsville news column ten years later. Originally appearing in the *Glasgow Times* published in Barren County, Kentucky, the article identified a market in the state for "conscientious white labor." Immigration was the obvious source for new workers. Immigration would solve the state's labor problem, attributed to black people, whom the writer called "lazy and shiftless," both in slavery and in the years of emancipation.[44] The article provided one more assertion of unyielding white racial judgment; its scornful attitude toward black people in the first generation of freedom was all the more contemptuous in view of its publication during Emancipation commemorations in western Kentucky.

In sharp contrast to the experience of African Americans, European immigrants and their children in the late nineteenth and early twentieth century nurtured a realistic hope that they might be able to find a respected place in the United States. That hope was predicated on their willingness to emulate through social assimilation the values and practices of established white Americans. Social assimilation, however, was not a possibility for black people, immobilized by the restrictions of color and caste. Remarking on this contrast, Toni Morrison has observed that "[o]nly when the lesson of racial estrangement is learned is assimilation complete."[45] The process of "whitening," a useful metaphor for the assimilation of twentieth-century European immigrants into the American middle class, thus entailed an internalization of the American racial calculus separating whites or "would-be" whites from all others.

Du Bois famously wrote of the psychic and social rewards of white status. That is, instead of a Marxist expectation of common class interest uniting black people and lower class whites, racial opposition was the norm. Whiteness paid "a public psychological wage," according to Du Bois, enabling white people of all classes to gain access to public facilities, good schools, and the like. European immigrants would also be included. Poor whites, despite whatever racial privilege they had, remained anxious at the possibility that even cheaper black labor might supplant them.[46] This fear diminished any possibility of a colorblind class-consciousness emerging.

In Hopkinsville, the racialized contrast between European immigrants and African Americans in the conventional discourse appeared in a series of sketches of the foreign born and former slaves published in the *Kentucky New Era* in 1934. The editor introduced various immigrants—people from such places as Germany, England, Russia, Latvia, Greece, France, Italy, Austria, and Poland—aiming to show how they "are doing their part in promoting the welfare of the county and city."[47] These immigrants were praised for qualities such as thrift, entrepreneurship, discipline, patriotism, and good citizenship.

Later, the newspaper briefly presented the personal recollections of thirty people who had been slaves in Christian County. Depicted were "some of the very few 'Black Mammies,' and ante-bellum 'Uncles' of Christian County."[48] The stories were concerned with establishing who their white folks were (their owners when slaves or, subsequently, their employers) but found none of the civic values exemplified by the immigrants. Instead, the former slaves were presented as people apart, known primarily through whites; they stood outside the circle enclosing white Hopkinsville and its European newcomers. Early in the series, the editor sounded the recurrent if false historical theme that pervaded white vernacular memory up to the 1960s: "There has never been any race trouble in the county. The races live together in peace and amity today."[49]

Beginning in the mid-nineteenth century, Jewish newcomers were the most prominent among the immigrants. On the whole, they encountered a town that was congenial, even philosemitic in some quarters, especially the business and professional segments of the community.[50] They were generally esteemed, and by the turn of the twentieth century the immigrants or their American-born children were enjoying commercial success as merchants. The two local newspapers respectfully noted the Jewish holy days each autumn. More deferential than informed, the *Kentucky New Era* reported in 1906, "Perhaps no religious anniversary in the Jewish church is held in more reverence than is Yom Kippur." The article went on to describe the observance, including a religious service scheduled at the home of a prominent member of the religious community.[51]

Jewish economic achievement locally is embodied along the north side of east Sixth Street, where two of five old, deteriorating buildings once signaled the economic advance of Jewish businessmen. Mssrs. Klein and Bohn each erected a multistory building at the end of the nineteenth century for their dry goods businesses and enjoyed the privilege of whiteness, unrestricted in place of residence and schools that their children could attend, or by discriminatory actions of any consequence. Their names remain visibly embedded in the stonework near the rooflines of their respective buildings.

At the corner of Sixth and Virginia, ending the block that begins at the Klein Building, stands the Postell Block, erected by Peter Postell toward the end of the nineteenth century. A former slave, Postell was an immensely wealthy investor in real estate. Among his tenants were the prominent African American attorneys Walter Robinson and Claybron Merriweather; the latter, during his long life, was also a newspaper editor, artist, and published poet. The three were recognized leaders in Hopkinsville's black community, and their achievements gained recognition well beyond its borders. Yet as colored men, they inhabited a fixed category of racial estrangement and separation from their white and whitened neighbors along East Sixth Street. Accordingly, they lived their minority status in ways very different from the minority experience of the Jewish merchants.[52]

An incident in Nashville in 1900 is particularly apposite of the very different standing of blacks and Jews in the South. The *Hopkinsville Kentuckian* reported on "the discovery" in Nashville that "one of the most proficient art students in the Peabody Normal College, Parmelia Williams, is a negress." She acknowledged her racial status after another student observed her in the company of two black men. Having studied at the school for an entire term, she had proven to be not only accomplished but also popular as "the young ladies became greatly attached to her." Recognizing that she was somehow different, they thought she was a "Jewess." The story concluded, "It is not known what steps will be taken in the matter."[53] Different but accepted, Parmelia Williams seemed on her way to becoming white, until exposed as a young black woman who was instead passing for white.

The contrast, evident in Hopkinsville, between the people of recent European origin and their children, on the one hand, and the large African American population, on the other, exposes a profound historic contradiction in the American value system. Enshrined in the melting pot metaphor born in the early twentieth century, a national discourse celebrates America for the unity it forges out of the diversity of people from elsewhere—a nation of immigrants, *e pluribus unum*, not a nation of English, German, and other peoples simply relocated. The American was a "new man," in the words of the eighteenth-century French gentleman-farmer Jean de Crevecoeur.[54]

The "melting pot" or the "new man" encapsulates what Gary Gerstle calls "civic nationalism," a universalist faith in human equality and therefore the right and the capacity of anyone, no matter his or her origin, to engage in participatory democracy. These values are articulated in the founding documents of the United States. For a brief time after the Civil War, Reconstruction seemed to promise that newly freed slaves might enter an inclusive circle defined by the rights guaranteed to citizens. Certainly, the laws sanctioning that new beginning were in place, as the recognition of slavery in the Constitution was rendered nugatory. Yet Gerstle also observes that civic nationalism as an ideal has coexisted with an oppositional and exclusive "racial nationalism," or the highly particular belief that only white people of European origin, specifically from northwestern Europe, enjoy the singular right to govern.[55] By the mid-twentieth century, of course, the matter of slavery had long been settled, yet black people remained in a category of civic exclusion. In the South they were mostly bound to the land, in what elderly former sharecroppers now resident in Hopkinsville describe as "another kind of slavery." In the North, black people for the most part comprised an unskilled labor force, severely exploited in the burgeoning industrial cities of the Midwest and East, where they did not have the prerogatives of full citizenship.

While the landmark civil rights legislation of the 1960s destroyed the legal, if not the social, foundations of racial nationalism, slavery continues to occupy a considerable space within American historical memory, especially in the South. Hopkinsville and Christian County are no exceptions. Celebrations of the Confederacy and "southern heritage"—itself a thinly shrouded racialized idea—the display of Confederate emblems, and the tending of monuments and historical markers commemorating southern heroes bring slavery and racial nationalism into the present, exposing a yawning chasm of difference in perception and feeling between black people and proponents of southern heritage. The Civil War as historical memory, for example, continues to resonate in southern references to the "War Between the States," or even occasionally the "War of Northern Aggression." In the decades after

1865, local newspapers reported regularly on the activities of Confederate veterans, including their reunions, organizations such the Sons of Confederate Veterans and the United Daughters of the Confederacy, commemorations of the Lost Cause, and the like. Also locally famous is the Orphan Brigade comprised of Confederate volunteers from Kentucky. They had to leave the state to enlist and train, usually in Tennessee, because Kentucky did not secede, and they could not return to their homes until the war ended. Comparable commemorations of the Union cause have been not-ably absent.

Following the 2008 celebration of the Jefferson Davis bicentennial at his birth place in nearby Fairview, several black people in Hopkinsville said that they had never heard a white person acknowledge the pain inflicted on the descendants of slaves by the continued display of Confederate symbols. At the bicentennial, the connection between the emblems of secession and slavery was scrupulously avoided, even denied, in favor of a celebratory southern memory. But the latter depends on severing the link between slavery and the Civil War, thus denying history in the interest of contemporary acceptability, which the descendants of slaves will not concede. Black people know full well that valiant service and self-sacrifice in the Civil War, key elements of southern memory, have been summoned in defense of racial nationalism.

Black people also find subtle legacies of slavery in the persistence of attitudes forged long ago. Thus, the city's rejection of a black-initiated proposal to commemorate Martin Luther King Jr., by renaming a major street in a black neighborhood in his honor rankled multiple black groups supporting the plan. They regarded the failed proposal as tantamount to a repudiation of the man most responsible for spurring the country to repair the broken promises following Emancipation. The city's decision implicitly endorsed the view that Martin Luther King Jr. was not a heroic figure acting in the spirit of the Constitution and national values but, rather, a man who stood only for narrow, inimical racial interests. Recalling the defeat of the proposal, a black observer said simply, "I guess they just couldn't identify with it," suggesting that African Americans once again found their claims to history, and indeed to the town, rejected.

While the racial binary has defined the town and county from their beginnings, native peoples of eastern North America also left their mark on Hopkinsville, as many individuals, black and white, proudly recount their Indian ancestry. The Trail of Tears Park on the east side of town commemorates the forced passage of Cherokee through the area in a particularly poignant way. A monument to a Cherokee chief stands in the Park, telling visitors that he died in the town when he and his people were making the bitter trek. Of course, the Trail of Tears marks the antithesis of contemporary multicultural strivings, for it sprang from a government policy bent on eliminating the native presence through coerced removal of the Cherokee in 1838–39 from the southeastern United States to eastern Oklahoma, or "Indian Territory." Now, the park is the site of an annual September Pow Wow, celebrating crafts, dancing, and other efforts at identity creation, recovery, or enhancement that are a staple of American communities according recognition to some variety of multiculturalism.

The multicultural discourse also resonates in town owing to contemporary immigration, which affects all areas of the United States, including communities outside of the larger metropolitan centers. Hopkinsville, accordingly, has added new demographic ingredients, modest in number, to the pluralist mix that has evolved all along. Chinese and Mexican restaurateurs, Indian motel owners and professionals, and Latin American laborers are now a part of the local scene. New in recent years is the prescription calling for respect for ethnically, racially, and religiously diverse peoples and their "cultures," while condemning public as well as private expressions of bigotry against any category of people. Indeed, civility generally marks the public, if not the private, conversation on race.

Although its public discussion is very constrained and circumscribed, race is never far from consciousness. As a result of the widely shared commitment to public civility concerning racial matters, black people may be left guessing about white attitudes and intentions. Separate toilets, waiting rooms, drinking fountains, schools, restaurants and all the rest of the Jim Crow past dictated behavior sanctioned in law and custom that codified white commitment to unambiguous racial hierarchy and social inequality. Black people always knew that separate was never equal, yet forty years of institutional integration has not indexed white racial attitudes with nearly the same clarity. In matters of race, there is much room for uncertainty and contradiction, so much so that a black businesswoman in exasperation said, "Maybe it was better when we knew our place." Motives, intentions, and ways of acting and speaking are now easily construed as efforts to maintain racial hierarchy, separation, and white control, as illustrated in the contentious debate over a proposal to build a municipal swimming pool and water park.

Public discussions before the city council in 2005 included alternatives to the proposed water park, including building a swimming pool at the Walnut Street Center, a recreational facility in a black, inner city neighborhood. The latter option would have cost much less than building the water park and would have offered much greater accessibility to minority youth. Against some considerable public opposition, the water park proposal was adopted and eventually completed; its location at an established city recreational site on the bypass circling the town limited accessibility except by car.[56] While the idea of a swimming pool on Walnut Street had some black support, much black opinion insisted that the motivation for the plan was to reinforce *de facto* segregation, to keep black youth in the inner city. At the same time, the location of the new facility outside of city neighborhoods and requiring transportation by car would present a considerable obstacle for inner city youth, and this fact, too, was "read" by other black people as yet another way of reinforcing *de facto* segregation and weighting use of the water park in favor of white youth.

The most striking departure from multicultural rhetoric is the sectarianism of Christian County's public life. The county is named for William Christian, a Virginian who served in the American Revolution and eventually settled in eastern Kentucky. Casual observers may be forgiven for momentarily linking the county's name to pervasive speech and practice normally occurring within churches. Fundamentalist Christianity is much in evidence, and any public meeting impinging on perceived moral issues promises to attract many often angry interpreters of the divine will. In fall 2005, for example, proposed Sunday alcohol sales in restaurants, promoted by the Chamber of Commerce and other business interests, riveted local attention when an enabling ordinance came before the city council. A council member in favor of Sunday sales traded biblical verses with a prohibitionist, each invoking scripture in support of his views. Reformed alcoholics were also present, publicly testifying that Christianity had pointed the way to their deliverance into abstinence and pure living and would do the same for all others in the town, if only they would open their hearts to biblical truth. At an earlier meeting, religious critics of Sunday sales brought their children, who publicly prayed for named city councilmen inclined to support the alcohol ordinance. Despite the strenuous efforts of the religious opposition, the city council passed the resolution legalizing Sunday alcohol sales.

Nonetheless, the presence of a very traditional protestant Christianity, based in the Baptist and Methodist Churches especially, remains prominent. John Shelton Reed, in writing of the dominating presence of Protestantism in the South, refers to its "Baptist-Methodist hegemony," which captures an important dimension of religion and public life in Hopkinsville.[57] Religiously inspired assertiveness on public issues can provoke acrimonious debates, public and private, as believers exhort nonbelievers to adopt the moral life of the faithful. Secular dissenters, cynics, liberal-minded Christians, and those of other denominations are much less organized in arguing for a diminished sectarianism in the discussion and formulation of public policy. Public meetings, including those of city government, as well as gatherings of clubs and voluntary associations, typically begin with a Christian invocation often led by a local clergyman. Periodic mention of the values of multiculturalism and tolerance notwithstanding, public Christian prayer and professions of faith have lost none of their customary southern vitality; however, their public policy implications are not always realized, as is evidenced by the passage of the alcohol ordinance. On the other hand, without apparent dissent, the city council has allocated over the past four years twelve thousand dollars per annum to a Christian outreach organization.[58] Discussing the role of Protestantism from Reconstruction through the Gilded Age, when it encompassed more than churches and prayer meetings, Edward J. Blum writes that "religious ideologies were at play in virtually every aspect of American life."[59] While this observation refers to a three-decade period in the late nineteenth century, it nonetheless resonates with contemporary Hopkinsville, and efforts since the 1980s to extend further the reach of religion into public life.

Notwithstanding the First Amendment, public prayer occurs as if Christian belief were universal. The white pastor of the Disciples of Christ Church registered a modest but unpopular protest against Christian sectarianism outside of churches. A southerner by birth and education, he accepted an invitation to offer an opening prayer for a Rotarian meeting. He purposely left out a reference to Christ in order to acknowledge that Hopkinsville is the home of people who are not Christians. He was upbraided by some of the members.[60] Far from divisive in the context of the racial binary, however, intense Christian faith among both black and white people more than any other factor smoothes over the deeply etched line of racial bifurcation. It has certainly played a substantial role, along with black fears of economic reprisal and job loss, in insuring racial peace, if not justice, even during the turbulence of the 1960s. The few protests that did occur in Hopkinsville at that time remained peaceful, as black ministers consistently counseled Christian nonviolence.

The pervasive discourse about shared Christian faith leaves little room for recognizing the presence of other beliefs, including those of Hopkinsville's recent Asian immigrants. An Indian physician reported in fall 2004 that her daughter's classmates informed the young girl that she and her family would go to hell. This remark and other instances of intolerance about Hinduism notwithstanding, the physician was positively disposed toward the town, feeling that she and her family were generally well treated.[61] She offered no criticism of the religious status quo but only sought wider recognition and understanding of her own faith. The physician did so by participating in an ecumenical study group at the local community college, where self-selected participants were already respectful of religious differences.

"WE KNEW WHO OUR WHITE PEOPLE WERE"

Whenever diverse peoples have come into sustained contact with each other, the movement of culture and genes—acculturation and miscegenation—between groups is inevitable, even in the American South where legal and customary codes of rigid social separation defined an ideal of black-white relations until the 1960s.

Yet a distinctive African American culture emerged as captive African peoples and their descendants recreated a world reflective of their experiences, direct and handed down, including those experiences of the religion, language, and culture of the slave masters. Indisputably, peoples of African origin were changed by their continuous contact with white people. But what has too often been missed is that processes of cultural change set in motion by the meeting of two peoples—the flow of culture—ran in both directions, even amid the sharpest differences of power and wealth. The dependency of slavery was never complete, nor was racial separation absolute. For example, South Carolina slave owners, initially unfamiliar with rice production, were dependent on slaves for the success of that lucrative crop, as Lawrence W. Levine points out. Particularly important were people from Sierra Leone and other rice areas along the Gambia River, not simply for their labor, but for their African expertise in cultivating a crop of long-standing importance in West Africa. Moreover, slaves understood local ecological and environmental conditions of the Carolina littoral and coastal plain that were similar to their homelands. Although it is impossible to quantify, black people brought Africa to the South and to the ways of living of the racial majority as surely as the latter was bound up in the black creation of African American culture.[62]

The historic affirmation of the values of segregation and social separation, both in this corner of Kentucky and throughout the historic South, was belied not only by the two-way process of acculturation but also by ubiquitous miscegenation. The town and the county are crosscut by many familial relationships, for the most part unacknowledged, across the line of race. The public library is replete with family and county history volumes as well as genealogical files that consider only the white holders of a particular family name. The official chronicles recount the migration from Virginia or the Carolinas to western Kentucky of the first representatives of the family. In a few cases, a family arrived with their slaves as early as the waning years of the eighteenth century when Hopkinsville was founded. Some narratives locate even earlier forebears in England or Scotland. No comparable account of black people exists.

Newspaper stories, the activities of the county genealogical society, and locally published family sketches of the town and county remain nearly silent about the social and kinship relationships between white people and black people who share a common name. Here, historical memory has given way to a consensual public amnesia, or even denial. Not unique by any means, this scrupulous avoidance of the interwoven family histories of blacks and whites helps to sustain the many fictions of local history. In reciting their histories, particularly in annual and biennial reunions, some interconnected black families, or what anthropologists call kindreds, regularly consult white family chronicles to glean some small insight about their slave antecedents and, perhaps, their white ancestry.

An interesting case in point of public identification of a white forbear by an African American family chronicler occurred at a book signing at the museum in Hopkinsville in June 2007. Charlene Hampton Holloway spoke about her family memoir, which featured her grandfather Charles Whitlock. Born in Hopkinsville, he later settled in Louisville, where he became the city's first black florist. Holloway identifies her grandfather Whitlock's paternal grandfather as John C. Whitlock (1818–1886), a prominent white physician who lived just outside of Hopkinsville.[63] About twenty-five people, mostly African American, attended the event. Among the few white attendees was at least one Whitlock descendant, who did not engage the author, a distant cousin. The newspaper announcement of the book signing indicated the author's grandfather was the grandson of a "Caucasian Hopkinsville doctor," a notice that the museum director, not a native of the area, expected to provoke some critical phone calls.[64] No one registered a protest or comment, preferring instead to ignore the matter.

Intense, even emotional resistance to the acknowledgment of miscegenation is not uncommon, particularly among white people. The relationship between Thomas Jefferson and Sally Hemings is the most well-known American example. Though it has been rumored since the nineteenth century, white historians until recently denied the relationship and hence the possibility that Jefferson was the father of Hemings's children. In bringing renewed attention to the story with the publication of her 1974 book, Fawn Brodie points out that black historians always found credibility in the evidence that an intimate bond united Jefferson and Hemings, his slave and the half-sister of his wife.[65] Brodie argued that a long connubial relationship joined master and slave, resulting in the birth of several children.

Early on, black oral tradition acknowledged Madison Hemings's own self-identification as Jefferson's son, along with his brother, Eston.[66] Until the 1960s, nondocumentary sources, such as transcribed slave narratives, had no credible value among historians, or at least white historians, who rejected out of hand oral traditions, folklore, artifacts and the like. Such sources, when located among black people, were even more susceptible to critical dismissal by writers who regarded slaves and their descendants as mere ciphers in history. Beyond their methodological skepticism and racial biases, the historical doubters were also resisting conclusions that might impugn Jefferson's character. Now, as a result of DNA analysis, professional historians by and large accept as a near-certainty Jefferson's paternity. Yet dissenters remain, arguing that DNA evidence points only to the possibility of a sexual relationship between Sally Hemings and one of several Jefferson kinsmen, but not the master of Monticello.[67]

The Jefferson-Hemings controversy is only one of many new cracks in a mirror that reflects an intricate multiracial, multicultural American past, more complex and surely more accurate than earlier sanitized and self-serving portrayals of unbreached separation. Of the controversy, Alexander Boulton observes, "the arguments swirling around Jefferson and Hemings are charged with the political and cultural biases of their age."[68] The same might well be said of any consideration of race and slavery, even in the twenty-first century.

"We knew who our white people were," older black people in Hopkinsville acknowledge, even today, but they continue to keep it among themselves. The reports about DNA evidence linking Jefferson and Hemings, and the more recent news that Strom Thurmond had fathered a black daughter, were hardly revelations to a black community acutely aware in their own family histories of a white grandfather or great-grandfather. Black people are equally cognizant of stories of other famous slaveholders who fathered children by captive black women. In Hopkinsville, some black people claim descent from Confederate icons such as Jefferson Davis and Robert E. Lee.

Despite the estrangement of the races, one is continually reminded of the social and symbolic affinities across the divide of color. In Hopkinsville, the genealogical intimacy of white and black impresses itself on anyone walking successively through Riverside and Cave Spring, the two prominent cemeteries in Hopkinsville. Shared surnames recur on the headstones and markers in both places. Riverside is the white cemetery, the resting place of those whose names are recorded in the public library's genealogical files and family histories. Many were slaveholders and veterans of the Confederate army or their descendants. Cave Spring is the black cemetery; it is the resting place of those not mentioned in the library files and family histories bearing their surnames.

The designations "white" and "black" in reference to the cemeteries hold more than historical interest, for they are municipal, tax-supported properties that remain segregated by custom rather than by law. Decades after the end of legal segregation, racial separation lives on in the present. Indeed, after many years of integration in restaurants, public accommodations, schools, and other public institutions, segregation in death remains as thoroughgoing as any form of racial separation prior to the 1960s. In a very real sense, the segregation of death is an extension of the sharp delineation between black churches and white churches. The descendants of slaves and the descendants of slaveholders of common name go about their business with only rare acknowledgment of their common ties, while the cemetery headstones of Riverside and Cave Spring literally through the decades inscribe and reinscribe that undeniable connection.

2

SLAVERY, THE TERROR OF IMAGINATION, AND EXILED FREEDOM IN LIBERIA

The centerpiece of this chapter is the unpublished journal/diary of Ellen Kenton McGaughey Wallace, a slave owner who resided both in Hopkinsville and on a nearby farm. Her private reflections about local and national events between 1849 and 1865 reveal the world of the slave owning elite and the ideology of slavery and racial domination. These reflections also embody the benign paternalism and expressions of constitutional fealty that underpin current celebrations of "southern heritage." The journal is one of many sources of those historic memories that are profoundly racialized. Wallace's reflections, however, outline contradictory images of the slave. On the one hand, she portrays the ideal bondsman, personified by her slave, Lewis, as passive and religious. On the other, she fears a nightmarish inversion of the faithful, childlike slave into an insurrectionist bent on vengeance and freedom. For that reason, the Wallace journal provides a valuable contemporaneous source on the suspected slave rebellion of 1856, a terror of imagination that spawned intense and grotesque violence against suspected plotters.

Wallace's private expressions of fear that bondsmen would violently seize freedom occurred at a time when a few slaves in Hopkinsville attained freedom through legally sanctioned manumission. But it was a freedom contingent on the slave's assent to resettlement in Liberia. This, too, was integral to the worldview of whites in Hopkinsville, as few slave owners considering manumission would accept free black people in their midst. The most extensive record of a Christian County slave bound for Liberia concerns Alexander Cross. He accepted manumission and emigration to Liberia under special circumstances; he was freed in order to become the first missionary sent to Africa by the American Christian Missionary Society, founded in 1849 by the Disciples of Christ Church. Extant documents depict him as a model of Christian faith, at once passive and compliant, in the ideal manner of Lewis, whom Wallace lavishly praised.

However, both the slave Lewis and the liberated Cross remain silent. They have no voices in effect, but instead are spoken for or about, respectively, by Wallace or various members of Cross's sponsoring church. Because no letters from Christian County slaves or former slaves have come to light, those from Rachel Eddington to her former owners in Ohio county (approximately sixty-five miles northeast of Hopkinsville) provide insight, through her own words, into a former slave's desperate life after Liberian resettlement, which seemed to her more akin to exile.

The drama of the lived experience of slavery is thus considerably more elusive than its objective demographic and ecological features outlined in the previous chapter. White voices dominate the documentary record of slavery, not only in Christian County but also throughout the South. A case in point is Liberty County, Georgia. Even amid an extensive record of the social life of the county's slave owners, Erskine Clarke remarks that "an act of imagination" remains essential if one is to penetrate their world. Indeed, a disciplined imagination enabling one to transcend his own time and discern the consciousness and outlook of people of the past is a vital tool for any historian. The problem, however, is all the more acute in regard to slavery, which demands even more resourcefulness in depicting the experience of bondage, given the dearth of documentary sources and the historical muting of black voices. Clarke thus calls for use of the widest array of evidence, or "witnesses," including not only rare slave letters and testimonies but also the findings about other communities of slaves, photographs, histories of slavery, and, if cautiously employed, the letters, court documents, and other materials written for and by slave owners.[1]

Melton A. McLaurin, for example, in his eponymous book, *Celia, A Slave*, reconstructs the trial and execution of a Missouri slave who killed her master after he raped her. Celia is not known through her own words but only through very limited historical evidence of the "manner in which others responded to her."[2] The author makes many inferences—acts of imagination in Clarke's terms—to fill the interpretive spaces that would not be so gaping if Celia's words had survived. This is precisely the challenge in understanding slavery in Christian County and environs, requiring as it does consideration of a range of sources, including letters, wills of slave owners determined to exercise even posthumous control of their bondsmen, slave narratives, and the Wallace journal.

THE JOURNAL: OUTLOOK AND REFLECTIONS

An invaluable resource for gaining insight into the ideology of slavery and racial domination, the Wallace journal also provides a day-by-day account of household and farm activities. Wallace writes of visitors, slaves, and family relationships, her impassioned reactions to the growth of Republicanism, alleged slave rebellion, the Lincoln presidency, and the Civil War as it played out locally and beyond.[3] Although Wallace's slaves are named, they are known only through her prefabricated attitudes toward black people as a collectivity. Yet this reveals the context in which slaves had to operate. The record set down by slave owners establishes the framework constraining without absolutely determining the actions of slaves. Whatever agency bondsmen exercised in relationship to white people always occurred within the narrow limits set and reproduced by the slave order. Of the words, actions, and relationships among slaves themselves—from "sundown to sunup," in George Rawick's apt phrase—little is known directly, but much can be inferred.[4]

Having lost four children, her parents, and a brother and sister within a relatively brief period in the early 1850s, Wallace is preoccupied by illness and mortality. On July 30, 1862, she notes the death anniversary of her father, who died only ten years before. Wallace's child, Robert, died later that day. On August 1, 1862, she noted that her mother had also died exactly ten years before.[5] On August 27, 1862, she records her melancholy and solitude, and then asks, "When will I cease to grieve for the dead?" Although rhetorical, her question is answered when she says that her burden of grief will end only when she dies.[6] Worried apprehension suffuses her journal, thus giving her ruminations an ominous, anxious character. In our own time, hers would likely be called a case of clinical depression, caused not only by personal losses but also by the false threat of insurrection and then the reality of the Civil War. It raged in the nearby Kentucky and Tennessee countryside and sometimes produced skirmishes in Hopkinsville itself, almost literally in her front yard.

Wallace supported the Union against the forces of secession, yet she staunchly defended slavery. As the war came close, her allegiance shifted from North to South. Likewise, other unionists in the county, including those in its northern reaches where slavery and tobacco were less salient economically, had no qualms about the institution. Slavery made possible the advantaged life Wallace and the Christian County elite enjoyed. Like so many others of her privileged station, Wallace offered rationales and justifications for slavery that thoroughly transformed the self-serving exploitation of human labor—the use of men, women and children literally as capital goods—into a benevolent paternalism that provided food, clothing, shelter, medicine, and, in the writer's view, a carefree life. The raw reality of slavery was further mystified by a sense of Christian mission and responsibility to bring enlightenment to those who had emerged from the heathen darkness of Africa to the radiance of Christian civilization.

Albert and Ellen Wallace owned as many as forty-one slaves who worked on their Christian County farm, which they maintained after moving to Hopkinsville in 1856. Their stately home in town still stands in the historic district. The farm, Winter Hill, lay west of town along the Newstead Road. Although the farm house no longer exists, the land remains unspoiled by rural development or urban sprawl. It retains the pristine beauty and obvious fertility that first attracted the Wallaces, McGaugheys, McCraes, Nances, and other early settlers to this portion of south Christian County. Near Winter Hill lay Steadfast, the farm owned and occupied for many years by Ellen McGaughey Wallace's brothers, John and Robert. John McGaughey's highly redacted diary can be found in the Hopkinsville–Christian County Public Library.[7]

Ellen Wallace records the births of eleven slave children, a remarkably small figure given the total number of slaves and the sixteen-year span of the journal. Indeed, James T. Killebrew estimates that many more children—perhaps as many as seventy-five—were born on the Wallace lands.[8] Following the prevailing pattern, the children are identified only as sons or daughters of their mothers without regard to paternity. As an institution, slavery rendered both social and biological paternity irrelevant.

Wallace's first mention of slaves and slavery occurs early in her journal, when she lauds her slave Lewis. He is very close to her ideal of a submissive bondsman resigned to a fate determined by his master or mistress but represented by Wallace as the will of God. She even holds him up as a model of forbearance, which in the entry below and elsewhere in the journal, she herself cannot follow. The diarist says nothing of his age nor of any characteristics except obedience. Although resistant, Lewis had no choice but to capitulate to the Wallaces' decision to hire him out, once again to a smelter, where he had worked on at least one prior occasion. An iron forging industry had developed around various locales on or near the Cumberland River in Tennessee and Kentucky. The first and lengthiest entry about Lewis, dated February 22, 1855, discloses his death following his return to a smelter, probably in nearby Stewart County, Tennessee where high quality iron ore was abundant:

> This evening we have heard the sad intelligence of Lewis's death at the
> furnace. We have the pleasing hope that he rest in peace with his God.
> Oh, Master's [*sic*] and Mistresses what a fearful responsibility rests upon

you. How much we need the strength and guidance of Almighty God. We think we see but we walk in darkness. I earnestly pray to my heavenly Father that I may be humble and always to have a spirit of prayer and supplication, grace and strength to discharge my duties to his glory and my soul's eternal salvation. I have had a fatiqueing [*sic*] day working at various employments frequently losing my temper at trifles. How beautifully, how gloriously the grace of God shone forth in poor Lewis's conduct when told he had to return to the furnace, he was very much opposed to going, but it was unavoidable. He went with resignation. Oh, that we all could walk in the thorny path thus supported, thus strengthened that poor slave though he could neither read nor write had any of the advantages of mental culture. How sublimely he carried out the principles implanted in his soul by the hand of God. He conquered his [illegible] by the grace of the Lord Jesus Christ and met his fate like a hero and a Christian.[9]

At other points in the journal, Wallace bemoans the worries and responsibilities shouldered by slave owners on behalf of their human property. Always knowing better than her slaves, she could not acknowledge responsibility for overt decisions that brought harm, such as sending Lewis to the punishing and dangerous work he did not want to do and from which he did not return. On February 25, 1855, she writes as if Lewis went to the smelter willingly, rather than as a reluctant pawn of owners determined to sell his labor. She says, "Poor Lewis died this day a week ago, how we regret that he left home to die amidst strangers."[10] As to age, illness, exhaustion, or accident as causes of Lewis's death, the journal is silent.

Wallace was an eyewitness to history, and her journal registers both quotidian practice and the momentous events in her corner of Kentucky. She remarks about the activities of some of her slaves—bringing food staples from the Wallace farm to her Hopkinsville residence, childcare, preparing a garden, and cooking. From the beginning, her bleak, melancholy outlook is apparent, often induced by thoughts of the death of loved ones, including another child, her young son, Johnny, in April 1855.[11] The journal is not simply descriptive. It is also introspective. Wallace continually plumbs her own haunted feelings of loss. She seeks consolation in Christian faith, but her despair frequently overwhelms the power of her religious beliefs to hold her desolation at bay, thus compounding her gloom.

At seemingly bright or hopeful moments, Wallace's dark feelings quickly take over, exposing to her the fragility of what she values. A telling entry on February 29, 1856, is not ostensibly about slavery but about the coming of spring, which Wallace marked as March 1. For her, expectations easily betray appearances, and the familiar metaphors of winter and spring as emblems of death and renewal reverse themselves. The barrenness of winter can evoke positive feelings, whereas the renewed life of spring can induce endless pain.

> The last day of winter. We have a very cold, but very healthy season. Old Winter good bye. I leave you like I would a safe harbour for the tempestious [*sic*] ocean. The cholera has prevailed here during the summer months to such an extent that I dread to see their return. Old winter . . . you brought me no bitter tear, save those of memory, but a bright beautiful boy that my heart delights in. Spring and summer I greet you with a frown. I hate your deceitful face, your [illegible] flowers and poisonous breath. Amidst your gaudy wreaths and glad promises I buried my dear little Johnny. And summer with your breezes ladened with death, how my heart aches at your approach. I would move you back like an unclean intruder if I could and it were the will of God. Did I not amidst your golden harvest and bright sunshine in ten days see Father, Mother, Sister and child laid in the cold sleep of death. How then can I love you?[12]

In the same vein, the familiar face of slavery—a source of comfort and a commonplace in her life—transforms itself when Wallace conjures the imagined terror of insurrection. While she never has misgivings about the legitimacy of slavery as an institution, she comes to doubt the devotion of her slaves in the pivotal year of 1856. Then, an imagined revolution transformed Wallace's trust into fear and her sense of security into profound vulnerability. Rumors of a slave uprising soon spread like a contagion.

In the latter part of 1856, Wallace's account, as well as newspaper stories, described the slave owner's worst nightmare—an organized slave uprising. Collective hysteria aroused by imagined enemies within the community resembled what anthropologists call witch-finding movements. The best-known movement within a European-derived community in North America to locate witches and to purge them occurred in Salem, Massachusetts, in 1692; similar movements to cleanse a locale of its witches are well documented in the anthropological literature on central Africa.[13] For slave owners holding up the ideal of the slave as passive and loyal, like a child or even a domestic animal dependent on a keeper for care and protection, a threatened inversion of servile virtues through revolt spawned reactive terror and extreme violence. Insurrection threatened the lives of white people, certainly, but it also negated the social, economic, and political foundations of a slave society. Moreover, slave risings transformed a self-justifying worldview into delusion. Accordingly, slave owners, their overseers, and other white people responded with swift, collective, and brutal measures. Writing in the midst of the ubiquitous dread in Hopkinsville and beyond, Wallace said simply, "I fear I shall never feel safe after this."[14] Both the invented slave revolt and, later, the Civil War gave particular clarity to Wallace's racial beliefs. Yet each crisis constituted an acute challenge to her convictions that slavery was essential for the care and protection of bondsmen whose incompetence and deficiencies ill-equipped them for independent survival.

THE JOURNAL AND OTHER ACCOUNTS OF THE IMAGINED SLAVE INSURRECTION

Wallace's intense preoccupation with an expected slave revolt in 1856 warrants discussion of various aspects of the phenomenon. Particularly salient are the origins of the rumored insurrection, the unfolding of events in Hopkinsville and nearby areas of western Kentucky and Tennessee, newspaper accounts of the events, reprisals against suspected insurgents, and, finally, its meaning both for slaves and slaveholders.

A number of scholars have examined the feared slave uprising. It long ago captured attention as historians, including Herbert Aptheker and Harvey Wish, argued that a genuine insurrection was brewing. In more recent years, the historians Charles Dew and Dan Carter have instead seen a frenzied white counteraction to an imagined revolt.[15] Widespread fear gripped white people in the counties of Christian and Trigg in Kentucky and in neighboring Tennessee counties, particularly Montgomery and Stewart. Anxiety and dread also seized communities elsewhere in the South.[16]

Antislavery political activities in the pivotal year of 1856 provided fertile ground for rumor and panic. The recently founded Republican Party ran its first presidential candidate, John C. Fremont, in that year. Although he lost the election, he captured most of the vote in the North. His candidacy alarmed white southerners and emboldened slaves overhearing nervous conversations of slave owners about the first candidate for president to proclaim antislavery in his platform. It is impossible to gauge fully the extent to which the rise of the Republican Party, Fremont's candidacy, and radical abolitionism motivated hopeful actions of one kind or another among bondsmen. But the intensifying feelings of relative deprivation, or the consciousness among enslaved people that slavery was under serious political challenge, doubtlessly inspired hope and overt opposition, if not outright revolt. Insurrection as a form of resistance to slavery was simply the most extreme action that slaves might take to liberate themselves as consciousness of the possibility of freedom intensified.

Newspaper reports about slave unrest began appearing in December 1856. An editor for *Le Courrier des Etats Unis,* a journal published in New York, was traveling up the Cumberland River to Nashville and disembarked at Dover in Stewart County, the epicenter of the panic; later he visited the Cumberland Iron Works. His *Le Courrier* account of December 11, published the next day in the *New York Times,* reports on his observations of December 2. Mindful of the possibility of exaggerated opinion, he relied only on what he saw and what eyewitnesses told him. Aside from his credulity about what were presented as first-hand observations, the editor provided a temperate account of the fear and vigilantism that swept through Dover and neighboring areas, including the iron forges along the Cumberland. He described white women and children assembled in Dover's only hotel and in neighboring homes, while armed men reconnoitered the countryside for rebellious slaves. He saw black servants obeying quickly and submissively. Guards with bayonets affixed to rifles held nine black prisoners captive. The editor reported that five of them would likely be released, but of the other four, "the chiefs of the conspiracy—they will in all probability become acquainted with the cord." One of the five was a black preacher who had delivered an abolitionist sermon.[17]

The writer also commented briefly on what he saw at the Cumberland Iron Works. Sixty alleged conspirators were under guard, while other slaves worked routinely and obediently. By December 20, ten slaves arrested at the forge were hanged after reportedly confessing to participation in a plot to commit "a horrible series of cruelties." Vigilantes were also driving free blacks out of the vicinity, and indeed free people of color in the South were consistently regarded with the suspicion that they actively encouraged discontent among slaves.[18]

The *Courrier* editor reiterated the observation that presidential politics had incited the fear he was witnessing:

> Much weakened by distance, the echo of the noise made in the North about the name of Fremont has extended to the banks of the Cumberland. It came in the track of the steamers . . . and then found itself in the centre of Tennessee. . . . Whether emissaries (as they affirm here) came or not from the North, it is nevertheless true that there have been certain indications of an approaching revolt. According to some, it was to be general and would extend to all the Slave States. According to others, it would simply be confined to Kentucky and Tennessee. This latter version appears to me true, and it is already more than necessary to exercise an active surveillance.[19]

The reference to emissaries concerns the alleged activities of slavery opponents in the South, including abolitionists, stirring the passion for freedom among black people. In a social world attributing little human agency or initiative to slaves, the source of black discontent was located in the incendiary words of northern white opponents of slavery and antislavery agents in the South.[20] A few whites accused of inciting slaves to rebellion were in fact arrested, beaten, or even executed. Three white "Free-Soilers" apprehended in Dover were assaulted, then given fifteen hours to leave Stewart County and thirty hours to get out of Tennessee.[21]

The correspondent for *Le Courrier* credits white provocateurs with some role in arousing expectations that Fremont would lead an army of liberation:

> The credulity of these poor people is such that, in the belief of the whites who excite them, they imagine that Col. Fremont with a large army is waiting at the mouth of the River Cumberland until the night of the 23d or 24th of December has arrived. Then all this army will help to deliver the slaves. They have been struck by the sudden swelling of the river, and attribute this circumstance to the great assemblage of men and ships at its mouth. Certain slaves are so greatly imbued with this fable that I have seen them smile while they are being whipped and have heard them say that "Freemont and his men can bear the blows they receive."[22]

On December 19, 1856, another report from the *New York Times* minimized the role of white outsiders in exciting discontent among the slaves. On the contrary, the newspaper argued that slave owners bore responsibility for the "reports of terror in the South." By their constant talk of Fremont and abolitionists determined to end slavery, slave owners were nurturing revolt.[23]

Resistance to slavery, however, did not require an external origin. Its genesis lay among the slaves themselves and took many forms. Opposition included malingering, feigned ignorance, and sabotage.[24] Acts of defiance that were not overtly violent represented "weapons of the weak," in James Scott's phrase.[25] Likewise, resistant folkloric tales that featured the slave as a trickster taking advantage of master, or identifying with small animal tricksters defeating the strong and powerful, codified ethical principles that stood against the moral calculus of the slave holder.[26]

The Bible, particularly the Old Testament, has long inspired colonized peoples in New World, Africa, and the Pacific to resistance, protest, and millennial expectation. Perhaps no segment of the Bible has resonated more with African Americans than the Exodus story. They could easily see, both in slavery and in the post-Emancipation world that betrayed the promises of freedom, their own lives in the travails of the ancient Israelites in Egypt. Identification with the oppressed peoples of the Bible prompted resistance among colonial peoples and represented the unintended consequence of the spread of Christianity. Paul Laurence Dunbar's poem, "An Ante-bellum Sermon," plays on an enslaved preacher's message about God's deliverance of his children from Pharaoh's bondage through Moses. Although the poem was written at least a generation after Emancipation, Dunbar captures the preacher's artful resistance and his self-protective but ironic admonition to his listeners: "I will pause right hyeah to say, Dat I'm still a-preachin' ancient, I ain't talkin' 'bout to-day."[27]

It is thus not surprising that suspicion fell on a number of preachers during the insurrectionary panic. Three were among six suspected slave conspirators executed in Dover in a single day. A free black preacher, Sol Young, was hanged in Cadiz, Kentucky (in Trigg County immediately west of Christian County), on December 16, and Ned Jones, a well-known black preacher in Hopkinsville, was jailed by the vigilance committee. On December 17, another free black preacher was executed by hanging at Pembroke in Christian County.[28] If Fremont did not prove to be a latter-day Moses leading the enslaved to freedom, he was nonetheless seen as an agent of deliverance. Like other near-messianic revitalization movements, the stirrings among slaves along the Cumberland invoked heroic, inspirational figures, either from the Bible or their own time.

The dread hanging over southwestern Kentucky, Tennessee, and much of the rest of the South led to extreme retribution against free and enslaved black people.[29] Throughout the South, the mythology of loyal and contented slaves was regularly exposed by the presence of patrols, which monitored the movements and activities of slaves against the possibility of organized resistance. The patrols, or vigilance committees, were particularly active when rumors of rebellion filled the air, but even in more tranquil times their existence embodied chronic white doubt about slave loyalty and even an obsession with the possibility of insurrection. Self-fulfilling prophecies were manifest as vigilance committees, fearful but determined to locate and kill would-be insurrectionists, interrogated suspected conspirators without restraint. Under conditions where interrogators freely threatened, beat, or tortured captives— not only with impunity but also with community encouragement and approval—it was certain that the inquisitors would find precisely what they were seeking. Defensive measures, however, exacerbated white fear by prompting the torture and confession of suspects, leading to new arrests, which in turn restarted the cycle.

When a slave was apprehended following his escape from the Cumberland Iron Works, he told his captors that he was fleeing from other slaves who promised to kill him if he did not join the insurrection. His avowed refusal to participate in the resistance probably spared him the swift and deadly reprisal of his questioners. After his interrogation, some eighty slaves were apprehended, all reportedly acknowledging collusion in a planned massacre of whites on Christmas and for a day or two on either side of the holiday. Readers of the *Le Courrier* or the *New York Times* did not learn how the incriminating confessions were elicited, nor did they find out how the slaves would accomplish their ends against white men who were organized and under arms.[30]

The correspondent for *Le Courrier* did, however, observe that in various places around the furnace industries slaves significantly outnumbered their white overseers, thus raising the possibility of overwhelming them by sheer force of numbers. But it didn't happen. On the contrary, the reporter discredited a rumor that he believed might have reached the East. He found no evidence that four hundred slaves had laid waste to farms in Middle Tennessee and killed the owners.[31] While the possibility of slave rebellion existed in all places throughout the South, the intensity of the reaction in settlements on the Cumberland River is not only closely related to the high ratios of slaves to whites but also to the nature of the work demanded. On either side of the Kentucky-Tennessee border, where tobacco dominated the rural economy, and along the river where the iron furnaces were operating, labor was grueling, severe, and continuous. At the furnaces it was often deadly, and slave discontent was most obvious to overseers and other whites. Although he did not resist, Wallace's slave Lewis dreaded her hiring him out to the iron industry. Restive slaves came to preoccupy white thinking as news and rumors of antislavery activity in the North proliferated.

On December 3, a day after observing conditions in Stewart County, the writer for *Le Courrier* disembarked at Clarksville, a town that appeared less agitated than Dover or the area around the Cumberland forge. Clarksville, he observed, had a larger white population and hence a less fearful attitude. Still, anxiety prevailed and the arrests there of thirty slaves and six white people "who stirred up the revolt have sufficed to suppress the commencement of an insurrection."[32]

Amid the panic, reasoned voices were raised. W. F. Cooper, living in Nashville, thus wrote toward the end of December 1856:

> We are trying our best in Davidson County to produce a negro insur-
> rection without the slightest aid from the negroes themselves. Whether
> we shall succeed remains to be seen, but it is certain no more effectual
> means could be pursued than those our wiseacres have adopted. The
> rack, the thumbscrew, and the wheel are looked upon, it is true, as
> instruments of justice belonging to the dark ages of barbarism—but
> then the lash properly administered is quite as efficacious. It breaks no
> bones, while it satisfactorily elicits whatever confessions or disclosures
> the ministers of extra-legal justice are anxious to procure.

There is, in sober seriousness, no shadow of foundation for any belief of domestic plot or insurrection. But the popular mind is in that excited state requiring the most trivial cause to set everything in a blaze. Our better citizens are at work and I hope will succeed in preventing an outbreak—*among the whites* [original emphasis].[33]

In a retrospective view forty years after the panic, J. B. Killebrew, living in Clarksville at the time, reflected on the imagined revolt and the outburst of extreme violence:

During the winter of 1856–57 there was great excitement growing out of the belief that a negro insurrection was imminent. . . . Firearms were secured and men enlisted for protection against a servile war. I never believed there was any serious intentions among the negroes to rebel. Some hot-headed white men . . . imagined that they saw indisputable evidence of an insurrection, and the poor negroes upon whom suspicion fell were . . . unmercifully whipped until they confessed that such a thing as an insurrection had been freely discussed. . . . they would often implicate others without any foundation, and thus the excitement and suspicion grew until whole counties were involved.[34]

By the time the maelstrom had spent itself through quasi-judicial hangings and mob execution, the number of victims in all likelihood numbered in the hundreds.

In Christian County the frenzy seized people in several locales including Hopkinsville and the small hamlet of LaFayette, lying eighteen miles south of Hopkinsville and twenty miles northeast of Dover. The Vigilance Committee of La-Fayette declared, "We are in great danger," in a December 2 message to Hopkinsville seeking assistance because of an expected attack the next day by slaves from the iron works. The secretary of the LaFayette committee stated, "The negroes of Eclipse, Clark, and La Grange [smelters in Tennessee] have united and are marching towards Dover, and were within eight miles of that place when last heard from. Their intention is to relieve the negroes [free the prisoners] at Dover, then march to the Rolling Mill, then to Bell-Wood Furnace, then through LaFayette on to Hopkinsville and the Ohio River."[35]

This message, as well as a report from Clarksville about an imminent insurrection, stirred "intense excitement" in Hopkinsville.[36] The Christian County court had already begun defensive preparations. Orders were issued appointing fifteen groups, each consisting of a captain and two assistant militiamen, to patrol designated sections of the county.[37] Reporting to the *Louisville Courier,* the

Hopkinsville correspondent stated in a letter of December 3, "Our little town is up in arms at the present writing. 'The negroes are marching upon us,' is heard from every mouth. This morning several messengers arrived from Lafayette, a small town eighteen miles south of Hopkinsville, calling on the citizens of this place to come to their assistance. They were momentarily expecting an attack from about 600 negroes. About 150 persons left immediately for the 'seat of war.' . . . Hopkinsville is strongly guarded. It is rumored we will be attacked to-night."[38]

Again, rumors were baseless. Neither LaFayette nor Hopkinsville was attacked. A correspondent from Louisville wrote from western Kentucky that a company of Hopkinsville men went to LaFayette and then returned home, having found only a frightened white population.[39] Likewise, Dover, Tennessee, and other Stewart and Montgomery County locales experienced only the mayhem of armed and desperate white people projecting their worst fears onto terrified slaves, whom they beat and killed mercilessly after extracting confessions.

Amid a frenzy of brutal retribution along the Cumberland and in nearby towns, the countermeasures taken in Dover were among the most macabre. Vengeance went beyond execution to include corpse disfigurement and decapitation in order to terrify the slaves. The grotesque abuses dramatically enacted the raw, unchecked power of the slavocracy. The following admonition in a Clarksville newspaper provided public sanction for what was about to happen in Dover to those regarded as beyond the ken of the human, considered, as they were, "maniacs" and their flesh like the meat of butchered animals:

> The crimes contemplated should be atoned for precisely as though those crimes had been attempted and consummated. Fearful and terrible examples should be made, and if need be, the fagot and the flame should be brought into requisition to show these deluded maniacs the fierceness and the vigor, the swiftness and completeness of the white man's vengeance. Let a terrible example be made in every neighborhood where the crime can be established and if necessary let every tree in the country bend with negro meat. Temporizing in such cases as this is utter madness. We must strike terror, and make a lasting impression, for only in such a course can we find guaranties [*sic*] of future security.[40]

According to the Goodspeed histories of the local area published in 1886, six "ringleaders" were hanged just before Christmas. A resident of Dover, still living at the time of publication, was said to have decapitated the corpses; he exhibited the heads atop poles and "paraded the streets during the day of the hanging, displaying the ghastly, gory objects to the terrified Negro population."[41] This travesty is independently corroborated in the journal of Eugene Marshall, a Union army soldier bivouacked in the vicinity of Dover in February 1862, at the time of the battle of Fort Donnelson. Marshall spoke with Stewart County residents who reported "great excitement in relation to slave insurrections" that he said, incorrectly, had occurred ten years before. Of his conversations, Marshall wrote that "they tell me that at the various iron works in the country many negrows [*sic*] were whiped [*sic*] to death, to make them confess the conspiracy, that the heads of several were cut off stuck up on a pole as a terror to the rest, and that at Hillman's furnace below here one negro jumped into the furnace while it was in full operation and was completely consumed. All these horrors they relate as coolly as any other matter which has ocured [*sic*] without seeming to feel that there is anything very terrible about it."[42] Horrific but not singular in its ruthlessness, the ritualized display of severed heads joined torture to fatal beatings and public hangings that aimed simultaneously to punish purported revolt and deter its repetition.

The testimony of Mary Wright of Hopkinsville, given to a WPA interviewer collecting slave narratives in the 1930s, indicates that beheadings occurred in Christian County. Raising a number of unanswered questions, Wright's claim is consistent with the Goodspeed account of Dover. The latter source was sufficiently credible that at least one major historian of slavery has accepted the report without independent confirmation.[43] Wright was born on August 1, 1865, in Gracey, a small settlement in Christian County. She told the interviewer that her mother had spoken of the black uprising, although no date is indicated. Wright also attributed the reprisals to the Ku Klux Klan, although it was founded after the Civil War. Her mother described how the heads of black people were placed on stakes and then planted along the road joining Hopkinsville to Cadiz (Trigg County) immediately to the west. Buzzards picked the bones clean.[44] The Fisk slave narratives describe similar events. An anonymous narrator spoke of beheadings at the Hillman furnace, reiterating Marshall's report. Another former slave mentioned Henry King, a preacher beheaded in Dover; the victim's brother was shown the mutilated corpse and threatened with the same fate unless he stopped speaking of freedom.[45]

Terrorizing a slave population through corpse mutilation had occurred in the largest slave rebellion in American history. In January 1811, some four to five hundred slaves in the vicinity of the parishes of St. Charles and St. John the Baptist, some thirty-five miles from New Orleans, revolted against the slavocracy. Arriving at the Andry plantation armed with knives, clubs, and axes, the insurgents seized additional weapons, including guns, wounding Major Andry and killing one of his sons. As the group moved through the countryside, other slaves joined the insurgents, and together the small army burned plantations and killed another person. Other planters, bolstered by state and regular army troops, organized themselves against the insurrectionists. Numbering more than six hundred, the combined forces put down the slave revolt by killing more than sixty, some in battle, others by summary execution. Some were captured and executed in New Orleans, their heads displayed along the route between the city and the Andry plantation.[46] The beheadings in Dover and near Hopkinsville four and a half decades later occurred in response to a rumor of revolt, confirmed by confessions extracted under torture; such was the panic of 1856 that it easily rivaled the fear provoked in Louisiana by an actual insurrection.

Reprisals and the atrocious retributions in various locales seized by collective hysteria are reminiscent of lynching as an extra-legal form of collective violence. The suppression of slave revolts and lynching, both before and after slavery, were determined efforts of the most extreme ferocity to maintain the supremacy of whites, first as slave masters and later as the sole arbiters and beneficiaries of the postbellum racial caste system. Richard Hofstadter and Michael Wallace have observed "there is a suggestive psychological similarity . . . between the psychology of lynchings and the pattern of suppression of slave revolts."[47] Wright has found this linkage particularly suggestive in his study of racial violence in Kentucky.[48] Very different from ordinary sanctions against individual slaves for theft or other prohibited acts, lynching and the suppression of revolt were filled with bloodlust without restraint. Their purpose was to maintain black people collectively in their lowly rank, lest others challenge the nearly absolute authority of whites or, before 1865, the legitimacy of the slave order itself. Mutilation of the physical body conveys enormous symbolic power, particularly if, as anthropologists suggest, the physical body stands in for the social or political body. Then, the act of decapitation, especially of leaders of an insurrectionary movement, is emblematic of the decapitation and destruction of the nascent political body of slaves, believed to be organized for a revolutionary overthrow of established order.[49]

While Wallace noted what she was seeing and hearing in Hopkinsville and near her farm, her diary entries in late 1856 also take account of newspaper reports of black unrest and white countermeasures, as discussed above. The various reports almost certainly played a part in shaping her fears and apprehensions. Wallace's journal and the news reports of an imminent slave uprising thus converge in recurrent themes. Consequently, it is difficult to sort through Wallace's spontaneous expressions of fear and the news reports that undoubtedly provoked or exacerbated anxiety in western Kentucky and Tennessee. That these themes recur in news accounts from all over the South strongly suggests an infectious apprehension sweeping through the slaveholding states as disseminated by the press and by word of mouth.

Wallace's journal entry of November 20, 1856, stimulated by a newspaper report, represents her first remarks about a slave rebellion. "The papers contain several alarming accounts of intended insurrections in various parts of the country. I earnestly wish my children maybe [sic] freed from the rankling cares and perplexieties [sic] that destroys the peace of a slave holder. The consientious [sic] master and mistress are less happy than their dependants, who have with moderate labour have [sic] all the comforts and some of the luxuries of life without thought or care. They know that their bed will be made for them in sickness, their doctors bills paid, their wants attended to and then taken care of in old age."[50]

Reflecting the ubiquitous fear in Hopkinsville and Christian County, Wallace's anxieties build throughout December.

December 3, 1856

The town and country in a great excitement on account of the Negroes. A general insurrection is feared. Ammunition has been sent for in Clarksville, and the citizens are preparing for any sudden alarm. Mr. Wallace [her husband, Albert] armed himself this evening, something very strange for him to do. One who has passed such an awful trial during Cholera as I did should be able to meet any crisis.[51]

December 7, 1856

Dreadful things are coming to pass. Seven or eight Negroes hung. The jails of the neighboring towns as well as this are crowded with Negroes suspected. Some have confessed their intention to rise and murder the whites and in a body gathering strength as they go to fight their way to a free state. The whole town, county and ajoining [sic] counties are in a perfect state of agitation and under the strictest patrole [sic]. . . . I do not feel alarmed. The danger may be greater than I imagine.[52]

Wallace's mood changes quickly in the space of a single day, perhaps as a result of seeing the apprehension and fear of others.

December 8, 1856

This has been a day of great anxiety to the citizens. Committees have been examining Negroes and commiting [sic] them to jails. . . . The news still fearful with regard to the Negroes. Old men look serious, and women fear. I fear I shall never feel safe after this.[53]

December 10, 1856

We live at present it is thought in the midst of danger. This state of affairs has been brought about by the great latitude given to slaves. The excitement and speeches during the presidential election and the pernicous [sic] influence of low forms [abolitionists and other whites allegedly encouraging slave discontent and action] mingling with the Negroes. Tonight is dark and stormy in accordance with the times. The grave has one comfort. It is free from care.[54]

December 11, 1856

There has been six Negroes arrested in town today. At Newstead [a small settlement west of Hopkinsville near the Wallace farm] they are making arrest [sic]. Danger seems to be thick around. There was to be a general raising [sic] on the 24th of December 1856, the plan universally known and finely arranged. Gentleman [sic] who laughed it to scorn at first are now active in endeavoring to ward off danger. I only wich [sic] I had half dozen revolvers and the heart and hand to use them, but I am as easily frightened as a kitten. I disgrace my ancestry.[55]

December 12, 1856

This day a Negro was hung for killing his Overseer. The excitement grows stronger and stronger. Had not the plot been discovered this region of country would have flowed with blood. White men who had fought in the Mexican War laid the plan and provided arms and ammunition for the Negroes. Committees of the most able citizens in every neighborhood and town have been sitting from day to day making investigations and the disclosures are truly fearful.[56]

That a slave was executed at this time inevitably associated him with insurrection in Wallace's view. However, the slave, Jacob, had killed a white man, Charlie Boyd, in early October, prior to the outbreak of panic. A jury, which included Robert McGaughey, Wallace's brother, rejected Jacob's claim that he killed Boyd in self-defense and sentenced him to death.[57]

December 13, 1856

Mr. Wallace went to the farm. . . . The accounts he brings back are truly awful. All the Negroes in the neighborhood implicated. The leading Negro in each family was selected to kill their owner's wives and children. The young girls to be made wives of. No exaggeration of imagination or language can equal the reality. Such are the confessions. All agreeing in the same thing though examined apart. What heart rending scenes would have been enacted had their scheme been put into execution. The time has not yet arrived when their plan was to be put into effect. Christmas was the time set apart. The punishment inflicted to extract information are terrible. But the occasion requires it and there is no alternative. . . . We have heard no news today yet I have a strong suspicions [sic] of one of our maids, Caroline. I may do her injustice but I think her in the plot, heart and soul. Our Negroes on the plantation, it is said, are implicated. To what extent we have yet to learn. The poor creatures have no doubt been instigated to such dreadful intentions by fiends in the shape of white men.[58]

In this entry, Wallace reiterates the anxieties reported in newspapers. The insurrection would loose the basest impulse of the slave that on other occasions would result in lynching. In the expected uprising, it was to be an organized assault on white families, not only to kill slave owners but also to ravage their daughters who, Wallace believed, would become the conspirators' wives. For Wallace and others, their dread was so intense as to conjure images of impossible realization.

Of course, the unchecked power of slaveholders—economic, physical, and sexual—was nearly complete, represented no more tellingly than in the sexual exploitation of female slaves. Yet a deeply rooted white anxiety transformed the reality of raw white racial and sexual power into an ever-watchful defense against the fearful figure of the black male. Driven by lust both in slavery and freedom, he would, if not controlled, transgress the most sacred of all boundaries—the white female body. In lynchings, real or imagined insurrection, or in Nathan Bedford Forrest's defense of his actions at Fort Pillow, one sees again the projection onto black men of a savage sexuality and power that demanded the most ruthless suppression.

Forrest lived in Hopkinsville with his wife and family as commander of six companies of cavalry quartered there early in the Civil War. He is commemorated on at least two historic plaques in town. In 1863, Confederate forces under his command killed surrendering black soldiers at the federal garrison of Fort Pillow on the Mississippi River some forty miles north of Memphis. Poorly armed black troops constituted nearly half of the Union force of 557 men. The Fort Pillow troops faced an overwhelming number of cavalry led by Forrest. While denying that his command had massacred black soldiers as they surrendered, Forrest gave "a little preface" to his self-serving postwar version of events by invoking alleged sexual depredations by these soldiers. Forrest, a trader in slaves before the Civil War and a founder of the Ku Klux Klan afterward, claimed that the black troops "had pillaged the whole country, and under the pretext of looking for rebel arms, had insulted women, abused old men, and in several instances had committed the most brutal outrages on highly respectable women."[59]

Wallace also expected the uprising to take place on or about Christmas day, as reported in the newspapers. A projected upheaval on that day was, paradoxically, consistent with normal Christmas celebrations by slave owners and their bondsmen. Aside from the terror induced by fear of insurrection, Wallace registered no particular outrage at what contemporary sensibilities might regard as a desecration of a holy day. Christmas had a very different meaning in Wallace's time.

Rule-breaking and symbolic inversions of normal activity during Christmas were widely accepted and actively cultivated by slave owners. As Stephen Nissenbaum has shown, contemporary Christmas celebrations are a relatively recent development, departing significantly from the carnivalesque excesses marking Christmas throughout much of the nineteenth century.[60] Of the ceremonial genre anthropologists have termed "rituals of rebellion," Christmas celebrations at one time licensed participants to suspend rules of normal social and political action and to practice what was normally prohibited. The ethnographic and historical literature is replete with cross-cultural descriptions of the breaking of taboos, rulers humbled by their lowly subjects, dominant men giving way to the aggressive and sometimes obscene initiatives of usually subservient women, and other symbolic attacks against the institutions of power.

In the antebellum South, the holiday suspension or reversal of normal order was much in evidence. Work-free days punctuated the lives of slaves during the Christmas season. Slave owners provided their bondsmen with alcohol, usually prohibited during the year, and drinking was accompanied with much raucous singing and dancing. Masters and mistresses distributed presents, including food and special items such as sugar, clothing, and baubles to their slaves; they even participated in the preparation and serving of special meals to their slaves, sometimes in the plantation house. As befits ritual inversion, white presentations to slaves were marked by deferential and respectful behavior.[61] For example, Kenneth Stampp cites a Mississippi slave owner who recorded a Christmas day spent "waiting on the negroes, and making them as comfortable as possible."[62]

In Christian County, John McGaughey remarked briefly in his diary about Christmas celebrations in the 1850s. Anything but solemn, the holiday seemed a combination of Halloween and July 4th. On Christmas 1854, the day was ushered in with "the boom of Christmas guns," canon perhaps, firing from 4:00 in the morning until daybreak.[63] Young slave children would cause much amusement by bursting inflated pig bladders outside the door and then demanding a gift.[64] He describes slaves in "excellent spirits" of expectation of the holiday. John McGaughey also assisted his brother-in-law, Albert Wallace, in "measuring a dozen patterns of calico intended for his Negro women" during Christmas 1855.[65] On Christmas Eve, 1860, McGaughey records that "Robert [his brother] dealt out sugar, coffee, and flour to the servants. They seem in pleasing anticipation of the holidays. On Christmas morning, John [a black child] honored us with several bladder explosions."[66]

Rituals of rebellion are assertive, oppositional displays of normally unacceptable behavior. That they occurred in rigid, hierarchical social formations such as the American South during slavery suggests a revolutionary potential inherent in these complex rites. Yet the paradox of their performance lies precisely in negating the revolutionary impulse. Slaves seeking to elevate themselves into masters and to seize the levers of economic and political power while disposing of their white overlords would no longer be players in a ritual drama but rather potential revolutionaries. Societies that not only tolerate but also actively encourage such performances rely on the unchallenged acceptance of existing hierarchies and arrangements. Slave owners as much as slaves thus valued the occasion. For the slave it was an opportunity for leisure, indulgence in food and drink, and freedom from the rigid restraints of the repetitive labor routine. In promoting a week or so of merrymaking, drunkenness, work-free days and the like, slave owners served their own interests by enabling slaves to canalize the frustration, aggression, and anger built up over the year, thereby helping to preserve the institution of their oppression.

Frederick Douglass explicitly claimed that without the revelry and drunkenness of the holiday season, encouraged by slave owners, insurrection would ignite immediately. His critical assessment foreshadows by many decades modern social science understandings of rituals of rebellion. "These holidays" he wrote, "serve as conductors, or safety-valves, to carry off the rebellious spirit of enslaved humanity." In Douglass's thinking, the Christmas bacchanal encapsulated "the gross fraud, wrong, and inhumanity of slavery." The excesses of the season, far from exhibiting the benevolence of the slaveholders, sprang instead from pure self-interest.[67]

For very different reasons, Booker T. Washington unsparingly criticized the Christmas celebrations of the slave era and their continuation after the Civil War. Rough dancing, or the "frolic," whiskey, firecrackers, work-free days, and the absence of religious observance were all inimical to Washington's purposes. Reform of the carnivalesque celebration thus became part of his larger plan of promoting work, sobriety, and discipline. At Tuskegee, Washington stated, "we made a special effort to teach our students the meaning of Christmas, and to give them lessons in its proper observance."[68]

When relationships between the powerful and the powerless are actively questioned, then rituals of rebellion are no longer tolerated. Under those conditions, they threaten to break through the innocuous fiction of ritual and the unreality of the scripted drama to ignite real, consequential resistance or aggression against the existing social formation. It is for this reason that the frenzy of December 1856, raising as it did the specter of an actual, organized revolution against the slavocracy, could not comport with customary Christmas practices. In Louisville, for example, the mayor issued a curfew order prohibiting slaves on the city streets at night during the Christmas holiday and "the annual Chrismas-Eve Negro Love-Feast was forcibly broken up in conformity with the Mayor's insurrectionary proclamation." The public, however, felt no anxiety in that part of Kentucky, as the "proclamation is satirized in the Press and derided by the people."[69] Even after the Civil War, the latent danger of actual revolt that came to be associated with Christmas continued to create fear. In the absence of evidence that Christmas violence was imminent, collective apprehension still drove former slave owners to consolidate their power against hopeful former slaves seeking to redeem federal promises of land.[70]

Wallace's anxieties, increasingly extreme and paranoid, continued throughout the Christmas holiday. She suspected that her slaves Elijah, William, Caroline, and Jack were complicit in the plot. Elijah and William were called before the Vigilance Committee and later virtually confessed to Wallace their sympathy for rebellion.

December 17, 1856

Mat arrived half an hour by sun this morning in great hast [sic] for his master. Elijah has been implicated, and is before the committee. I do not know what they will do to him. I hope he will be cleared. I doubt his innocence, as he is fond of bad association. I was in a great passion with my maid, Caroline, also this morning. The Negroes have got to such a pitch of impudence that farther [sic] forbearance is degrading to the whites and a serious disadvantage to the servants.[71]

December 19, 1856

Tonight is dark and stormy. The state of the community in general is in the same condition. Committee still making investigations. Elijah and William confessed . . . that on the 23rd of November a certain Negro preached in the neighborhood, took up a collection for the avowed purpose of obtaining arms and ammuntion for the Negroes in their intented [sic] rebellion. [T]hese meetings were held secretly at various houses in the neighborhood where ever the Overseer or master were most indulgent. The Negro is now in jail awaiting trial. [This may have been Ned Jones, reported by the *New York Times*, December 24, 1856, to have been arrested.] This disturbance has occasioned great suffering. I hear of executions every day or two. I have some idea of changing my cook. Caroline is not of an obliging turn neighter [*sic*] is she brisk or handy.[72]

December 21, 1856

Sunday Evening. Yesterday I was very unwell having a bad cold and otherwise indisposed. Today is the calm Holy Sabbath. There is snow, the weather very cold. As we sat around our well filled table, our children laughing and enjoying their dinner, a perfect picture of domestick [*sic*] happiness without a dark shadow. My thoughts for contrast turned to the dark prison in town with darker spirits and I raise my heart in humble supplication that the wrath of the Almighty not descend upon his unworthy children.[73]

December 23, 1856

Last night I was unwell and very wakeful. I never fully realize our perilious [*sic*] situation except when lying awake at night. Then the least noise is startling. We do not know but the next moment we may be face to face with death in its most terrible form and accompanyment [*sic*]. Tomorrow night was the time set apart in the plot.[74]

December 24, 1856

Christmas Eve. The night the Negroes intended to have risen and murdered the whites had the plot not been discovered. Two of ours had agreed to join. Elijah said he was getting old, but he would help all he could. Jack said he would promise to stand where any other man would stand. There are now 30 in jail, 5 committed this evening.[75]

Wallace says nothing of the immediate aftermath of the interrogations of Elijah and William by the Vigilance Committee, nor of the consequences of Jack's defiance. It is not known if they were beaten or otherwise punished, but they did survive. William is mentioned in a journal entry of January 1863, and Jack a year later.[76] It is likely, then, that Wallace did not press for severe punishment, either of Caroline or Elijah.

December 25, 1856

Christmas, the town very quiet. No security. I hear nothing like life or animation, but a company drilling, the beat of the drum and the roar of cannon.[77]

December 30, 1856

Robert and John dined with us. We have need of grateful hearts for the forbearance and mercy of God manifested in the discovery of the late plot for an insurrection of slaves. Their intentions were of a horrid and awful character, to provide poison for all the cooks on the day preceed-ing the night of general massacre. This is all true.[78]

A letter to the *Canton Dispatch* (Trigg County) of December 13, 1856 captures the full extent of white paranoia during that month. Writing from Pembroke, ten miles south and east of Hopkinsville, the commentator puts forth an extraordinary claim about the reach and scope of the alleged plot.

I have no doubt but that it [the plot] is a universal thing all over the Southern States and that every negro, fifteen years old, or older, either knows of it or is into it; and that the most confidential house servants are the ones to be the most active in the destruction of their [masters'] families.[79]

It was widely believed, as Wallace indicates, that conspiratorial participation of trusted house slaves included a macabre role for cooks. They were to transform nurturance into death by poisoning the household. In this respect, the dread of 1856 came to resemble ethnographic cases detailing a collective nightmare about ene-mies within. Such settings induce deep apprehension by giving people a sense that their most fundamental assumptions about the world—their social and psychologi-cal moorings—are no longer secure. Panic is the likely outcome of a realization that slave loyalty is a fiction, exposed by the certain belief that bondsmen closest to the master were the most treacherous. The witches of Salem or the malefactors of innu-merable other places who corrupt or betray basic rules of comity and commensality are kinsmen, neighbors, and even friends.[80] Of the old planters to whom Wallace refers on January 14, 1857, disillusionment followed in the wake of "discovering" the treachery of their domestic servants. Once again, the homology between the social and physical body is apposite. Conceived for so long as benign, the enemy masquer-ading as friend, solidary kinsman, or loyal servant within the intimate circle of the family carries out her lethal work by insuring that the boundary of the physical body is fatally breached by noxious adulterants in the place of wholesome food.

On January 14, in her last journal entry on the subject, Wallace referred to the "late insurrection movement." The crisis had for the most part passed. But even after the executions and the export of the remaining problem—the selling of particularly recalcitrant slaves southward—Wallace was discomfited at the remaining sympathizers, including some of her own slaves.

> January 14, 1857
> A number of the Negro leaders in the late insurrection movement were hung in the surrounding counties. Those next implicated were or are to be sent to a southern clime [to be sold]. Four from our immediate neighborhood in the country are of the number. There are many equally guilty left behind. I fear some of our family are of the number. This movement has fallen stunning blows to many old planters who had looked upon their servants as only second to their children. A remarkable feature in the case was that those who were kept about the house and had had the entire confidence of their masters were generally most guilty.[81]

Wallace believed that the alleged conspiracy had penetrated her innermost domestic space and that her maid, Caroline, had joined the plotters as a potential poisoner.

THE JOURNAL AND THE CIVIL WAR

Although insurrection was a chimera, it exacerbated racial fears, latent or overt, but always present. The Civil War came to Hopkinsville and further undermined what Wallace had come to expect regarding black people. The looming specter of anti-slavery actions, whether in the form of abolitionism or other rumored hope, increasingly emboldened the slave population in Christian County, especially as the war came close to home. Wallace's forebodings intensified as visible challenges to her racial views were manifest. Some of her slaves were reportedly very restive, and increasing numbers of slaves throughout the county were fleeing to Union lines, some to enlist and others to work for the army. At base, Wallace feared a loss of control over black people, signaled by runaways, the memory of the 1856 panic, and, in the latter part of 1862, the imminent Emancipation Proclamation freeing slaves in the states in rebellion. Although Kentucky's slaves were to be excluded from the emancipation order, Wallace portrays the impending mass liberation of slaves in apocalyptic terms. The idea of emancipation in her view could only stir up black people, still legally enslaved.

September 29, 1862

Lincoln's Proclamation emancipating all the slaves is justly creating great indignation. The consequences of it are too awful to contemplate. The blood of women and children and helpless aged will flow in torrents if its carried into effect. The foul wretch ought to suffer all the torments that could be inflicted on him, body and soul. Then to place innocent women and helpless infants at the mercy of black monsters who would walk in human shape.[82]

December 13, 1862

These are days of midnight darkness for this Republick [sic]. God only knows upon what awful calamities we are drifting. A band of robbers came in last night. Only ten in number. Broke open stores or rather ordered them open. Took what they wanted and left. I am afraid to put on my night gown for fear of sudden alarm at night . . . We live as it were by chance without any security from the law, but only by the mercy of God. The President from his message to Congress still intends carrying out his infamous proclamation. For this one act he should be impeached and incarcerated in a dungeon the remainder of his miserable life. Servile insurrection will be the consequence unless the strong arm of the nation prevents it, and the blood of the helpless women and children will flow in torrents if his wicked and fanatical policy is not over ruled.[83]

December 23, 1862

We are alone tonight. This Christmas and the first of January '63 will be remarkable in coming years for its connection with Lincoln's infamous proclamation. The Patrole [sic] has to be very vigilant and watchful in the country. And if it were not that there is several military companies [U.S. troops] stationed here at this time none of us could lay down at night without a shudder at what might happen before morning. St. Domingo over again. [Here Wallace refers to the slave insurrection and revolution establishing an independent Haiti out of the French colony of Saint Domingue.][84]

February 17, 1863

A dark rainey [sic] day. The town dull and gloomy. Gloom, gloom pervades the town and country. The President and his cabinet can think of nothing but the Negro, Negro. The Constitution made by our fathers and sealed with their blood is nothing with them compared to the Negro. The laws of this once glorious Republick [*sic*] compared to the Negro. The interest of the white man is nothing in comparison to that of the Negro. There seems to be but one idea in the head of Lincoln and his cabinet, and that is the liberation of the slaves at the cost of everyting [*sic*] held sacred by the white race. All must give way to the superior rights of the Negro. What can save the Republick [*sic*] under such an administration. Nothing but hurling them from power as madmen should be hurled.[85]

By early 1864, Wallace was recording her desperate feelings about black troops as well as the loss of her slaves.

January 20, 1864

My chief fear is of the Negro soldiers at Clarksville, Fort Donelson and other places along the border of the state. Should they become insubordinate or be headed by desperate Abolitionist[s] and over-run the country, our condition would be fearful.[86]

January 21, 1864

I have just heard of a great stampede of Negroes which took place last night. Capt. Campbell lost forty-six. They took wagons, mules, and baggage. I expect everyday our turn will come. . . . We can hardly hope to retain ours when they are leaving all around.[87]

Wallace and her husband, like some other white people in Hopkinsville, were slave-owning unionists. They opposed secession, but at the same time were committed to slavery as an institution. Steadily, her hatred for Lincoln, whom she referred to as "the Negro President," grew along with admiration for the southern armies and their leadership.[88]

March 5, 1864

Silent, burning indignation against Lincoln and his administration is the prevailing feeling among the better class of citizens through out the country. But they dare not give expression to them for his hireling soldiers are stationed at the corner of every street and every by-way in the country, exciting the Negroes to leave their owners and all manner of high handed insolence.[89]

In March, Wallace noted that her slave, Jack, who took a risk eight years before when he said he would support rebellion, was urging Wallace's other slaves to join him in fleeing to Clarksville, where federal forces were in control. She writes on March 24 that slaves "are leaving nightly in large numbers." Their overseer also decamped, and Wallace observed "no prospect of making a crop this year."[90]

The challenges to the familiar racial order haunted Wallace's dreams as well as her waking hours, which prompted the particularly bitter and sarcastic entry of June 7. Again, the slave owner is portrayed as victim of overweening federal power incarnate in Lincoln.

> June 7, 1864
>
> I could not sleep last night for thinking and dreaming of the draft which is to take place Saturday. Those drafted cannot pay off as formerly, but must furnish a substitute or go into Lincoln's Army side by side and shoulder to shoulder with the Negro troops. [Wallace's racial fears did not comport with the reality of black men in the Army of the United States. They served in segregated units, commanded by white officers; they did not as an order of battle fight alongside white soldiers.] The master and his former slave must keep time to the same musick [sic], share the same rations if there is any advantage the Negro must have it. His family must certainly be looked after they are more worthy than than [sic] the white mans [sic] in the eyes of the Abolitionist. What a pity after taking them from their rightful owners and making soldiers of them, they cannot send a delegation to heaven demanding of the Almighty to change their ebony skins to snow white or suffer the consequences, such is their presumption.[91]

By the autumn, black soldiers had entered Hopkinsville.

> September 22, 1864
>
> The long dreaded event has at last occurred, a company of Negro troops now occupy the town. . . . I fear we will have to take Julia and Alfred from school, owing to the town being filled with Negro soldiers. It will be unsafe for a decent woman to walk the street.[92]

> September 23, 1864
>
> Mr Wallace just from downtown reports that prospects are dark indeed. White men coming to town were insolently stopped in the road by gangs of armed Negro soldiers who are going through the country

at will, persuading the Negroes or forcing those who are not willing to join them.[93]

Throughout the fall, Wallace complained about slaves running off, as well as the importuning by federal soldiers in the town, especially black troops. On December 12, Wallace reported that two thousand Confederate soldiers had taken control of the town. She wept with happiness because no longer would black Republican outrages occur. Yet her happiness was quickly tempered by the harsh reality of military occupation, even by Confederates. Two drunken soldiers, cursing and threatening, pounded on the Wallace door late at night demanding food. The "reign of terror" continued as southern forces conscripted the young men who had not fled. Two days later, southern troops seized two of the Wallace horses, but the writer comforts herself in the knowledge that the horses "have gone to the right side."[94]

Wallace's penultimate entry about Lincoln occurs on March 4, 1865, the day of his second inauguration.

This day Lincoln is inaugurated for his second term. Another four years of darkness, tryrany [sic] and blood if they bear any resemblance to the past term. The South is gathering her strength for the last desparate [sic] struggle. Sherman is marching his victorious barbarian hords [sic] through South Carolina taking and destroying city after city. Charleston, Wilmington and Columbia. Grant is holding General Lee in check at Richmond. It is the opinion of the people that the Confederacy is in the last ditch. But General Lee is the greatest general of the age, and his principal officers are men of undaunted courage and great ability. This of its self [sic] is reason for hope even though the case otherwise seems hopeless.[95]

The last weeks of the war brought Wallace the regular importuning of federal soldiers seeking food and, in her view, an opportunity to steal. Wallace suffered a fate that was "provoking," for the Yankee soldiers "get all their information . . . from our Negroes. Oh, the humiliation and degradation of the present times for people who have always been true to the constitution and laws of their state and country."[96] Here, Wallace reflects a ubiquitous southern view that persists to this day among Lost Cause apologists. They argue that southerners were always faithful to the principles of the American Revolution and to the Constitution, believing the South to have stood up for individual liberty against usurping radicals from the North. Whether in the writings of Jefferson Davis or other secessionist partisans, the full humanity of black people was never accepted. Otherwise, the spectacular contradiction between the passionate espousal of liberty and human rights, on the one hand, and slavery on the other, could not have been so casually sustained.

On April 6, Wallace recorded the fall of Richmond and noted that "Lincoln now issues his commands from the deserted mansion of Jeff Davis." Hopkinsville, by military order, was to be illuminated, but Wallace put no light in the window, because "there was no corresponding light in the soul." She relented when ordered to do so by soldiers.[97] News of Lee's surrender to Grant on April 9 reached Hopkinsville by telegraph the next day.[98] Despite or perhaps because of the venomous hatred Wallace held for President Lincoln, she said nothing about his assassination on April 14; nor did she mention him after she recorded his issuance of orders from Richmond on April 6. A woman of deep religious conviction but always faint of heart, Wallace, it may plausibly be speculated, bore some sense of shame that an assassin had acted on sentiments precisely her own. She felt implicated, perhaps, in the violent death of a president, even one whom she reviled so intensely.

ALEXANDER CROSS: CHRISTIAN MISSIONARY IN LIBERIA

At the beginning of Black History Month in 2001, the *Kentucky New Era* featured a story about Alexander Cross. The article began, "On Oct. 5, 1853, Alexander Cross walked out of the Christian County Courthouse a free man."[99] His manumission, however, brought him only a contingent freedom, dependent as it was on his willingness to emigrate to Liberia. To the supporters of Liberian colonization, free blacks could never gain the same domestic and political privileges of white people, and indeed Kentucky law from the end of the eighteenth century through the Civil War never granted free blacks the privileges of whites. The colonization movement from its beginnings sought to allay anxieties among slave owners that a move toward emancipation was afoot. Accordingly, the Kentucky Colonization Society assured the slave owner by stating that its intent was to protect individual rights to property by "removing free blacks from association with his slaves, thereby silencing that discontented spirit which their connexion does engender."[100] Henry Clay, a founder of the American Colonization Society, explicitly disavowed any intention by the colonization society to encourage the wholesale manumission of slaves: "It is not the object of the society to liberate slaves or to touch the rights of property." "Slaves," declared the First Annual Report of the Kentucky Colonization Society, "become what are *erroneously* called '*freemen*.'"[101] The lives of free blacks were controlled at every turn, and the same rights of citizenship held by any white person far exceeded those of free blacks.[102] In a social order of entrenched slavery, darker skin was virtually tantamount to a condition of servitude, and free blacks, constrained by many legal restrictions, were an implicit contradiction

Alexander Cross was born in 1810, either in Clarksville, the home of his owner, Thomas Cross, or in nearby Trenton, Kentucky (Todd County), where Thomas Cross also owned land.[103] As a house servant, Cross learned to read and write before his move to Hopkinsville. Thomas Cross permitted Alexander to work in Hopkinsville as a barber and as a servant in a hotel dining room. Slave owners frequently hired out the labor of their slaves, sometimes giving their bondsmen a small portion of what they had earned.[104]

Regularly attending Hopkinsville's Ninth Street Christian Church, Cross impressed the membership with his biblical knowledge and his considerable abilities as a preacher. Other slaves attended the Hopkinsville church as well, although their seating was strictly segregated in the gallery overlooking the sanctuary where white congregants assembled. Cross made an equally strong impression on D. S. Burnett of the American Christian Missionary Society when Burnett visited Hopkinsville in 1853. Burnett heard Cross deliver a sermon on temperance and then set in motion the plan for Cross's manumission and emigration to Liberia. The American Christian Missionary Society prevailed on the Ninth Street Church to arrange Cross's freedom. In light of his skills as a barber, his value was estimated to be $1500. His owner, Thomas Cross, although not a member of the church, set the price at $530 when he was told of the church's aim of sending Alexander Cross to Liberia as a missionary.

Other Christian County churches contributed toward the purchase, executed by Robertson Torian on behalf of his fellow parishioners of the Ninth Street Christian Church. Torian was reputedly one of the wealthiest men in the church and a donor of a significant portion of the money needed to purchase the slave. On October 5, 1853, Torian went to the Christian County court, where he officially manumitted Alexander Cross, subject to several conditions. Thomas Cross was to receive $530 from the church by January 1, 1854. The court also stated explicitly that it was Thomas Cross's understanding, on selling his slave to Robertson Torian, that the impending manumission required the church to provide the would-be missionary with the financial means of getting to Liberia.[105] Although not mandated by the court, the newly freed slave received funds from the American Christian Missionary Society and the Ninth Street Christian Church to sustain him and his family for the first year in Liberia.

In preparation for his missionary work, Cross studied with Enos Campbell, minister of the Ninth Street Church. Cross apparently proved to be an apt pupil, as an "association with the best cultivated white society, as a servant [rather than as a field hand] gave him a degree of culture very much above those of his station in life." He was described as "a gifted orator," a "splendid conversationalist," a speaker of "extraordinary power," and "as being kind and gentle as a woman," a telling metaphor emphasizing his compliance and resignation. He was ordained in a large ceremony attended by white and slave congregants at the Ninth Street Church in early October 1853.[106]

Together with his wife, Martha Ann, a free woman of color, his young son, and other former bondsmen, Cross sailed from Baltimore to Liberia in November 1853 on board the *Banshee*.[107] Nothing is known of his brief life in Africa. Cross and his family arrived in Liberia in January 1854, and he was dead of fever a month later. He died in that part of Liberia known as "Kentucky" because it contained the town of Clay-Ashland, named for Henry Clay's Kentucky estate.[108]

After his death, an affectionate "tribute of respect" adopted by the Ninth Street Church referred to him as "our esteemed brother." He was praised for his Christian devotion, which led him to turn away from "his future ease and comfort— to abandon the society of a large circle of friends by whom he was universally beloved, and which urged him to migrate to the land of his forefathers where he met his untimely fate, to preach to his benighted brethren. . . ."[109]

The benign view of Kentucky slavery draws its support from these kinds of examples. Reference to "his future ease and comfort" did not refer to freedom but to continued slavery. Many slaveholders simply regarded their obedient human chattel as carefree and childlike, living in happy dependency on their masters for food, clothing, and other necessities.

Cross by his actions did nothing to challenge that conception. Quite the contrary; on the available evidence, he evinced Christian piety and submission, fulfilling public expectations of the slave as passive and acquiescent to the will of the white majority. However sincere the tribute to Cross, the document ultimately tells us much more about those who drafted it. Cross remains unknown, except through the words of people who defended racial hierarchy as natural law and slavery as a just condition of "lower races." While he may have accepted freedom solely for its own sake by agreeing to the religious designs of his white patrons, one cannot be sure. If Cross wrote letters either to those who had held him in slavery or to Hopkinsville's Christian Church, those documents have not survived. Rather than remaining in slavery, Cross accepted manumission, but only on the condition that he leave Kentucky for Liberia. It was hoped that "his labours as a missionary would result in much happiness to his race—the advancement of pure & undefield [*sic*] religion in downtrodden Africa and to the ultimate savation [*sic*] of many of her benighted children . . ."[110] Absent contrary evidence, it is likely that Cross shared these sentiments.

The admiration of Cross expressed by the Christian Church and its missionary arm stopped far short of welcoming "Brother Cross" as a free man into the community, even on a strictly segregated basis. Although he was fit to risk early death in Liberia, Cross and many other Kentucky slaves were not regarded as racially "fit" to live as free men and women in their native land. If the law could technically end an individual's slave status, neither law, nor custom, nor Christian piety could obviate the certain impediment of color and its meanings in a slave society.

The paradoxes and questions surrounding the historical record of Alexander Cross, including his motives for resettlement, remain in place, but popular memory embodied in the Hopkinsville newspaper story of 2001 has elided these uncertainties for a largely sectarian public, black and white. What remains is a story of contingent freedom and human inequality. Focused on a pious slave freed by a religiously motivated white congregation, historic memory remains silent about the implacable opposition of the racial majority to black freedom in its midst.

A KENTUCKY VOICE FROM LIBERIA

Alexander Cross's death from fever after only a short time in Liberia was not unusual. Tropical disease was only one of many hazards the resettlers had to face, amid the formidable challenges of a culturally and ecologically alien place. The proponents of colonization were well aware of the dangers and asked rhetorically: "If they had no sufferings in Liberia, would it not be contrary to all history of new colonies? If the emigrants were not attacked by death, would it not be a denial of the great law of nature in acclimating in a new country?"[111] The sponsors of Liberian colonization remained unmoved by threats to the lives of others, convinced as they were by the righteousness of their cause and what they regarded as the inevitable human costs of progress, which they did not have to bear.

Beyond the pronouncements and reports of the Kentucky Colonization Society and its parent body, the American Colonization Society, the emigrants themselves wrote of their struggles to lead a normal life through letters to their former masters. Over more than two decades of archival research, Bell Wiley reports finding some three hundred letters from resettlers, including those from Virginia, Maryland, Louisiana, and Mississippi, to their own kinsmen and friends, but mostly to former masters and mistresses. His published collection contains very few letters pertaining to Kentucky.[112] A small collection of letters from a slave manumitted to Liberia from Hartford, Kentucky (Ohio County), adds to the corpus of first person accounts. They were preserved by the Stevens and Belt families and bound together with a much larger body of family correspondence.[113] The letters provide insight into what Alexander Cross might have faced on arriving in Liberia, although he began with the advantage of missionary patronage.

Rachel Eddington disembarked in Liberia in May 1857 on board the *M. C. Stevens*. Her husband, Sandy, had preceded her. The ship's manifest lists her as Rachel Belt, age 40, accompanied by her children John, Joseph, and Samuel. Additionally, Atha Belt, age 40, whose relationship to Rachel is unclear, arrived with the same group. Rachel Eddington corresponded with the Stevens and Belt families of Hartford. Eight letters written from Clay-Ashland, the capital of the larger area designated "Kentucky," survive. Her letters provide a poignant firsthand description of the ordeal of sustaining a family in a place where disease was an endemic threat and familiar Kentucky farming practices, such as plow agriculture, were unworkable. It was very difficult to wrest a living from the thin tropical soils of Kentucky in Liberia. Likewise, unfamiliar foods and lack of wage labor compounded the desperation many of the newcomers felt. The despair suffusing the letters is intense. Rachel Eddington wanted to return to Kentucky, knowing full well that it would mean a return to slavery. She encouraged her brother, Adam, to remain in bondage rather than to live freely and desperately in Liberia. That plea, as well as her longing to escape Liberia through re-enslavement, is extraordinary. Wiley found only a single writer seeking a return to servitude.[114]

The first letter was sent to Charlotte Stevens Belt on August 17, 1857, reporting on the struggle to make a living. Rachel Eddington and her children did not have enough to eat and depended on the charity of others. She quickly exhausted the small sum of money she had on arrival. Without fixing blame, it is likely that her complaints implicitly point to the Kentucky Colonization Society, which depicted Liberia in terms very different from what she encountered, as her opening line suggests.

> This is not the country that was recommended to me. You know the condition that I was sent here on. When I landed I had but three dollars and some cents, and now I have spent all that for the nourishment of the children. I have nothing left . . . We staid in the receptacle 11 days, and all the time we were there our children were crying for bread; after we left we did not get any provisions for 2 weeks and had to beg everything we eat. . . . I have to pay for my washing and live in a house where we are compelled to pay rent. Some assistance to build a house is greatly needed 2 acres, 2 hoes, and 1 spade was all the children get to farm with, no cutlass, no grass scythe, no mattock. I did not get even a water bucket. My respects to all. Rachel Eddington[115]

This letter sets the tone for subsequent ones, which lament hunger, lack of money, and a scarcity of paid labor.

On July 19, 1858, she wrote to Henry Stevens, brother of Charlotte, having received a response from him to a prior letter. Here, she says that slavery in Kentucky is preferable to her life in Liberia.

We vary in our views as regards africa being as good . . . as Kentucky. There is no work for one to do. One must make their own work or go without. The people are nearly all poor and do their own work. Their farms are small patches, not farms as with you for there is nothing raised in this country but vegetables. There are no horses, no working cattle. The land is prepared with the hoe and a newcomer can't go to work as soon as they get here. They will have the fever which will lay one up for months. You speak of washing [to earn a living]. I did not have strength . . . to wash. If I did, I should not have sold the bread out of my mouth to pay for washing. I did see Mr. Cowan [Rev. Alexander M. Cowan, Kentucky Colonization Society agent] and talked with him. I told him that I wanted to go back. Being here a year makes me more anxious to return. I and my children want to return for we do suffer for bread and meat, and there is no hope for a change. There is no work for the boys. You must understand that the natives here do all the work for what they can eat and don't want any clothing. Some of the missionaries have 10 to 20 of these natives laying around and would not have an American boy. The native is the same as a slave. How are my boys to get work? If we must stay I shall do all I can. But we want help; without it we must suffer. Meat is 25cts a pound, fish 12 cts a pound . . . A man when he can get a day's work gets 25cts a day. . . . Sandy [Rachel's husband] has been laid up for the last 2 months with a wound or ulcer. Joseph has been sick nearly all the time since we came.

Apparently chided by Henry Stevens to be "industrious," she says that because of sickness she has been unable to work since arriving in Africa.

I want to come back to my old home for this is a poor place. You speak of me being industrious; that is all right but when a man does all he can, what more is to be done? I labor, I am prudent, and use all the economy in my power. I plant as other men do, but my family is large and has been sick. I have feelings for my children. But they suffer here from hunger. They can't do no worse as slaves and get something to eat. You can't form any idea how hard it is for the people to get something to eat in this place. Adam [Rachel's brother in Hartford, Kentucky] for the Lord's sake, stay where you are. There is no money here.

Yours most Respectfully, Rachel Eddington[116]

Her desperation is so intense that she sees only two alternatives: re-enslavement or starvation. Accordingly, she advises Adam to stay in place, enslaved. Her experience provides the kind of evidence J. Winston Coleman, Jr., utilized in characterizing Kentucky slavery. In his introduction to the letters of the Stevens and Belt families, he says that, "In some cases manumitted slaves preferred to return to the benign bondage in Kentucky rather than live as free people in the semi-savage condition in their African home."[117]

But of course, Rachel, Sandy, their children, and all the rest were not at home in Africa. They were native Kentuckians, and Liberia was as foreign and alien to them as it would have been for the Stevens and Belt slave owners and the sponsors of the American Colonization Society. Such was the distorted but always self-interested perception of race and culture in the mid-nineteenth century. That Rachel Eddington was willing to return to slavery is a particularly stark indication of the desolation and anguish she felt in Liberia. It is a dramatic exception to Booker T. Washington's observation, lest any reader of his autobiography misinterpret some of his remarks about servitude, that "one may get the idea that some of the slaves did not want freedom. This is not true. I have never seen one who did not want to be free, or one who would return to slavery."[118]

Two letters were sent on August 19, 1859. The first, to her husband, Sandy Stevens, who had returned to Kentucky within two years of Rachel Eddington's arrival, upbraids him for not responding to her prior letter. It communicates the almost frantic needs of the family while still maintaining the dignity of social manners and concern about other newcomers to Liberia.

I should like to hear from you as soon as possible. You know my cir-cumstances as well as I do. You know wat Africa is. It is as you left it . . . I look for you or good news by Christmas. If you come or not . . . I want meat and a barrel of flour for a Christmas gift without fail. I want a bolt of shirting for boys shirts. I want 3 white dress patterns. . I want a few bottles of black pepper. I want some indigo 1 Box of candles & soap. . . . Mr. Duncan sends his respects and hopes to dine with you on Christmas day. Mr. Duncan wants you to inquire for his uncle in Russellville, Daniel Duncan. Mr Calwell sends his respects. He is well. Mr Holcom's family are quite well or as well as could be expected under the circumstances. If you send means for me and the children to return I can come with the children and you need not come it would be a waste of money.[119]

It can be inferred that Sandy had established friendships with the Calwells (Cain and Kesiah) as they were from Kentucky and emancipated prior to settling in Liberia. They had sailed with Sandy on the *General Pierce* in December 1854.[120] Mr. Duncan was probably John Duncan, a freeman from Kentucky, who had emigrated to Liberia in December 1852. J. W. Holcom, Martha Holcom, and their four children were freemen from New York State, having sailed with Rachel. A postscript states: "If you make up your mind to return you must bring nails. I have nearly sold all the nails and want needles & pins a keg of lard and butter. The small pox is in the vacinty I have had the children vacinated Your most affectionate Wife Rachel Eddington"[121]

There is no evidence of Sandy's return to Liberia or of her ever having received a communication from him. The second letter to Mrs. Stevens, [née Hannah Bennett], the wife of Henry Stevens, describes her disillusionment with Liberia. Her homesickness was intense. Rachel Eddington conceives of herself as an American, not an African, and thus suffers the psychological dislocation of exile. She also succinctly describes the emergent system of stratification in Liberia that consigned indigenous groups to social and economic positions useful to missionaries and eventually to the elite of Americo-Liberians. In spite of the difficulties of living, she carries on as a dutiful mother, seeing to her children's schooling and civility.

Dear Madam,

I can't earn a living as I could in America. This is a hard country for a poor person. There is no work for Americans. The natives do all the labor. As for farming, this is for those that have money to have their farms cleared and planted. All land is to be cleared. There aren't any plows in use here. The hoe is the plow, the native the horse and the ox of Africa. [Plow agriculture did not exist in sub-Saharan Africa, partly because of the prevalence of animal diseases.] Please give my love to all inquiring friends. All the children send their respects to their mistress. The girls go to school every day. The boys are a little careless about going to school. Tell Adam that he can't make a living in this country. He had better stay where he is. . . . I expect Sandy has seen you and told you all about me and the country. I don't expect that you will believe a word he says. But it is just as true as the sun. I could not have believed that this country was so hard. But I have seen for myself.

Yrs most Respectfully, Rachel Eddingon[122]

After several years, and with no word from her husband, Rachel Eddington wrote to him on January 23, 1860, reporting that she and the younger children were ill and hungry. Her oldest boys were idle and received very little pay when they could find work. She wonders what has happened to her husband and asks that he send food. The letter seems desperate in its brevity.[123] Her continuing disappointment at not receiving any letters from her husband prompted her complaint to Charlotte Belt in July of 1860. She again lamented her poverty and hunger, the low pay for her sons, the scarcity of work, and her loneliness. She asked Mrs. Belt to give her news of various neighbors in her next letter. There is no indication that Sandy sent supplies to the family.

Many months later, February 28, 1861, Rachel Eddington again wrote to Charlotte Belt to report her own ill health, her daughter Caroline's death, and a growing despair and loneliness. Without specification, she desperately says, "send me something, anything for my children and myself will be thankfully received." She asks that Mrs. Belt convey her love to her friends and her desire "to see them all once more if it is the Lord's will."[124]

The last letter from Liberia is dated October 3, 1863. Sent to Henry Stevens, the letter reports her general good health after recovery from a chronic wound, but she also informs him of the deaths of two more of her children. Joseph, about sixteen years of age, was killed, probably while working, on board a ship on the Liberian coast. Her daughter died in September 1861 of sunstroke.[125]

Despite Rachel Eddington's desperate pleas from Liberia, her letters also point to the personal dignity that freedom could bestow. They indicate the overt markers of respect among men and women that were denied them as slaves. She thus refers to her friends as Mr. Duncan, Mr. Caldwell, and Mr. Holcom. In the same way, lists of names of Liberian arrivals in the years from 1843 to 1865 reveal an obvious difference from the names appearing in slave owners' wills, diaries, and other documents. Men and women liberated from slavery were free to control their names for the first time. Diminutives and mocking titles that were bestowed on slaves give way in the Liberian rosters to the predominance of decorous formal names—Robert, Thomas, Daniel, Elizabeth, Catharine, Cynthia, and the like. The folklorist Newell Niles Puckett identified similar patterns of formalization in his collection of black names from before and after the Civil War.[126] Lieberson has most recently discussed the convergence of black and white names from emancipation into the early decades of the twentieth century.[127]

The Eddington letters consistently express positive feelings toward kinsmen back in Kentucky, as well as solicitous, even affectionate, inquiries directed to her former master and mistress. In requesting that her correspondents convey love to "inquiring friends," Rachel may well have had in mind other white people as well as black people, given the complexity of emotions infusing relationships within the slave system and the dependency it spawned. However, those affectionate expressions in no way diminish the raw reality of slavery as a system nor the obdurate and callous attitudes of slaveholders unable to accept or even consider the full humanity of black people. Rachel's former master and mistress also conveyed news from Liberia to her family and friends remaining in Kentucky. Supporting as they did the colonization enterprise, cooperating former masters and mistresses may have portrayed to those remaining in captivity a gentler, less disillusioned view of Liberia than their former slaves and others expressed. To do otherwise would call into question the virtue of their own motives. For a similar reason, Wiley made little use of letters from Liberia published by the American Colonization Society in its periodical, *African Repository and Colonial Journal*. Redacted and highly selective, those letters served the ACS's purpose in conveying the most positive picture of the society and its mission.[128]

Masters and mistresses manumitting slaves to Liberia have frequently been portrayed as benevolent figures. This is certainly the case with Alexander Cross's sponsors. Edith Bennett, one of the compilers of her forbears' Liberian letters, explained their value in conveying what she calls "the other side." Remarking on the interest in slavery stimulated by Alex Haley's *Roots*, Bennett observed that the emphasis has been on "hatred and abuse of the slaves." But the letters in her collection, she points out, show that the slave owners "loved their slaves and did everything they could for them, and the slaves loved their masters."[129] She ignores, however, the dire conditions under which the Liberian resettlers lived, as well as their pleas for help. Bennett's assessment of motives and sentiments accords well with a vernacular memory of southern heritage and gentle paternalism, and with older scholarly views of slavery, particularly in Kentucky. In his introduction to Bennett's collection, Coleman regards Kentucky slavery as "its mildest form."[130] Yet the pestilential conditions and the economic and social barriers faced by the newcomers to Liberia were well known to their former masters and mistresses and to the American Colonization Society. Manumitted slaves were effectively banished from their country. Their exile was the high cost of freedom.

With the end of the Civil War, Wallace's world and that of her fellow slaveholders in Christian County and throughout the South had crumbled, while Lincoln's declaration of a "new birth of freedom" promised bondsmen an end to the long night of slavery. But there was no end to the hatred and scorn provoked by their very color and the effrontery to the defeated South of black emancipation and, soon after, citizenship and the franchise. The end of Reconstruction brought a laissez-faire federal policy toward the South, which suppressed by law or by extra-legal means the aspirations of American citizens of African descent. For that reason, emigration to Liberia continued, but never as a large-scale movement. In the postbellum years, settlement in Liberia was a self-determined effort at a fresh beginning in West Africa; it was no longer a condition of freedom dictated by white people, whether in defense of slavery or as an act of misplaced benevolence. Interest in emigration to Liberia was particularly strong during periods of pernicious racial conflict.[131]

The failure of the federal government both to provide land to former slaves and to carry through the promises of Reconstruction, including civil rights enforcement, is a story well and frequently told by historians. It does, however, have a twist in Kentucky. African Americans in the state maintained the franchise, and although efforts were made in particular elections to discourage black voting, intimidation was not sufficient to prevent black people in Christian County from voting and electing black candidates in the nineteenth century, even after Reconstruction. Black voting and the seating of black officeholders in Kentucky occurred for the next century, even as such developments continued to be unthinkable elsewhere in the South.

Still, it must be emphasized that black officeholders in Kentucky up to the present are elected for the most part from black majority areas; such is the continuing legacy of segregation and racial feeling. Penny Miller characterizes the historic pattern as black enfranchisement without empowerment.[132] In Hopkinsville, this has meant that black political aspirants have aimed for city council seats through election from predominantly black wards. They are less likely to achieve elected offices having the entire city or county as a constituency.

Hopkinsville home of Ellen McGaughey Wallace, journal author. She lived here during the imagined slave insurrection of 1856. The home still stands in the historic district.

Christmas Eve D[o] 24. 1856

This night the negroes intended to have risen and murdered the whites had the plot not been discovered. two of ours had agreed to join. Elijah said he was getting old but he would help all he could. Jack said he would promise to stand where any other man would stand. There are now 20 in jail & committed this evening D[r] Wallace spent the with us. to day Robert and the D[r] dined with us. Julia has hung up her stocking also little Alfreds to be filled with nick nacks and is now sleeping and dreaming about the expected treasures. Dec 25. Christmas the town very quiet no merriment I see nothing like life or animation. but a company drilling the beat of the drum and the roar of cannon Julia met with an accident this evening she fell and cut a gash in her forehead just above the eye. D[r] E dressed it. I have a harrassing Cough.

dec 26. Elijah came up to day it has been a very dull one to me. D[ec] 27 had a cooking stove put up. I feel peevish and irritable life has but little sunshine for me. the morning has long since past its beautiful flowers are withered. ~~The~~ its early buds of promise yielded only gall and wormwood. so far as this life is concerned D[ec] 28 this is the last sabbath in the year it has been a dull unprofitable day to me I thank thee my heavenly Father for the blessed sabbath of this year and pray for a heavenly spirit

Ellen McGaughey Wallace's December 24, 1856, journal entry. (Kentucky Historical Society, MSS 52.)

Historic Marker, Stewart County, Tennessee.

Remnant of the Great Western Furnace, Stewart County, Tennessee.

James Walter Bass (1860–1925) ca. 1887, Princeton, Indiana. Born in slavery, he attended Oberlin College 1884–1886 and started a laundry in Princeton. He was settled in Hopkinsville by 1890. (Courtesy of Margaret Bass Wilkerson.)

Johnnie Fiser Bass (1870–1927) ca. 1915, Hopkinsville. Born in Springfield, Tennessee, she married James Walter Bass in 1890. (Courtesy of Margaret Bass Wilkerson.)

Idella Bass (1891–1973) ca. 1920, Indianapolis. Eldest child of James and Johnnie Bass, she joined the Great Migration in 1910 to attend high school in Chicago. (Courtesy of Margaret Bass Wilkerson.)

Peter Postell (1841–1901), grocer and real estate investor, seated right, with his family at home in Hopkinsville, ca. 1895. At his death, he was reportedly the wealthiest African American in Kentucky. (Courtesy of Pennyroyal Area Museum.)

Claybron W. Merriweather (1869–1952), Hopkinsville poet, artist, and attorney, ca. 1910. Courtesy of Pennyroyal Area Museum.)

Sharecropper cabin, Newstead Road, Hopkinsville.

Corn wagon, once commonly used at harvest time, Newstead Road.

Crispus Attucks, black patriot killed in the Boston Massacre, 1770, after whom Hopkinsville's black high school was named in 1916. This image appeared in the first Attucks High School Yearbook, 1927.

Two commemorative panels of old Hopkinsville, Ninth and Main Streets.

Farmers Loose Floor Tobacco Warehouse, one of the few remaining in Hopkinsville; Marby Schlegel (owner) and Michael Dillard (warehouseman) in 2005.

3

INSCRIPTIONS OF FREEDOM: THE MAKING OF AN AFRICAN AMERICAN COMMUNITY

This chapter examines efforts of former slaves in the years immediately following the Civil War to construct community institutions and lives of freedom. Facing a mix of white hostility, paternalism, and indifference, black people in the town and county sought ways of establishing a sense of personal and communal agency. They proceeded fully aware that achieving any level of autonomy and self-determination would necessitate an accommodation with the racial majority on whom they were economically dependent.

Slaves in Hopkinsville and Christian County, along with other bondsmen in Kentucky, were officially manumitted by the Thirteenth Amendment on December 18, 1865. For nearly three years after the Emancipation Proclamation, slavery continued throughout the state.

Once federal forces entered the state early in the Civil War, slaves began to flee toward Union army lines. Escaped slaves, both men and women, earned menial wages working for individual soldiers. The army itself employed escaped slaves in constructing roads, fortifications, and the like. Increasing numbers, accordingly, were emboldened to escape their masters, expecting that they would find safety, which was generally the case. Ellen McGaughey Wallace's distress about her inability to retrieve escaped bondsmen mirrored the prevailing feelings of impotence among slave masters when they failed to recover absent slaves. But more than this, the exercise of will and agency by escaping bondsmen fundamentally exposed the fiction of contented, passive slaves. Wallace's fulminations against Lincoln and emancipation only grew more intense with the rampant defection of Christian County slaves to Union lines. Among slaveholders and secessionists, her "silent, burning indignation" was a general sentiment. The slave order on which she had constructed her life of advantage was crumbling around her, spawning shock, bitterness, and rage. Angrily protesting the impending loss of the natural racial privilege she regarded as her birthright, Wallace seems dissociated, assuming as she did that slaves, rather than facing desperate circumstances in seizing freedom, actually had the upper hand in relationship to their owners.

In reality, escaped slaves had to cope with squalid living, insufficient work, sometimes brutish treatment by Union soldiers during and after the War, and all the debilities of an indigent, powerless, and reviled class. Writing in the *Atlantic Monthly* in 1901, W. E. B. Du Bois portrayed the harsh world of the refugees in starkly human terms: "They came at night, when the flickering campfires of the blue hosts shone like vast unsteady stars along the black horizon: old men, and thin, with gray and tufted hair; women with frightened eyes, dragging whimpering, hungry children; men and girls, stalwart and gaunt,—a horde of starving vagabonds, homeless, helpless, and pitiable in their dark distress."[1] They had seized their freedom, lurching toward a hopeful but uncertain future despite the privation and danger of their new conditions.

While the Union lines generally offered safe haven, escaped slaves remained vulnerable to recapture. The army admonished soldiers not to interfere with slavery or with an owner's effort to reclaim an escaped slave. Soldiers, however, were by and large sympathetic to the escapees and in many instances ignored army policy by forcibly preventing slaveholders or local authorities from capturing escaped slaves.[2]

Runaways also joined the Union army in increasing numbers to destroy slavery directly by taking up arms against the Confederacy. Black men volunteered for army service throughout the state. Some 60 percent, qualified by age, served in the military.[3] In Hopkinsville, a recruitment center opened in 1864, as federal forces in their continuing need for manpower encouraged black enlistment among the large slave populations of the state's western counties.[4] Toward the end of the war, an act of Congress emancipated the families of black soldiers. Besides spurring further enlistments, this action assured would-be soldiers that through federally guaranteed freedom their families might gain protection from slave owners' reprisals.[5] The Thirteenth Amendment in effect ratified by law the *de facto* freedom gained by escape and reiterated the legally free status achieved by black army recruits and their families. Nearly three quarters of the slaves in Kentucky had gained their freedom legally shortly before the end of the Civil War.[6]

Still, the vindictive malice of slave masters against their former bondsmen, including the wives and children of black Union soldiers, was ubiquitous, both during and after the war. Proslavery sentiment was so strong that Clinton Fisk, the Commissioner of Freedmen's Affairs for Kentucky and Tennessee, shortly after the war predicted accurately that Kentucky would not support the upcoming vote on the constitutional amendment abolishing slavery. Writing to the Freedmen's Bureau on July 20, 1865, Fisk reported a mass movement of black people across the Ohio River abetted by an order from General Palmer freeing all slaves leaving the state. Palmer also mandated that a black person could secure a pass from the commander of any military post in Kentucky. The *New York Times* commented on Fisk's account and reported that throughout the state "the most cruel and fiendish atrocities are being visited upon the slaves by their maddened and despairing ex-owners. Especially is this the case when the males of families have been enlisted in our army."[7] In Du Bois's words, "former slaves were intimidated, beaten, raped, and butchered by angry and revengeful men."[8]

Whether outright secessionists or Unionists opposed to the Republican administration, the whites of Hopkinsville and Christian County were decidedly sympathetic to slavery and its political and ideological underpinnings. Like Wallace, many Unionists undoubtedly softened their views of the Confederacy as the war proceeded. When southern forces captured Hopkinsville in August 1862 and seized weapons originally intended for the Home Guard defense of the town, the *New York Times* observed, "Hopkinsville is well known for its secession sentiments."[9]

For months after the conclusion of hostilities, the county court continued its routine of ordering appraisals of estate property, including slaves, detailed in wills under probate. For example, the Christian County Court in August 1865, more than three months after the end of the war and in the wake of massive defections of black people to Union lines, recorded one of its last appraisals and divisions of human property. George King bequeathed thirty-seven slaves to his heirs. Court appointees valued the slaves at $11,875. Their values ranged from $600 for "one man, Ben" to $75 for a young boy, sums only somewhat less than the dollar value of slaves at the onset of the war.

Slavery in Kentucky, although in ruins even before the Civil War ended, continued in a formal, legal sense until the end of 1865. Some people harbored a vain hope that the federal government might reimburse slave owners for the loss of their human property. Up to his issuance of the Emancipation Proclamation at the outset of 1863, even Lincoln had promoted compensation to slave owners, as well as the assisted colonization of areas outside the United States by former slaves.[10] Others held a faint belief that slavery might somehow persist in Kentucky, as reflected in the state legislature's vote against the Thirteenth Amendment. In either case, the documentation of the ownership of slaves and appraisal of their monetary value remained in place up to the statutory demise of slavery in the state.

The will of J. J. Rogers illustrates a slave master's expectation, however dim, that his nearly absolute prerogative to punish, to profit from, or to liberate his slaves might survive in some form. Written in August 1864, his final testament also exemplifies both the benign paternalism once regarded as the norm in Kentucky slavery and the unforgiving, punitive attitude toward those who refused to submit or ran away. Rogers bequeathed most of his money, land, and assets to his wife, nephews and nieces. As to the fate of the Rogers's slaves, he says, "I gave [sic] . . . my old servant Munford his freedom and his wife and three children Fannie, Tom, Bartley, and Henry five hundred dollars. I also appoint Armistead G. Rogers to attend to them and see that a proper use is made of the money for his use and the use of his wife and children and to keep others from taking . . . advantage of them."

Rogers also freed two servant women and their children, as well as his blacksmith. Four slave girls were to be cared for by his nephews, who were instructed to free each one when she reached the age of twenty. Although written in August 1864, Rogers at that late date nonetheless concluded that his heirs still might impose an owner's sanction against four runaway slaves: "I gave [sic], if anything can be got out of the Government for the four boys that has [sic] enlisted in the Federal Army, to [names six heirs] to be equally divided as they shall be sold if they return."[11]

Economically ruined and embittered by the war, many former slaveholders sought to continue controlling their erstwhile slaves, especially in regard to labor. The loss of the capital value of their slaves, the new necessity of paying wages, and a fundamental refiguring of the social system only emboldened efforts to restore the privileges of their old way of life. For example, former slave owners in Christian County in October 1865 asserted a peremptory right to hire their former bondsmen. Only if the former master had no need for the labor of a black person he had once owned could the latter seek other employment, but not without a written release from his former owner. General John M. Palmer, a Kentucky native, implacable opponent of slavery, and the ranking officer in an Illinois regiment in the Civil War, had become the Union commander in Kentucky. He quashed the effort of Hopkinsville's former slave masters to retain control of the labor of those who were recently their human property.[12]

Joab Clark, a Hopkinsville Universalist minister writing to his brother in Illinois in December 1866, captured particularly well the malevolent attitude in Christian County. He described "the political feeling in Kentucky at this time," stating that:

Kentucky being a slave state was from the beginning of the rebellion sentimentally largely disloyal and in feeling was in full sympathy with the Rebels; but whilst the war raged, it was the policy of many enemies of the Government to profess great loyalty to the Federal government— but when the war ceased and the war power of the Government no longer terrified them, they threw off their mask of loyalty and Kentucky is now acting in the interest of and cooperating with the defeated Rebellion which is bent if possible to get control of that Government they vainly endeavored for four years to destroy.

Continuing, Clark described the enraged cruelty of one of his neighbors, when the emancipation of Kentucky slaves was at hand:

Just about last Christmas when the Proclamation of Universal Liberty was published, Austin Dulin flew into a fit of wrath like most . . . Rebel slaveholders, drove his negroes out of their cabins and out in the winter weather and told them to shift for themselves, and advised a certain negro woman to come to me for protection as I was a friend of negroes. The woman came to see me, told me she had seven children, most of them small and helpless and that she wanted me to give her shelter . . . Those negroes worked all their lives for Dulin; they filled last year his granaries and meat house; and just as this was done he turned them out in midwinter with but little to eat.[13]

Other former slave owners committed acts even more atrocious than those of Clark's neighbor. Violence against freedmen was widespread in Christian County and other western counties of the state, and no area of the state was immune.

In the wake of the Civil War, freedmen daily confronted new dangers that they did not face as slaves. Human chattel represented a capital investment for slave owners whose interests depended on the lives and vitality of their human property. Although they enjoyed precious few protections in law, bondsmen were not the victims of wholesale starvation or murder, nor would they live without shelter or clothing. Once the self-interested restraints of ownership and investment were removed, however, the full force of violent retribution and reprisal was set in motion. Arrayed against black people seeking greater control over their own lives, enraged whites were determined to maintain white domination. They remained wedded to the deeply entrenched racial ideology that rationalized human enslavement and hence motivated determined resistance to the advancement of black freedom.

THE FREEDMEN'S BUREAU IN CHRISTIAN COUNTY
AND WESTERN KENTUCKY

Formed by congressional action in March 1865, the Bureau of Refugees, Freedmen, and Abandoned Lands became an agency of the War Department. Known simply as the "Freedmen's Bureau," it aimed to normalize as much as possible the lives of four million newly emancipated slaves. As its formal name implies, the bureau was also charged with the administration of lands either abandoned by owners or seized by the army during the Civil War. General O. O. Howard by presidential appointment served as head of the bureau from its creation until its dissolution in 1872. Vulnerable in every respect, freed slaves looked to the bureau for medical care, as well as clothing and provisions. They sought bureau support for fledgling black schools. Black Civil War veterans turned to the bureau for help with their claims for service pay. The bureau also promoted the formal registration of marital unions established in slavery and supervised labor contracts between ex-slaves and white employers, often their former owners, in order to prevent new forms of servitude.[14]

In effect, the bureau undertook a program of social service that had no instructive precedents to guide the implementation of such a radical undertaking. The bureau emerged well before such agencies, mostly private, developed in urban America toward the end of the nineteenth century. Under the best of circumstances, the challenges by themselves would have been extraordinary, but the ameliorative task was all the more formidable in the face of uneven leadership at every level, inadequate funding, and variable commitment to the plight of the freedmen. Likewise, corruption in the bureau further undermined the hopes of the ex-slaves.

The Freedmen's Bureau agents in Hopkinsville and throughout the central and western parts of Kentucky reported relentlessly on the defenselessness of freed slaves in the aftermath of the Civil War. With brutality and unrestrained violence, white antagonists robbed, intimidated, and killed black people in what the bureau called "outrages." Whites who provided assistance to black people might also suffer threats if local "regulators," as the vigilantes were known, wanted black people to vacate an entire locale. White veterans of the Union army as well faced intimidation, violence, and even murder.

The Freedmen's Bureau represented the only institutional buffer between former slaves and malicious whites bent on retribution. The latter made no distinction between people liberated after the Civil War through passage of the Thirteenth Amendment and those who had earlier escaped bondage, or secured freedom for themselves and their families through enlistment in the Union army. All were equally vulnerable to vengeful fury. Throughout western Kentucky, former slave owners counted among their sympathizers civil authorities and institutions.

Thus, county sheriffs and courts often refused to act in the face of violent assaults against black people, even when pressed to do so by bureau agents, who were generally reviled.

From the earliest days of freedom, former slaves throughout the South demonstrated the most intense desire for basic education. Literacy was a "coveted possession."[15] That value was prominent, as reported by a number of Freedmen's Bureau correspondents. The drive for education was all the more dramatic in light of the many obstacles freedmen faced, none greater than recurrent violence. Writing in August 1866, a little more than a year after the bureau's founding, General John Ely, Chief Superintendent for Kentucky, reported to General Davis, Assistant Commissioner, on the results of an inspection of bureau operations in the state. Particularly in regard to black efforts to form schools, he found intense and violent resistance in many areas of the state:

> This inspection revealed a very unsettled and unsatisfactory state of affairs, both as regarded the interests of the Freedmen and the sentiments of the people toward them, the bureau, its Officers and agents . . . There is a very general desire on the part of the colored people to obtain knowledge and . . . [there is] a commendable interest and effort on the part of a large majority of the colored people . . . to provide suitable means for the education of their children. These reports also show that the children themselves evince remarkable zeal and ambition in their studies. Many of these schools have met with strong opposition from a class of white malcontents who style themselves Regulators and aside from the assistance and protection afforded by the bureau the colored people meet with but little encouragement in their efforts to organize schools. In some places they have been broken up and the teachers driven from their posts.

Beyond reporting on the formation of schools, Ely described the "intensely hostile" feelings of white people toward the freedmen, as well as toward officers of the bureau. He believed that only troops could restrain the many acts of violence.[16] Nelson Lawrence, headquartered at Russellville (Logan County) and overseeing Christian County, likewise felt that matters were very serious in that county and "someone, a resident of the place to look after matters all the time would have a very good effect."[17]

Daniel L. Hays, veteran of the War of 1812 and a septuagenarian major general in the Union army, became the Hopkinsville agent in October 1866 amid the turmoil and violence against freedmen and federal army veterans in Christian County and the southern subdistrict of Kentucky. Perrin, an early historian of the county, described Hays as "the friend and the attorney for widows and all poor people," who would represent them without charge.[18] Lawrence observed, "There is a great deal to do in Christian County." Young white men for amusement were harassing black people and shooting at them.[19] At various times Hays complained of noncompliance with his orders owing to the absence of troops. For example, in trying to force payment from white farmers to freedmen for a season's labor, he remarks that "I am unable to get the sheriff and other officers to execute process, and the system of findings by a rebel county judge and of private hearings is now producing great difficulty . . . and a great many persons have failed to pay the Freedmen for their labor last year and are again hiring for this year—strangers to their last year's conduct, and when I give orders as I do daily—they give no attention to my order."

The agent pled with Ely for soldiers to help him enforce "many writs of *habeas corpus.*" These included demands that slave owners release children whom they had kept in bondage after ratification of the Thirteenth Amendment and despite their having been freed earlier as a result of their fathers' army service.[20] Hays also continued to seek enforcement of orders, based on affidavits of complainants, against whites who had robbed, assaulted, or intimidated black people or against employers who had refused to pay the freedmen whom they had hired.

While freedmen might swear an affidavit before a bureau officer or even before a grand jury, they were barred in Kentucky from giving testimony at court against white people. White crimes against black people, even when witnessed by many black people, went unpunished by courts and further emboldened vigilantes and Regulators. In a statement made to the Christian County Court and in a separate, more detailed statement to Hays, Oliver McReynolds explained that his employer, Robert Baker, had not paid him, except with "one pair of indifferent shoes and one pair of cheap cotton pants" for work done over the previous seven months on the Baker farm. He sought one hundred and sixteen dollars and fifty cents. Seeing McReynolds calming an animal team fearful of plowing a ditch, Baker severely beat McReynolds with sticks and switches, then threatened McReynolds; if the latter left the farm, Baker said "he would land me in hell." Two other freedmen supported McReynolds's sworn statement, seeking "indemnity and protection from the bureau."[21]

There is no evidence of black people in Christian County engaging in collective self-defense against vigilante depredations. However, it is plausible that former slaves and army veterans individually might have taken up arms to protect themselves and their families. More organized black resistance occurred in other places, but, according to the Freedmen's Bureau, such action was exceptional. Ely reported violent attacks on freedmen's schools in Glasgow, Bowling Green, Paducah, and

Mt. Sterling. He observed that under these conditions black people were reluctant to attempt to educate their children, but the bureau was making preparations to reopen each school by force. On black counteractions, Ely stated that "the colored people have not themselves resorted to any measures of self defence [*sic*] but they passively submit to outrages upon their schools and persons (the case referred to as having occurred at Glasgow being the only exception reported)."[22] Freedmen were not the only targets of the Regulators. In Christian County and elsewhere in the state, white veterans of the Union army and whites who permitted freedmen to live on their land were subject to violent reprisals. Bureau agents were also vulnerable to attack.

Shortly after requesting that Ely send troops to Hopkinsville, Hays contacted General Sidney Burbank, the new head of the Freedmen's Bureau in Kentucky. He provided additional details about the severity of the problems he faced:

> Permit me to say that there now exists a state of things in our county that requires immediate attention. Our court officers are all Rebels and do not execute process for Union men and particularly the defrauded Freedman.
>
> I have not out of many cases in this and Trigg Counties got them to execute . . . Habeas for the Parent to obtain the possession of his child.
>
> And still there is now a state of affairs existing—about ten days since Mr. Everett living six miles west of Hopkinsville Who had been a Union solder [*sic*] while at work in his field was shot—six balls taking affect and instantly killed, no one present but it is well known to have been done by a returned Rebel . . . living within four miles of Town—he has been in Town several times since and no effort made to investigate the affair.

In the same report, Hays went on to say that "a gang of Rebels" had threatened a recently discharged Union army captain. Considering his life in danger, the former officer sold his land and relocated to another farm; he was again threatened in the form of "written notice . . . to leave, together with two other Union army veterans." They had not yet vacated the land, but they informed the agent that they were afraid to work their fields. Hays concluded his letter by telling Burbank that the Union men would band together to protect each other and to "hunt up these desperadoes." Once again, Hays requested troops and informed Burbank that he had managed to keep the Union veterans from acting only by promising to seek military relief.[23] There is no evidence Hays's request was granted. On the contrary, at the time of his request, plans were afoot to reduce the policing function of the bureau. In December 1867, a circular from O. O. Howard, the head of the Freedmen's Bureau, stated that except for superintendents of education, bureau officers and agents in Kentucky would be withdrawn by February 1868.[24]

S. F. Johnson, writing to General Davis just months after the formation of the Freedmen's Bureau, expressed the desperate fears of white loyalists in Logan County, particularly, but also in other southern counties of the state, including Christian County. He said simply, "the truth is, there is a reign of terror in this country, such as has never been before." His letter is especially compelling for its depiction of the hatred, intimidation, and violence on the part of recalcitrant Confederates. Johnson said that any man who served as an officer in the Union army "is not safe in life or property." He, along with others, had received threats stating that they had to leave the area. Black people were robbed and shot each day.[25] "Terror" was a common designation by bureau agents for what freedmen and federal army veterans were facing. Just three months later, writing from Russellville, Nelson Lawrence added to his report on schools in the southern subdistrict that "there is a band of outlaws in Logan Co. and one in Christian."[26]

Whites who were not army veterans also received threats. Moreover, hatred of the Freedmen's Bureau focused not only on its would-be beneficiaries but also on bureau personnel charged with implementing policy. M. E. Billings, a sub-assistant commissioner, encountered a threatening mob in Elkton (Todd County) during the course of a tour of schools in the southern subdistrict. He addressed a large assembly of black people regarding their school, for which "every effort has been made to break up this school by the rebels . . . ." The officials of Todd County also refused any support for the school, although a special "colored school fund" had been established. Of the threat to himself, Billings continued, "The K.K.K. with their murderous missives are continually threatening Weir [the teacher] and have succeeded in frightening away . . . his pupils. While addressing the meeting . . . a crowd of lawless men gathered around the Church making threats so I retired to my Hotel. I was followed by this rabble. The[y] entered the Hotel shouting Ku Klux Klan, and Nigger bureau. No serious violence was offered although the leader who was oddly disguised proposed to compel me to leave town that night. I however remained at the Hotel until morning. . . ."[27] Scarcely two years after the founding of the Ku Klux Klan, the organization had quickly spread throughout the South. Nonetheless, Klan robes and regalia were still sufficiently novel that Billings remarked on the "oddly disguised" leader.

Instances of compliance and cooperation of the white people of Christian County and Hopkinsville with the bureau were uncommon, or at least rarely remarked on in the face of the extensive violence and mayhem against the bureau's clients. One such instance involved the indenture of Ambrose Watkins, a black youth brought to Christian County by George Killibrew and his son, William. Sometimes negotiated with a parent or guardian, an indenture represented a contract for a youth's labor in exchange for food, board, clothing, and sometimes a promise of instruction in reading and writing. At this time, few questions were raised about work contracts centered on children. Although it was acknowledged by the Killibrews and the Freedmen's Bureau in Prince Edward and Cumberland Counties that the youth was running away from his home in Virginia, a contract was still negotiated. William Killibrew consulted with the bureau, not to secure parental permission but to ascertain that the youth was not encumbered by any prior labor agreements.

The case was brought before agent Hays in Hopkinsville because the young man's parents were seeking his return. William Killibrew was amenable to their request but did ask for a return of the cost of transportation in bringing Watkins to Christian County. It was only after agent Hays received instructions from O. O. Howard regarding the minor status of Watkins that Hays raised the issue with William Killibrew, who felt that the bureau personnel in Virginia should have addressed the matter of age before granting permission for the contract. In any event, this particular case stands out for the high praise Hays reserves for the Killibrews and the fairness and decency they showed to the freedmen. Their employees received very ample food three times daily and were provided individual plots for tobacco cultivation, as well as the time and tools for working the crop, the proceeds of which they would gain independently of their wages.[28]

Notwithstanding the humanity of the Killibrews, the entire system of labor contracts supported by the Freedmen's Bureau in Kentucky and throughout the South risked the principle of free labor. There were too many opportunities for exploitation and unfairness regarding black farm workers since many contracts were negotiated outside of bureau supervision. Unregulated contracts gave advantages and prerogatives to employers, who, for example, could reduce a worker's wages should he miss work for any reason, including illness. Some contracts threatened physical punishment for infractions. Others specified that employees would have to maintain a proper attitude of respect toward the employer. Husbands and wives could be engaged through a single contract specifying farm labor for the man and domestic work for the woman.

No evidence indicates that the Freedmen's Bureau approved of the contract between W. H. Wilson and Harrison, a black man for whom no surname was given. The labor agreement proposed by Wilson in Harrison's name illustrated how deeply chattel slavery as the condition of black people remained embedded in white consciousness. Dated December 30, 1865, the one-year contract was submitted, although not drafted, by the illiterate Harrison. He agreed to give Wilson one third of the tobacco and one third of the corn crop he produced on the owner's land using Wilson's team, plows, and other tools. Wilson was to provide Harrison, his wife, and two sons with bread and meat, if all of them worked. Harrison's wife, Bettie, was to cook, wash, and perform all kinds of housework "without murmur." For every day he didn't work for any reason, Harrison would pay seventy-five cents; the two boys twenty-five cents. Breakage was to be charged at double the cost of replacement. An old woman, perhaps Harrison's mother, was expected to work as well, making soap, candles, and the like in exchange for her board. Should she not work, Harrison would pay Wilson forty dollars for her upkeep. For theft "the said Harrison is to pay double for the first offence [sic] & second is still to pay double & the party guilty of steeling [sic] is to have 39 lashes & for the 3 offence the party gilty [sic] is to be shot."[29]

Some bureau agents, such as Daniel Hays of Hopkinsville, showed an estimable commitment to the welfare of the former slaves. Nonetheless, much remained beyond local control as agents on the ground faced frequent changes in personnel at higher levels, ineptitude, bureaucratic delay, and corruption. Hays counted his assistance to former slaves who had won their freedom through military service as one of his most important duties. Specifically, that assistance centered on securing back pay, or "bounties," for black veterans. But the Freedmen's Bureau had to contend with deceptive brokers, promising to assist the claimants while intending to defraud them. Major Benjamin Runkle, appointed in November 1867 as the superintendent of the bureau in Kentucky, ended his tenure ignominiously, as he was caught up in a fraudulent scheme.[30]

In a particularly telling letter, Hays took Runkle to task for the latter's earlier remarks mocking attempts of black veterans to secure their money and finding amusement in the indifference to duty shown by some of his subordinate officers:

> . . . sir I think it very strange indeed that an officer of the bureau whose duty I thought was to facilitate the Disbursement of Bounty money to the colored soldier should throw difficulties in the way or be negligent in answering their communications in regard to the condition of their claims or delay and make sport of their demand and that of their friend[s].
>
> These men look to me for Justice, they are my citizens and friends, they fought for my country for which my government has allowed them a bounty which after much delay by the proper officer should not be withheld by subaltern officers and not disbursed without delay.[31]

Runkle was later separated from the army following his court-martial conviction for "fraud against colored soldiers." He was fined $7000 and sentenced to four years in prison.[32]

HOPKINSVILLE SCHOOLS AND
THE FREEDMEN'S BUREAU

Throughout Kentucky, bureau personnel reported that former slaves were very eager to establish schools, despite widespread resistance. B. S. Newton of the Methodist Episcopal School, responding to a monthly query from the bureau about the public view of colored schools, reported in February 1870 that "the sentiments are generally against us."[33] Hopkinsville and Christian County whites were in many respects antagonistic, sometimes violently so, toward black education. In procuring a room for Lucy Hughes's class, Daniel Hays regarded the rental as a favor from the landlord, as "we have here to encounter much violent opposition from the Rebels."[34] Nevertheless, the dominant theme in reports on the schools from teachers, agents, and others was a lack of resources. Bureau neglect was the critical obstacle facing the fledgling black schools, which therefore had to rely on the freedmen, who were least able to raise money to sustain them. Highly praised by Hays, Hughes was a white teacher who had come to Hopkinsville after attending Oberlin College in 1866.[35] She struggled to support herself by teaching at the AME Zion School but was dependent on the freedmen, not the bureau, for her salary. After about one year of teaching, Hughes reluctantly tendered her resignation saying, "I am compeled [sic] by the meager support which I receive from the col. people in this place to seek another situation." Hoping to find a position in a black school with better salary prospects, she sought help from the bureau agent supervising the southern subdistrict.[36]

James Bell, who also taught at the Methodist Episcopal School, complained of a lack of books and reported that some of the students need "decent and comfortable clothing," thus further underscoring the desperate conditions of the freedmen. He concluded his report, saying that "the teachers of this school as well as the other colored schools in this city are in much need of such increase of pay as will enable them to support their families."[37] Likewise, Christopher Malone, teaching at the freedmen's Baptist school, stated, "I was the first colored man that ever taught a colord [sic] school in Hopkinsville . . . and I need Books of various sorts." Malone went on to say that the freedmen of the Baptist church who were attempting to support the school could not pay him and that he might have to give up teaching.[38]

The freedmen were sometimes unable to pay the school fees for their children, which were assessed monthly in amounts ranging from twenty-five cents to a dollar. All of the schools suffered a chronic shortage of funds. The Freedmen's Bureau supported education in principle but provided little money. In Hopkinsville, the bureau paid rent for schoolrooms but little else. By April 1870, as schools were seeking their own permanent space rather than rented quarters or church rooms, Charles Smith, teaching at the Baptist school, reported, "The school is progressing finely only we lack for school accommodation." At the same time, in response to the monthly query about "public sentiment toward Colored Schools," Smith noted some improvement in the atmosphere, stating, "Encouraging evincing no signs of antipathy."[39] Repeated pleas from teachers, lower level bureau personnel in the southern subdistrict, and from sympathetic members of the community to provide teachers' stipends, books, paper, or slates went unanswered. Freedmen's schools in Hopkinsville continued to struggle financially.

Problems attending the lack of bureau financial support for freedmen's schools in Kentucky are summarized in a letter from Ely to the National Freedmen's Relief Association. He was soliciting philanthropic assistance, particularly for education. Writing of the thirty schools for black children existing in Kentucky in August 1866, Ely explained that,

> All of these schools are supported by the Freedmen, there being no pro-
> vision made by the state or county authorities to have free schools for
> black children . . . The Law establishing this bureau does not provide the
> payment of School Teachers and for this reason the Superintendents
> of this bureau are unable to obtain teachers, there being no money to
> pay them. Most of the Freedmen are not able to spare money for this
> purpose, consequently their children cannot go to school. Much good
> could be done in this State by sending money here to pay teachers as
> several schools have been closed on that account.[40]

Despite many obstacles, a black school began in Hopkinsville as early as February 1865. Although it provided little support, the bureau continued to seek monthly school reports from teachers. These were supplemented by observations by the local agent, as well as other interested parties from whom the bureau solicited information. Among the latter was William T. Buckner. "I am," he wrote the bureau agent in Russellville, "a native born Kentuckian and have been a large slave holder—and as they labored faithfully for me and mine while they were slaves—I am now willing to do everything in my power to elevate them morally and mentally." Beyond his reporting to the bureau about the state of black schools in Hopkinsville, particularly their lack of adequate funds, it is unclear how much further his helpfulness extended. Nor are there additional statements that might explain Buckner's apparent epiphany about former slaves at a time when many suffered retributive action from their erstwhile masters. Like Ellen McGaughey Wallace, he was a Unionist and a slave owner. He also served in the Union army, but unlike Wallace, he accepted the end of slavery without apparent rancor.

In response to a bureau inquiry about the state of black schools, Buckner reported,

> I have called together at my office some half dozen of the leading and influential black men of this county and talked freely with them. I have never seen any people so fully alive to the importance of education as these people are. They have never, so far as I can learn, recieved [sic] any aid from the bureau or any society—and still their children are attending school of their own and learning quite well in spite of many disadvantages. They need suitable books above all else—cannot these be supplied in some measure by your bureau? The teachers seem to be laboring faithfully—cannot they recieve [sic] some compensation from the bureau.[41]

In a second letter four days later, Buckner provided a candid, sympathetic assessment of teachers, schools, former slaves, and pupils, who, despite hindrances, "are learning fast and doing remarkably well." Once again, he pleads for assistance to the freedmen for school supplies and stipends for the teachers, three black men and the "white lady from the north," struggling to support themselves. Calling Christian County the largest slaveholding county in the state before the Civil War, he described the freedmen "as quiet and industrious," showing "a most earnest desire to educate their children." Buckner's praise for the freedmen also included great admiration for their self-directed efforts to build a community:

> If your bureau has any funds with which to assist these people it is time they were letting it be known in these parts. They have formed a benevolent society among themselves & have done much good from their scanty account in feeding the hungry clothing the naked & especially in burying the dead. They have purchased & enclosed a piece of ground as cemetery—but many calls have exhausted their means, & after paying half the purchase money I fear they will lose this land by default.

In light of the failure of the bureau to provide the much needed help specified on several occasions, Buckner reported that the freedmen

> have lost all hope of being benefited by the Freedmen's Bureau, & unless they can be assured by *you* that some of their prayers . . . can be granted, that they will consider the whole thing as "played out," to use their own expressive language.[42]

The bureau officer in Russellville responded fecklessly. Praising Buckner for providing more information about Christian County than any other correspondent, the officer explained that his connection to the bureau and its workings was very new. He promised, however, to bring Buckner's concerns to his superiors.[43] Two years later the teachers were still pleading for assistance.

CIVIC ASSERTION, AUTONOMY, AND THE EMERGENT COMMUNITY

In Christian County and elsewhere, people newly freed from slavery by their own actions or by law sought to establish some degree of autonomous control, both as individuals and as members of a racial community. Nascent independent black social institutions emerged to provide mutual support, education, and religion. Autonomous action also included attempts to reconstitute families torn apart by slavery and war, part of a continuing reiteration of the primary value of kinship. The self-determined actions by freedmen to renovate their lives are all the more remarkable in light of the forces of Confederate reaction organized against them following the Civil War. The intensity of hatred, cruelty, and murderous violence directed at former bondsmen defines the leitmotif of Freedmen's Bureau records.

Assertions of individual and communal agency did not, however, spring suddenly from the fact of emancipation. Rather, they derived from deep-seated human characteristics that survived under conditions of bondage. As restrictive as it was, slavery did not foreclose the possibility of bondsmen having some room for maneuver in light of the importance of reciprocity in every human relationship, including that of master and slave. Given the highly personal social bonds often embedded in the owner-slave relationship, particularly if a slave were either a house-servant or a skilled artisan, diffuse feelings of affection sometimes emerged, giving even greater salience to reciprocity. However asymmetrical the quid pro quo relationship, the social connections between master and servant admitted some possibility of the slave turning that relationship to his benefit, within the severe limits of the institution of slavery.

Ellen McGaughey Wallace struggled with the question of reciprocity. She was unable to understand slave discontent, when their "moderate labour" was rewarded by the alleged largesse of their owners who provided clothing, food, medical attention, and what she regarded as a carefree life. Wallace could not comprehend ingratitude when so much, in her view, had been given to her slaves. It was their reciprocal obligation, she thought, to appreciate all that had been given to them. Reciprocity, however, did not mean the same thing to slaves and slave owners.

Slaves accepted the doctrine of reciprocity, but with a profound difference. To the idea of reciprocal duties they added their own doctrine of reciprocal rights.

To the tendency to make them creatures of another's will they counterpoised a tendency to assert themselves as autonomous human beings.[44] That autonomy and sense of rights extended from a profound feeling of inviolable kinship—that a family should not be fragmented by sale—to religious belief expressed in a black idiom of worship; the latter spoke to spiritual needs wholly different from anything available in white churches.

Two examples serve to illustrate the anguish of family separation in the face of slave owners' willful ignorance or outright denial of the humanity of their slaves. Both Moses Slaughter and Amy Elizabeth Patterson told their stories to a WPA interviewer in Vanderburgh County, Indiana; the interviewer's race is unknown, although it is likely that she was white.[45] That fact did not appear to inhibit either interviewee's condemnation of slavery, although other slave narratives, including a number in the Fisk series collected by an African American interviewer, were more graphic and bitter in their depictions of slave owner cruelty.[46] Nearly seven decades after Wallace expressed her sense of betrayal by ungrateful slaves, Moses Slaughter, born in Montgomery County, Tennessee, contiguous to Christian County, told the interviewer of the fallacy of the "good master." "No master was really good to his slaves. The very fact that he could separate a mother from her babes made him a tyrant. Each master demanded exact obedience from his slaves." He spoke of separation from his own mother, owned by Joseph Fauntleroy. "When I was a good sized little boy Miss Emily Fauntleroy married G. H. Slaughter and Master Joseph gave me to Miss Emily for a bridal present. That was my first real sorrow, having to leave my mother and the other children." Stressing that his mother was a "loyal slave, a Christian, and always ready to help the children pray," Moses Slaughter establishes the fundamental injustice and violation of human values implicit in owning slaves. Having enlisted at Clarksville in the federal army, he fought in the Civil War, married another former slave, and settled in Evansville, Indiana. First baptized as a slave in the Cumberland River, he was baptized once again in the Ohio, thus inscribing his freedom by immersion in the river that had meant liberation to so many bondsmen. Not only free, he belonged to an independent black Baptist church.[47]

The personal quality of the relationship between slaves and their owners was particularly important, for otherwise how might slaves exercise any will against masters and mistresses? Without standing in the law, without institutional protections, without rights guaranteed by any mechanism other than a diffuse personal bond with a powerful individual, a slave could do little to affect his or her world. That slaves tried to exercise some efficacy was certain, but the outcome of their actions was quite variable. Moses Slaughter's mother, for example, could not prevent her separation from the child, presented as a wedding gift.

On the other hand, Amy Elizabeth Patterson, born a slave in Cadiz, Kentucky, in 1850 was, while still a child, kept by her father and master, John Street, who wanted to prepare her for life as a housemaid and seamstress. He had sold all of his other slaves, including Patterson's mother and twin sisters. However, her mother was so distraught in her new home that she was unable to work. The child, too, was inconsolable. As a result, Street agreed to sell Patterson to her mother's purchaser. About the inhumanity of slavery, Patterson shared Moses Slaughter's sentiments and indeed those of every slave who suffered family loss through sale when she said of her own purchase, "that was the greatest crime ever visited on the United States. It was worse than the cruelty of the overseers, worse than hunger, for many slaves were well fed and well cared for; but when a father can sell his own child, humiliate his own daughter by auctioning her on the slave block, what good could be expected where such practices were allowed?"[48] Heartfelt and profound in its expression, Amy Elizabeth Patterson's judgment points to the slave owners' denial of the inclusive humanity of the people they claimed as property. Slaves certainly did not share this view of themselves.

Whereas slaves had once masked resistance to white domination through expressive techniques such as sermons, songs, and stories, emancipated men and women could at least publicly act on their freedom and on their own sense of humanity. Both collectively and individually, self-determined actions began to redefine their position in the southern social order. As an early step in affirming their new lives, Hopkinsville's freedmen began by making provision for burial and the management and memorialization of death in a way they could not as slaves. Freedom, in effect, meant ownership, both of one's life and one's death within the emergent black community.

The landscape of Christian County is dotted with hundreds of white cemeteries dating from before the Civil War. These are usually burial grounds of extended kin situated on land once owned by a constituent family. Sometimes surrounded by stone walls or iron gates, often in disrepair, or otherwise set in a cluster without a marked perimeter, the gravestones record the names and dates of the dead, and include perhaps a religious verse, homily, or laudatory thought; sometimes a bas relief or engraving depicts a popular motif of its time. Of course, many such monuments are severely eroded or broken, but they nonetheless record a life whose traces do not depend solely on the memories bequeathed to descendants. Rather, it inheres in the materialization of the stone monument, a written record in a family Bible, a newspaper, or other repository. The county genealogical society, for example, attempts in its publications to preserve the identities of the cemeteries and those who lie within.

By contrast, numerous slave cemeteries lie anonymously across the county, probably in close proximity to the burial places of slave owners. Originally identified by wooden markers, now long decayed, and without iron or stone enclosures, slave burials namelessly contrast with the material and documentary evidence of white graves. Unless preserved in a diary of a slave owner or in plantation papers, the historic documentation of slave burials must await the archeologist. Archivists and other custodians of local records in the decades after slavery made no effort to tap the living memories of former slaves nor to map slave burial sites before their deterioration into invisibility.

Thus, the 1867 purchase by recently freed slaves of four acres of land in Hopkinsville in order to establish a burial ground represents a signal event. It is the earliest recorded corporate act of Hopkinsville's freedmen. Newly empowered to enter into legal contracts and other civil agreements, former slaves effectively proclaimed a kind of collective self-determination, whether in regard to labor, family, education, worship, or, in this instance, disposition of the dead. While their impoverished state and vulnerability to violence were certainly limiting factors of great moment, collective action nonetheless proceeded.

In October 1867, Nathan Bailey, a thirty-year-old carpenter and "President of the Union Benevolent Association (colored) of Christian County," contracted with Ann Montgomery, a white woman, for the cemetery land. Purchasing four acres for five hundred dollars on behalf of the association, Bailey paid one hundred dollars in cash and agreed to pay an additional one hundred and fifty dollars by Christmas 1867, as well as a final installment of two hundred and fifty dollars on or before January 1, 1869.[49] The extant record does not detail the number of participants in the Union Benevolent Association or the nature of assessments that made the land purchase possible. Despite William Buckner's fear expressed in his letter to the Freedmen's Bureau agent in Russellville that the freedmen might default on their payments, title to the cemetery land eventually passed to the Union Benevolent Association. Burials in that cemetery continued well into the twentieth century.[50] The Union Benevolent Association was not a singular development in Christian County. Rather, organizations with a similar name emerged throughout Kentucky over the two decades following the Civil War. Lucas suggests that the Union Benevolent Society of Lexington, founded in 1843, became the model for similar welfare organizations of freedmen.[51]

Two other self-help communal institutions among freedmen in Christian County provide a clearer picture of assessment and membership. In 1876, ten men, led by Ross Metcalf, formed the Loving Sons of the Union for "the mutual improvement of each other, taking care of [the] sick, the relief of our distressed members and the buryil [sic] of our dead." Membership was open to anyone at least sixteen years of age and willing to pay a two-dollar fee and a monthly assessment of twenty-five cents.[52] It is unclear if the name, "Loving Sons of the Union," indicated that the charter members were veterans of the Union army or simply citizens avowing their loyalty to the government that had effected their liberation. In either case, "Loving Sons of the Union" was a self-assured declaration of autonomy standing in sharp counterpoint to its members' lives as slaves and to prevailing local allegiances to the Lost Cause. In 1879, the Loving Sons of the Union reincorporated itself with the Daughters of Zion, also referred to as the Daughters of Liberty. The purpose of the new organization remained precisely the same as its predecessor, with membership remaining open to "any colored person of good moral character of the age of sixteen and voted on by a majority of the membership."[53]

In 1881, the mutual aid and welfare provisions of these early voluntary associations in Christian County expanded considerably with the formation of the Grand Lodge of the Union Benevolent Society. Its purpose was "to manage the affairs pertaining to a benevolent order and to grant charters to subordinate lodges." Acting as a governing body, the new organization led by A. C. Banks, a carpenter, would establish rules for smaller lodges and would also "support the indigent or needy brethren and sisters [and] provide for the burial of the dead of its membership and the support of the surviving member or members of the family of a deceased brother or sister and to do and transact all business . . . for the mutual protection and employment of its members and their families." Additionally, a benefit association within the larger group was organized as a kind of precursor to an insurance cooperative. Members were assessed a minimum of twenty-five cents per month. At a member's death, his or her heirs could receive a sum totaling fifty cents per member to an unlikely maximum of fifteen hundred dollars, "provided . . . that the benefit may be paid to any person designated by the brother or sister in his or her life time by a writing properly signed and attested."[54]

KINSHIP, MARRIAGE, AND FAMILY

Marriage and the family among freedmen also achieved institutional status and legal recognition in the wake of the Civil War. During slavery, domestic life built on the relationship and emotional bonds between spouses, children, and other kin lacked all legal recognition. Bondsmen were enumerated in the slave schedules of 1850 and 1860. Each schedule resembled a livestock census, identifying owners by name and then enumerating each nameless slave by sex, age, and color (black or mulatto). Nonetheless, bondsmen might enact their humanity through a marriage ritual or ceremonial of their own design, such as "jumping the broom," probably the most ubiquitous of folk legitimations of the marital bond. "Jumping the broom" was important, according to Annie Morgan of Hopkinsville, an informant in the WPA slave narrative project, because preachers were not often available.[55] However meaningful to the participants, clergy-sanctioned slave unions, like folk rituals of marriage, remained outside the formal strictures of state law and commanded no civil recognition.

Like marriage, social paternity lacked civic relevance, reflected for example in the contrast between the registration of births, white and black, in some Kentucky counties, during the slave era. Sometimes the name of the slave mother along with the sex of the child appeared; occasionally the child's name was listed. Neither mother nor child had a surname. Each white child in the Todd and Christian County listings appeared as the legitimate offspring of a married couple. The mother's maiden name was recorded, and the name of the father appeared in a column labeled "father or owner of the child." Although the county registrar erratically recorded the names of the slave mother and child, he consistently listed the name of the owner.[56] County birth registrations encoded institutional values and arrangements of the South, denying black paternity as a social category in favor of "owner." At the same time, the registrations perpetuated the public fiction that masters did not cohabit with female slaves, as the heading "father or owner" designated mutually exclusive categories.

If the slavocracy did not grant civil recognition to the conjugal relationships of bondsmen, many slaves fully recognized and prized marriage and family. At the same time, the absolute power of masters to sell their slaves or posthumously to disperse their estate property, including people, meant that slaves could maintain only the most tenuous hold on stable family relationships. Those relationships continued at the pleasure of the slave master. Here, the quality of the personal connection between slave and owner was all that stood between the continued integrity of the slave family and its fragmentation through sale of its members.

Less than a year after the Civil War's conclusion, newly liberated slaves in large numbers took the opportunity to transform their own self-defined marriages into legal unions recognized by the state. Legislative action by the Kentucky General Assembly in early 1866, a year after Congress recognized slave marriages, provided former bondsmen the means to do so. Black ministers were authorized to perform marriage ceremonies. Shortly after the state acted to sanction marriages contracted during slavery, the Freedmen's Bureau advised people to secure a marriage license if they wanted to record their marital bond. Otherwise, those living as husband and wife since before the war would be guilty of a misdemeanor if they failed to secure legal recognition.[57] On March 24, 1866, Dudley Short, a laborer in Hopkinsville, and Matilda Short, a housekeeper, were the first couple to state publicly and officially before the Christian County clerk of courts "they have heretofore cohabited as husband and wife and that they now desire to continue to live together as such."[58] Many hundreds of other Christian County men and women over the next twenty-one years, who had "jumped the broom" as slaves or had been married by a black or white preacher, followed suit. Some declarations indicated how long the couple had lived as married people and how many children they had.

In Christian County and elsewhere, the decision of couples to declare their marital commitment involved some sacrifice. Besides the trip to Hopkinsville if they lived in a rural area, people had to pay a registration fee of fifty cents, not a small sum for former slaves in 1870. This inscription of freedom, however, was more than an expressive act. Some suggestion of self-interest, beyond a desire to avoid a misdemeanor charge, resonates in the following declaration at court on August 21, 1873: "Robert Downey and Mary Ann Downey (both of color) . . . allowed that they have lived together as husband and wife for the past 21 years and over and desire to continue in such relations [and] they further declared that they have the following named children who are legitimate, to wit Georgella Downey aged 21 years on 15 May 1873, James Downey aged 18 years on 2 March 1873, and Texanna Downey aged 15 years, 6 March 1873."[59] This and other assertions of civic status in effect were statements of entitlement to the kinds of rights enjoyed by all other citizens. These included the right to own property in one's name and to bequeath it to one's children, pronounced legitimate in this official statement.

In 1870, a detailed demographic profile of the black population appeared in the federal census, the first one following emancipation and recognizing the new civic identity of former slaves. Overwhelmingly domestic servants, unskilled workers, or farm laborers, very few former slaves owned land or other taxable property. However, a relatively small number of exceptions to this pattern appeared. The county numbered 23,227 people, of whom 9,812 were black. The census ascertained the value of real estate and personal property for those enumerated. Black people five years beyond slavery registered few entries under either category. The census lists 137 black owners of real estate; the value of holdings ranged from one hundred to over one thousand dollars. Among these was Robert Downey, who owned real estate valued at eight hundred dollars and personal property worth three hundred dollars. It is unclear how he acquired what may have been as much as thirty acres of land, but certainly protecting his interests and those of his children was served by registering his marriage and otherwise assuming the rights of citizenship. Leon Litwack sums up the self-interested implications of which former bondsmen were well aware in registering their marriages: "The insistence of teachers, missionaries, and Freedmen's Bureau officers that blacks formalize their marriages stemmed from the notion that legal sanction was necessary for sexual and moral restraint and that ex-slaves had to be inculcated with 'the obligations of the married state in civilized life.' But many of the couples themselves, who needed no instructions in such matters, agreed to participate in formalizations of their unions for more practical reasons—to legitimize their children, to qualify for soldiers' pensions, to share in the rumored forthcoming division of the lands, and to exercise their newly won civil rights."[60]

Although the family life of slaves was always at risk, emancipated people used their freedom to legalize and protect these primary relationships. The census of 1870 did not ask explicitly about relationships among people within a household, but one can nonetheless make reasonable inferences from the information given. The relative ages of the oldest male and female household members as well as a common surname provide some indication of a marital relationship or at least a family unit. In these terms, the census shows the two-parent family as the prevailing mode of domestic life regardless of color, an unlikely outcome if marriage either as an actual bond between a man and woman or at least as a value had not been widely accepted among slaves. The postbellum legitimation of marriages, some growing out of relationships that had lasted for decades, sprang from custom and personal attachment reinforced by legal pressure and self-interest. But the opposite was also the case amid the institutional denial over generations of social paternity and responsibility. That is, under conditions of slavery, irregular unions and unstable relationships could only flourish alongside the committed conjugal bonds among other slaves.

It is the former condition, however, to the almost complete exclusion of the latter, that white chroniclers of black life in slavery and freedom fastened on. A century of postbellum repression found many popular rationalizations. As Blight has demonstrated, the South achieved control over the discourse on race and the Civil War following its military defeat. The North readily capitulated to the southern view in the interests of reconciliation and reunification.[61] The southern perspective, which became the national perspective, was abetted by historical and social science scholarship produced by numerous southern historians, amateur and professional, and sociologists emphasizing black familial instability, illegitimacy, dependency, irresponsibility, immature temperament, and a host of other negative traits, argued by many to be biologically based. This pattern thoroughly veiled the usable past discussed in Chapter 1.

By the 1960s, when biological explanations of human behavior had abated, a new conventional wisdom had emerged, focused on alleged cultural deficiencies in the black family. In this view, self-perpetuating cultural processes—a "culture of poverty"—were invoked to explain black family fragmentation and instability with their origins in slavery.[62] Those persistent cultural features, it was claimed, remained fully in evidence in the 1960s. The Moynihan thesis famously propounded this viewpoint.[63] It generated enormous controversy and critical rebuttal, particularly from social scientists. Some of the latter saw it as an attack on women, who often headed black households; the report was also taken as an overly narrow, ethnocentric view of what constitutes "the family." The critique was all the more intense because of the report's implications for public policy. Would government programs focus on interrupting the self-perpetuating behaviors associated with the "culture of poverty" across generations? Or would government programs instead locate the causes of the "culture of poverty" in the structural problems of unemployment, underemployment, and poverty?[64]

Anthropologists Carol Stack and Eliot Liebow provided powerful refutations of the arguments deriving from the "culture of poverty" thesis. Each drew on field research and the personal lives of real individuals, rather than on statistical profiles of impoverished urban locales. Stack looked closely at black family life and the putative pathology of matrifocal families and absent males. She found highly functional coping strategies of single mothers bound by poverty but still resourceful in using extended and fictive kinship, as well as friends, to create networks of support and assistance. She showed how government assistance programs provided incentives for men to absent themselves from the household, since families with resident working males could not qualify for welfare.[65]

Liebow likewise focused on people whose repeated failures in procuring jobs and a stable way of living was not due to the continuing reproduction of a culture of poverty. The street corner men of Liebow's study were in chronic economic crisis that was not self-induced. Able-bodied men willing to work simply could not earn enough to support themselves and their wives and children; even support of a single child was not possible. Liebow wanted to understand their world and how they thought about it, including the effects of economic struggle on their social relationships with kin and friends. Moreover, honesty was often penalized, since employers depressed wages on the assumption that their workers would steal merchandise.[66]

In addition to seminal anthropological criticism of the Moynihan thesis, historians also weighed in. Herbert Gutman, particularly, drew on demographic data, plantation records, naming practices, probable kin networks, and the like to turn the Moynihan argument on its head. He argued that black family and kinship bonds were remarkably tenacious in the face of the destructive environment of chattel slavery. Problems within modern black families thus were not the historical legacy of slavery. Gutman found that the two-parent black household was the norm between 1880 and 1925, whether the family was part of the lower class majority or the more privileged class of artisans or skilled workers.[67] Blind to the historical realities of black life, many contemporary observers continue to err in projecting backward the current blight of inner city black communities ravaged by poverty, out of wedlock births, multigenerational welfare, and despair. This only diverts attention from the structural and economic sources of the devastation.[68]

The value of conjugal bonds, parenthood, and sibling relationships among slaves finds its most enduring and moving expression in numerous black newspaper notices seeking information about particular kinsmen separated by sale during the slave era. Such efforts to locate family members continued for decades after the Civil War. The following request in the "Lost Relatives" column appeared in the *Freeman* in 1896: "I want to my find brother, Gilbert, who was sold with my mother, Lettie Mitchell, about 1847, from Trimble county, Ky., by one Daniel Trout. Last accounts he was a dray driver in Memphis . . . Any information will be thankfully received. Thornton Mitchell, Madison, Ind."[69] Particularly tragic was the separation of children from mothers, as indicated in this heartfelt plea, also issued more than thirty years afterward: "I will be very thankful if anyone can give me some information of my mother whose name was Lucy Barns, and lived in Haywood county, Tenn. The last time I saw her was in 1861. I was the only child at the time I was brought to Texas. My name is John Dennis, and has never been changed. J.S. Dennis, Rice, Tex."[70] Lengthier notices implored readers for help in locating multiple relatives by providing their names, dates of separation, and other identifying information about owners and their families.

RELIGION

While former bondsmen, for both emotional and practical reasons, sought to confirm or reconstitute their kinship ties following emancipation, their efforts to reconfigure the organization of religious practices were equally consequential in the formation of free communities. Once again, a desire for self-determination, both in behavior and belief, was paramount in repudiating the powerlessness and humiliations of servitude, yet those assertions were constrained by the racial realities of the early postbellum period. Part of that reality included cooperation with former slave owners, a factor in the formation of the first independent black Baptist and Methodist churches.

Hopkinsville's oldest black congregation—the Virginia Street Baptist Church—began in association with the white New Providence Baptist Church in 1850. The white congregation emerged in 1818, later becoming the First Baptist Church. Admitting black participants in a segregated gallery from the beginning, it eventually permitted the freedmen to conduct their own service in the basement before eventually assisting their move to a former tobacco barn.[71] The slavery issue divided Baptists in the 1840s just as it divided Methodists. Black Baptists of the north insisted on a strong denominational stand against slavery. Southern whites in 1845, opposing antislavery policies, formed the Southern Baptist Convention. In the early formative years of free African American communities, slavery's ideological legacy preserved a large space for white patronage and what James Washington calls "denominational racism."[72]

The tension between self-determination and white patronage played out clearly among Hopkinsville's black Methodists just after the Civil War's conclusion. Prior to the war, the slavery issue had split American Methodism, when in 1844 northern Methodists called on Bishop James O. Andrew of Georgia to resign because he owned slaves. Having inherited them, Bishop Andrew and his many southern supporters claimed slave ownership did not violate the key provision of the church's rule, which opposed "the buying and selling of men, women, and children, with an intention to enslave them." Unmoved by Andrew's casuistry, northern Methodists resisted, and the schismatic southern Methodist Episcopal Church broke apart over slavery and formally established the Methodist Episcopal Church South as a separate entity in 1846.[73]

In 1858, the defense of slavery by the Methodist Episcopal Church South deepened when the phrase condemning the commerce in people was expunged from the General Rules (the "Discipline"). The southern church did not want to imply that it was "antagonistic to the institution of slavery, in regard to which the Church has no right to meddle, except in enforcing the duties of masters and servants as set forth in the Holy Scriptures."[74] The rule had not referred to domestic slave trafficking but explicitly to the African slave trade, outlawed in any case by the federal government in 1808. Still, a hardened segment of the new southern church not only supported slavery but also repudiated the federal prohibition against the overseas commerce in slaves.[75]

An institutional apologist for slavery before the Civil War, the Methodist Episcopal Church South continued to reflect regnant racial attitudes afterward. The demise of slavery left intact all the predicates of color, hierarchy, and power within the church; they remained unquestioned and too deeply rooted regionally to be influenced by the federal statutory edicts that transformed the legal and political status of black people. It remained for black Methodists to define their relationship to the white parent church. Accordingly, the case of black Methodists in the immediate aftermath of the war is particularly pertinent to the question of autonomy in the face of disparaging racial attitudes. By 1867, black Methodists had begun withdrawing from segregated attendance at Methodist Episcopal South churches. In that year, Peter Freeman and five other men living in Hopkinsville founded the eponymous Freeman Chapel, which affiliated in 1870 with the newly formed Colored Methodist Episcopal Church (CME). Freeman Chapel remains Hopkinsville's second oldest postbellum black church. The six organizers had all married as slaves, and then declared their marriages as freedmen early on. They had also reached an economic level exceeding the vast majority of unskilled laborers and domestic workers, both on farms and in town.

The 1870 census provides some clue about the nature of leadership in Hopkinsville's community of freedmen. While the census does not record an occupation for Peter Freeman, it does note his ownership of real estate valued at three hundred dollars. Nelson Cross, a barber, and perhaps a kinsman of the missionary to Liberia, Alexander Cross, owned real estate valued at one thousand dollars. Ben Phelps, at thirty-nine the youngest of the founders, worked on the railroad. George Crutchfield, although a farm laborer, possessed real estate valued at four hundred fifty dollars.

Phil Bell was a blacksmith whose real property, a house and/or land, was worth eighteen hundred dollars. Kit Banks, at seventy the eldest of the charter group of Freeman Chapel, worked as a mason; his real estate was valued at five hundred dollars.[76] Additionally, three other men, all ministers, participated in the founding of Freeman Chapel. Two do not appear in the 1870 census, but a third, David Ratcliff, is listed as a grocer with personal property valued at five hundred dollars. He and his wife, Martha, had also officially registered their marriage.[77] That people so recently freed from slavery managed to own personal property or real estate, some valued in excess of one thousand dollars, is arresting. Four of the founders had skills that liberated them, as least partially, from unskilled labor; they were likely able to earn more money than average. Additionally, as noted in the will of J. J. Rogers, slave owners might bequeath money to bondsmen they were liberating, and this, too, may account for the economic standing of the church founders. Moreover, for years after the Civil War, some black institutions, including churches, received support from interested white people.

For example, the Church of the Good Shepherd, a black Episcopal institution, was built in 1896 with the assistance of Hunter Wood, Sr., the publisher of the *Kentucky New Era,* and Nat Gaither, a Confederate army veteran and president of the Bank of Hopkinsville. Both men were active members of the Grace Episcopal Church. Gaither had successfully arranged for a large number of fellow Confederate army veterans to contribute one dollar each toward the building of the black church.[78] In related instances, the First Baptist Church and other white donors contributed funds to the construction of the Virginia Street Baptist Church, completed in 1893, and the CME Church partly owed its existence to material aid from the Methodist Episcopal Church South.

White patrons of black institutions usually included former slaveholders, combatants in the Lost Cause, and other arch-segregationists. John C. Latham, Hopkinsville's wealthiest benefactor, and a Confederate veteran, contributed to the M and F College, a black institution teaching basic trade skills.[79] Absent explicit statements about these contributions, the donors acted on motives, seemingly paradoxical, that can only be inferred. A free black population was a visible and constant reminder of defeat in war, regional economic devastation, and repudiation of a way of life as old as the town itself. While there was no dearth of vindictive reprisal by former masters against freedmen, assistance to fledgling black institutions was not unusual. In the case of churches, newly freed black people argued that the whites still had a Christian obligation to see to their religious well-being, and this appeal undoubtedly moved some white patrons.[80] Carter Woodson found a mix of motives among white people supporting and sometimes contributing money to the formation of independent black churches. Woodson suggests that the departure of black members from white churches found approval among many former slave masters, since "they could no longer determine their faith and how it should be exercised." On the other hand, "some benevolent southern men felt it was the best way for black people to develop their religious life after emancipation."[81] Whatever the mix of individual motives among white people actively or passively supporting new black churches, their actions had important consequences not only for the free community of African Americans, but also for the social and economic life of the town. It was above all in the interest of white people to have a large, available source of easily exploitable labor—domestic and service workers in Hopkinsville and agricultural laborers in the rural areas of Christian County, where sharecropping quickly supplanted chattel slavery. In this context, the support of black institutions, particularly churches, would help to stabilize the emergent free population whose labor was essential to rebuilding white prosperity. It was, in short, an effort, thoroughly mystified by Christian charitable sentiment, to control a black labor force and to help insure its quiescence.

The continuation into the postbellum period of relationships of racial hierarchy established in slavery appears, on the face of it, inconsistent with the assertion that the CME represented an inscription of freedom. Its founding reproduced the old pattern of southern racial paternalism, according to Reginald Hildebrand in his study of Methodism following emancipation. For example, the CME Church began life through the auspices of the Methodist Episcopal Church South. White bishops supervised the ordination of the first CME bishops and oversaw the first General Conference of the CME Church. Moreover, the early CME leaders were resolute in establishing cooperation with the white Methodists, notwithstanding pervasive racism. One critical dimension of that accommodation concerned political activity within CME churches. Glenn T. Eskew has pointed out that the fledgling CME Church received property from the white parent church on condition that the CME leadership refrain from using the new church for activist purposes.[82]

In cultivating an informal, friendly relationship with the white Methodists, the CME Church suffered derision from the African Methodist Episcopal Church (AME), a northern organization that had sent missions and teachers southward after the Civil War. Beginning in Philadelphia, the AME Church protested slavery and ill treatment of free blacks in the United States. The black Methodists also complained of the derisive treatment they were receiving in the white church and their lack of participation in its affairs. The political genesis of the northern AME Church was thus fundamentally at odds with the southern CME Church and its strategy of adapting to new forms of white domination in the postbellum world. Consequently, in Hopkinsville, the AME Church made no substantial inroads, although it sent at least one teacher to the town just after the Civil War. The freedmen's actions suggest that they felt more comfortable dealing with familiar white patrons than with black strangers with outspoken political opinions. The northern black missions, for their part, were critical of the CME accommodation to a church thoroughly imbued with southern values and to which many former slave masters affiliated.

Yet Hildebrand's discussion supports an alternative view consistent with the argument here that inscriptions of freedom and self-determination were prominent spurs to action among the freedmen, including the early members of the CME Church. He refers to the relationship of the Methodist Episcopal Church South to the fledgling CME Church as a new kind of patronage—at a distance. Nonetheless, the freedmen's new relationship to whites did not entail an abandonment of the personal and collective agency, however limited, within their reach. Early members of the CME Church reproduced neither the precise form nor content of antebellum race relations. Instead, the young CME Church rejected any official relationship with the Methodist Episcopal Church South, despite the desire of the latter to establish a connection. Furthermore, the new church's initiative in organizing itself included its self-designation in contrast to the original name—Colored Methodist Episcopal Church South, which suggested it was simply the segregated section of the southern white Methodist church.[83]

In all of this, the early CME Church made the kinds of choices they could not have made in slavery, and these choices were conditioned by a desire for independence from white control. It was an independence black people effected through negotiated concessions from the white Methodists, who ceded some church properties and money to the new denomination. The young church called in this way on recent slave masters, as a matter of obligation, to show special consideration for the continuing spiritual comfort of those whom they had enslaved.[84] Paternalism was certainly woven into the relationship between white and black Methodists; it could hardly have been otherwise. But since minorities always understand majorities more thoroughly and with more nuance than the other way around, the former slaves of the young CME Church used their knowledge and their prior relationships to navigate to their self-defined advantage within the new but still asymmetrical world of racial politics.

Finally, the emergent Colored Methodist Episcopal Church surely represented a declaration of spiritual independence from southern white Methodism. The latter's preaching and evangelism among black people was yet another expression of racial domination, aiming to use religion both to blunt slave discontent and abolitionist messages rippling through Kentucky and to inculcate an acceptance of bondage as part of the divine plan. Slave owners, accordingly, often strongly supported such missionary efforts among their bondsmen.[85] Yet the entire enterprise assumed that the messages preached from a white pulpit would be received and interpreted precisely as the preacher intended. Bondsmen, in this view, were only malleable listeners who would be molded by the sermons, homilies, and biblical texts propounded by white apologists for slavery. But as noted in Chapter 2, the promotion of Christianity among colonized peoples of the world has often produced unforeseen and liberating consequences as narratives of missionaries and evangelists undergo a process of reinterpretation. Whatever bondsmen heard from white preachers could only have been mediated by their lifelong experience of slavery. Few would have thought that involuntary servitude was their inevitable, divinely sanctioned human destiny, that God could sanction abuse, degradation, beatings, and separation of families through sale. Instead, they prayed that freedom might still deliver them in this world rather than in the world to come. Slaves and then freedmen thus sought to shape a useable religion, not unlike the usable history long obscured by the ideology of racial domination. To paraphrase the anthropologist Paul Radin, the religious fashioning for slaves was not so much through their conversion to God as presented by slavery's defenders, but rather their conversion of God to themselves.[86] At emancipation, that process continued unimpeded in religious institutions under black control.

THREE LIVES IN BRIEF

Inscriptions of freedom recorded in family, welfare, and religious institutions defined the lives of many individuals, the vast majority of whom will remain anonymous to history. Peter Postell, Claybron Merriweather, and James Bass represent three known lives. All three were affiliated with the CME Church. Unique in their own ways, each man acted within the shared experience of postbellum white racial domination in Hopkinsville and Christian County. Postell and Bass were born into slavery, Merriweather shortly after the Civil War. In one important respect, their lives were atypical of the black majority, whose labor was under the strict control of white employers, whether farmers, merchants, or householders. Postell, Merriweather, and Bass had sources of income or livelihoods that limited to varying degrees, or in the instance of Peter Postell, cancelled, their economic dependency on the racial majority. While Postell and Merriweather achieved some celebrity beyond Hopkinsville, Bass established himself in a much less public manner. But like Postell and Merriweather, he showed a remarkable capacity for seizing opportunities under circumstances that more often than not conspired to maintain the black population as a pool of unskilled labor for town and county.

PETER POSTELL

Despite his social standing, economic position, and fame in the last decades of the nineteenth century, very few details about the life of Peter Postell survive. Black Hopkinsville in the 1890s witnessed the emergence of a very small middle class, but Peter Postell exceeded all expectations of black achievement by reaching a level of wealth exceeding that of many affluent whites in the county. At the time of his death in 1901, the *New York Times* identified him as "the wealthiest Negro in the state," estimating his assets at between $100,000 and $125,000. Robert E. Park, aide to Booker T. Washington, put the Postell fortune at $300,000.[87] A rare photo held by the Pennyroyal Museum in Hopkinsville pictures the elegantly attired Postell family at home amid the late Victorian opulence of a well-appointed parlor replete with piano, hearth and mantle, carpeting, long curtains, and other decorative features.

Postell was born in 1841. P. J. Glass bought the young Postell in Virginia and came to Hopkinsville in 1858. Once the Civil War began, Postell, then known as Peter Glass, ran off, eventually enlisting with many other Kentucky escaped slaves at Clarksville, where he joined the 16th Colored Volunteer Infantry of the Union army. After the war, he started a grocery in Hopkinsville, which became the seedbed of his fortune. By 1870, he and his wife, Pauline Buckner, had one child and personal property valued at five hundred dollars.[88] He regularly expanded his food business and invested in bonds, stocks, and real estate throughout Hopkinsville, including lots and rental houses. A generous contributor to many public improvement projects, Postell was described as "among the city's most public spirited citizens" and whose gifts went "largely to public improvements."[89]

Postell's ascendancy from slavery to Civil War soldier to wealthy Hopkinsville grocer and real estate investor was singular. At the same time, he embodied an image of black Hopkinsville that both black and white leaders wanted to portray. That is, if emulating his wealth was not possible, his civic-mindedness and gentlemanly conduct could serve as a model of good citizenship, promoting positive relations between the races. Postell, both in his stunning business success and civic spirit, exemplified the values espoused by Booker T. Washington in his public pronouncements about black enterprise and advancement. Through self-determination, discipline, and probity in all facets of life, black people would progress and would do so without recriminations about slavery. Thus, the preamble to Postell's will revisited the trauma of boyhood separation from his mother through their sale as slaves. Writing without vindictiveness, Postell described his own moral compass and his triumph over bleak circumstance: "From the time I was placed on the sale block in the slave market of Virginia, and through that instrumentality was seperated [*sic*] from my mother, I have endeavered [*sic*] by industry, honesty, and gentlemanly conduct to win the battles in this life. . . ."[90]

CLAYBRON W. MERRIWEATHER

Born in Christian County in 1869 to freed slaves, Claybron W. Merriweather achieved a very different kind of reputation that also extended beyond his native area. Freedom meant achievement in multiple endeavors, despite the extreme deprivation of his early life. Merriweather became a man of letters, publishing his first of several books of poetry in 1907, although he did not come to the literary life easily.[91] He attended rural schools after 1874 when the state of Kentucky established severely underfunded common, or public, schools for black children. Young Merriweather worked on farms in the rural area before going to Earlington, Kentucky, in adjacent Hopkins County, to shine shoes in a barbershop operated by his brother. He also worked as a barber and by 1889 was able to attend State University in Louisville, an institution founded by black Baptists and renamed Simmons University in 1918. He returned to western Kentucky, where he taught school in Christian and Hopkins counties. He founded and edited the *Paducah Bee* in 1899 and shortly thereafter co-founded the *New Age,* a Hopkinsville weekly. He eventually studied law and set up a practice in Hopkinsville. Merriweather's artistic inclinations also found expression in oil painting, but it is in published verse that Merriweather is best known and where he wrote of the meanings of freedom in the decades after the Civil War.

Merriweather's most immediate literary influence was his celebrated con-temporary, Paul Laurence Dunbar. Like Dunbar, Merriweather sometimes wrote in black dialect and made ample use of natural images. Their immediacy and evocative quality give Merriweather's poetry a mystical cast, which often trends toward doggerel. Deeply Christian, he wrote poetry, often maudlin, and in this respect his verse brings some of Dunbar's more sentimental lines to mind. None of Merriweather's verse, however, exhibits the political edge and sharp race consciousness and pride apparent in much of Dunbar's poetry, whether written in black dialect or standard English. Dunbar's just renown derives from such famous poems as "We Wear the Mask." In allusion to that poem, Merriweather in his lengthy, lyrical ode, "The Declaration of the Free" declares,

> The right to be and call'd a man,
> Is all we ask;
> The chance to be the best we can,
> Without a mask;

To have the right to do or die
As we should like, beneath the sky.[92]

Yet nowhere in his poetry does Merriweather follow Dunbar in laying bare the pain of injustice or black dissembling under the force of white domination. Nor does "the right to be and call'd a man" convey Du Bois's highly assertive political stance in defending the manhood of the race.[93] In Merriweather's independent voice, the realization of freedom's promise occurs only through will, determination, and faith alone. Politics is absent. Although slavery is acknowledged, Merriweather considers it only elliptically. Earlier in the poem, Merriweather writes of black people "bowed in pain," who "toiled and wept," yet he insists that the "past is dead" and, in the manner of Booker T. Washington, that "We have no grievance to adjust, no charge to make."[94] For Merriweather, black emancipation emerged from Christian-inspired faith and hope, not from resistance, political struggle, or war. In this respect, his embrace of accommodation rather than opposition and resistance to white domination marks the prevailing black viewpoint of his time and place.

JAMES WALTER BASS

James Walter Bass's move "up from slavery" chronicles a life of determined confidence amid the frustrations he faced in Jim Crow Kentucky. Born a slave in the hamlet of Kirkmansville in northwestern Todd County, Bass lived his early years in an area with relatively few slaves compared to the southern, tobacco growing reaches of Todd and Christian counties. His parents were Julia Smith and Green Bass.[95]

In mid-September 1860, two months before James Bass's birth, the official federal slave count proceeded in and around Kirkmansville. The Slave Schedule of 1860 tallies nameless human chattel, identified only by approximate age, sex, and color. Joseph C. Bass, more frequently listed as J. C., owned ten slaves living in two dwellings. The schedule provides no key to the precise relationship among the slaves or their family organization. One can only speculate, uncertain about the anonymous adult slaves and who among them were James's parents, Green and Julia, which dwellings they inhabited, or if in fact they were both Bass slaves. Green was an itinerant preacher permitted by the slave master to travel between farms.[96] As a very young child, James Bass may have become literate through the instruction of Mary Bass, the daughter-in-law of J. C. Bass. Kentucky did not criminalize teaching a slave to read and write, so Mrs. Bass's instruction was not a sub-rosa act. James Bass's great-granddaughter reports that as a child her great-grandfather was favored by his owners, who referred to him as "our Jimmy."[97] But because the former slave master died in 1880, fifteen years after the end of slavery in Kentucky, his will took account only of money, moveable property, and land, which he divided among his few immediate survivors. Like most other erstwhile slave masters, he chose to bequeath nothing to his former slaves; his will, accordingly, is silent about James Bass and others who became the free black Basses at the end of 1865.

Within a few months of J. C. Bass's death, James Bass, a young man of nineteen, was counted in the Federal Census of 1880 in Gibson County, Indiana, ninety miles north of Kirkmansville. Granted freedom and a civil identity by the same government that had once effaced the names of his parents and other forbears and countenanced his own servitude, he was in the process of inscribing his freedom, first through labor and education and eventually entrepreneurship and land ownership. Neither a documentary record nor the memory of descendants records his activities between 1865 and 1880.

According to the 1880 census, Bass resided at the home of his employer, David Stormont, a resident of Princeton, Indiana, and locally famous as a white abolitionist and Underground Railroad conductor in the slave era. James Bass also found support in his association with people in the neighboring settlement of Lyles Station, a once-flourishing black community. Now partially restored by the state of Indiana, the community was founded by Joshua Lyles, a freed slave from Lyles, Tennessee, with whom James Bass was acquainted.[98] The town initially grew as escaped slaves found a safe haven there. Joshua Lyles periodically made forays southward to assist fugitive slaves bent on crossing the Ohio River into Indiana. Gibson County was an important route along the Underground Railroad and counted many abolitionists among its population.

Bass became the proprietor of the City Laundry in Princeton, located just a block from the main square, beginning in 1881. By 1884 he was studying at Oberlin College; he continued at Oberlin for two years. According to Bass family tradition, he came to the college through the assistance of a German immigrant woman in Princeton. Southwestern Indiana was the destination of a large number of German newcomers in the nineteenth century, many of whom were of a progressive persuasion and whose political aspirations were frustrated by the failed liberal revolution of 1848. The visible markers of Bass's days in Oberlin are in the surviving recitation books kept by his instructors in Latin and Algebra and in a brief notation in a treasurer's report that Bass received support from Oberlin through the Avery Fund.[99] The Fund was a bequest of $25,000 for "the education and elevation of the colored people of the United States and Canada."[100]

In these two faint traces from Bass's life—assistance from a German immigrant and receipt of a small stipend from the Avery Fund—white patronage is very much at play. It stands here as elsewhere as a kind of tense complement to a prominent African American value Bass shared with so many of his contemporaries, namely self-help and independent action. To the extent that white patronage was available, African Americans pragmatically and often of necessity availed themselves of the opportunity, as suggested in the complex relationship of the CME Church to the Methodist Episcopal Church South, and in the support black Baptists and Episcopalians received from white contributors, including former Confederates. Black Episcopalians in Hopkinsville, through white patronage, founded the primary school where Mr. and Mrs. Bass educated their children.

Yet white patronage in the founding of schools for black children was certainly the exception in Kentucky and elsewhere. On this point, R. R. Wright, Jr., the long-neglected early black sociologist, detailed the gross inequities in the allocation of tax dollars for the education of black and white children. By community self-help, often through the church to which schools were frequently attached, newly free black people organized the education of their children and hired teachers, as the Freedmen's Bureau records for Hopkinsville attest. According to Wright, the number of black teachers nationwide was 1,000 in 1866; by 1907 the number had risen to 28,000, a remarkable increase that would be unaccountable without the assiduous self-help efforts within African American communities in the Reconstruction and post-Reconstruction eras.[101]

After two years at Oberlin, James Bass returned to Princeton, and in 1887 reopened the City Laundry for another year. With confidence and in entrepreneurial spirit, his ad in the December 15 issue of the *Princeton Clarion* reads: "The City Laundry is again in operation and ready to receive work. The proprietor takes this method of announcing that all work entrusted to him will be promptly attended to, and that satisfaction will be given in all cases."[102]

Just before his return to Princeton following study at Oberlin, Bass was advised by an Oberlin acquaintance about a good job in Tennessee. He wrote a letter sufficiently persuasive to elicit a job offer. Assuming he was white, Bass's would-be employers on his arrival advised him with thinly veiled threats to leave town immediately.[103]

In 1890, he married Johnnie Fiser of Springfield, Tennessee, another tobacco center not far from Hopkinsville, where they settled. They raised their children on seventeen acres of rich farmland on West Seventh Street, then at the edge of town, which Bass had purchased in 1900 for the large sum of $1,500. He also earned off-farm income working for many years at the Metcalfe Laundry in downtown Hopkinsville. He died in Hopkinsville in 1925 and is buried in the family plot that he had purchased in 1915 in the newly established black cemetery, Cave Spring, where Postell and Merriweather are also buried.

Bass believed, with so many of his contemporaries born in the Civil War era, that genuine freedom required not only personal liberty but also economic emancipation. This was very much in keeping with Booker T. Washington's formula for the black future. Bass regularly pressed on his family the value of owning one's home or land, stating, "You must have your own roof."[104] His experience at the Metcalfe Laundry gives special relevance to his advice. After some fifteen years at the laundry, where he served as the unofficial manager because Metcalfe also operated an adjacent floral shop, a young white man, twenty-five years Bass's junior, was elevated to the managerial position after working only briefly at the laundry. Frustrated by the situation, Bass eventually left Metcalfe's for other off-farm work in a tobacco warehouse. Land ownership gave him some freedom from wage labor dependency, as the Bass family raised much of their own food, including livestock, and leased some of their acres for pasturage.

REPROBATES AND EXEMPLARS

It is difficult to discover the fate of other former slaves owned by the white Basses of Todd and Christian counties. In examining the lives of particular slaves, researchers rather quickly face the likelihood of learning much more about the slave masters than about those whose lives they are trying to uncover. For example, J. C. Bass, his wife, son, and daughter-in-law are buried in a peaceful forest in the hamlet of Kirkmansville, their graves recorded by Todd County genealogists who have mapped family cemeteries throughout the area. Moreover, various county histories document the white Basses. But of the date, place of death, and burial of Green and Julia Bass, James's parents, nothing is known. Before 1865, the lack of civil status as voters, property owners, taxpayers, employees, spouses, parents, and the like conspired to efface the identity of slaves. Unless mentioned in personal letters, plantation records, or similar sources, the anonymity of the vast majority of slaves was nearly complete. Still, in the case of the enslaved and newly free Basses, a few faint footprints can be discerned, including some that lead dimly along very different paths from the one that James Bass was able to take. Such is the case of Peyton Bass.

J. C. Bass was the son of Jordan Bass, Sr., who died in 1862. Jordan lived in the northeastern corner of Christian County, on a farm abutting the land in northwestern Todd County owned by his son. Jordan left a sizeable estate in land and property, including slaves, to his eleven children. None of the slaves is named, except in a separate bequest where he said, "I give and bequeath to my son John N. Bass, my Negro Boy Peyton."[105] By 1870, according to the Federal Census of Christian County, Peyton Bass was fifteen years of age and living in the household of Barbe Bass, listed as "housekeeper," with four girls of the same surname. Because the 1870 census did not explicitly delineate relationships within a household, one can only surmise that Barbe and the girls were Peyton's mother and sisters.[106]

In 1879, Peyton Bass met a violent end. He was killed in an altercation with a white man. The only extant account appears in the *South Kentuckian,* a Hopkinsville newspaper, which described a "difficulty" between George Knight and Peyton Bass: "They were engaged in a quarrel and Bass knocked Knight down with an axe handle. Knight arose threw a stone at Bass striking him in the face, and then shot him in the side with a shot gun, and cut his throat with a knife after he fell. The negro died in a short while. Knight, who is only about twenty years of age, has not been arrested. The negro was a notorious desperado and public sentiment is largely in favor of Knight. If the report given us of the affair is correct it was a case of self-defense, and the negro got what he deserved."[107]

The tone of this account of the violent death of a young former slave is indicative of the public portrayal of African Americans in newspapers and other publications written by and for the white populace. Criminal activity among black people regularly found its way into Christian County newspapers, which in the post–Civil War period showed only slight hesitation in justifying mob retribution. On January 20, 1880, the *South Kentuckian* reported that "Charles Smith, a negro, an escaped convict . . . was hanged by a mob in Boone county for arson and other crimes. As a general thing mob law should be disapprobated [*sic*] but when the law neglects its duty, the people ought not to be severely censured for avenging their wrongs."[108]

The *South Kentuckian* also portrayed black people in positive terms but no less stereotypically than the image of criminals, desperados, or fiends regularly sketched. Black people in the white press could also be exemplars of work and struggle along the path to good citizenship and improvement, although the portrayals were thoroughly condescending in their representations of an entire class of people suffering severe limitations. The *South Kentuckian* wrote in approving, patronizing terms about black teacher, George W. Belt, called "George," and his pupils:

> On Thursday and Friday nights concerts were given at Mozart hall, to which many white persons listened. These concerts were conducted in a quiet and orderly manner, and the dislogues [*sic*] and songs evinced that colored people can be taught these things, and to those who are unprejudiced can acquit themselves in a commendable manner. George is an intelligent and educated man, polite and courteous in his bearing, and has made a success of his school. . . . We are not one to let blind prejudices smother all merit in the colored people, but believe that our people, Democratic especially, should encourage them in their laudable

efforts to secure education, for this will be more to make good citizens of them than every thing [*sic*] else.[109]

The continuing bifurcation of society into white and colored in the post–Civil War era was promoted and reproduced at many levels. Social institutions and community consciousness were predicated on a sharp racial divide into "we" and "they." Thus, the news story about George W. Belt, although positive, nonetheless reported to "our people" about "them," and "their laudable efforts" toward self-improvement did nothing to mitigate the culture and social organization of inequality, social separation, and racial difference.

Even the respect accruing to Hopkinsville's most renowned black citizens was always refracted through the prism of race. Thus, the distinguished attorney, Robert N. Lander, a man born into slavery who unsuccessfully sought appointment as United States ambassador to Liberia, could not escape racial classification. The *Kentucky New Era* pronounced Lander "educated, dignified and reserved and . . . ventures the assertion that no man applying for the office which he aspires is more qualified to fill it with credit." The newspaper pointed out that "Bob Lander is a man of influence among his people and a man who is generally respected." Yet had Lander aimed for a posting to someplace other than Liberia or Haiti, the newspaper would likely have remained silent. Supported by the newspaper, he also won the endorsement of the "best and most influential citizens of the county . . ." whom readers would certainly know were white.[110]

After 1865, the hardened ideological underpinnings of slavery remained in place. Black achievement or independence always occurred within a framework of white efforts to typify black people as indolent, childlike, or dangerous, on the one hand, or, less often, "credits" to their race, on the other. The latter encomium depended on their progressing in endeavors and at a pace meeting white approval. Nonetheless, a collective racial deficit far exceeded the number of "credits." No better example occurs than in one of the standard histories of Christian County published in 1884. William Perrin concedes that there are "enterprising and industrious families of colored people" and that "several colored men . . . are doing well and may be classed as energetic and prosperous farmers." Well regarded by white people, the latter should be models for colored people. But Perrin concludes: "When the colored people learn to help themselves and show a disposition to become worthy citizens instead of loafing about town and lying around doggeries, they will find ready help from all intelligent white people. But to accomplish such a result they must display some efforts in this direction. The great majority of whites wish them well, and when it is deserved will not refuse a helping hand." But Perrin remained skeptical of black progress, even stating that the value of emancipation twenty years after the fact had yet to be determined in view of "unbridled inclinations."[111] Alleged indolence and other characterizations of individuals en masse mystified the severe structural-racial inequalities that effectively limited black mobility; at the same time, the victims of social inequality bore responsibility for its consequences.

When work was available at a living wage, black people took advantage of it, thus giving the lie to stereotypic beliefs about black propensities to idleness. Yet the stereotypes persisted. Black and white labor recruiters seeking black workers for the Mississippi cotton fields at wages higher than the local standard had some success in enlisting Christian County agricultural laborers, including entire families, in 1904.[112] Local labor shortages sometimes drove up wage rates, and black men did not hesitate to take advantage of the market for scarce labor. In 1906, the *Kentucky New Era* reported that the early maturing tobacco crop and the devastation of worm infestation "caused the farmers . . . to offer almost unheard of prices for workmen to go into the fields in an effort to save their crops." Farmers had to outbid each other to secure enough field hands, with the result that "Ninth street which is usually filled with idle negro men and boys is deserted today."[113]

Inscriptions of freedom after the Civil War occurred within the tight constraints of continued racial domination. The latter was justified as the logical outcome of racial differences that were conceived as natural rather than historical and cultural. But beyond the ideological dimensions of control, race supremacy and economic domination were mutually reinforcing. The harsh effects on the living standards and education of black people could then be invoked to demonstrate innate racial deficiency at a time when the conventional wisdom of the majority attributed poverty to individual failings. That black people remained dependent on white people for their livelihoods represented the single most significant factor in restricting the autonomy people were seeking in their individual and communal lives. Although emancipation effected physical freedom in the most literal sense, it did not bring to black people the degree of self-determined command over their own labor that they would have achieved had vast numbers secured ownership over their own land through compensation for a lifetime of arduous, unpaid labor.

Leon Litwack describes the distress and anger that met General Howard, the head of the Freedmen's Bureau, when he addressed two thousand freedmen on Edisto Island, South Carolina, just after the Civil War. He had come to inform them that they would have to yield the land, which they had farmed and claimed as their own, after their masters had abandoned it to fight in rebellion against the United States. In direct protest and religious lamentation, they reminded Howard of their fidelity to the government. But that same government had decided that the freedmen would receive no compensation in money or land for their years of labor as slaves. Instead, it was their disloyal former masters who would be rewarded.

General Howard advised the freedmen to return to work for those who had enslaved them.[114]

While there is no record of a comparable scene playing out in Kentucky, similar feelings of rage must certainly have swept over many former slaves after 1865. While Kentucky was not in rebellion, many of its Christian County citizens were ardent apologists for slavery and took up arms in support of the Confederacy. After the war, they too returned to their lands, worked in many cases by their former slaves through unfair labor practices, including asymmetrical contracts that the Freedmen's Bureau was supposed to prevent.

Despite the intimidation and violence of the early postbellum years, newly free men and women founded autonomous churches, schools, and other black social organizations in a determined effort to create an African American community. But the latter had to exist within the limitations imposed by a social order built on racial inequality. The possibilities and limits of black aspiration recall Marx's justly famous pronouncement: people are free to make history but they cannot make it any way they please.

4

FREE BUT NOT EQUAL

Institutionalized social and economic inequality for a century after emancipation betrayed the ideals of freedom and the postbellum constitutional guarantees that black people believed were theirs. Beginning in the early twentieth century, W. E. B. Du Bois articulated activist strategies challenging the status quo, but it was Booker T. Washington to whom most black people in the town and county looked for a model of accommodation. Washington reiterated his well-known program when he spoke in Hopkinsville in 1909. In this period of American apartheid, black social capital, rooted in the early years of freedom, advanced further through community institutions. Churches, schools, lodges, social clubs, a literary society, a Union veterans' organization, and fraternal associations met the social and cultural if not the economic needs of a severely segregated black community. A small but economically weak black middle class was emerging amid a much larger black population of urban service workers and rural sharecroppers. The vitality of these institutions was especially important when Jim Crow became entrenched during the 1890s. At that time, black attorneys and their allies in Hopkinsville mounted a well-publicized legal challenge to one of the more flagrant Jim Crow statutes— Kentucky's separate coach law. Throughout these decades, racial violence, including lynching, continued unabated, even as black farmers cooperated with white farmers in trying to break the economic grip of the Duke tobacco trust in the early years of the twentieth century. The discussion of these themes begins with a particularly clear ideological justification of segregation, social inequality, and public policies based on the racial theories of the time.

"THE WHITE RACE IS DOMINANT IN KENTUCKY"

Appearing before the United States Supreme Court in 1908 on behalf of the state's right to enforce segregation in private education, Kentucky Attorney General James Breathitt of Hopkinsville defended social inequality as a natural principle. In its single-minded determination to maintain legally sanctioned white racial privilege, the state had extended its reach from the strict segregation of public life to private institutions. The Day Law, passed by the Kentucky legislature in 1904, underscored the near-sanctity of racial inequality in governing virtually all domains of social life. It was one more indicator that segregation was growing even more severe in the late nineteenth and early twentieth centuries. Berea College, a private school, had for five decades existed as a successful but radical social experiment in interracial education, until the Day Law declared integrated education, even if privately funded, illegal.[1] Berea failed in its appeal to the Supreme Court to invalidate the Day law.

Breathitt's brief forcefully defended white supremacy by arguing that its tenets emanated not from law, reason, or custom, but rather from nature. Race supremacy as ideology was thus rendered self-evident and timeless, just a matter of common sense. Racial coeducation, Breathitt argued, was the beginning of a process that could lead only to social equality, personal attachments, and licentiousness, since the law against intermarriage would not be repealed. The certain risk to white racial purity through racial amalgamation was a particularly dire prospect since "the historian and the adventurer found the negro race centuries ago in barbarian darkness, and the race, as a whole, so remains, a warning . . . against social advancement and equality."[2]

A year later, an audience of a thousand African Americans from throughout Kentucky belonging to the Grand Lodge of Free and Accepted Masons assembled on Sunday, August 8, 1909, at Hopkinsville's venerable Virginia Street Baptist Church. Lodge members gathered to conduct the annual business of the organization and to hear addresses from local black dignitaries, out of town delegates, and other guests. Featured speakers that evening included Edward B. Davis of Georgetown, Kentucky, the African American Grand Master, and Lucian H. Davis, a Democrat and white member of the Hopkinsville City Council. Their shared surname was only one of several ironies at the Masonic gathering.

Councilman Davis presented an encomium to equality, color-blind educational policy, advancement, individual worth, and human brotherhood. In light of the day-to-day life of black people or Breathitt's rationale for shutting down integrated education, Davis depicted an imaginary world. His buoyant remarks bore no relationship to the early-twentieth-century black experience in Hopkinsville. Stark social inequality legitimated by law and custom at every level as well as the concentration of black people in domestic service and manual labor in town and countryside had severely limited the terms of black freedom after 1865. Underfunded black education also gave the lie to the city councilman's remarks. Spasms of extra-legal violence against black people in the town and surrounding areas further rendered the councilman's observations illusory. Still, he asserted, "We know no creed, we draw no lines." Forty-four years had elapsed since the end of slavery in Kentucky, but few whites in Hopkinsville would have subscribed to this quixotic declaration.

Yet his speech, according to Horace Slatter, the African American journalist writing the story for the Hopkinsville newspaper, the *Kentucky New Era,* set "an encouraging tone and breathed much of the friendly spirit that exists in Hopkinsville between the races." Slatter's newspaper byline added yet another layer of incongruity to the rhetoric of the evening, as his name was in parenthesis; this marker always called reader attention to the rare appearance in the white newspaper of an article by an African American writer whose topic inevitably centered on stories about black people. It is particularly ironic that the Masonic gathering occurred on August 8, still celebrated in western Kentucky and much of Tennessee as Emancipation Day. On August 8, 1864, word spread that Tennessee's military governor, Andrew Johnson, had freed the slaves in his jurisdiction.

Grand Master Davis responded with thanks for the councilman's welcome to Hopkinsville and then praised a number of highly regarded black and white citizens of the town. He made a special plea for black people to be able to advance themselves without the impediments of discrimination and race prejudice. Davis went on to declare, "We yearn not for social equality, but only want to work out our own salvation unhampered by prejudice and other restrictions." Then, in blunt terms thoroughly at odds with the spirit of the councilman's remarks, the grand master simply stated what everyone in the sanctuary had always known and had lived with each day—-that "the white race is dominant in Kentucky." Without challenging the legitimacy of racial hierarchy and the social inequality that Breathitt and others proclaimed as the natural order of things, he embraced moral suasion in appealing to the higher inclinations of whites. He requested that the "examples you set before us be one [sic] of purity, uprightness and truth. One man can only keep another down by staying down with him."[3]

Black people, in other words, had the personal resources to move forward in all domains, but only if the fetters of racial prejudice and discrimination binding them in place were severed. But with little political power, African Americans could only seek, in the terms set by Grand Master Davis, amelioration through the benevolence of white people. Recognizing that the legal and customary restraints on freedom would likely remain, Grand Master Davis could only issue a moral appeal to white authority. Although acknowledging the social and political status quo built on race, he asked white people to yield what conscience and charity, not law, dictated. The Masonic leader's address echoed the influential exhortations of Booker T. Washington, who visited Hopkinsville three months later, and whose formula for black advancement was already well known. His program of self-help and moral improvement without disturbing the fixity of social inequality insured the broadest possible support among whites.

Although a spirit of comity prevailed at the Virginia Street Baptist Church, African Americans in Hopkinsville daily bore quiet witness to the indignities of exclusion and economic marginality thinly veiled by the kind of public rhetoric Councilman Davis's remarks embodied. On the surface, racial peace and courteous interactions enforced in part by the gross asymmetries of power were routine, leading white people particularly to laud the state of race relations. But Horace Slatter, the black journalist reporting on the Masonic assembly, did as well.

Other black people of relatively high profile, such as Claybron W. Merriweather, also embraced this viewpoint, at least publicly. For Merriweather, a profound Christian faith provided an enduring rationale for racial amity under almost any terms. Many black people, on the other hand, who might assent by their silence or even echo Merriweather before a white audience had no illusion about the role of political and economic power, as well as extralegal violence, in enforcing the rigid hierarchy of race. Likewise, many black people have recognized what George Wright has termed, "polite racism," the white conceit that what passed for racial peace and progress was only possible if black people would continue to accept their secondary place.[4] At the Masonic assembly and in all other mixed race settings, Paul Laurence Dunbar's bitter words of racial dissembling, "We wear the mask," were apposite.[5] Such divergent views on race along the black-white divide persist.

In 1909, despite a very large African American population that constituted 41 percent of the Christian County total of 38,485 in the 1910 census, a black person could not acquire a secondary education anywhere in Christian County.[6] The kind of advancement Councilman Davis heralded was hardly possible without black educational opportunity on a par with what was available to white children. Any young black men and women able to reach for a secondary education had to leave Hopkinsville. Underfunded primary schools in the city, and especially in the predominantly rural county, were also the order of the day. At the primary level, the severe differential in tax allocations to white and colored schools was acute, guaranteeing the perpetuation of white racial privilege at all levels and frustrating black educational efforts.

Beginning shortly after the Civil War, the Kentucky General Assembly mandated that the support of black schools derive exclusively from black tax revenues. The racialization of tax collection and tax allocation for education resulted in a gaping discrepancy between funds available for the support of black and white schools. In

Hopkinsville, for example, the personal and property taxes levied on whites and blacks for the year 1907 totaled $3,371,260, comprising $2,085,585 in real estate tax receipts and $1,285,675 in personal property receipts. Total black tax receipts were $169,685, broken down into $162,900 in real estate taxes and $6,695 in personal property taxes.[7] The value of black assets, including real estate and personal property, was a mere 5 percent of that for whites. The white population of Hopkinsville exceeded the black population, but not by much and in a proportion very much smaller than the ratio of white to black tax receipts.

In a particularly telling account of the growth of black education in Christian County, Merriweather described with little critique the parlous state of black education in comparison to that of whites. He preferred instead to praise white generosity and good will in combating the legacy of slavery, rather than criticizing, even in the mildest terms, the inequity of law and public policy. He attributed to the first educators— "the most unselfish souls of both races"—the sacrifices needed to counter "the degrading and demoralizing after-effects of slavery." Writing of the early 1880s, Merriweather observed that the state appropriation to the county was approximately $2,236, or less than fifty cents per pupil, for the cost of educating 4,542 enrolled black children. In Hopkinsville, a series of ad hoc responses to the absence of a permanent schoolhouse meant that classes were held in shifting locations, wherever a spare room in a church or residence was available. The situation had hardly improved over the previous two decades since the Freedmen's Bureau in Hopkinsville paid rent on a series of temporary quarters for black schools, while providing no stipend for teachers in those schools. In the early 1880s, "our colored leaders, assisted by a warm spirit of sympathy on the part of white friends," acquired a lot for the construction many years later of the Booker T. Washington School. Merriweather's account, "Hopkinsville Colored Schools," appeared as a section of Meacham's *History of Christian County*.[8]

In describing the penury of black schools, Merriweather does not take corresponding note of how the state of Kentucky after emancipation had racialized the educational budget and tax policy to favor white schools. As early as 1882, a federal court ruling declared that educational funds must be equally provided to white and black schools. There could be no racial discrimination in the use of taxes raised for schools, yet throughout the entire history of segregated education in Kentucky, black schools continued to be unequally funded in violation of the law.[9] Nevertheless, Merriweather conveyed a conciliatory message of asymmetrical racial accommodation, echoing the sentiments of Booker T. Washington and the Masonic assembly in 1909. If Merriweather refrained from even the mildest criticism of racial inequity in educational funding, the Kentucky Colored People's Convention as early as 1869 was not so chary. Leaving aside the unfairness of segregated taxation, the convention complained to the state legislature that throughout Kentucky black tax collections were held back; they were not distributed to black schools and, were it not for federal aid, "our children would be left to a great extent to grovel in ignorance, as in the dark ages of slavery."[10]

The racial discrepancy in education, supported in law as well as by actions outside the law, was only one of many indices of the subordination of black people. Amelioration depended on the working out of "our own salvation," in Grand Master Davis's words. These words are redolent with religious meaning, since salvation promises heavenly deliverance from sin, destruction, or even failure. But despite the setting of the Virginia Street Baptist Church and the deep religiosity of black personal and institutional life in Hopkinsville, Davis's invocation of salvation implied something quite different from divine action as the sole instrument of uplift. His was instead a confident belief in the capacity of black people, absent white prejudice and other racial constraints, to make their way through their own agency. But was that possible amid a regime of social inequality that few black people were willing to challenge for fear of economic reprisal or the eruption of personal or collective violence?

BOOKER T. WASHINGTON AND W. E. B. DU BOIS

Two distinct visions of the black future envisioned at the dawn of the twentieth century turned on the answer to that question. Booker T. Washington emphasized racial conciliation without overtly challenging the regime of racial hierarchy and social inequality embedded in segregation. Beginning with his famous Atlanta Compromise speech in 1895, he emphasized accommodating black life to the social and political realities of race.[11] That meant an acceptance of white domination and black quiescence in the face of the denial of civil rights and the ballot throughout the South. This was the framework of Grand Master Davis's remarks. Moreover, accommodation in Washington's terms also entailed support for black common schools and industrial training, while directing black youth away from higher education.

W. E. B. Du Bois offered a very different vision of the black racial future. The brilliant sociologist, critic, and activist famously proclaimed in *The Souls of Black Folk* that "the problem of the twentieth century is the problem of the color-line." He rejected Washington's program of black submission to white domination in favor of an assertive push for political power and civil rights, as well as a relentless challenge to the continuation of psychically damaging acts of discrimination flowing from social inequality. Du Bois also advocated higher education for African Americans, not simply the industrial or agricultural training or other preparation that would lead only to service work or farm labor. Although Du Bois admired Washington's advocacy of black business formation, property ownership, and skilled labor, he argued that these economic achievements were impossible to sustain without black political efficacy. Black workers and business owners could not, in his view, protect their rights without the vote. Du Bois asked rhetorically: "Is it possible, and probable that nine millions of men can make effective progress in economic lines if they are deprived of political rights, made a servile caste, and allowed only the most meagre [*sic*] chance for developing their exceptional men? If history and reason give any distinct answer to these questions, it is an emphatic *No*."[12]

Moreover, the personal toll on black people of stoically enduring the daily insult of "civic inferiority" would "sap the manhood of any race in the long run."[13] Du Bois asserted that the destiny of African Americans lay not in their own hands, as Washington claimed and as Grand Master Davis reiterated, if they continued to stake their future on moral appeals to those in power. Without the force of law or a political voice that could be heard through elected representatives, moral petitions could not command consistent results. Such pleas simply put power into the hands of others. The African American future, in other words, should depend not on white benevolence, where it could be found, but on less capricious and more sweeping and lasting initiatives to gain civil rights, enforced legal protections, and a black political voice. For Du Bois, any black person assenting to social inequality—in effect accepting pariah status—"is forging the chains of his social slavery."[14] Quite obviously, Du Bois's demand for an end to public policies predicated on racial hierarchy met the strongest resistance among whites.

In sharp contrast, Booker T. Washington enjoyed enormous celebrity, not only among black people but also among whites. He made no demands on white people that would in any way challenge segregation and the social and racial principles of inequality supporting it. He absolved white people of any important responsibility to the black community. He consulted with presidents and dined at the White House as the guest of Theodore Roosevelt, although that precedent-shattering event provoked white outrage, especially in the South. Because political leaders frequently sought his counsel, he exerted a critical role in the appointment of particular African Americans to federal offices; he also advised white philanthropists about the black causes they would support.[15] Large receptive audiences, regardless of race, welcomed Washington's program. He was by far the most influential black figure on the American scene, although he faced growing challenges to his strategy of accommodation and his acquiescence to race-based civic and political exclusion.

Du Bois's increasing fame as a black leader and militant spokesmen in the opening years of the twentieth century soon led to a breach in his once amicable relationship with Washington. Both men shared a commitment to black self-sufficiency, but Du Bois came to deplore Washington's apparent inaction in the face of racial injustice. By 1909 their estrangement was complete. Du Bois and more than fifty other African American men had organized a meeting in 1905 at Niagara Falls in formal opposition to Washington's strategy of accommodation and unfailing advocacy of submissive racial conciliation instead of racial protest. The Niagara Movement stood for sustained agitation against racial humiliation, discrimination, and denial of civil rights.[16]

In the wake of continuing disenfranchisement of black people in the South and the Atlanta Riot of 1906, Washington's opponents saw a deepening crisis. In the summer of 1908, a smaller scale reprise of the Atlanta violence occurred in Springfield, Illinois, replete with the kind of rumors that fueled white rage and racial violence in the South—black men assaulting white women.[17] Springfield, however, lay in the North, and the freighted symbolism of Lincoln's home was hardly lost on Du Bois and well-known figures in the Niagara Movement, including the interracial group that founded the National Association for the Advancement of Colored People (NAACP) in early 1909. A growing number of African Americans, particularly among the generation born after the Civil War, simply could not endorse Washington's accommodation to racial inequality, the caste-like position of black Americans, color prejudice, and political weakness. They rejected the idea that the potentialities of the race, once amicable personal relationships with whites were in place, would then devolve to the exclusive control of a black community denied civil rights and the franchise in many parts of the country.

Beginning in mid-November 1909, Washington made an "educational pilgrimage" to fifteen towns and cities across the state of Tennessee. It was yet another opportunity to propound his blueprint for black advancement and thus to respond, at least implicitly, to the formation of the NAACP earlier that year. Despite or perhaps because of intense challenge from Du Bois and a younger generation, Washington at the time of his "pilgrimage" remained the most widely respected black person in the United States. He wanted to use his tour to continue his promotion of African American education and racial harmony. Prior tours two years before had taken him to Arkansas and Oklahoma, and to Mississippi, South Carolina, and parts of Virginia. For his Tennessee visits, he traveled with a distinguished party of African American business leaders, including members of the National Negro Business League, which he had founded in 1900. African American bankers, educators, ministers, doctors, attorneys, and other professional men from throughout the state were also part of Washington's entourage. Horace D. Slatter of Hopkinsville, the African American journalist who had reported three months before on the Masonic gathering at the Virginia Street Baptist Church, likewise traveled with the Washington party. Along the route, other eminent black leaders from around the country came aboard Washington's train. Speaking at Knoxville, Memphis, and cities and towns in between, Washington wanted to observe and comment on the varied conditions of the black communities of Tennessee.

A correspondent from the *New York Evening Post* was also present, thus assuring wide press coverage of the tour. A series of articles appeared in the *Post* between November 22 and December 2 describing the enthusiasm of audiences, black and white, to Washington's message of racial amity and his exhortations to his black listeners about personal and social improvement. On December 2, the *Post* editorialized on "Booker Washington's Greatest Service." Following the many accolades from local white leaders along the tour, the *Post* concluded that, however valuable Washington's work at Tuskegee or his discussions with presidents about the federal appointment of blacks, his most important service lay in enabling southern white men "to break away from the conventions, even the terrorism, which have kept them silent heretofore." A lesser leader, the *Post* argued, could not win the same enthusiastic endorsement. The implication of the editorial was that Washington enabled white people to speak in more benign terms than usual about race relations.[18] Washington's standing among white people was apparent from the outset of his tour in Bristol, Tennessee, where Judge Price, the son of a slaveholder, said, "I don't know what he is going to talk about, but I am willing to endorse anything he says, before he says it."[19]

The response of white people seemed particularly notable to Robert E. Park, the sociologist, who would go on to found the field of urban sociology at the University of Chicago and to make signal scholarly contributions to the study of race. In 1909, he was serving as an aide and ghostwriter for Booker T. Washington. At the conclusion of the Washington tour, Park observed, "The paradox of Southern life, from the point of view of a Northerner who does not understand the local conditions, is that while Southern people frequently seem opposed to Negroes in the mass, the personal relations between the races are on the whole kindly. These friendly personal relations between individual colored men and individual white men, Mr. Washington insists, must be made the basis for the final reconstruction of the Southern States."[20]

Horace Slatter's observations about the friendly spirit between the races in his report of the Masonic gathering at the Virginia Street Baptist Church exemplify the public rhetoric emanating both from black and white spokesmen. Washington's views had taken hold long before his Tennessee tour and resonated in Hopkinsville well after the focus of ameliorative action was shifting from Washington's politically submissive philosophy of accommodation to the overt protests and demands by Du Bois and the NAACP. The latter challenged opposition to "Negroes in the mass," codified in custom, law, and other institutional and political arrangements that seemingly did not compel Washington's attention.

Great anticipation marked the days leading up to Washington's Hopkinsville visit. Readers of the *Kentucky New Era* saw a story on November 19 about Washington's opening address in Bristol, Tennessee. "I told President Taft that the

Negro is well off in the south and that the races are harmonious. I told him that there is no spot on earth where the outlook for the race was better."[21] Such publicly expressed sentiments, optimistic to the point of fantasy and devoid of any hint of recrimination or demand, guaranteed his support among white people who, like Judge Price of Bristol, had full confidence that the racial status quo would remain unchanged. Indeed, large numbers of whites attended his speeches along the route. Of course, Washington's public pronouncement or reports of private conversations were calculated actions to advance his program by maintaining the good will of white people.

Less visible were Washington's quiet, unpublicized efforts on behalf of the kind of initiatives his strongest critics could endorse. For example, he actively supported appeals to the Supreme Court to rule against peonage and the debarment of black people from juries. He retained a lobbyist to stifle a bill mandating racial segregation of rail travel in the North despite his publicly expressed commitment to racial separation. Washington also provided financial support for legal briefs opposing black disenfranchisement in Louisiana and Mississippi. Washington's long-term goals and those of his critics were not so disparate—equality and full civil rights for black Americans. But his conflicts with the activists in the Niagara Movement and the NAACP were profound at the level of tactics. A post-slavery generation could not abide the praise, so apparent in his Hopkinsville speech, of southern whites of the "better class," or his disregard of black higher education.[22]

Following a morning visit to Springfield, on November 22, the Washington group aboard its specially chartered train crossed into Kentucky, stopping first at the small Todd County town of Guthrie, just north of the state line, where he briefly spoke to several hundred people at the station. Disembarking that afternoon in Hopkinsville, twenty-five miles to the northwest, Washington rode in an open carriage through city streets alive with the cheers and excitement that marked his visits to the towns and cities of Tennessee. Exuberant and welcoming, substantial numbers of Hopkinsville's black population gave a tumultuous greeting to the founder of the Tuskegee Institute. Many people, black and white, were expected to hear him in Hopkinsville. The *Kentucky New Era* carried brief notices over the previous week advertising Washington's imminent appearance at the Union Tabernacle.

The Tabernacle stood on West Seventh Street near the site of the present Christian County Justice Center. It was a popular venue for large public meetings, performances, school exercises, and other events. The advance notices informed people that tickets at the door for adults would be either fifty or twenty-five cents; children's tickets were fifteen cents. In those segregated days, half the ground floor of the Tabernacle was reserved for black people and half for whites. Reserved seats for fifty cents were also available, and segregation extended even to those advance purchases. White people could buy reserved tickets at Anderson and Fowler's Drug Store, African Americans at the People's Drug Store.[23]

Washington found his reception particularly gratifying, anxious as he was that the social and economic character of black Hopkinsville, as he perceived it, might limit the appeal of his message. He thought that black people in Hopkinsville might reject the kind of program of agricultural and industrial training in place at Tuskegee. After all, black people in Kentucky possessed the franchise; a black man held an elected seat on the Hopkinsville City Council, and a small aspiring black middle class had developed, although lagging well behind the income levels of their white counterparts. They made their way in small businesses as merchants, self-employed artisans and semi-skilled tradesmen, as well as teachers and other professionals. A very few black people had risen beyond middle class status, even by white benchmarks.

Washington's speech elicited the same kind of enthusiasm that greeted his arrival in Hopkinsville that afternoon. According to Park, the audience of thirty-five hundred was perhaps the most enthusiastic of the tour up that point. While most of the black people in attendance were from Hopkinsville, a few hundred had arrived from the countryside, either driving their own wagons or riding in railway cars, especially chartered and discounted for the occasion. A mine owner with a progressive outlook, J. G. Atkinson, gave his workers the day off if they wanted to attend the evening program culminating in Washington's speech.[24]

The local reception committee consisted of luminaries of the city's early twentieth century African American community. Prominent among these leaders was P. T. Frazer of the M and F College, the institution sponsoring Washington's visit. Frazer was a graduate of Simmons, a black Baptist college in Louisville founded in the 1870s. The M and F College taught the Bible, some trades, and basic courses that would have been available to secondary students, had there been a black high school. Also on the committee were several ministers, as well as Edward W. Glass, an undertaker and a member of the city council. Prominent local businessmen and tradesmen included George Leavell, a carpenter; H. S. Smith, a well-known stone mason; and A. C. Brent, a prosperous grocer who served both black and white clientele in a store in the downtown area.

By any measure—publicity, organization, attendance, and press coverage—Washington's visit to Hopkinsville was a major event. In 1909, the city's population was nearly 10,000 people.[25] Conservative estimates of attendance at Washington's evening address put the number at 4,500.[26] The Tabernacle program began with a song performed by the students of M and F College followed by a prayer. Another song, "The Old Time Religion," was sung, according to a Kentucky New Era writer caught up in the stereotypes of the time, "as only Negroes can sing that wonderful old song." Following brief introductory remarks by W. H. Lewis, a prominent African American attorney from Boston, Frazer and Reverend Williams also spoke briefly. Then for two hours, Washington delivered his address, advancing the philosophy made famous in his 1901 autobiography, *Up From Slavery,* and repeated subsequently in many articles and public appearances.

Washington expressed no recrimination over Jim Crow laws, the denial of civil rights following Reconstruction, or slavery itself. On the contrary, Washington argued that slavery had provided the crucible in which black people forged an ethic of unremitting hard work, giving them the mettle to succeed through their own efforts. Only forty-four years after the end of slavery in Kentucky, a Hopkinsville audience that included people who, like himself, had been born into servitude heard Washington. One can only wonder how they reacted to the assertion that something good might have come out of the shame and injury of bondage. At the same time, Washington did not reprove white people nor make special demands on them, except to be examples of propriety to their black neighbors. Aiming to secure white financial support for black enterprises, Washington was keenly aware of white sensibilities and patronizing attitudes, and he played to them. He acknowledged the personal benefaction of whites, stating that "colored men . . . could not have reached their present degree of success in your city without the help, encouragement and protection of the best white people."

In Hopkinsville, Washington disclaimed any interest in social integration. He had espoused this view in his Atlanta Compromise speech nearly fifteen years before, when he said "the agitation of questions of social equality is the extremest folly."[27] He thus tried to set to rest once again the primordial fears and anxieties of white people regarding the social mixing of the races. "I am constantly mingling among members of my race, North and South, and of all the subjects discussed that [social equality] is very rarely referred to. Let me say emphatically as I can, that judging by my observations and experience with my race, no where [*sic*] in this country is it seeking to obtrude itself upon the white race, and especially here in the South."[28] In a well-known metaphor on racial separation and community development, Washington often said, beginning in his Atlanta Compromise speech, that "[i]n all things purely social we can be as separate as the five fingers and yet one as the hand in all things essential to mutual progress."[29]

Unfailingly conciliatory, Washington's Hopkinsville speech praised whites and exhorted black people to hard work, thrift, and right living. The progress of one race, in Washington's formulation, was intimately bound up with the progress of the other, just as failure would be collective. "[T]he Negro is very much what the white man is. I find that on going into a community where the white people are ignorant [and] lawless, the negro will be found leading the same kind of life; on the other hand, where you find an intelligent, cultured, law abiding class of white people you will find the negro leading the same kind of life." At the conclusion of his speech, Washington applied this line of thinking to Hopkinsville. "We have here in proportion to their number probably the very highest type of Negroes to be found anywhere in the country. This is very largely due to the fact that we also have the very highest type of white people."

Washington claimed "the individual relation between the black man and the white man is the basis for the settlement of whatever problems that are remaining."[30] If Washington could persuade a white community that its progress depended on the progress of the black community and vice versa, white people might come to see that the advancement of black Americans was not only a moral obligation but also a matter of their own self-interest.

Whatever his African American contemporaries may have thought about his publicly expressed political, economic, and social viewpoints, none could deny the remarkable achievements of Booker T. Washington, the man. That, as much as his message of accommodation and acceptance, was surely what was celebrated in Hopkinsville in the autumn of 1909. Even Du Bois, before the breach in their relationship, acknowledged the older man's origins in slavery and how he therefore hesitated "to criticise a life which, beginning with so little, has done so much."[31] At Washington's death, the *Crisis* in reiteration praised his achievements in promoting black ownership of land and property but "in stern justice" found him responsible "for the consummation of Negro disfranchisement, the decline of the Negro college and public school and the firmer establishment of color caste in this land."[32]

Even before Washington's death in 1915, the center of black leadership in the United States was shifting toward the young NAACP and its activist founders. Hopkinsville's African American community was caught up in the transition, if not in overt or frequent demonstration against social inequality, at least in a clear awareness of the NAACP and its activism on the national stage. An effort to halt the Hopkinsville showing of *The Birth of a Nation,* the infamous silent film extravaganza glorifying white supremacy, probably brought the petitioners into contact with the NAACP. One surviving copy of the Hopkinsville black-owned newspaper, *The New Age,* is revealing, carrying as it does several stories in the April 25, 1924, issue concerning protests of the NAACP, including a report on the successful campaign to secure a War Department commutation of a life sentence of a black soldier. Readers also learned of discrimination in the allocation of educational funds for black schools and black teachers in Georgia. Another column described an interracial dinner in New York City, where W. E. B. Du Bois was honored "as one of the greatest living Americans." From a black news service, *The New Age* carried a scathing portrait of an Alabama senator describing a divinatory technique for determining the guilt of black suspects. The story concluded by saying that, if all the people of Alabama could vote, proponents of such retrograde practices would never be elected.[33] This kind of news was unavailable to black people reading Hopkinsville's white-owned and operated newspaper. Beyond the social notices and reporting on religious activities, *The New Age* reflected a strong race consciousness that in some degree was present in the black community all along.

DEMOGRAPHY AND EXPERIENCE
IN THE COUNTY AND TOWN

The black population of Hopkinsville appeared to Washington and Park as very different from the desperately poor and deprived people to whom Washington frequently directed his message of industrial and agricultural training and service work. In the unsigned "Special Correspondence of *The New York Evening Post*," probably written by Park, the challenge the town presented is described as follows:

> Hopkinsville . . . where the evening meeting took place presented a
> more complex problem [a few hours before, Washington had spoken in
> Guthrie to an audience comprised mostly of farmers and farm laborers].
> . . . Kentucky Negroes are in a class by themselves. They are clannish to
> a great degree. They remember that before the war they were largely of
> the house-servant class, and they are apt to take advice slowly. There
> has never been any difficulty about their voting either.
>   "Any man who knows a log cabin where he sees it can vote," is the
> way they put it. The log cabin is the Republican emblem in Kentucky,
> and this county has only gone democratic once since the war; that was
> last year. All this made it seem probable that the Negroes at least would
> hesitate about accepting Dr. Washington's strictures as applicable to
> themselves.[34]

Here, Park was caught up in the then common view that Kentucky slavery was essentially a domestic institution, rather than the basis of large-scale agricultural production, as it was in much of Christian County. Under his own name, Park also wrote briefly about black people in the rural areas of Christian County, some of whom came to hear Washington's Hopkinsville address.

Implicit in his view of town and county is the positive relationship between the races that Washington so frequently portrayed. Washington's aim was to identify black progress, marked by land ownership and business formation, and to promote amicability across the color line in order to garner white support for his program.

As adviser and personal secretary to Washington, Park of course sought to advance Washington's ideas and to highlight black progress:

> The colored tobacco farmers in this region are doing particularly well, and one of them, Tom Wright of Cerulian [sic] Springs, is said to have taken the prize regularly for a number of years for the best sample of dark tobacco produced in Christian County. Near this city, also, is the famous St. Bernard mining company's properties, where 3600 colored and 2000 white miners are employed. The head of this company, J. G. Atkinson, is recognized as a friend of the colored people. For example, his private secretary, bank boss in one of his mines . . . the man that has charge of all the operations below ground, and a number of other men occupying responsible positions are Negroes. Mr. Atkinson employs three Negro electricians who were educated at Armour Institute, Chicago, at his expense.[35]

One need not gainsay the validity of Park's depiction of the favorable circumstances of some segments of the black population in the town and in the rural area to ask how representative those observations were in a county that in 1910 numbered 15,956 black people out of a total population of 38,845.[36]

In that year, often regarded as the beginning of the Great Migration of southern blacks northward, black dissatisfaction with life in both the town and county was manifesting itself in a small population loss of 641 people. In the same period, the white population increased by 1,523. The loss of black population, although negligible, is noteworthy because it marks the first downturn in black numbers since the census of 1870, when black people, as citizens, were first counted.[37] Between 1910 and 1920, more than 3,000 black people left the county, the largest decline in any ten year period. Black population loss continued in each decennial census until 1960.

The Christian County census of 1910 included 304 black farm owners, the second largest county total in Kentucky, giving some justification to Washington's buoyant outlook and Park's portrayal. Black tenant farmers, on the other hand, numbered 571, the largest number for any county in the state. The count of white farm owners and white tenants was 1,905 and 1,065, respectively. The data do not permit a more microscopic view of these figures that would reveal average holdings of white and black owners. But clearly, the ratios of owners to tenants by race nearly reverse themselves. Whereas white farm owners constituted approximately 65 percent of white farmers, with the remaining 35 percent cultivating the land as tenants, black farm owners number 37 percent and black tenants 63 percent.[38]

"Tenancy" in the South referred to several possible arrangements. In some few instances in Christian County, tenants might simply rent farmland from the owner and have no further obligation. Other tenants, sometimes called "share croppers," "croppers," or "share tenants," would receive shelter, food, and provisions, including tools, from the landowner. Once the final crop was marketed, the owner would deduct from the tenant's share the value of the goods advanced to him. After the deduction, the tenant might receive half the value of the crop. If, on the other hand, the tenant were not down and out, he would require less provisioning from the owner and could then realize a greater percentage of the return, assuming an honest accounting. Black sharecroppers or tenants of limited education often feared challenging the authority of a farm owner or manager controlling a system rife with abuse.

Personal narratives inevitably humanize the raw aggregate statistics and the broad outlines of a severely exploitative system of labor extraction. They lay bare the hardscrabble lot of sharecroppers and their families. Sometimes unable to read or write, black tenant farmers in any event were at the mercy of those in charge of keeping accounts and settling up after the harvest. The owner or manager kept track of the advances but was not answerable to anyone. Sarah Nance includes among her most vivid and troubled recollections the "settlement" in the mid-1930s that a white farm owner made with her father, a "share-cropper," as she described him.

Mrs. Nance began her account with her own exploitation as a child of twelve by the farmer's wife for whom she worked. She and her sister received only scraps of clothing, empty perfume bottles and candy boxes—"I guess she was givin' us that to play with." She continued,

> I got tired and one morning I said I was not going. I didn't want to go. I knowed I was bein' cheated. But my dad was 'fraid of white people. He was on the farm, and he didn't want trouble. And he had a hard time anyway. And my Daddy come off of slavery, you know. He just didn't want no parts of it. He'd tell us, you all go back. She ask what y'all charge. He always want us . . . y'all just tell her whatever you want to give us. And so we told her that and that's what she give us cause she didn't have to sack 'em up cause they was already sacked up [ready to throw out]. She'd reach into the bag and give 'em to us. And we'd walk a long way, too, to get back home.
>
> So then she had us over there—we had to clean out her toilet, clean out the hen house, and that's the time I went over there, and I didn't wanna to go. And my Daddy told me if I didn't go I wasn't gonna stay here. If you don't go, you ain't gonna stay here. I knew then he's gonna whip me if I didn't get out the house.

So we got ready and went direct by the garden, and my mother was workin' there, and she told us, she said, now this time if she ask y'all what y'all charge, y'all tell her a dollar. And I told her OK. I looked down. I was half scared to death. When we got through, I had to clean her toilet out, she said, why how much do I owe y'all? And I said a dollar. And she went in there and got it and give it to us. We had fifty cents apiece. It felt good, I had some money, cause a nickel was a whole lot to me anyway. I had fifty cents.

The narrative then takes up one of her father's particularly bitter experiences in sharecropping, made all the more disturbing in her memory by a one-sided show of respect in death. That is, Sarah Nance's parents paid their respects at the death of the white farmer's mother, but a corresponding expression of condolence was not forthcoming from the farmer or his family when Mrs. Nance's father died:

He raised 'bacca crops and one time he raised a crop and he promised my brothers—two boys—some overshoes, and they was glad to get some overshoes. So when he sold his 'bacca, they got back home around noon, and they settled up, and he had eleven cents from paying up his debt what he owed. That's all he had left but eleven cents. And he stayed in the woods over there until dark, 'til night. Just couldn't come home and tell his sons he didn't have money. So that hurt me. I always thinks about that. A whole lot. He didn't get to get the overshoes. My daddy was a sharecropper. He would get flour over there [from the land owner]; my daddy would get flour once a month to feed ten of us. He had to pay for that; he had to pay for fertilizer. I don't know, whatever he got over there. And we got our oil from over there; we used lamps.

When his [the owner's] mother died, my mother and father got in the wagon. It was raining, cold, and ride over there in the wagon. They had her funeral in the house. So they went over there. My mother and father had to sit in the kitchen. And they was in there having the funeral. I don't know why my daddy and mother went there. Bin me, I'd astayed home. I wouldn't have went. So they set there in the kitchen while the funeral was goin' on. And when the funeral was over, they got in the wagon and come home. My daddy died. This man did not send us *nothing;* this man did not come over to see us, to tell us he was *sorry;* this man never done *nothin'* and did not come to his funeral.[39]

Sarah Nance's personal account is not unique. The recurrent motifs among those who worked on farms as sharecroppers are struggle and arduous labor, sometimes compounded by broken promises and outright fraud by owners and managers. The vulnerability of black people bound to land owned by white people grew out of a combination of fear and limited access to legal redress. Mr. Wilson, Sarah Nance's father, was so fearful of white people that he threatened to beat his daughter if she did not comply with the white lady's request for domestic service. In asking for a dollar for the day's work she and her sister performed, Sarah Nance was also afraid to make her wishes known to a white woman. Had she not exercised her will, emboldened by her mother, she and her sister might again have received nothing for their labor.

While life on the land owned by others had its share of misery, there were other stories of black success in the rural area, as recounted by Park. Likewise, it is possible to sketch the more positive aspects of economic life in the town. Although a net outmigration was taking place for the county as a whole, a close examination of the black occupational profile in Hopkinsville in 1910 suggests that a number of people, but certainly not the majority, worked beyond the unskilled level. The 1910 City Directory of Hopkinsville included the names of 2,815 black people and specifies residence, name of spouse, and occupation. The black population of the town in 1910 was 4,187, or 44 percent of the total of 9,419.[40] The discrepancy between the directory listings and the city total of black people can be attributed to the absence of children from the survey, as well as to an uncertain number of people who simply escaped notice. Those in the unskilled categories such as domestic, houseman, laborer, porter, cook, and laundress predominate, but it is not stretching a point to identify a small black middle class at the time of Washington's speech. They were among the early leaders who welcomed Washington and headed various institutions within the black community.

Among the leadership were skilled or semi-skilled individuals such as painters, plasterers, masons, and bricklayers, including brick contractors, tailors, dressmakers, and shoemakers, some of whom owned their own businesses. Thirty-two independent farmers also lived within the city limits as well as fifty-three teachers, thirty-four carpenters, twenty-five barbers, and seven independent grocers. Not surprisingly, the obstacles to advanced training and the limited venues for securing it strictly limited the number of black professionals, which included only three attorneys and two physicians in the 1910 directory.[41] Although later generations of black people would count prominent lawyers and doctors among race leaders, the early twentieth century continued the post-emancipation pattern of black leadership clustering among artisans, teachers, undertakers, and clergy.

Young black people aspiring to professional careers aimed for a very narrow range of occupations open to black people and guaranteeing an exclusive black clientele. Segregated schools and the black church assured that a career in teaching or the pastorate would not invite interference or competition from white people. Likewise, the black body was the nearly exclusive concern of black physicians and morticians. While some white doctors would set aside office hours exclusively for black people, there is no evidence that the addition of black doctors in the town at any point caused competitive friction with the white medical establishment.

Still, the psychological heritage of slavery also accounted for the small number of black lawyers and physicians, according to Francis Eugene Whitney, a prominent black leader in Hopkinsville from the early 1950s until his death in 2005. Whitney served on the city council for twenty years, beginning in 1952, and had a very successful career as an accountant and real estate investor. A Hopkinsville native, Whitney recalled his own father's initial inability to earn a living as a lawyer. James T. Whitney is listed in the 1910 directory as a mail carrier; he was one of the first black postal employees in the town.[42] It was a coveted position for a young black man, although the elder Whitney originally settled in Hopkinsville in order to practice law. He had prepared near his home in Barren County, but with a black population of about 16 percent, that county offered no opportunities for an aspiring black lawyer. The senior Whitney hoped that his move to Hopkinsville, with its much larger black population, would offer greater promise, but he faced disappointment. The younger Whitney explained that his father encountered a black community much more likely to trust the legal skills of a white rather than a black lawyer.[43] By the 1920s, however, J. T. Whitney was a practicing attorney.

F. E. Whitney's characterization of black attitudes toward black professionals in the early twentieth century undoubtedly captured some and perhaps a majority of black opinion in the first decades following emancipation. That opinion could not help but be affected by white sentiment. After all, an antebellum public discourse ranging from local newspapers to churches continued long after the Civil War and relentlessly insisted that black people suffered from inherent limitations. But other factors were certainly at play regarding black attitudes toward black professionals. Those people retaining white attorneys recognized that "skills" also included white racial privileges of credibility before all-white juries and judges, as well as access to racialized social networks of personal and political influence closed to black professionals. In other words, a basic pragmatism and calculation also shaped the choice of legal counsel. This may be discerned in the experience of James Bass, who faced a serious legal problem in 1891, shortly after he purchased a home for five hundred dollars in cash. The sellers did not disclose to Bass that their outstanding financial obligations had resulted in the placement of a lien against the property. While the race of the sellers is uncertain, the lienholder was a white woman. In seeking relief from the sellers' debt obligation, Bass might have sought the aid of the respected black attorney Robert Lander. Instead, he chose James Breathitt, the widely known and politically connected white attorney who later was instrumental in shutting down integrated education at Berea College. The court record is incomplete and family memories do not include this case, but Bass's effort to protect his property against the lien was successful.[44]

Not only white professionals, but also white storekeepers and others counted black people among their clientele. By and large, the opposite was not the case. The small black middle class provided goods and services for other black people with little crossover to a white clientele. For the most part, black merchants and artisans made their living in what would later be called a "ghetto economy," the resources of which were much smaller than what white people controlled.[45] The city tax receipts for 1907, cited earlier, provide a telling index of racial disparities in wealth.

E. Franklin Frazier's classic characterization of the black middle class captures the economic profile of black Hopkinsville in the early twentieth century. Black businesses were generally small scale and undercapitalized; they were dependent on a segregated clientele of limited means, and their income lagged far behind their white counterparts. Collectively, black businesses controlled little wealth and had little impact, either on the American economy as a whole or on the economic standing of black people, beyond a very small number. Frazier was particularly critical of the liberal definition of "business" utilized by the National Negro Business League, founded by Booker T. Washington, which included peddlers and newsboys as businessmen. For these reasons, Frazier disparaged such businesses as "a social myth," although one which was widely promoted by Washington and other black leaders.[46]

J. T. Lynch, when he was a student at Crispus Attucks High School, prepared a map in 1925 showing the location of black businesses and the offices of black professionals. In the early twentieth century, Main Street marked a divide between a largely black east side and a white west side.[47] Black businesses tended to cluster east of Main Street, where most black people lived. Lynch identified thirty-seven black-owned businesses and professional offices. One can infer a minimal white racial crossover occurring in those black businesses west of Main Street. These included a sheet metal shop, a tailor shop, and the Buckner and Brent Grocery. By that time, A. C. Brent, an early twentieth century leader in the black community, had built a commodious two-story brick home on the East Side that could match in size and cost some of the homes of Hopkinsville's prosperous whites. On the east side, where little crossover occurred, the businesses included six groceries, four barber or beauty shops, including one designated "whites only," four restaurants, three undertakers, two physicians, and three attorneys, including J. T. Whitney. He was eventually able to give up postal delivery in favor of the profession he wanted to pursue on coming to Hopkinsville some twenty-five years before. An eastside, black-owned barbershop catering exclusively to a white trade was not unusual in the South, where shops with multiple barbers and service personnel for shining shoes, could attract a large white clientele, provided of course they did not also serve black customers.

Like the marginal black middle class, black schools were equally disadvantaged through the system of segregated funding, as discussed earlier. Prior to 1916, black students had no opportunity to attend secondary school. A lack of funds and diffuse white attitudes that black youth did not require a high school education precluded the possibility of building a black high school until the second decade of the twentieth century. Then, white support was forthcoming, not as a generous civic act but instead as a result of converging white and black self-interest. In 1915, the city council put before the voters a bond issue to raise a hundred thousand dollars beyond normal tax revenues to be collected. The money was to be used to retire a debt of sixty thousand dollars on Hopkinsville High School built in 1912. Twenty thousand dollars would be used to construct a new white primary school, and the remaining twenty thousand would be earmarked for the building of the first and only black high school in the town. Two thirds of the voters were required for approval of the bond issue. Given the population of the town, which approached racial parity, black votes were essential, and indeed the measure passed. Reflecting on the ways ameliorative changes had come about in Hopkinsville, F. E. Whitney indicated that a considerable amount of discussion behind the scenes had taken place prior to the proposed bond issue. In other words, according to Whitney, whose father, J. T. Whitney, served on the segregated black school board in 1915, the town through its white representatives on the city council and school board committed itself to building a black high school as a condition for black support of the bond issue.[48]

BLACK POLITICAL AND LEGAL ACTION IN THE AGE OF JIM CROW

Washington's politics of accommodation was the order of the day in Hopkinsville and Christian County. Du Bois's compelling critique of racial conditions no doubt appealed to many African Americans in Hopkinsville, but his call to political protest was another matter. Kentucky differed from the Deep South in not depriving black people of the franchise after 1870. Of course, the state's black population was proportionally much smaller than in the states of the old Confederacy and the black vote, accordingly, less consequential statewide. Still, a black population approaching racial parity in Hopkinsville and Christian County could exercise some influence, exemplified by the political maneuver that brokered the building of the black high school. This kind of action does not seem to have happened with any frequency, although black people in Hopkinsville and Christian County managed to field candidates for office and to win elections, even as early as the 1880s. Except for consistently supporting Republicans in a county whose majority white population was largely Democratic, black political action neither organized opposition to Jim Crow custom nor elected people to the city council who actively opposed the segregationist patterns of the town.

To oppose the racial status quo within the town would simply have put too much at risk, including, particularly, employment. Actions that in any way challenged the familiar order could have severe economic consequences, for the vast majority of the black population in the city and in the rural area was wholly dependent on white people for employment. Without factories or an industrial base, Hopkinsville for at least the first half of the twentieth century was made up of small businesses that employed a few black workers in various capacities. Domestic work, moreover, was a vital source of income for many black women. In each instance, the relationship between white employers and black employees lacked the impersonal quality of the factory floor; instead, oppositional political or other untoward activity had a personal face and a possible economic cost, and activist black people could quickly suffer punitive job loss. Hattie Oldham, a Hopkinsville native now living in Frankfort, noted the very limited black political activity in Hopkinsville during the civil rights activism of the 1960s; she emphasized how black women working in white households strongly discouraged their children from confrontational political protest.[49] With job insecurity as the backdrop, Ed Owens, a longtime resident of Hopkinsville and now retired from the housing authority, recalled a planned march instigated by a young pastor in the late 1960s. The marchers were to carry their grievances directly to city hall where they would demand better jobs and an end to discrimination in hiring. There seemed to be considerable support in the black community, but on the appointed day, fewer than thirty people assembled. The minister called off the march, saying that such a low turnout would do more harm than good.[50]

The interconnection of race and politics in the town and county has been a constant, although at each historical juncture that relationship has taken its own particular turn. Beverly Kelly became the first black elected official in the county when he assumed the position of coroner in 1882. A blacksmith by trade, he won the office by a margin of thirty-four votes, yet it was an inauspicious victory. Like the other early black officeholders and community leaders, Kelly was light complexioned.[51] A number of voters who cast a straight Republican ticket in the party's strongholds in the northern part of the county learned only after the election that Kelly was black. They petitioned to have their votes withdrawn, but the clerk did not comply and the victory stood.[52] Whatever the strength of the Republican Party in the northern half of the county, voting for the party of Lincoln among white people did not *ipso facto* entail benign views about race. Indeed, Republican voting in Christian County more likely meant opposition by small, less prosperous farmers to the large landowners and tobacco interests who long dominated county affairs. In a particularly insightful remark that anticipated the observations of later professional historians, Perrin in 1884 characterized non–slave owning whites as resentful at the pretensions of slave owners, who expected them as well as black people to show a proper obeisance. Writing of the poorer, non–slave owning class, Perrin notes that they "did not object to slavery but to the 'aristocracy of slave owners.'"[53]

Hopkinsville's best-known black officeholder in the early years of the twentieth century was the undertaker Edward W. Glass. He was first elected to the city council in 1898. In that year, black officials also included the coroner, a constable, and pension examiner.[54] City council minutes document Glass's service on a number of subcommittees and his consistent record of votes with the majority. He represented a black ward on the east side of town, and his initiatives on the council often served very mainstream interests within the black community. As an undertaker, Glass enjoyed an independence from white control, but that latitude never extended beyond the moderate positions he took. For example, Councilman Glass called attention to certain violations of a city ordinance referring to "Bawdy Houses [and] Lewd Women, etc." He was concerned about a lack of enforcement of the ordinance on the east side and therefore proposed a resolution to the Council, adopted without apparent dissent, directing the chief of police "to strictly enforce the provisions of said chapter against colored women as well as white women."[55] Glass's resolution had the potential of exposing a degree of official indifference to what occurred east of Main Street, that is, among black people. But his plea for across the board enforcement of the ordinance did not lead to action on other issues of race and the law.

By contrast, although the record is scanty, a protest with obvious racial overtones came before the council in 1916. Edgar Foreman, a coal dealer, and Peter Moore, a teacher, joined other black petitioners in protesting the impending showing of *The Birth of a Nation*. The text of their complaint does not survive, although cancellation of the showing was the implied goal of the petitioners. At the same meeting, the film's local promoter requested deferral of the request for several days. The mayor pro tem and one council member approved the request; it isn't clear what role other council members might have played.[56] The matter did not come back to the council, and the film showing occurred two weeks later. Black Hopkinsville was hardly alone in its objection. Protests sponsored by the NAACP occurred across the country. In Springfield and Lawrence, Massachusetts, NAACP objections succeeded in shutting down the film. In other places, some of the most egregious scenes were cut before the film was shown. The NAACP called for "continued and determined action." It was especially concerned with showings in places such as Hopkinsville: "The play is leaving the cities and going into the smaller towns where its influence may be greater than in the larger cities."[57] The racism of *The Birth of a Nation* was magnified in Hopkinsville because the film was lavishly advertised with newspaper notices promising "a symphony orchestra of twenty-five New York musicians and a carload of special electrical and stage equipment."[58] The *Hopkinsville Kentuckian* printed testimonials, including praise for the Ku Klux Klan, from other places in the South.[59] Carter Woodson regarded the film "as a shocking measure of public credulity for racist fantasies." That assessment was one of his reasons for founding the Association for the Study of Negro Life and History.[60]

The earliest black protest against Jim Crow statutes in Kentucky occurred on the heels of the state's passage of the separate coach law in 1892. Conflict over the coach law festered into the twentieth century. Rationalized as separate but equal, Kentucky's coach law was a particularly emotional issue, for it relegated black people to railcars that were dirty, ill kempt, and anything but equal. Black travelers had to pay the same fare as whites, and their protests to ticket agents or conductors were frequently met by racial slurs and personal humiliation. Whereas black people could find accommodations, meals, entertainments, or spiritual solace in black institutions, there were no alternative black railroads where personal dignity might be respected. Travel from one town to another subjected black people to the vagaries of white-controlled railroads and white personnel. The coach law was part of a larger legislative process to enact laws institutionalizing racial separation in schools, restaurants, and public accommodations.[61] The anger and sense of humiliation among African Americans is captured in a *Freeman* editorial: "The South is in the throes of diabolism; the idea that ladies and gentleman must, because of the hue of their skin, be separated in public conveyances partakes of the most depraved and diseased condition. . . . Is the Negro human, an American citizen or is he an animal with only instinct?"[62]

Ironically, this degree of segregation marked by Jim Crow and separate coaches was a new phenomenon, one that departed from social patterns prior to the Civil War. As C. Vann Woodward has pointed out, the regime of slavery in the rural south was antithetical to strict segregation, since the master-slave relationship was predicated on social contact. Whites supervised black labor, white owners or doctors provided care for sick bondsmen, slaves and masters might worship in the same churches, and slave domestic service often included residence in the master's house. It was in regard to domestic service that the matter of social contact was most pertinent. Likewise, urban arrangements in the South after the Civil War continued a pattern of residential propinquity; that is, daily attendance in the master's house had entailed immediate availability. Newly freed slaves, entering paid domestic work, often continued the earlier arrangement, living very near their former owners who had retained them as employees. Independent of domestic service, southern cities before and after slavery were much less segregated than northern cities.[63] In some places, black people could even attend theaters, enter hotels, or book train travel on an equal basis with white people.[64] The latter right was painfully foreclosed by law once Reconstruction was dismantled. Thus it seems paradoxical that the institution of slavery was built on social contact, which in its own way enabled masters to exercise a direct and personal control over slaves, yet post-1865 social arrangements moved toward greater separation, segregation, and social distance.

The enactment of other Jim Crow laws in the 1890s throughout the South thus effectively hardened racial lines, limiting association and reinforcing social inequality. Kentucky's separate coach law was a particularly egregious example. It mobilized legal action and protest in Hopkinsville on at least two occasions, beginning in 1898. The Hopkinsville attorney Robert Lander and his wife Fannie sued the Ohio Valley Railway in Christian County court following the ouster of Mrs. Lander from the first class, or "ladies'" coach. Lander had purchased a first class ticket for his wife, who was traveling from Hopkinsville to Mayfield, Kentucky. That this was an intrastate journey would eventually prove legally decisive. Ignoring the conductor's request to remove herself to a car reserved for black people, Mrs. Lander eventually left the first class coach when, as she alleged, the conductor returned with three other railroad employees who forced her removal. According to the suit, "It was very warm weather, and the compartment to which she was . . . assigned was small and illy [sic] ventilated, and that it was unclean and equipped and fitted with accommodations greatly inferior to the ladies coach from which she was ordered . . . and was occupied by colored passengers of all classes, sexes, and conditions, and persons were allowed to smoke and indulge in other practices without restraint . . . offensive to ladies and children, and which was not permitted in [the] ladies' coach."

In response, the Ohio Valley Railway denied all of Mrs. Lander's charges and her account of conditions and events on the train. She was not touched by employees, according to the railway, nor treated in any impolite ways. Informed that the law required that she ride in "the smoker," or black coach, Mrs. Lander voluntarily and without protest complied, according to the counterclaim. The railway also contended the black coach was "as comfortable, clean, and as free from offensive misconduct . . . as the coach provided for first-class white passengers." Having sought $10,000 in damages, the Landers were awarded $125.00 in a trial in the Christian County court.[65] The Ohio Valley Railway in 1898 successfully appealed the Christian County decision. In 1900, the United States Supreme Court sustained Kentucky's separate coach law. In each instance, the separate but equal doctrine established by the well-known Plessy vs. Ferguson decision was invoked.[66]

Fannie Lander's complaint not only registered her protest against racial exclusion but also against her forcible association in the "smoker" with black people whom she considered beneath her station, including those who smoked and engaged in other unspecified "practices offensive to ladies and children." That black women throughout the South had to endure such assaults against their dignity as women in the wake of separate coach laws prompted a campaign of protest by Carrie Williams Clifford, civil rights and feminist activist and president of the Ohio Federation of Colored Women's Clubs.

In "A Plea to Colored Men," printed in the *Freeman,* Clifford called for protection of colored women, declaring, "Of all the infamous schemes which the white South has devised for the humiliation of self-respecting Negroes, the 'Jim Crow' car is the must [sic] infamous." Particularly victimized were colored women, "whom white Southerners have studiously and systematically degraded and insulted for nearly three centuries." Consequently, Clifford felt that black men had a duty to confront these conditions and to demand a proper respect for black women. She concluded: "You are no longer slaves . . . but free and able to act of [sic] you will do so." Her appeal was yet another echo of Du Bois's frequent exhortation to African Americans to reestablish the "manhood of the race."[67]

The degradation that the separate coach laws inflicted on black people compelled the attention of Booker T. Washington in 1914. He declared "Railroad Days," described by the *Freeman* as "the combined protest of the race against the unspeakable, indefensible, and hatred-engendering iniquities of the separate car laws as at present enforced in the Southern States." Washington asked black people around the country on June 6 and 7 to bring to the attention of the railroad companies the deplorable condition of rail cars set aside for black people. Protests in various towns and cities included mass meetings, petitions, and conferences with railroad superintendents and passenger agents. The *Freeman* reported that the railroad representatives in each town were cordial and expressed a commitment to improve accommodations. Disingenuous for the most part in their appearance of cordiality and cooperation, railroad officials in the past had appeared in court, where legal rulings pressed them to provide equal facilities. Only a few had complied with court decisions.[68] Washington characteristically wanted to take advantage of what he took to be the good will of the railroad companies, believing as he did that "the thing of last resort is the court, but before this we should try by whatsoever means in our power to get what is wanted."[69]

A few months before Washington proclaimed "Railroad Days," litigation in the Christian County court protesting the unequal treatment of black people by the railroads again proved successful. On March 9, the court issued eight indictments against the Louisville and Nashville, Illinois Central, and Tennessee Central railroads "for discrimination practices in the quality of the cars and service given to the colored people in the jim-crow cars." Separate was clearly not equal, owing in this case to the observably inferior facilities for black people, rather than any perceived contradiction in principle of the separate but equal doctrine underlying segregationist laws. That doctrine was not questioned in the Hopkinsville court case. Rather discriminatory action marked by a failure of the railroads actually to provide "equal" facilities was the issue, constituting a misdemeanor under state law and requiring fines of up to fifteen hundred dollars for each violation.

Prior to the indictments, black people in Hopkinsville had vainly sought amelioration from railroad management and the State Railroad Commission. Besides the Landers, Phil Brown, an African American active in the state Republican Party and the editor of the Hopkinsville *Saturday News,* pressed the cause. Brown complained of the basic injustice to black people, who were restricted to dirty and inferior accommodations while paying the same fare as whites. According to the *Freeman,* Brown's paper had a large readership among whites, and the state attorney, Denny Smith, took up the case and secured grand jury indictments. He had the cooperation of Judge John Feland, "one of the leaders of the Kentucky bar and a warm friend to the colored people," and of the black attorneys Claybron Merriweather and Walter Robinson. The black businessmen Edward Glass and Peter Postell's son, also named Peter, assisted in the case. Feland had represented the Landers more than fifteen years before.

The *Freeman* story reported on the racial harmony in a community where black people and white people, or at least the "the better element of the white race," publicly expressed feelings of amity and cooperation. The article was not signed, but may well have been written by the Hopkinsville journalist, Horace Slatter; the tone of the *Freeman* article echoes Slatter's report of the 1909 Masonic gathering in Hopkinsville. But more than lauding a seeming racial accord in the town, the news story recalled Booker T. Washington's Hopkinsville speech in presenting Hopkinsville as a race relations model: "The people here are congratulating themselves upon the fact that the most tangible movement toward securing equal accommodations upon the railroads in Kentucky emanates from Hopkinsville, where the feeling between the races is better than that of any place south of the Ohio river. It is not believed that these indictments could have been secured in any other county in the State of Kentucky, or elsewhere in the South."[70]

The case against the railroads was also a matter of the enforcement of existing state law. It did not challenge social separation, only the grossly inferior and humiliating facilities assigned to black rail passengers at a time when it was still widely believed that separate could in fact be equal.

Despite the 1914 court victory in Hopkinsville, black people continued to suffer humiliation and abuse in southern rail cars, as punitive sanctions against the railroads were insufficient to deter continued abuse. Regarding Kentucky,

Wright points out that "in 1939 blacks were still pressuring the railroads to improve conditions."[71] In three successive issues of the *Crisis* shortly after the Christian County court success against the three railroad companies, NAACP investigative reporter T. Montgomery Gregory traveled by rail in various parts of the deep South, witnessing the deplorable conditions of antiquated coaches reserved for black people, who were further degraded by surly and contemptuous ticket agents and conductors. Unlike the Hopkinsville litigators and much of the black citizenry for whom they acted, Gregory articulated a more far-reaching view consistent with the outlook of *Crisis* editor, W. E. B. Du Bois. In the first part of the series, Gregory wrote: "This so-called 'Jim Crow' car system is a disgrace and a blot of shame to this nation.... We are not contending against the system of *separate* accommodations as practiced by these roads, although such a practice is in violation of every principle of American democracy and justice. We accept it for the present as a necessary evil. But we do maintain that the laws requiring *equal* accommodations for both races be upheld and enforced to the last jot and title of the law."[72]

Sentiments challenging "separate but equal" occurred only rarely in Hopkinsville. While racial injustices had long provoked some individuals to risk speaking up on their own behalf, such actions risked reprisal of one kind or another. Individual or family narratives often recount people who had to leave town to avoid extra-legal violence, either for speaking disrespectfully to white people or otherwise breaching racial etiquette. Charles Nance, husband of Sarah Nance, recalled his uncle, Prentice Nance, who left Christian County very quickly and without explanation, probably in the 1930s. He did not return. It was known that he had settled in Indianapolis, but the reasons were unclear to his nephew's generation.[73] Older people said little. Black people who breached the racial code certainly endangered themselves. For example, Alison McGregor, longtime resident of Detroit, now in his nineties, described several confrontations with whites during his youth in Hopkinsville. He recounted in 2006 his departure from the town in the 1930s:

> A white girl and a white boy was coming down the street, and they took up all the sidewalk and they want to make me get off and walk in the street while they come down. Well, I didn't think that was right and we got into an altercation about it. I told my father I don't want to live nowhere where I gotta get off and let somebody have the whole sidewalk. So I left and come on up here, and I been up here ever since. My daddy, for him to stay down there, he always went along with the white people ... so they wouldn't bother him. So he told me, "Son, it might be better

... you might have to leave 'cause I don't want to see you get in more trouble." I never stood for white people running over me when I was coming up.[74]

Less common than direct personal confrontations over racial matters were activist political and legal responses to discriminatory practice. A case in point of politically engaged protest is the *Hopkinsville Contender,* a newspaper founded in 1919 by Robert and Ulysses Poston, shortly after their discharges from the army. Under their influence, younger brother Ted Poston said that he became a journalist. Born in Hopkinsville in the 1890s, Robert and Ulysses were the children of college-educated teachers originally from nearby Clarksville. After a brief life, the *Hopkinsville Contender* ceased publication following Robert Poston's editorial protesting a parade in Hopkinsville of returning World War I soldiers that consigned black veterans to the back of the march. The *Negro World,* the voice of Marcus Garvey's Universal Negro Improvement Association, reported, as a result of the brothers' protest, that printers in Hopkinsville would no longer produce the *Contender.*[75] It seemed that sharp or sustained criticism of local racial conditions would preclude the Poston brothers from continued residence in Hopkinsville, if they wanted to write the kind of news stories and editorials that were their passion. The *Contender* enjoyed a brief rebirth in Detroit until the brothers ultimately settled in New York, where they became associates of Garvey and wrote for the *Negro World.* Robert and Ulysses eventually grew disillusioned as they came to regard Garvey as a demagogue, but they maintained their political edge.[76] The Poston brothers' protest against discrimination sprang from an intense race consciousness and a determination to act on it. They sought the kind of black empowerment that not only provoked white opposition but also, in all probability, frightened numbers of black people in Hopkinsville. Giving up on a façade of racial amity for the sake of accommodation to social inequality, the Postons assuredly did not "wear the mask."

Ulysses Poston took up his brother Robert's complaint about the treatment of black veterans, but he did so in New York rather than Hopkinsville. Writing in 1923, his remarks were part of a larger critique of racial conditions in America that stifled black economic and social development; he described black people in America as living in a state of "semi-slavery." Yet black institutions of the time, according to Poston, including the press, churches, business groups, and the "negro wing of the American Legion," were working strenuously to improve conditions. Of black veterans he stated that "an organization which should symbolize patriotism is utterly disgusted with every effort it made during the war to insure the security of America, and if America ever goes to war again some men of this organization will die martyrs rather than fight again for the country that offers Germans more advantages to become prosperous and respected citizens than the negro, who never betrayed his trust."[77]

Poston's bitter statement resonates with other African American laments, both before and after, about how black loyalty and service to American institutions had not won for African Americans their just entitlement to the rights any citizen should expect. His words recall the shock registered in speech and song when General Howard spoke on Edisto Island to freedmen forced to abandon the land they were farming to those who had gone to war against the United States. Forty years after Poston's article, Martin Luther King, Jr., reiterated these themes on the steps of the Lincoln Memorial, seeking to redeem a long overdue promissory note from the United States to American citizens of African descent.

TERROR AND RACIAL DOMINATION: LYNCHING AND ITS REPORTING

The constant threat of harassment and violence against black people constituted the starkest contrast to the public discourse about racial harmony. Six months prior to Booker T. Washington's celebrated paean to race relations in Hopkinsville, a black youth was lynched at Flat Lick, then a thinly populated wooded area lying on the southwestern edge of Christian County. A century later, the woodland has given way to housing developments, roads, and other indicators of modern suburbanization and population growth. Flat Lick has a familiar prosaic quality that belies the outburst of vengeful killing that took the life of a terrified youth a century ago. That the youth, Benjamin Brame, was also known as "Booker," adds a particularly tragic irony to his murder. Some fifty years before, Flat Lick lay on the supposed route of the slaves of Stewart County, Tennessee, believed to be bent on fighting their way to Hopkinsville en route to freedom across the Ohio River. As noted in Chapter 2, Ellen McGaughey Wallace claimed their intent was to take young white girls as their brides. From the template of the frenzied white imagination, the sexually dangerous black man periodically materialized, only to be destroyed by white mobs in a collective paroxysm of lethal violence. That was the gruesome fate of the imagined plotters of 1856 and of Benjamin Brame, a teenage day laborer in 1909.

The record of events in early April 1909 survives only in newspaper accounts, including a brief report in the *New York Times*.[78] Black people now of middle age that grew up in the vicinity of Flat Lick and LaFayette recall that in their youth in the 1960s, elders without elaboration sometimes quietly mentioned the event, which now evades virtually all local memory.[79] Hopkinsville's two newspapers reported over the course of three days Brame's alleged offense, the chase and apprehension of the youth, his lynching, and the postmortem inquest.

Alleged on April 8 to have grabbed Ruth Gee as she and her younger sister, Sallie, were in their rural yard, Brame was reported to have fled after the younger girl fought him off with a hatchet.[80] A later version reported at the inquest indicated that the younger girl was attacked, yet the inconsistency of the narratives, which would have had some value in a just court of law, was unimportant. There was no trial, even in a court tainted by racial bias. With the large headline, "Lynching Bee in Flat Lick," the *Hopkinsville Kentuckian* on April 10 reported Brame's apprehension and hanging the previous day, following identification by the Gee sisters. The newspaper stated, "The lynching was done in an orderly and determined way."[81] The *Daily Kentucky New Era* also found decorum in the mob, whose work was "Quickly Done and Quietly." The latter newspaper said that after his capture "the negro began moaning and praying and begging to see his mother, but a deaf ear was turned to his entreaties." Then, attempting to shoot Brame, the girls' father was reportedly restrained by the posse "just in time to prevent him taking vengeance with his own hands."[82]

The body remained undisturbed for nearly two days, as crowds flocked to the site from Friday afternoon until Sunday morning. The news stories explained that no shots were fired into the body nor was it in any way mutilated, implying that those mob actions were the expected accompaniments of vigilante execution, as indeed they often were.[83] Leon Litwack has observed that lynchings in the late nineteenth and early twentieth centuries, while hardly novel, did mark a new level of white sadism and exhibitionism.[84] Not so in the lynching of Booker Brame; mob action though it was, his murder was portrayed in the Hopkinsville newspapers as closer to a civic duty than to an extra-legal vigilante attack.

On Sunday April 11, J. L. Allensworth, the elected African American coroner of Christian County, went to the lynching site. He immediately impaneled seven men, including A. M. Henry, who had summoned him from Hopkinsville, to serve as jurors for a summary inquest. At its conclusion Coroner Allensworth cut the body down and buried young Brame in a nearby wooded area.[85] Allensworth, a minister, had been elected for a second term in 1897 and was one of four black elected officials in Christian County.[86]

Two jurors, apparently selected on the spot, were African Americans, and two were close kinsmen of the Gee girls. Those who carried out the lynching allegedly were not recognized. The *Hopkinsville Kentuckian* reported, "They were not masked, but it is claimed came from some other locality. The large crowd was ordered to stay behind, while the smaller crowd took the negro to the place where he was hanged."[87] In a perfunctory manner, the jury quickly decided that those responsible were strangers in the area and that Brame's death by strangulation resulted from hanging "by parties unknown to this jury," a formulaic conclusion repeated frequently throughout the South.[88]

That Allensworth was a black man, and even a black officeholder, had no apparent effect on the foreordained outcome of the inquest. No evidence survives to provide any insight into the compelling question of Coroner Allensworth's frame of mind in presiding over the ritual of exoneration; nor is anything known of the two black men who served on the coroner's jury. In this and other cases of lynching of black men in and around Christian County, the record is equally vacant regarding the response of black people. One can only guess that actual lynchings achieved their immediate, desired effect of terrorizing the black population into public silence and extreme circumspection. Silence and fear, however, are not tantamount to assent, and resistance to terror or violent threats in Christian County undoubtedly took many of the same oblique, "everyday forms" of protest that occurred during slavery when outright insolence or rebellion could be fatal.[89] On the other hand, the uncomfortable fact must be acknowledged that some black people found some kinds of mob action justified. After all, five years earlier, black vigilantes in nearby Guthrie killed a black murder suspect in his jail cell. In a different vein, W. Fitzhugh Brundage briefly describes two cases of lynching in Georgia where black people publicly supported the action of white mobs in lynching black victims. In his view, that support is not an act of legitimation but rather a compliant attempt to assuage and conciliate the supremacists.[90] However one may wrestle with these difficult problems, the racial majority in Christian County strongly sanctioned mob action and took at face value Allensworth's legitimating action in discharging his official duties. Likewise, black support of vigilantism in Georgia could only reinforce for the majority the justice and legitimacy of the mob.

Several aspects of the Brame lynching bear all the earmarks of the ritualized actions identifiable in other lynchings throughout the South.[91] That is, mob executions followed an almost formulaic routine, which might add or subtract particular elements, but was nonetheless recognizable as a particular type of deadly extra-legal action. The *Hopkinsville Kentuckian* described the mob murder of young Brame as a "lynching bee," emphasizing a communal, almost celebratory aspect of the murder. Although no pictures of the execution have come to light, there are numerous instances in other cases of lynchings of horrific photographs that sometimes were turned into post cards.[92] Moreover, collectively restraining the elder Gee from shooting Brame repudiated private retaliation in favor of prompt, self-legitimating public vengeance accepted as justice. Throughout the South, it was the customary obligation for white men corporately to punish real or imagined affronts to white women. Any untoward behavior could be interpreted as an imagined prelude to rape, and nothing less than the terror of summary execution, collectively inflicted, could palliate feelings of racial outrage.

Typical of lynchings throughout the South, the body of the victim remained suspended, in this case for forty-four hours. People came from the vicinities of Christian and Trigg Counties to see the result of Brame's alleged transgression. For white men, it bound them together once again in a shared racial commitment to keeping black men in their place; that solidarity could again reactivate and reinforce itself in the next mob action. In this respect, but certainly in others as well, lynching was a metaphor for race relations.[93] The newspaper accounts say nothing of the racial makeup of the viewers, but one can have little doubt that news of the lynching spread quickly among black people. Each lynching reiterated in the strongest way possible the warning to all black men of what awaited them if they breached the most guarded line of racial separation. The Brame murder also reminded readers that other black men in the vicinity were dangerous. The newspaper accounts carefully pointed out that the Gee farm lay only two miles from the home of a Mrs. Watson, reportedly assaulted in early January 1909. Before that, a young woman "barely escaped a negro who attacked her on the public road."[94]

The lynching of Wallace Miller four months after Brame's mob execution may give some hint of the internalization of white racial ideology. His murder occurred just four days after the conclusion of the black Masonic conference at the Virginia Street Baptist Church. The *Hopkinsville Kentuckian* reported that Miller, "a mulatto about twenty years of age," made "an indecent proposal" to a nine-year-old white girl near Caledonia in Trigg County west of Hopkinsville. She ran home and reported the incident to her older brothers, who set out to capture Miller. They apprehended him soon after, and he denied the charge of importuning the child. The brothers returned him to their home, where the child identified Miller. He then reportedly confessed, saying that he could not account for what he did and that it was just "the negro in him." If one can accept this account, it is a particularly severe instance of how the ideology of race inferiority and savagery could be internalized by its victims.[95] The statement might also be interpreted differently—as an effort by the captive to forestall what must have seemed inevitable. In either case, white readers of the *Hopkinsville Kentuckian* would have found reinforcement of their most basic assumptions about black men. Miller's lynching played itself out in predictable fashion. As the brothers were taking him to Cadiz, the county seat, they were intercepted by a gang of fifty men, who seized the victim and hanged him. The body was on display for another twenty-four hours. Again, the news report reminded readers that within a ten mild radius the lynching was the fourth vigilante action in eight months, including the killing of Benjamin Brame.[96]

It is impossible to know precisely how much newspaper reports led public opinion or simply reflected the popular view. Doubtless newspaper readers found their own prejudices reinforced while the news source claimed to represent local opinion. After reporting on the killing of Wallace Miller and relating it to other alleged local abuses of white women by black men, the *Hopkinsville Kentuckian* concluded by saying "the promptness with which Miller was put to death shows that there is to be no trifling with rapists in that section."[97] Through their approving tone in reporting lynchings, the two newspapers in Hopkinsville were complicit in sustaining a social atmosphere in which acceptable forms of "justice" included vigilantism against black men suspected of "outraging" white women. The two newspapers lost few opportunities to reinforce the regnant stereotypes of black people, whether as inferior to whites or variously childlike, indolent, clownish, improvident, and sexually immoral.

Although victims of lynching included both blacks and whites, blacks are disproportionately represented in the existing record. Between 1866 and 1934, Wright records 353 lynchings, comprising 265 black victims, or 75 percent of the total.[98] The majority of victims, black and white, were suspected of committing murder or rape. Yet black people might also perpetrate vigilante action. Lynching in western Kentucky thus created its own insidious contagion capable of channeling the vengeful anger of black people into killing blacks suspected of heinous crimes. For example, in Guthrie in early 1904, Lewis Radford, a black man, was jailed on suspicion that he murdered a young retarded black woman. While the marshal was at dinner, a black crowd assaulted the black jailer who had initially refused to turn over the keys to Radford's cell. They could not have issued this demand to a white jailer and certainly not to a white officer. Radford would not leave his cell and was immediately shot eight times. His body was hanged from a tree near the entrance to the jail.[99] The perpetrators suffered no legal consequences, and the established pattern once again unfolded, including the subsequent report by the Todd County coroner declaring "the victim was killed by person or persons unknown."[100]

Relatively rare and remarkable, five cases of black victims lynched by either black or integrated mobs occurred in Kentucky between 1882 and 1930. Four of the five took place in western Kentucky. Throughout the South in that same period, 148 black victims were killed by black vigilantes or by blacks and whites acting in concert. Black mob violence against black people tended to appear in counties with large black populations, such as Christian, Todd, and neighboring western Kentucky counties. Where the justice system was regarded as indifferent to violence committed by black perpetrators against black victims, then vigilante action was more likely to occur, especially if black people had the numbers to mobilize themselves for direct action.[101]

VIGILANTISM AND RACE IN THE BLACK PATCH WAR

Lynching sprang from the violent template of western Kentucky history. Such extra-legality marks what anthropologists call "self-help," or the practice of acting on one's own or in concert but outside the strictures of constituted authority. It occurs when the institutions of the state and orderly procedures of law are feckless, undeveloped, or regarded as illegitimate. Beyond institutional deficiency as a cause of endemic extra-legal violence, the cultural genesis of personal and collective aggression in western Kentucky is also relevant. Suzanne Marshall proposes that "the culture of violence was primarily created by white men in order to maintain their power over their families, blacks, and the community."[102] That power was abetted by a fundamental faith in the vengeful morality of the Old Testament.[103]

In 1908, prominent articles in *Harper's Weekly* and the *New York Times* reported on anarchic conditions in Kentucky, where disrespect for the rule of law was common. *Harper's Weekly* declared, "There is war in Kentucky. In a score of towns what is virtually a state of martial law exists."[104] The *New York Times* described a menacing lawlessness imperiling people and property throughout the state. In dire terms, the article began, "There now exists in the State of Kentucky a condition of affairs that is almost without parallel in the history of the world. Disrespect and disregard of law and order prevail; . . . the taking of human life is alarmingly frequent and, in some sections of the State, men and women dread the hours of darkness."[105]

Public complacency in the face of extra-legal violence stood in the way of improvement, but still more worrying was the fact that many people in the state did not believe the rule of law ought to prevail in every case. Rationales for lynching in the popular press up to that time certainly corroborate that view. Indeed, vigilantes and Night Riders in particular had won much popular sympathy.

Both articles were written during the raging "Black Patch War," when lawlessness in western Kentucky reached its zenith. The "War" refers to the early-twentieth-century vigilante attempts to break the economic grip of the James Duke monopoly.[106] In brief, Duke's American Tobacco Company, founded in 1890, aimed to control the tobacco market, setting wholesale prices and driving out competitors. The American Tobacco Company entered into an agreement with the Regie Tobacco Company of Italy, agreeing to avoid competition in the purchasing tobacco. They in effect were controlling the wholesale price of tobacco, which dropped sharply as a result of their action. By the first years of the twentieth century, tobacco growers were unable to make a profit or even recoup the cost of production. The burden imposed by the agreement between the two companies fell very heavily on small farmers who could cultivate, usually as share croppers, only a few acres owing to the intensity of labor that tobacco commands. In reaction to the Duke effort to control the market, growers in western Kentucky and nearby counties in the Tennessee Black Patch organized the Planters Protective Association in Guthrie, where thousands of tobacco farmers gathered in 1904. Of course, much organizational work had been done in advance in various Black Patch locales. The association pledged its members not to sell their harvest to the Duke Trust in order to break the hold of the purchasing monopoly. The association called on members to pool their tobacco and withhold it from sale until market conditions improved. On the eve of the Guthrie meeting, a Hopkinsville newspaper reported much optimism: "Already there exists an anticipation of approaching good times among the planters, and it is estimated that the present crop of tobacco, which is now being housed, will bring better prices than for years."[107] Growers of burley tobacco in central Kentucky also joined together to form an association to hold back their tobacco from the market until demand would effect a reasonable price. As in the Black Patch, vigilantism emerged to punish farmers if they sold tobacco on their own, thereby weakening the market boycott. In writing of both movements, Tracy Campbell thus refers to the "Tobacco Wars."[108]

Any boycott depends on widespread compliance if it is to succeed, and the actions against the Duke trust were no exception. But not all farmers cooperated, since the trust offered acceptable prices to particular farmers as a way of breaking the solidarity of the planter association. Farmers doing business with Duke prompted vigilante action by people long accustomed to ignoring the law. Violence by Night Riders ranged from "scraping," or destroying tobacco seedbeds, to beating farmers, to burning their homes and tobacco barns, to murder. Night Riders also attacked warehouses storing tobacco owned by the American Tobacco Company. Secretive, hooded, armed, and violent, the Night Riders resembled Klansmen, who doubtlessly were well represented among the vigilantes. Intimidation extended even to judges and juries.[109] The association, however, regularly disavowed the threats and intimidation serving its interests. For example, in the wake of the destruction of plant beds of L. L. Leavell, one of the largest growers in southern Christian County, officials of the association stated that "every right-thinking member of the organization absolutely condemns any sort of lawlessness." Leavell did not belong to the association, although J. T. Garnett, whose beds were destroyed along with Leavell's, had been a member since the association's inception.[110]

Likewise, the beds of Garnett's black tenant, Gent Sanders, were destroyed. Sanders was probably a member of the association, but certainly the destruction of Garnett's plant beds indicates that the vigilantes acted for reasons unrelated to the Duke boycott. My particular concern in this discussion is the experience of black farmers. In the case of the attack against Garnett, one can plausibly interpret the destruction as punishment of Garnett for having a black rather than a white tenant. This would have been nothing new, having begun immediately after the Civil War when any degree of black economic independence provoked intimidation and violence. Although prolonged vigilante actions occurred ostensibly to punish those who refused to pool their tobacco, the reprisals and brutality frequently had a clear racial dimension that often had nothing to do with the conflict over tobacco.

Out of a mix of fear and self-interest, many black farmers supported the boycott and joined the association at its founding, but this did not protect them from violence.[111] Vigilante intimidation also included threats against whites such as J. T. Garnett who hired black labor or otherwise had black tenants. The manager of one of the largest farms in Christian County received the following warning, signed "Night Riders;" it is reproduced as written. "We take this way to let you know that you are not to have any negro croppers for next year; now if you think anything of your back you had best ter git rid of thim negroes and tell all of yur neighbors and friends the sae for we are coming through there soon and you better be right or you better have a lot of them dam soliders to gard you every night."[112]

Such threats against black sharecroppers, farm workers, and those who supported them were widespread in the Black Patch. The association in Trigg County denounced intimidation by mail for any reason. "[W]e call upon all true citizens to openly and honestly condemn all anonymous letter-writing . . . in regard to the employment of negro labor on the farms . . . The negro has been true, and no instance is known where he ever violated his pledge [not to sell tobacco to the Duke Trust] and the association is in honor bound to protect him."[113]

Night Riders had nonetheless seized the opportunity to terrorize black people. Whether it was the settlement of old scores, reprisal for breaches of racial etiquette, action motivated by hate-filled envy at the sight of independent black farm families, or the belief that black labor limited opportunities and wages of white labor, Night Rider violence against black farmers resembled the pogroms of the time occurring in eastern Europe. Black people were ordered to vacate their homes and property under threat of death. In early 1908, two white farmers in Marshall County were tried for beating a black man. They were identified as part of a gang determined to drive black people out of the county.[114] In March 1908 one hundred Night Riders entered Birmingham, in Marshall County, where they shot six black people and whipped five others. Shooting into every black cabin in the town, the Night Riders killed one man and wounded his wife, three children, and a granddaughter. Two weeks before, black people in Birmingham were warned to vacate the town.[115] Sixteen Night Riders were indicted for the attacks.[116] The raiders were identified as members of the Ku Klux Klan.[117]

Racial purges or separate incidents of racial terror also occurred in other parts of western Kentucky. Along with Marshall County, Lyon County is notorious for several vigilante actions aimed at driving away black people. The legacy of that intimidation is the sparse black population in the two counties, even now.[118] Some of the refugees sought safety in Hopkinsville.[119] Just west of Christian County, in the land between the Cumberland and Tennessee rivers (Trigg County)—now known as the "Land Between the Lakes"—racial terror was also concentrated. Night Riders attacked the small settlement of Golden Pond, initially burning a warehouse belonging to a farmer who was not a member of the Planters Protective Association. In March 1908, some forty raiders made "grim sport" of Tom Weaver, a black man, who was a servant in the local hotel. He also worked at a tobacco facility, but one owned by the association. He was shot down, having refused to run from his captors.[120] A particularly ghastly instance of Night Rider violence also unrelated to the boycott occurred in Hickman, located in the far western corner of the state. The *Hopkinsville Kentuckian,* a newspaper that did not always distance itself from vigilantism, printed a story headed, "Fiends Wipe Out Family," and reported on an "unheard of atrocity" and the "massacre of Negroes by the Night Riders." David Walker, his wife, and five children were murdered by Night Riders because Walker was "said to have cursed a white woman and charged also with having drawn a revolver upon a white man." The vigilantes doused the Walker cabin with kerosene, ignited it, and then shot the entire family as they fled the flames.[121]

In surveying the history of the area that was eventually flooded by the Tennessee Valley Authority in creating Lakes Barkley and Kentucky, J. Milton Henry found significant differences in white attitudes toward black people in the rural areas:

Negroes once lived on the dividing ridge between the Cumberland and Tennessee Rivers. After 1905, no Negroes could be found; indeed, were not allowed to live in this area. There was even a rumor that members of the Negro race would be dealt with summarily if they were found passing through the region. . . . Many of the wealthier families opposed the vigilante action against the Negroes. The origin of the anti-Negro feeling in the area may [have] been largely economic. Certainly the motives of the whites who defended the Negroes were largely economic. The lesser white people considered the Negroes as both economic and social competitors, while the wealthier whites looked upon them as a source of cheap labor.[122]

The intimidation of black farmers could thus expose some of the class divisions among the racial majority, as well as the resentments of economically marginal whites against black people. For poor whites, their racial privilege—the "wages of whiteness"—bought very little. As tenants or sharecroppers, they continued to suffer cycles of debt and dependency as the large planters prospered. Their hostility toward black people on the land only diverted their economic concerns away from the class-based sources of their misery.

Racial violence in the Black Patch War can thus be seen as continuous with the violence and intimidation against freedmen in the years immediately after the Civil War, particularly in regard to the fear of poor whites that blacks would depress wages. Additionally, black political and economic success could provoke assaults. Because black people had the franchise in Kentucky, large voting blocks of black Republicans could affect the outcome of an election. Summed up by Miller, racial violence aimed "to stave off economic and political competition from blacks after the Civil War. The Ku Klux Klan and the Night Riders roamed at will, driving away blacks who had become successful landowners, businessmen, or politicians."[123]

In Hopkinsville, much concern centered on the business implications of the violence and destruction throughout the tobacco-producing counties, particularly in regard to the insurability of tobacco. However, a local newspaper reported in late 1906 that fewer than four small insurance companies among the more than sixty engaged in writing local tobacco policies had cancelled coverage or declined to write new policies. With considerable self-satisfaction and complacency, the story continued: "There is no disorder in Hopkinsville or Christian County. None is expected. The high feeling exhibited in some parts of the district . . . has never existed here. The people of this county are law abiding. They are not going to commit outrages and they will not permit them to be committed by outsiders. The tobacco stored in Hopkinsville, whether it belongs to the association or to the trust, is safe."[124] Ignoring evidence to the contrary, this exceptionalist claim for Christian County appeared six months after Night Rider vandalism against tobacco grown by Leavell, Garnett, and Sanders.

Exactly one year later, a very different account appeared in the Hopkinsville newspapers. On the night of December 7, 1907, four hundred raiders with military precision attacked Hopkinsville and burned warehouses containing tobacco purchased from growers who refused to join the Planters Protective Association. The Night Riders severely beat and pistol-whipped a tobacco buyer. Windows in banks and other commercial establishments were shot out, yet remarkably no one was killed amid the mayhem and gunfire. City and county officials requested that the governor call out a local detachment of militia to secure the town. The *New York Times* observed that the Hopkinsville attack was to that time the "most daring raid in the history of Kentucky night riding," and that "Christian County and the western part of the State is [*sic*] in a condition of terror, no one knowing where the next outbreak will occur."[125] Night Rider violence seems to have worked. In August 1908, Duke's American Tobacco Company directed its purchasing agents to suspend their activities. The *New York Times* reported that, "[i]t is generally accepted that the numerous 'Night Rider' troubles and the intense feeling that exists against the American Tobacco Company . . . have caused the officials of the company to withdraw . . . agents from the state."[126]

Hopkinsville, Christian County, and the entire Black Patch region were caught up in fundamental economic changes, both complex and threatening to individual farmers. Since the Civil War, a gradual but inexorable shift was underway. Market forces well beyond the control of local farmers were determining prices. Changes in the money supply, begun during the Civil War, diminished the availability of credit for small growers and made it more expensive. Many independent farmers were driven into tenancy. Moreover, the grower's options for selling his crop narrowed severely as the Duke Trust successfully eliminated local competition among multiple purchasers.[127] The trust was a manifestation of the external forces that had begun to take root in the 1870s, and by the first decade of the twentieth century, violence in Kentucky was having international repercussions. For example, the burning of large stores of tobacco in the Hopkinsville raid in December 1907 provoked the Italian and French governments to protest to Washington about the destruction because it was depreciating their trade interests. President Roosevelt charged Governor Willson with suppressing the vigilante violence.[128]

While fear was widespread in western Kentucky in the early years of the twentieth century, the alarm raised by the *New York Times* article of July 26, 1908, about anarchy and local sentiments favoring vigilante action requires some qualification. Hopkinsville's banking and commercial sectors knew that extra-legal violence was decidedly not in interest of the town or county. The town was growing rapidly, increasing its population from 5,833 to 9,419 in the twenty-year period from 1890 to 1910.[129] The City Directory of 1910 boasted that "Hopkinsville has made wonderful strides during the past decade, and it has a bright future before it." Among the reasons for civic pride were plans for a new post office and a new high school (the all-white Hopkinsville High School), street improvements, a doubling of building permits from 1908 to 1909, plans for two new primary schools (divided by race), an expansion of the Imperial Tobacco Company, and a remodeled city hall.[130] The much-heralded progress of Hopkinsville was, however, imperiled by vigilantism. For example, farmers in Christian County and the wider Black Patch zone withheld their 1906 and 1907 crops, which meant that approximately thirty-five million dollars did not enter the state economy. Without tobacco income, farmers were denied credit from the banks, and insurance companies surveying the violence were canceling policies and refusing to write new ones after the Night Rider attack in December 1907.[131] Accordingly, organized civic resistance to citizen-initiated violence and other actions outside the framework of established law and institutions coalesced in the founding of the Law and Order League of Hopkinsville and Christian County in the closing weeks of 1907, just after the Night Rider attack. The pronouncements of the Law and Order League stood for "the best types of citizenship in this community," and it would be "a powerful force for peace and good order."[132] Still, fear gripped the League when it sent to the Kentucky General Assembly a plea for immediate but unspecified action to restore order and tranquility since "an uninterrupted reign of lawlessness has disgraced many counties of this state for nearly two years."[133]

For black people, the convulsion of racial violence during the Black Patch War was nothing new. Threats of violence and harassment persisted, particularly in the rural areas of Christian County and more widely in western Kentucky. In Hopkinsville proper, the town continued to promote its commercial progress. But racial hierarchy and an entrenched social inequality remained, along with a generally mannerly racism and a dominant discourse praising the positive quality of race relations.

Freedom without equality carried its own enormous burden of disappointed hope once Jim Crow restrictions began. The end of slavery and the passage of the Fourteenth and Fifteenth amendments had promised incorporation into an evolving civil society wherein rights would be a function of citizenship rather than race or ethnicity. The broken promise of civic inclusion damaged black lives in innumerable ways, frustrating human aspiration and consigning people to low, fixed positions in a caste hierarchy. Black religious and political leaders observed that whites also paid a price for the injustice. The Masonic leader, Edward Davis, told his Hopkinsville audience that "one man can only keep another down by staying down with him;" he was reiterating a message frequently delivered by Booker T. Washington, who impressed on his audience in Hopkinsville the linked fates of all people in the South. That is, black uplift would also benefit white people. In light of the longevity of Jim Crow, it seemed, however, that only black people were listening carefully. Recognizing in the post-Reconstruction decades a regression into social patterns of cruelty not exceeded by the slave regime, Paul Laurence Dunbar wrote of a South degraded by its postbellum racial practices. To paraphrase the poet, many of the events depicted in this chapter might best be described as a newer bondage and a deeper shame.[134]

5

THE ENACTMENT OF MEMORY: MONUMENTS, CEMETERIES, REUNIONS

The examination of slavery and its aftermath taken up in previous chapters is essential to an understanding of race and power in western Kentucky, for in slavery we find the historical roots of persistent racial attitudes and behaviors. That the United States continues to grapple with the problem of black-white relations one hundred and fifty years after emancipation underscores the fact that race and slavery remain inextricably bound to each other. But the challenge of understanding both history and current conditions requires sorting through popular memory, the focus of this chapter, particularly in regard to how memory is objectified in places, events, and things. People read or remember the past through various political and social lenses of the present, and few topics are as vulnerable to the distortions of popular memory as race and slavery. Contemporary interests provide a focus for memory, which might otherwise remain an inchoate or dimly lit feature of a distant past. Those concerns weave themselves into politics, community values, and personal identity, thus giving the past an immediate relevance. The historian's past, on the other hand, is the record at a distance of persons and events that the scholar critically orders and interprets. Scholarship, seemingly cold and analytic, bears little on the quotidian interests of most people. For that reason, it is largely through memory, not history in the strict sense, that people understand the past. Memory keepers may thus remain indifferent or resistant to historical correction because their understanding is self-justifying and consistent with their social experience. But social experience changes, and thus memory requires constant tending and validation. In effect, memory is as much process as repository, and it functions, "not to preserve the past but to adapt it so as to enrich and manipulate the present."[1]

Writing of the polarity of history and memory, Ira Berlin concludes, "they desperately need one another." Otherwise, history, distant from the affairs of ordinary people, will remain extraneous, except to its academic consumers. Memory that turns away from history will continue to validate presentist concerns in an exercise of "wish fulfillment." In regard to slavery, Berlin imagines the salutary consequences of a meeting of history and memory to "embrace slavery's complex history and the difficult realities of this extraordinary and extreme form of domination and subordination and to accept the force of slavery's memory and the passionate legacy it necessarily entails ... only by testing memory against history's truths and infusing history into memory's passions can a ... collective past be embraced, legitimated, and sustained."[2]

Some of my older informants described their anger and sadness in visiting southern plantations where slave quarters still survive, or their relief at the news that an American president, although falling short of an apology, called slavery "one of the greatest crimes of history." Speaking at Goree Island, Senegal, once a holding area for Africans captured by slavers, George W. Bush also acknowledged that "the racial bigotry fed by slavery did not end with slavery or with segregation."[3] My informants' feelings did not spring from an analytic interest in slavery and its complex history, in its variations between Kentucky and the Deep South, or its presence in the North, or in estimates of mortality in the Middle Passage. These sentiments were, instead, emotional expressions on the part of people who had lived through Jim Crow and had personally experienced the humiliations of that time, knowing full well its continuity with the enslavement of their forbears. It is still a living past. In these instances, an interplay of memory with history would not constitute a very formidable challenge, for both African Americans and historians of all ethnic and racial backgrounds begin in fundamental agreement about the brutality, degradation, and profound moral travesty of slavery. That of course was not always the case, as discussed in Chapter 1.

The African American memory of slavery may at times stand uneasily against historical scholarship, but whatever tension exists is episodic. Much closer, immediate, and consequential for local politics and the possibilities of civic comity in diverse communities is a very different but equally passionate historical remembrance. Southern memory, as previously noted, continues to embody popular representations of an antebellum world of benevolent masters, devoted slaves, and valorous defenders of states' rights. Most apparent in the small but vocal neo-Confederate movement, white southern memory also encompasses a broad segment of conservative opinion united around opposition to federal authority. As such, it stands in sharp opposition to the historic memory of black people, who, for a century and a half, have seen the federal government as an instrument of liberation and southern states as the agents of racial repression, legitimated by a doctrine of states' rights.

The rhetoric and representation of contemporary southern memory tends for the most part to walk lightly around the matter of race in the wake of many changes following the civil rights legislation of the 1960s. Yet race is always present, although unspoken and frequently coded. With surprising frequency, politicians and others who do not walk lightly embarrass themselves and hastily retreat from statements that overtly ally them with retrograde racial views. Trent Lott, for example, at a celebration of Strom Thurmond's hundredth birthday, said that the country would have avoided many problems if it had followed Thurmond in his bid for the presidency in 1948. His words very quickly provoked a reprimand from President George Bush, who declared that Lott's statements "do not reflect the spirit of our country."[4] Lott hastily corrected his "poor choice of words" and averred that he did not embrace "the discarded policies of the past."[5] Thurmond was an arch-segregationist, the assertive spokesman for white supremacy, and in 1948 terror still stalked black people in the Deep South. Lott had already compiled a record of similar statements before his obeisance at the Thurmond centenary.[6] There are many other instances of politicians beating embarrassed retreats from public statements that can no longer be countenanced by public opinion. The model for the political capital that conservative office-seekers can accrue by appealing to southern values, such as states' rights, is of course Ronald Reagan. He capitalized on Richard Nixon's "southern strategy" to turn the solid Democratic South into the solid Republican South. Reagan's message was subtle, whereas Lott's statements were direct in their appeal to racist sentiments. When he launched his 1980 presidential campaign in Neshoba County, Mississippi, where three civil rights workers had been murdered sixteen years before, Reagan declared, "I believe in states' rights" and promised to "restore to states and local governments the power that properly belongs to them."[7] The strategists of the Republican Party could then leave to their growing southern constituency the implication of those remarks for civil rights enforcement and black empowerment. Reagan's words would have received favorable local notice wherever in Mississippi they might have been uttered. But speaking at the Neshoba County Fair gave the speech an even greater force, since the fair for over a century has represented an anachronistic celebration of a racially homogenous community of shared white identity and tradition, the latter including the suppression of black people.[8]

The collision of memories, especially in regard to such emotional issues as slavery, race, diversity, and southern heritage, defies immediate resolution. Postmodernist cultural currents over the past thirty years have elevated popular memory to a new level of authority rivaling professional scholarship. Contests over ownership of the past and the right to represent it are widespread. Consequently, testing memory against history's findings is unlikely to prompt people to reformulate cherished understandings, regularly confirmed within their communities of common interest. A new legitimacy attaching to personal or communal self-representation only reinforces the truth-value of shared remembrance within a group. Recalling Berlin's observations, memory, personal and communal narratives, and self-fashioning of one kind or another may thus compete with the analytical and more disinterested understandings of historians, anthropologists, or other scholars.[9] But more than this, multiple popular interpretations of the American past are highly politicized in the wake of the pivotal changes in the United States since the 1960s.[10] Under these circumstances, the materials of history can become key elements in the creation of contemporary political ideologies that erase the distinction between truth and falsehood, history and myth. This phenomenon places a special responsibility on historians, as Eric Hobsbawm has argued: "I used to think that the profession of history, unlike that of, say, nuclear physics, could at least do no harm. Now I know it can ... This state of affairs affects us [historians] in two ways. We have a responsibility to historical facts in general, and for criticizing the politico-ideological abuse of history in particular."[11] These observations have a special cogency when considering contests over southern memory and their implications for contemporary politics.

Disputation over the past hardly occurs in human communities of relatively small scale, once the staple of anthropological research. Such communities are circumscribed by shared memories and meanings that are compelling and immediate. Embedded in the public discourse of ritual, ceremonial performance, storytelling, and even prosaic conversation, those memories of experience and meaning continually revalidate themselves. Collective memory is after all the common patrimony of relatively like-minded people. But in communities differentiated along lines of religion, class, or race, the memory of a dominant group will face inevitable opposition. These challenges in a place such as Hopkinsville have long existed, but they have sustained themselves sub-rosa, mainly in restricted gatherings of people who see themselves and are seen by others as separate and distinct. Different experiences spawn different historic memories, often mutually inconsistent. Such has been the commanding influence of race in the United States, but increasingly dissenting remembrances of the past find places for themselves in the public conversation.

THE CONFEDERATE MONUMENT
IN RIVERSIDE CEMETERY

Material representations provide some insight into the way people think about experience. Because a sense of finality inevitably settles on the cemetery and the monument, people can enshrine their most abiding values and attitudes in the objects and dedicatory inscriptions of those enduring settings. Ideas about race find a place there as well. Cemeteries and monuments provide mute witness to social relations among the living when those artifacts were created, yet they may also undergo a continuing reinterpretation in light of experience, thereby making them particularly relevant to the present. In some instances, symbols may fall from memory, yet in their material persistence, they record the regnant values and attitudes at their creation.

The Civil War remains a reference point for many pivotal turns in local history, fixing in time events occurring before, during, or after that epochal struggle. The newcomer from north of the Ohio River soon learns that "the War" does not refer to World War II or to more recent conflagrations. The Civil War has a palpable presence nearly a century and a half after its conclusion in the visible mnemonics of historic plaques, cemetery headstones, and monuments in Christian County and throughout western Kentucky.

The living past is particularly resonant in Riverside Cemetery and its Con-federate commemorations. The cemetery is a municipal property, with neat grounds and carefully maintained gravesites. Its monuments and headstones have not suf-fered the deterioration and neglect of other historic sites. According to William T. Turner, the county historian, many people in Hopkinsville look on Riverside Cemetery as "historic ground," where the memory of the Civil War is particularly conspicuous.[12] It is tightly interwoven for many with a sense of personal, familial, and regional identity, heavily laden with symbolic meaning. Included here are people belonging to the Sons of Confederate Veterans (SCV) and the United Daughters of the Confederacy (UDC). Joined by others, they associate themselves with the Civil War heritage of the town, particularly its Deep South sentiments. Those feelings embody a personal and communal self-definition closely linked to the racial sensibilities that dominated the past.

The most dramatic symbol of "historic ground" in the cemetery is the Con-federate Monument, sometimes referred to as the Latham Monument. The tallest and most commanding structure in Riverside, the monument was dedicated in 1887 with the lion's share of funds provided by John C. Latham, a Confederate veteran, tobacco magnate, Wall Street broker, and principal Hopkinsville philanthropist. He not only contributed money for the building of the monument; he also provided funds for its maintenance and for other civic uses. Latham was one of a number of former Confederates who settled in the North following the Civil War.[13] The Latham Monument became a focal point for observances by the UDC and SCV after those organizations were founded in the 1890s. A major observance for these organizations is June 3, Jefferson Davis's birthday, which became Confederate Memorial Day in a number of southern states, including Kentucky. Called Confederate Decoration Day in Tennessee, it continues to be an observance separate from the national Memorial Day, originally designated for May 30 as Decoration Day, a time for tending Civil War graves and placing flowers. The monument and other Confederate graves throughout the cemetery are still adorned each June 3 with flowers and Confederate national flags. Awareness of its significance has been broadened by its placement in the late 1990s on the National Register of Historic Places. It is particularly ironic that Decoration Day originated among black Americans and that the Confederate anthem, "Dixie," was in all likelihood composed by a black man. However, these facts are either ignored or simply denied in Old South vernacular memory.[14]

The Latham Monument stands over the anonymous remains of several hundred soldiers, primarily from Texas, Mississippi, and Kentucky, who died in Hopkinsville of disease, exposure, and other non-combat causes during the winter of 1861–62. Prior to the completion of the monument, the unidentified remains were exhumed from their original gravesite and reinterred in a circle around the base of the proposed memorial. The dedication of the Latham Monument attracted an extraordinary number of people—an estimated twenty thousand when the population of the town was approximately 5,800 in 1890.[15] Coming from throughout Kentucky, Tennessee, and Indiana, participants included such dignitaries as the Kentucky governor. The celebration was "intended to have no political significance." As reported in the *New York Times,* "Every residence in town was open wide, in keeping with true Kentucky hospitality, and sumptuous feasts were spread and declared free to everybody."[16] In this world of white southern hospitality and celebration, "everybody" was certainly circumscribed by race, as black participation would have been confined to domestic service. That was not the only effacement of race associated with the Latham Monument. Disavowal notwithstanding, the celebration was intensely political in its depiction of dutiful and heroic Confederate soldiers acting without regard to the issues of slavery and insurrection that precipitated the war.

The dedication program featured several speakers, including James Breathitt, the Hopkinsville attorney and later Kentucky attorney-general; Charles Deems, Latham's pastor at New York's Church of the Strangers; and W. C. P. Breckinridge, a Confederate colonel, congressman from Ashland, Kentucky, and cousin of John C. Breckinridge, a former vice president and a presidential candidate in 1860. Regretting that business obligations would keep him in New York, Latham sent a letter of apology to the city council of Hopkinsville.[17]

The speeches emphasized gallantry and courage on both sides, and, above all, reconciliation. Latham's original intent was to construct a monument dedicated to the unknown dead of the North and South, as a number of Union soldiers had been buried in the cemetery. But because the federal government exhumed many of the remains of Union soldiers for reburial at nearby Fort Donnelson, Latham constructed the monument to commemorate only the Confederate dead. Still, Breathitt acknowledged, without names, the few remaining graves of Union soldiers.[18] In keeping with the spirit of reconciliation, Latham's letter to the city council leveled the differences between the soldiers who perished, regardless of their loyalties, "for in the death they suffered there was hardship, heroism, and valor, costing precious lives of true-hearted American citizens."[19]

Rationalizing southern resistance as a just response to an overreaching federal government, Breckinridge dismissed slavery as simply a fact of life.[20] There were few references to slavery in the orations. Breckinridge cast black people as inferiors, thus enabling him to dispose of the contradiction between slavery and the much-vaunted southern value on liberty. Acknowledging without apology the deep racial feelings of the South and its passion for race purity, Breckinridge observed, "For the individual slavery of the black was held to be a distinct conception from the political freedom of the citizen and the national independence of a country." The defeat of the Confederacy did nothing to change white southern attitudes, for "the liberation of the slave did not change his race nor obliterate from the white race intense race-feeling." More than twenty years after a war of unprecedented carnage and the adoption of three constitutional amendments that quashed slavery and severed in law racial limitations on citizenship, voting, and political rights, Breckinridge and the other participants in the monument dedication remained recalcitrant defenders of white supremacy. He believed that the "educational power of American slavery" redeemed African peoples, "savages without traditions and without hopes."[21]

Breckinridge and the other speakers riveted their attention on collective national sacrifice and heroism, not on the preservation of slavery and white supremacy as the motive forces of secession and civil war. He asserted, "We did not fight for slavery . . . but we fought for the dear old freedom of our fathers. . . . It was that fundamental principle declared when our fathers organized into States possessing political autonomy and declared themselves free to choose their own government as to them seemed best."[22]

By the time of the dedication of the Latham Monument, the promulgation of the southern version of the Civil War was well advanced and has provided the substance of modern neo-Confederate memory. Central to the story is the claim, explicitly stated by Breckinridge, that slavery did not motivate the War. It was instead states' rights against intrusive federal authority that was the *raison d'être* of the Confederacy.

The narrative of defending individual freedom, of fidelity to the Constitution, and of state sovereignty lent itself to the apotheosis of the southern cause in a way that defending slavery did not. The ennobling process began at the war's conclusion. Initially, both Jefferson Davis and his vice president, Alexander Stevens, identified the South's commitment to slavery as a cause of the Civil War. But with the southern defeat, as Charles Dew has pointed out, "frank discussion of the slavery issue disappeared," and Davis and Stephens pressed instead states' rights as the sole issue provoking the war.[23] Dew provides definitive evidence that should sweep away any lingering doubt that the South's commitment to slavery ignited secession and the Civil War. The secession ordinances of the states that formed the core of the Confederacy are telling.

In the months following the election of Lincoln and prior to the start of the war, five Deep South states seceded from the Union. Each of these states dispatched secession commissioners to the remaining slave states that had not seceded in order to persuade them to follow the actions of Mississippi, Alabama, South Carolina, Georgia, and Louisiana in leaving the Union. The arguments are clear, passionate, and unambiguous, emphasizing the perpetuation of slavery as essential to the maintenance of a southern way of life, including its prosperity. Without slavery, moreover, the South would face the apocalypse of racial equality, race war, and race mixture.[24] Supremacist racial obsessions were not unique to the South. By the 1880s, many northerners were disturbed by the expansive and troubled development of their cities following the arrival of polyglot and unfamiliar immigrant masses, regarded as racially different from white people.[25] They were coming from the farther reaches of a Europe, then little known to Americans. Northerners were in effect finding more to admire than to criticize in the southern racial worldview.[26] Shared racial sentiments could only facilitate the process of sectional reconciliation.

The speakers at the dedication of the Latham Monument joined the legion of other northern and southern commentators in emphasizing selfless dedication on both sides, followed by national unity. James Breathitt provided the most maudlin example of reconciliation. He spoke of two soldiers from New Hampshire and Georgia who reportedly had mortally wounded each other on the battlefield and, as they lay dying, pledged mutual forgiveness.[27] A similar conceit appeared three decades later in the silent film epic *The Birth of a Nation*.

Both northerners and southerners, as David Blight has shown, embraced postwar reconciliation, although the process took time. Aging veterans on both sides came to emphasize shared memories of valor; differing views of the war's causes in the first decades after 1865 eventually gave way to a moral unity defined by courageous self-sacrifice in both armies. Of the aging veterans, Blight observes that "the differences in their remembrance of cause . . . could not hold back their own and the culture's need to cultivate the mutual ties in soldiers' memory. The national reunion required a cessation of talk about causation and consequence, and therefore about race. The lifeblood of reunion was the mutuality of soldiers' sacrifice in a land where the rhetoric and reality of emancipation and racial equality occupied only the margins of history."[28]

Consequently, the cost of national reunification was the sacrifice over a century of the civil rights of the freedmen. Even Ken Burns's celebrated public television series on the Civil War in 1990 recapitulated, as Eric Foner has shown, the view of the war as a family conflict among white people with little discernible relevance to the fate of black people afterward.[29] If the North won the war, the South effectively won the early postwar struggle over interpretation, providing a victory that would last a century.

WASHINGTON HALL AND THE "SECOND BURIAL": THE CONFEDERATE DEAD IN THE TWENTY-FIRST CENTURY

In 2001, the Sons of Confederate Veterans paid renewed homage to the Confederacy in the form of a collective "burial" at Riverside Cemetery. The ceremony honored the southern soldiers whose anonymous remains had been reinterred at the foot of the Latham Monument just before its 1887 dedication. The identities of the dead came to light a decade later.[30] At the ceremony, some three hundred identical headstones were dedicated. Laid out in orderly columns and rows, the headstones give that portion of the cemetery an unmistakable military appearance. That of course was the intent of the organizers, and each year since 2001 Confederate flags have festooned these markers on or about June 3. Yet no one is buried in any of the new spaces. The empty plots somberly provide yet another ironic twist to local history, for the mock graves lay nothing to rest, certainly not the contested past that continually attempts to make a place for itself in the moral and civic landscape of the present.

Increasingly, celebrations of the Confederacy and Old South historic memories encounter public resistance, although that was not the case when the new Confederate "burials" at Riverside were established. The quietude was most likely the result of a marked lack of publicity, despite the highly newsworthy quality of the event. Beyond the participants representing the SCV and the UDC, the funeral without bodies and the headstones without graves attracted little attention from the press or other media. A local reporter, invited by the SCV, was present at the dedication of Camp Alcorn, the original name of the Confederate encampment in 1861 and now the name of the new commemorative site in Riverside. But no news story appeared to the disappointment of SCV attendees.[31] The reporter offered no explanation, although she conceded that the decision probably aimed to avoid provoking a controversy over "heritage" that periodically roils the South, including Christian County.[32]

The plots at the new Camp Alcorn were donated by the city after a request to the city council from the SCV. The city incurred no costs, and the Veterans Administration reportedly provided the inscribed headstones. Without discussion or dissent, the council, including its four black members and two frequently allied colleagues, ceded the land to the SCV organizers of the memorial. One council member recalled that she and her colleagues were led to believe that actual, identified remains lay under the headstones.[33] She indicated that the decision would have been the same in any case, as no one on the council wanted to contest the land donation for fear of provoking a public furor among proponents and their likely critics. Like the placement of the headstones, the council decision received no publicity, and no conflict ensued.

Each marker is inscribed with the soldier's name, company, state regimental unit, and date of death. Three headstones contain additional inscriptions on the reverse side of the marker. One inscription contains a brief annotation, sparely acknowledging the virtue of one who had hardly lived: "Age eighteen, Good boy." A second headstone simply notes the soldier's age, eighteen, without comment. The third headstone with a double-sided engraving offers its own compressed depiction of the relationship between a black slave and his owner that typifies Confederate historic memory. One side has the following inscription:

> Pvt
> Washington Hall
> Co H
> 7 Texas Inf
> CSA

The opposite face reads:

> Man of Color
> Hills Company,
> Gregg's Regiment,
> 7th Texas "This old man was a
> faithful servant to his master and died much
> beloved by his Company."

While honoring the Confederate dead and identifying them in a mockup of a military cemetery, the sponsors of the current Camp Alcorn have also re-enshrined the loyal slave as an enduring feature of southern memory. In that view, a slave such as Washington Hall might follow his master to war, and even receive a military rank. But it was his master whom he served rather than the cause of arms directly. Southern memory also preserves an image of the devoted slave caring for the master's wife and children, hearth and home, while the master was away at war. Of Washington Hall's thoughts or those of countless other slaves praised in southern memory, we can only wonder.

In reporting on Civil War veterans, the Hopkinsville press occasionally carried stories well into the twentieth century about former slaves living out their old age in the care of those who once owned them. Some had gone to war, like Washington Hall, as servants to their soldier-masters. "Black Man in Gray" headlined a story in the *Kentucky Daily New Era* in 1904 that reported that at Eddyville, in nearby Lyon County, "A Negro Confederate Veteran Passes Away." The story continued: "'Uncle' Ike Copeland passed away a few days ago at the home that had been provided for him by Gen. H. B. Lyon."[34] General Lyon was known as the "Court House Burner," having burned the Christian County courthouse, which had quartered Union soldiers, and eleven other Kentucky courthouses in 1864.[35] The news account indicates that Ike Copeland entered the army as a body servant and "served faithfully." In his declining years, he was cared for by the Lyon family. At his impending death, the old man was said to have expressed regret that he would not live long enough to accompany General Lyon, "Marse Hiram," to the Nashville reunion of their unit, the Eighth Kentucky Cavalry, where he was "always given a place of honor by Confederates." The death notice indicated that the old man, proud of his Confederate record, would not associate with those he reportedly called "ordinary niggers" and was "a true type of the old-time southern Negro."[36]

The loyal slave, "the true type," and sometimes the slave allegedly at arms in service to the Confederacy continue as regular features of Old South nostalgia and popular memory. Efforts by organizations such as the UDC to support "a truthful history of the War Between the States" carry on this tradition.[37] Such artifice props up identity formation in a sedulous resistance to academic history. Personal relations between slaves and owners in some instances certainly had an affectionate quality. That fact is not at issue. Of the world from which the freedmen emerged, Du Bois remarked, "here and there much of kindliness, fidelity, and happiness—but withal slavery."[38] But the loyal slave as an emblem of the institution of slavery, or worse, as a rationale for its continuation on the grounds the loyal slave wanted enslavement, is pure fiction. Likewise, claims of large numbers of slaves serving as soldiers in the Confederate army are little more than desperate efforts to perpetuate an invented antebellum polity of racial harmony in which black slaves shared with whites an equal stake in its survival.

PATSY BRENT AND THE SEGREGATION OF DEATH

Besides Riverside, Hopkinsville has another major cemetery, Cave Spring. The two cemeteries are divided by race. Supported and maintained as municipal properties, they can no longer be segregated by law, as they once were. Theirs is instead a segregation by custom, akin to the unenforced segregation of memory, and as strictly observed as any legally sanctioned segregation before the 1960s. Nonetheless, the faux grave of Washington Hall and the actual grave of another black person, Patsy Brent, in Riverside fully reinforce the traditional white racial calculus.

The grave of Patsy Brent, who was buried in Riverside Cemetery in 1921, is especially indicative of the racial asymmetry that defined the town for much of its history. She was born into slavery in 1841 in Trigg County, just west of Christian County. The spare written evidence of her life is silent about the unprecedented and extraordinary circumstance of her burial in an all-white cemetery during the strict social regime of Jim Crow. Her name appears in census records, in Hopkinsville city directories, in a petition she successfully brought to the city council to lower her property tax, and in a death certificate. The latter lists no next of kin and Edward W. Glass, the black undertaker, provided the little information appearing on the document.

Each record indicates Patsy Brent's race, since black people always inhabited the marked category, colored, made explicit in every public document or newspaper story. The cemetery register of her burial, however, provides only her name and the plot number, without the inveterate race designation, nor is information about the purchaser of the plot included. The instigators of her burial in Riverside most certainly did not wish to publicize an event so spectacularly contrary to custom and thus likely to provoke controversy, or even outrage. Patsy Brent's racial effacement from the cemetery record virtually transformed her symbolically into a white person. But the geography of her gravesite says something very different.

A visitor to Riverside might reasonably wonder about her identity in light of the spatial oddity of her burial. Like many other cemeteries, Riverside is arranged with a few narrow roads to accommodate slowly moving automobiles or service vehicles. Along the back periphery of the burial ground, the road demarcates the cemetery itself from a large open area that contains no burials because of the possibility of inundation by the flood-prone Little River. The sole exception is the grave of Patsy Brent, separated by the road from the familiar community of family plots with their markers, flags, and flowers. Standing at the edge of the tarmac facing the headstone, however, one sees a single grave in an otherwise empty field. The inscription reads "Patsy Brent, 1841–1921." Her grave and headstone, as physical objects, are unambiguously within Riverside, a short distance from the new Confederate headstones, yet so eccentrically placed as to invite the conclusion that she was in some way marginal to the community. The disposition of her grave, in other words, condenses a small part of the white representation of black-white relations. To the observer aware that a black woman is buried in that space, the plot and marker palpably say that Patsy Brent was in but not of the community, which, at the time of her passing, was ordered by an encompassing system of white racism always determined to have its way, even in death.

Oral tradition provides the sole answer to the obvious question—how did a black woman come to be buried in a white cemetery in a rigidly segregated town in western Kentucky? William T. Turner, the Christian County historian, related the oral tradition regarding Patsy Brent. His account points to familiar obstacles in researching black history, when based on documents or oral traditions outside the black community. Libraries and archives of earlier generations did little to preserve primary materials germane to the African American experience. Consequently, black people are depicted as props in the life histories of white people. Such portrayals inevitably reveal much more about the architects of racial hierarchy than about those subordinated by Jim Crow law and custom. The extant oral tradition thus says little about Patsy Brent as a person, or as an actor exercising her own choices, however narrow the range of her options as a black woman. Instead, the active lives of two generations of old white families, the Andersons and Gaithers for whom she worked, are much more transparent in the documentary and oral record. Except for the local historian and those who may have attended his various talks or cemetery tours, Patsy Brent's story is now, for the most part, opaque, virtually unknown among black and white citizens alike. What is known of this woman's history, to modify Weber's famous dictum about meaning, suspends her in webs of significance spun not by her, but by others.[39]

When Patsy Brent died in 1921, the most influential man in Hopkinsville was Dr. Gant Gaither, the only person, according to Turner, capable of forcing the unprecedented burial of a black person in Riverside Cemetery. The decision had to gain approval of the city council, which may well have been the case, although council papers for 1921 record no discussion of the burial. Dr. Gaither's father was Nat Gaither, a Confederate veteran and the president of the Bank of Hopkinsville. Economically and politically influential, Nat Gaither was the recipient of the "iron cross of honor," an award given to him and twenty-six other "veterans of the Lost Cause" by the UDC in 1904. At the ceremony, a young Gant Gaither praised his father and the other veterans "who followed the banner that inspired deeds of heroism 40 years ago." The newspaper report describes Gant Gaither, then nineteen years old, as "a young man of much promise."[40]

The family of Nat Gaither's mother, the Andersons, resided in Cerulean Springs, a nineteenth-century spa in Trigg County, where they owned a hotel. Patsy Brent worked for the Andersons, and then worked for the Gaithers in Hopkinsville, where they lived in a stately antebellum home still standing in the historic district. The oral tradition is silent about whether Patsy Brent was an Anderson slave before the Civil War. Eventually buried in Riverside, the Gaithers and Patsy Brent continued their association in death, with her subordination represented by the isolation of her grave. More than ninety years after Patsy Brent's passing and decades after the civil rights movement, death remains a racialized event. Any effort to contravene the customary separation of the dead through the burial of a black person in Riverside would, even now, meet a "storm of protest," in Turner's view.[41]

A storm of protest in fact surrounded the burial in 1967 of Hopkinsville attorney and civil rights activist Louis McHenry in Green Hill Cemetery just west of Hopkinsville. His was the first black burial in that cemetery, where some congregants at his church, Freeman Chapel, thought that even in death McHenry wanted to make a statement. There was a police presence, and a number of people from his church who would normally have attended the McHenry burial remained at home for fear of racial violence. Prior to the funeral and that evening, the McHenry family received numerous crank calls and threats.[42] It was not the first public controversy for the McHenry family. Linda McHenry was one of three young black children who integrated two Hopkinsville schools in 1958.

Invoking "historic ground" as the basis of opposition to a black burial in Riverside reads black people out of the very history that African Americans have also shaped, usually anonymously, in Hopkinsville and Christian County. In this view, the white cemetery should have an inviolate, even hermetic quality, sacred in a cultural, religious, and racial sense. It is the final resting place of the white establishment through the generations, many of whom saw service in the Confederate army and owned slaves or were descendants of those who did. Although knowledge of the specific details of local Civil War history, beyond what appears in the documentary record, is diminishing with each generation, sentiment and emotion toward "the War," "heritage," and "southern tradition" still define a segment of Hopkinsville for whom black history, if it is considered at all, represents a thing apart. Yet the reality of the African American past in the city and county, including Patsy Brent's, is bound up with the political, economic, and social lives of the Andersons, the Gaithers, and many others buried in "historic ground."

In light of the continuing segregation of death, it is not surprising that Riverside remains *terra incognita* to most black people with whom I spoke. The sisters Emma Jordan and Thelma Moore, for example, grew up less than a mile from Riverside but had never walked through the grounds. We went there together after I had told them of what I was learning about Washington Hall and Patsy Brent. As we walked about, the novelty of their visit to the white cemetery was very clear. Their experience of death has taken them only to Cave Spring or to the resting place in nearby Trigg County of a number of their maternal kin. Although they count white people among their acquaintances, those relationships have not included participation in white funerals, beyond mortuary visitations.

Of the two Riverside headstones for black people, Patsy Brent's sustained the sisters' interest and attention to a much greater extent than Washington Hall's marker. Hall, after all, "lay" among others and was identified, acknowledged, and valued, however patronizing the sentiments. Patsy Brent, on the other hand, is buried in grim loneliness, the starkness of the scene relieved only by the poignancy of artificial flowers set next to the headstone either by the cemetery groundskeepers or an unknown person. The austerity of the inscription—name and dates of birth and death—seems to compound the loneliness and isolation, unmitigated by the comfort a biblical inscription or other annotation might provide. For black people, particularly, unceremonious or isolated death—precisely what the headstone and its geography evoke—is unacceptable and unseemly. My companions were very disturbed. As Karla Holloway has observed, dignity in death is a kind of birthright, and the black funeral historically has often represented the sole occasion in which one is accorded respectful tribute.[43]

In subsequent conversations, Thelma described her feelings as "sad and angry," knowing at the time from what I had told her that neither the oral tradition nor the death certificate yield anything about Patsy Brent's kin. None came forward to provide information when the certificate was prepared, and she apparently did not marry or have children. Thelma initially thought, generously, that Dr. Gaither's influence was sufficient to break Riverside's racial barrier but that even his community standing was insufficient to have Patsy Brent interred in the family plot. In that way, she would have been fully integrated. But Thelma then considered it more likely that Patsy Brent was buried precisely where the Gaithers intended, in but not of the community of the dead. That our cemetery visit occurred on August 8, Emancipation Day in western Kentucky, added a layer of irony. Although we can't be certain about their motives, the Gaithers were doubtless well intentioned in terms of the racial paternalism of their era. They were seeing to the burial of a black woman, apparently without close kinsmen, who was associated with three generations of their family. While the burial pressed beyond the limits of segregation and especially segregated death in the 1920s, it was at base another expression of race and power. The gravesite was now "read" by black observers concerned only with Patsy Brent and hardly at all with her white employers.[44]

The next day Emma brought her daughter back to Riverside, and, like her mother and aunt, she was deeply affected by the burial site. "Look," she said to Emma, "they hate us, even when we're dead."[45] But of course the Gaithers did not hate Patsy

Brent. Quite the contrary. Had that been the case, she certainly would not occupy a place in the white cemetery. The burial was instead affection at a distance, affection in white terms, affection circumscribed and constrained by the estrangement of race and the leitmotif of social inequality running through Hopkinsville history.

The isolation and separation in death as in life of a black person deeply affected three contemporary black women as well as their friends and family to whom they recounted their visits to Riverside. Yet the sadness of it all and the silence of earlier generations of black people "in but not of" Hopkinsville is now counterpoised to their own more assertive sense of self, belongingness, and black history. In later reflecting on the cemetery visit and the power a wealthy white family could exercise over African American death, Thelma said, "This is my town, too." Coming of age in the 1960s and after, Emma, Thelma, their siblings, and their children scorn the white racial calculus that long ago cast Patsy Brent into a marginal position, both in life and in death.[46]

The sense of Riverside as racialized "historic ground" again appeared when a primary school teacher asked students in her class to arrive on an assigned day dressed in some manner reminiscent of their ancestors. She described the kinds of attire that might be worn by affluent eighteenth-century Virginians or Kentuckians. Shirley Shelton, a black mother and teacher, accompanied her children to class, having dressed them as field hands and house servants. She discussed the matter with their embarrassed teacher, whom she informed, "This is how our ancestors dressed. We didn't have powdered wigs." This particular school project included a field trip to Riverside Cemetery, where the intent was for the children to get a sense of Hopkinsville history. Again, Shirley objected, pressing the point that many slave owners are buried there and that black children could only find an exclusionary and oppressive history in that place if it were the sole destination on the field trip. To her regret, the visit to Riverside was canceled. She felt it could have had some genuine value both for black children and white children, but only if a complementary field trip to Cave Spring, the black cemetery, were also scheduled. There, the children could have visited the graves of notable black figures in Hopkinsville history, such as Peter Postell, Claybron Merriweather, and Ted Poston, and learned of their accomplishments.[47]

THE JEFFERSON DAVIS MEMORIAL AND BICENTENNIAL

In early June 2008 over the course of two days, the state Parks Department hosted the Davis Bicentennial in Fairview, a short distance from Hopkinsville. It is the birthplace of Jefferson Davis and the site of the Jefferson Davis Memorial. The historic site consists of open, well-tended green space, a small pavilion for picnics, and a visitors' center with a modest museum and gift shop. The focal point of the site is a 350-foot obelisk. Robert Penn Warren, a native of nearby Guthrie, described it as "a faint white finger pointing skyward."[48] The monolith eerily interrupts the gentle roll of the rural landscape of this agriculturally rich area along State Route 68, long ago designated by the UDC as the "Jefferson Davis Highway." The bicentennial promoted southern historic memory amid flags, military displays, and other activities burnishing the Confederate image.

Construction of the obelisk began in 1917 with contributions from private donors, the UDC, and survivors and admirers of the Orphan Brigade. The latter refers to Kentucky units that fought on the side of the Confederacy, "orphaned" because they could not return to Kentucky, which remained in the Union, until after the war. They also contributed funds to the building of the monument. The Ku Klux Klan, which had been particularly active in this area of Todd County after the Civil War, burned a cross at the monument to celebrate its impending completion in 1924.[49]

The Davis obelisk was dedicated on June 7, close to Davis's birthday and Confederate Memorial Day. Fairview, then populated by about one hundred people, attracted thousands to the ceremony. The governors of Kentucky and Tennessee attended, as well as many aged Civil War veterans. By then, the emphasis on reconciliation of North and South was firmly established, and it was on ample display at the dedication. The *New York Times* reported that, "Places high in honor were given gray-clad veterans, and by their side were blue uniformed veterans of the North who joined in honoring Davis." Financing had been a problem, but a Union army veteran and member of the state general assembly from Hopkinsville "introduced a bill under which Kentucky pledged itself to take over and permanently maintain Jefferson Davis Park."[50]

In a profoundly ironic valedictory toward the end of his life, Jefferson Davis pleaded for a united country by declaring, "the past is dead, let it bury its dead, its hopes and aspirations." These words appear on a plaque at the entrance to the obelisk, yet long after the Civil War, Davis remained an unapologetic Confederate, convinced of the rightness of his cause.[51] Each June, his acolytes will not permit the past to bury its dead. They aim instead to revitalize the past and the ideology and rationale of states' rights and secession. That the past lives in the present is defiantly summed up in a popular bumper sticker in the area, "Forget, Hell."

In 2008, bicentennial activities included talks by Davis descendants, book signings, a Miss Confederacy pageant, and a reenactors' ball. Musicians in Confederate bandsmen uniforms played music of the time on vintage brass instruments. One could observe encampments of Confederate reenactors, some of whom fired deafening Civil War–era artillery and participated in military drills. Reenactors in appropriate costume portrayed Jefferson Davis and Varina Davis. A black participant was very prominent throughout the observance, declaring himself a "black Confederate." He wore a Civil War uniform of the South and carried the Confederate battle flag during much of the first day. When I asked why he would associate himself with a symbol representing the enslavement of black people, he responded, "You've been talking to a Yankee." He relished his role as the loyal slave, a central part of the mythos of the Lost Cause and its vision of an antebellum idyll of contented servitude.[52]

The official press release of March 7, 2008, emphasized the educational value of the bicentennial events "designed to interpret the role and impact this Kentuckian made on the nation's history."[53] At the Davis Monument particularly, but also at other state facilities with Civil War–era relevance, the Department of Parks faces the challenge of preserving legitimate historical sites while controlling the potential for controversy and negative publicity, given the deeply emotional sentiments that Confederate symbols provoke. Attempting to minimize the possibility of public controversy, the state limits the selling of Confederate memorabilia to only three places, including the Jefferson Davis Historic Site. The Davis memorial thus flies the Confederate national flag, and the visitors' center sells various souvenirs such as mugs, postcards, flags, t-shirts, and other paraphernalia evoking the southern cause during the Civil War. Given the state's interest in peaceful assembly without racial controversy, events at the bicentennial were closely planned and monitored by a Kentucky Parks Department employee with the slightly ominous title "Director of Recreation and Historical Interpretation."

State control of commemorative activities at the Davis memorial is relatively new. Beginning in 2006 the Parks Department took over planning of the annual Davis birthday commemoration, which had previously been organized by the SCV. The latter complains that too much state control and insufficient advertising limit attendance at the Davis site. The SCV has customarily advertised the annual event very widely on many small rural radio stations. Seeking to circumvent conflict of any kind, the state nonetheless remains susceptible to pressures from various sources, including the SCV. The organization protested strenuously when a member of the state's planning team for the bicentennial proposed an invitation to a Lincoln reenactor, who might debate the Davis reenactor. Irate emails from the SCV condemned the idea, insisting that nothing connected to Lincoln appear at the bicentennial. The SCV protest was effective, and no Lincoln reenactor appeared. A parks employee summed up the goal of the bicentennial as "commemoration without controversy."

In an effort to diminish the possibility of conflict, the park manager stated that the bicentennial did not aim to celebrate Jefferson Davis as the president of the Confederacy but rather as a constitutionalist. Two descendants representing the

Davis Family Association concurred. Davis's allegiance to the founding document is one of the staples of the neo-Confederate defense of secession and the Confederate leadership. Davis, in this view, was more faithful to the Constitution than was Lincoln. The Davis descendants also emphasized that the bicentennial would honor Davis's leadership before 1861, as a soldier in the Mexican War, a senator from Mississippi, a secretary of war, and a national political figure instrumental in founding the Smithsonian Institution. The Department of Parks likewise notes Davis's pre–Civil War political life and describes him as a "reluctant secessionist," thus dampening his leadership role in the Confederacy.[54]

In this vein, Jefferson Davis's great-great-grandson protested to a sympathetic audience that his efforts elsewhere to highlight his ancestor's achievements prior to the Civil War were ignored. In his view, "political correctness" has effaced these contributions in favor of a singular focus on Jefferson Davis as president of the Confederacy. Ironically, William C. Davis, unrelated to Jefferson Davis and the only author of prominence appearing at the book signing, has written of the Confederate president, "there is one reason, and only one, for writing or reading a biography of Jefferson Davis, and that is his quadrennium as leader of the Lost Cause. Without this vital element, few if any Americans would ever have heard of him, or wanted to." Except for his leadership of the Confederacy, Jefferson Davis's earlier political activities were unremarkable. Details of his career are included in William C. Davis's biography only because they illuminate the historic Davis's values and temperament that would later exercise such a telling influence on the Confederacy.[55] Despite rhetorical pleas at the bicentennial for attention to Davis's pre–Civil War activities, those features of his earlier life paled to invisibility against the continuing reminders and reenactments of the Civil War, including Confederate flags, mock artillery fire, period military drills, and other martial performances.

Davis's descendants further complained that misrepresentations of Jefferson Davis resulted from books written only from the vantage point of the present. They did not consider Jefferson Davis in the context of his own time. One might observe, of course, that Abraham Lincoln, Frederick Douglass, and the abolitionists were also part of the context of Davis's time. Moreover, Davis's great-great-grandson claimed that those books are nearly all written in Boston or New York, a charge inconsistent with even a cursory perusal of the modest display of books for sale at the visitors' center. The books include well-regarded southern university press publications by academic historians. Other books on display show the imprint of obscure partisan presses that assertively appeal to the neo-Confederate movement and its determination to rehabilitate secession as the just effort of southerners to maintain their constitutional rights. The partisan claims include assertions of mass volunteer service by slaves in the Confederate army and that slavery did not motivate the southern rebellion. At least two authors of neo-Confederate volumes were on site to sign their books.[56] The presentist claims on behalf of southern memory at the bicentennial challenged the legitimacy of history as a disinterested discipline; instead, the keepers of southern memory expose history as another means of northern domination, akin to the federal overreach that not only caused the Civil War but also continues to quash states' rights.

A few days before the bicentennial celebration, southern memory received the candid but unintentionally amusing support of a news headline in the weekly *Todd County Standard,* "Davis Presidency Marred by War Outcome."[57] Additionally, neo-Confederate sentiment was promoted by the free distribution during bicentennial activities of the quarterly publication of the League of the South. The issue available for distribution contained crude, stereotypic African imagery of Barack Obama. The league promotes secession and a romantic nostalgia for an imagined antebellum monoculture of universal Christian faith, contented slaves, and manly honor.

The bicentennial encomium to Davis and the Confederacy attracted little attention, a complaint made both by the SCV and the Davis family in attendance. Even in Hopkinsville, the nearest town, the weekend events, reportedly attended by a thousand people, generated little interest or news coverage. A portion of a news story in Hopkinsville captures the sense of temporary wish fulfillment in the reenactments: "Get 'em boys. A thunderous blast, then another and another. Smoke filled the air. The wind carried the stench of gunpowder, a man exclaimed from the crowd. The crowd cheered. There was no one to 'get,' however. The men in gray uniforms fired simulated cannon blasts at an empty field. Although everyone knew the outcome of the war the Confederate soldiers were re-enacting, they still cheered for the South, seemingly hoping the outcome would be different this time."[58]

OLD SOUTH, NEW SOUTH

The Lost Cause attitudes and symbols on display at the bicentennial encapsulate once ubiquitous and publicly unchallenged sentiments throughout the Old South. Those sentiments, materialized in public monuments or in unashamed displays of Confederate flags, flourished for nearly a century after Reconstruction. It is the South of states' rights, segregation, veneration of southern Civil War heroes, and justification of the southern cause.

Such attitudes and symbols now incite substantial public controversy throughout the post-1960s South, whereas the locus of dissent once lay primarily in the intramural confines of African American communities. Despite strenuous neo-Confederate denial, the Lost Cause and its visible symbolism evoke an historic memory of slavery and racial hierarchy. In the New South, citizens and leaders across racial lines recognize that public celebrations of the Confederacy risk damaging the image of inclusion, diversity, and welcome that they hope to project. Restrictive and exclusionary racial attitudes of earlier years, especially when roiled in public controversy, can imperil a community's reputation and therefore its potential for economic growth and prosperity.

This phenomenon is a product of black empowerment born over the past half century. Changes in the law, reluctantly accepted throughout the South, made possible the now routine features of contemporary southern life—integration of schools and public accommodations, the signal expansion of the black middle class, black police, and black elected and appointed officials at every level of government. These momentous changes are the centerpiece of what brochures and convention bureaus from the Carolinas to Louisiana herald as the "New South," a term once reserved for the economic rebirth of the South following the Civil War. In terms of racial attitudes, the New South of that time was not new.

The South of the last half-century, however, has had to contend with voices continually asserting that southern heritage is black as well as white. Kentucky fully associates itself with these changes. Politicians in their official capacities and public pronouncements embrace all of the legal victories that dismantled the system of American apartheid. Accordingly, the once widespread and unchallenged display of Confederate emblems and the staging of public events memorializing the Lost Cause no longer occur without public challenge or political intercession. For example, a marble statue of Jefferson Davis, a gift to the state of Kentucky from the UDC, remains in the rotunda of the state capital, but not undisturbed by contrarian viewpoints and the affirmation of a very different remembered history.[59] Likewise, the control the state exercises over the Jefferson Davis Memorial Park seeks to avert controversy and resurgent, publicly visible racial animosities. Even in Davis's adopted state of Mississippi, the legislature was sensitive to possible controversy attending the bicentennial and took no action on a proposal that would have created a commission to plan bicentennial commemorations. Nor did the Davis Family Association have any success in persuading the Department of Defense to commemorate Davis's role as secretary of war in the 1850s.[60]

Sometimes an almost studied neglect can accomplish the same purpose, as in the dedication of Confederate graves in Riverside. No stores or other places of business in Hopkinsville advertised the Davis bicentennial with posters or other announcements on their premises. Little advance or follow-up coverage appeared in the newspaper. The attitude in Hopkinsville seemed to be one of collective indifference. People from the Hopkinsville Convention and Visitors Bureau were on hand at some remove from the monument in order to distribute pens, rulers, and other small utilitarian items promoting the community rather than the event itself. In establishing a discreet physical distance from the Davis commemoration, the convention and visitors bureau hoped to advance tourism, not exclusion and separation.

The only black people I saw over the course of two days were two Parks Department employees and a young Hopkinsville mother with her toddlers. She had gotten off the highway to see what the gathering was about. A number of black people in Hopkinsville told me at no time would they go to Davis Park where they would be surrounded by Confederate emblems. Yet the Parks Department in 2010 appointed an African American to manage the Jefferson Davis historic site. Ronald Syndnor, a long-time resident of Christian County, idealistically hopes to overcome black resistance to anything associated with the Confederacy. His aim is to make the memorial a site for educational programs relevant to all people.[61] However, the polarity of white southern and African American memory and the burden of symbolism at a locale where secession and slavery's arch defenders are honored insure that African Americans will keep their distance from the site.

Increasingly, the contests over memory and interpretation in the South reach some resolution by what serves the pragmatic interest of civic organizations and the commercial sector. In Little Rock, for example, Confederate Boulevard underwent a name change in 2004, as officials realized that street signs were among the first city markers observed by visitors. Attuned to sentiments of tourists, conventioneers, and others—none of whom is exclusively white—the city took a very practical view in looking after its economic health.[62] Yet the Old South has hardly disappeared and reminders of its presence, proclaimed and euphemized in the anodyne term "heritage," regularly surface. When that occurs, critical observers with very different historic memories challenge the legitimacy of any public or official embrace of symbols associated with slavery or insurrection.

Prior to its reopening in 2004, the Jefferson Davis Monument underwent several years of renovation at a cost of three million dollars of public money that many contested.[63] Much better known are the disputes elsewhere. Flying the Confederate flag over the South Carolina State House and disputes over Confederate emblems appearing on the state flags of Mississippi and Georgia drew considerable press coverage. Members of Congress, such as Trent Lott and former congressman Bob Barr, the 2008 Libertarian presidential candidate, have spoken before the Council of Conservative Citizens, the successor to the White Citizens' Council. In Memphis, a downtown development office pressed the city council to change the names of Forrest Park, Confederate Park, and Jefferson Davis Park. A long and contentious debate on Forrest Park ensued. A large statue of Nathan Bedford Forrest on horseback surveys the park, and Forrest and his wife are buried there. The resourceful cavalry general lives in white southern memory, inscribed on historical markers in Hopkinsville, Memphis, and other sites in Kentucky and Tennessee.

Forrest also lives in an altogether different southern memory as the founder of the Ku Klux Klan. It is the memory of a once-terrorized black South, which now publicly confronts racially charged celebratory monuments and any implied veneration of the Lost Cause.

More than a name was at stake in the Forrest Park controversy. Also proposed was removal of the statue and disinterring the bodies for reburial elsewhere. While proponents focused on Forrest as a slave trader, instigator of the Fort Pillow massacre, and a Ku Klux Klan founder, a black mayor temporized over concern that Memphis once again would attract national headlines because of racial turmoil.[64] When historical events or persons provoke disputes over the meaning of the past, it is the present that comes into sharpest focus.[65] In early 2009, Forrest Park entered the National Register of Historic Places after an application for that status was submitted by the SCV. While the memorial to Forrest now has National Park Service sanction, the acrimony is certain to continue.[66] Also certain is a continuing clash of interpretations over historical memory in relationship to race, slavery, and the Civil War.

INVENTED MEMORY

The contest over emotionally charged symbols can sometimes turn deadly. Such was the case in early 1995 in Todd County, where the Davis memorial is located. As reported from Guthrie and Elkton by journalist Tony Horwitz, a car with several black teenage friends chased the truck of a white teen couple, husband and wife, because the truck was flying two Confederate battle flags. One of the black youths, Freddie Morrow, fired a shot at the truck; it struck the driver, Michael Westerman, who later died of his wound. The flags provoked Morrow's action, taking one life and committing Morrow and another occupant of the car to life in prison. A particular irony is that the black youth knew virtually nothing about slavery, the Civil War, or the Confederacy. But he did know that young blacks get angry when they see the Confederate battle flag, and he acted in deadly accord with those sentiments. It is doubly ironic that Morrow had grown up in a violent Chicago environment of drugs and gangs. His mother had sent him to Guthrie to live with relatives in order to insulate him from those destructive forces.[67]

Horwitz describes a process that made the victim a Confederate hero like the southern fallen of the Civil War, not simply a victim of senseless teenage violence prompted by a symbol that neither assailant nor victim really understood. A re-membrance at the Jefferson Davis Park featured a second transformation, with the victim cast as a "frontline soldier in a contemporary war, one that pitted decent God-fearing folk against [what one speaker called] 'an out of control government and its lawless underclass.'"[68] A number of speakers, including someone from the secessionist League of the South, fulminated against the NAACP and others "fomenting hatred against the honorable culture of the South." Klansmen without robes were present, and members of the Aryan Nation were also in attendance.[69] This event condenses many passionate, if less deadly encounters over historical memory and a past kept alive by the present. Old symbols and vernacular memories, even when the latter are at odds with history or perhaps because they are, press themselves into the service of a contemporary culture war over race.

In contrast to the vitality of Confederate symbols and sentiments Horowitz described in 1996, Robert Penn Warren provides a different portrait of local history and memory in Guthrie, his hometown, in the early twentieth century. Jim Crow was in full force, and racial feelings and sentiments were openly expressed without challenge. In those years, the present was not a battleground of contending historic memories. Guthrie was a railroad town more than anything else and not given to obeisance before the memory of native son Jefferson Davis and the Confederacy. The building of the nearby monument meant jobs, and no one was interested in refighting the Civil War or determining whose forbears were Confederates and whose were Yankees. Writing in 1980, Warren observed, "to a certain number of contemporary citizens the Civil War seemed to have been fought for the right to lynch without legal interference."[70] It was a right desired by local Unionists and Confederates alike, whose political differences about secession were leavened by shared racial animosities.

Although the people whom Horwitz interviewed claimed that Todd County had always identified itself with the cause of rebellion, this is an invented tradition of recent vintage. Kentucky never seceded, most Kentucky combatants fought in the federal army, and Todd County itself, like Christian County, was divided between a northern section of small farmers owning few slaves and sympathetic to the Union and a southern section of large farms with many more slaves. In each county, the southern area of slave-dependent large farms nurtured Confederate sympathies. But as the diary of Ellen McGaughey Wallace makes clear, Unionist sentiment was hardly incompatible with a commitment to white supremacy and the continuation of slavery.

In this vein, a Civil War letter of Mitchell Andrew Thompson, a Union soldier in the 83rd Illinois Volunteer Regiment, makes clear the proslavery sentiments of many Kentucky volunteers in the Union army. Engaged mostly in the vicinity of Fort Donnelson and Clarksville, Thompson writes of the ill will between Kentucky troops in the federal forces and the Illinois soldiers, whom the Kentuckians regarded as abetting runaway slaves:

Their Col. who is a slave owner says he would sooner shoot a nigger than a rebel and a great many of them seemed as if they have lost all human feeling. It would have been much better if the state of Kentucky had gone with the rebels for we could fight them much better if they were in the rebel ranks than in our own. [Their Adjutant said] they would show that G-d d-d abolition, nigger stealing 83rd a trick or two. . . . There has been more than one revolver drawn on them by our men.[71]

Support of the Union and of slavery of which Thompson wrote was particularly manifest in the presidential election of 1860. A number of western Kentucky counties, including Christian and Todd, voted for John Bell in that four-way contest. Antislavery and proslavery factions in the Democratic Party were divided between Douglas and Breckinridge, respectively. A slave owner from Tennessee, Bell ran on the short-lived Constitutionalist party, which opposed secession without opposing slavery. Its short platform was silent on the slavery issue. With the election of Lincoln, southerners who had supported the Union and slavery by voting for Bell "moved toward proslavery fire-eaters pressing the cause of secession.[72] Yet as Carl Degler has argued on the basis of a close analysis of the election, voters for Bell were concentrated in the counties of the middle and upper South with large black populations and a planter class, which had long opposed the Democrats in favor of a Unionist Whig party that was defunct by 1860.[73] It was the heritage of Unionist and anti-Democratic sentiment, not antislavery, that motivated the Bell vote. Although Kentucky did not secede, sentiment in the largest slave-owning counties such as Christian and Todd strongly favored slavery's perpetuation. Writing a local history in 1884, Perrin observed that in Todd County "opposition to emancipation was unanimous and determined."[74] That determination manifested itself in a profound bitterness and hatred after the Civil War when black people in Todd and other western Kentucky counties suffered a "reign of terror" at the hands of former slave owners, as Chapter 4 discussed. Todd County acted on a very old template, not of secession, but of racial antipathy shared alike by wealthy planters and poor whites. These feelings were revitalized and updated for a post–civil rights era when aggrieved whites could graft them onto the symbols of the Lost Cause to transform personal tragedy into white political martyrdom. This process is a particularly graphic illustration of the interplay of past and present in the formation of popular memory.

BLACK MEMORY AND REUNIONS

For obvious reasons, black memorialization of slavery and the Civil War and its aftermath did not take the form of massive public monuments. People impoverished by caste, economic dependency, and political weakness could hardly muster the resources necessary for these kinds of public mnemonics. In Christian County, one does not see acknowledgment of black heroism or achievement, past or present, even in more modest public forms, such as historic plaques or visible street names. Instead, black memory often inheres in the more intimate, restricted domains of church or family reunions.

Reunions tend to follow a common pattern, yet each family gathering develops its own distinctive character. The dominant themes emerging from the reunions of the Bingham and McCray families are renewal—of acquaintanceship with widely scattered distant cousins, of commitment to family solidarity and the bonds of kinship, of religious faith, and of pride in accomplishment. The very old and the very young assume particularly valued places, as they are the visible nodes in a line of continuity from the earliest, remembered forbears to the family's future. Families tend to have one or more historians charged with assembling documents such as marriage licenses, obituary notices, and the like. Their efforts find their way into the reunion in the form of family trees, genealogies, or narratives printed in a booklet or reunion program. Emphasizing family continuity through time, each reunion recognizes those who have died over the previous year, establishing where that person stands in the genealogy. Rendell Thomas, acting as master of ceremonies at the 2006 McCray reunion in Hopkinsville, asked for statements of tribute to accompany the death announcements. Tribute and praise infuse black historic memory, providing visions and narratives of black experience very different from its historic renderings by white people.

This alternative discourse becomes apparent when comparing the 1947 newspaper obituary of Ned Bingham of Trigg County with the family memory of Ned Bingham. The oral recitation of his life materializes in each biennial Bingham reunion that gathers his many widely scattered descendants. The *Cadiz Record* reported the death of Ned Bingham at one hundred years of age in the same paternalistic terms marking the obituary four decades earlier of Ike Copeland, reported to be a black Confederate loyalist. Each was cast as a racial exemplar, both subordinated by the ironic kin term, "uncle." It is of course their subordination that helps to make them laudable. Described as an "interesting type of his race," Ned Bingham was born into slavery in Sherman, Texas, and came to Trigg County, Kentucky, with his Bingham owner. The obituary continued: "Uncle Ned Bingham was a good man, a good farmer, and a good type of his race." A faithful member of the Bloomfield Baptist Church, Ned Bingham's depth of religious feeling also contributed to his commendable reputation as an exemplary Negro. His obituary recounts his often told narration of coming to Kentucky as a young boy in the 1850s from Texas by way of rail, boat, and horseback, sometimes riding behind Jabes Bingham, his young master.[75] The implication of the brief account of his life in the *Cadiz Record* is that slavery was merely an unremarkable, passing condition of his birth and early experience that led to his praiseworthy life as a farmer, husband and father, and ideal representative of his race.

While these features and events in Ned Bingham's life are well known to his many descendants and are publicly recited at Bingham family reunions, the cruel and degrading aspects of slavery are also recounted, although briefly. He carried scars on his back from the beatings he had received in his youth and was not loathe to show them to family and friends. Thus marked literally by "the peculiar institution," he too was figuratively marked, although neither inscription had any significance for the *Cadiz Record* writer or his assumed readers. Instead, it has been left to the Bingham family to recount and interpret their forebear's experience of servitude. Its manifest cruelty did not divert Ned Bingham from becoming "a serious and kindhearted man" in the view of his many descendants.[76] But while Ned Bingham told his family of the bitter experience of slavery, on the whole little was communicated by former bondsmen to their children and grandchildren. Silence, not a narrative reliving of degradation, became much more meaningful than the occasional pithy recitations handed down from former slaves.

Historical memory remains active and present in Bingham reunions. Participants in these gatherings are descendants (with their spouses) of Ned and Ollie Bingham. Usually held over a weekend, reunions typically include visiting with near and distant relatives, communal meals, recreation, entertainment such as singing, dancing, or dramatic performance by family members, recitation of family history, and prayer. A written program outlines the weekend schedule of activities and reprises family history, later recited publicly. Religious observance is integral to the reunion, sometimes including a special family service for the attendees at one of the home churches in Hopkinsville or in the host city. Anthropologists at least since Durkheim have described rites of intensification, those ritual actions that induce a feeling of acute consciousness of the group and its shared values and beliefs. The Bingham reunion and four other black reunions I attended in and around Hopkinsville and in Milwaukee are quintessential rites of intensification that merge the individual and the group. The observances proudly acknowledge the sum total of individual achievements within the family circle, made possible by the force of tradition, including deep Christian faith, and the diffuse support of kinsmen, beginning in slavery.

In a Friday evening family church service in Hopkinsville, which ushered in the weekend Bingham family reunion in August 2005, Paulette Robinson, great-granddaughter of Ned and Ollie, led a memorial candle lighting. Like Ned Bingham, her great-grandmother, Ollie, was born into slavery on the Grooms plantation in Trigg County, where her owner had fathered her. Her people lived near Cadiz, Kentucky, some twenty miles west of Hopkinsville. Paulette asked a descendant of each of the ten children of Ned and Ollie to describe to other reunion attendees the place they share with their siblings in the family genealogy. Following that public declaration, each of the ten descendants came to the front of the church and, facing the congregation, lit a candle in remembrance of their forbears. A very solemn occasion, it resonated with forms of ancestral veneration ubiquitous throughout black Africa.

At the service, honorific ritual and oral narrative gave way to history as Shirley Shelton reported the results of her research on Ned and Ollie, as recorded in the census and slave records of Trigg and Christian counties. As in prior reunions, her reiteration of known history emphasized the "up from slavery" struggle of Ned and Ollie as the wellspring of values that empowered many Bingham progeny to become teachers, attorneys, nurses, physicians, and business people. The family reunion is thus suffused with the particularism and distinctiveness of blackness from the bitterness of slavery and Ned's physical abuse to his own triumphs in freedom centered on family solidarity. At the same time, the assembly of Bingham kin celebrated achievements in the wider society and made explicit the inspiration Bingham descendants had gathered from previous generations. The next day's visit to the family cemetery and the graves of Ned and Ollie enabled assembled kin once again to pay homage to the founders.

Like the Bingham family, the McCrays try to gather annually or at least biennially in a southern or midwestern city. Hopkinsville, "where it all began," is a preferred locale. There is much visiting and kinship renewal, eating, and retelling of family stories. A McCray family pastor, Reverend Haskins, took the lead in prayers, emphasizing the bonds within the wide circle of kin. After his death in 2007, his son, Reverend Michael Haskins, assumed that responsibility. Like the Bingham descendants, the McCray kindred acknowledges, without dwelling on it, the slave experience. Each McCray reunion also establishes the African origin of their earliest forbears, beginning with Billy McCray, a young slave descended from "an African family group brought to the United States" and auctioned to a Virginia slave owner named McCray. The number and identity of the genealogical linkages between Billy McCray and his African forbears are unknown.[77] Here, memory diverges from historical experience since the havoc of capture and the decimation and mortality of the Middle Passage virtually foreclosed the possibility that an intact family in Africa could survive those ravages. Yet the historic memory is resilient, not because of its fidelity to events, but because it distils with deep feeling the supreme value of familial continuity, loyalty, and commitment in the face of destructive forces. Just in the way Ned Bingham's descendants acknowledge the experience of slavery,

McCray kinsmen likewise note what occurred in order to show how they have transcended it.

For the McCrays, the recitation and recording of family history and genealogy begins with Billy's marriage to Patsy Ann Whitlock while they were both in slavery. They eventually had two daughters and five sons born in the 1860s and 1870s. The genealogical record focuses on the largest segment of the family— the descendants of Billy's son, Tom, or Tommie as the family tree and family stories designate him, and his wife, Lular. Pictures of forbears and facsimiles of documents, such as the marriage license of Tommie and Lular, appear in the reunion program. Known white ancestry is identified. Interestingly, the latter aspect of the genealogy is presented without comment since the fact of sexual exploitation of black women, in slavery and after, by white men is burned into the African American vernacular memory. Abiding Christian faith, moreover, within the religious atmosphere of the reunion, spurns racial recrimination in much the same way that Claybron Merriweather's poetry is silent about slavery's local architects.

More triumphant narratives of hard work, education, and all that marked the movement out of slavery characterize the program notes and oral recitations at the family reunion. Tommie and Lular, for example, after many years of working as sharecroppers on a white-owned farm, finally were able to purchase a home in Hopkinsville. Tommie's daughter, Dorothy Quarles, observed in 2002 that her father always realized less return on crop sales than he knew was fair. His experience with white farm owners was a reprise of Sarah Nance's narrative in Chapter 4 of her father's experience as a sharecropper. Both men had little recourse.

The reunion programs retell the story of Tommie's late teenage years, when he worked as a field laborer on the Christian County farm of Arthur Henry. There, he met and married Lular Averitte, the daughter of Drucilla Averitte and Aaron Hester, a white man whose father had owned Drucilla. Aaron took a particular interest in his black daughter. When Lular was four years of age, Drucilla died and eventually the child's white father placed her in the home of an elderly black midwife after witnessing her stepfather beating her. Lular, at that time unaware that he was her father, later told of a white man coming to visit and bringing food. When Lular's guardian died, Aaron Hester again intervened, placing his daughter, Lular, with the Henry family, with whom she lived in the family residence as a house servant.

What has not appeared in the reunion programs is an account of the death of Lular's white father. According to the oldest McCray family members, Lular was well treated by the Henry family because of the special concern of her white father. Aaron Hester's interest in his black daughter of course did not extend to taking Lular into his own home. However lightly complexioned, Lular was black and publicly unacknowledged by Aaron Hester. What transforms a descriptive account into a narrative of resistance is the added detail about Tommie's action during Aaron Hester's last days. It suggests a race antagonism that McCray program planners prefer to leave in the oral tradition, recounted by Dorothy Quarles. She described her father's reaction to Hester's effort to see Lular. Living south of Hopkinsville, very ill and near death, Hester sent word to Lular that he wanted to see her. Mrs. Quarles said that her father was well aware of Lular's paternity but angry at the summons: "My dad wouldn't take her. 'I'm not taking you down to that white man.'" Although Lular was ready to comply, Tommie's insistence apparently did not provoke an argument.[78]

While she attributed no explicit motive to her father's adamant refusal, Mrs. Quarles's recitation of her father's life-long experience of subordination and unfairly compensated farm labor was of a piece with the exploitation of Lular's mother by Aaron Hester. He would be a father to Lular only on his own private terms, assertively negated at the end by Tom McCray. It is therefore particularly interesting that the abrasions of paternalism, exploitation, and racial animus constitute only a negligible part of the work of memory at these black reunions. But they have hardly slipped from consciousness. Rather, the reunion is a public, ritualized enactment of the triumphant aspects of black experience.

BLACK MEMORY AS COUNTER DISCOURSE

Black popular memory as counter discourse long antedates the current contention over the meaning of race and slavery. It always stood opposed to the more public and widely sanctioned commemorations of the southern cause that cast African Americans as a people apart from southern history. Whether in the stories, both documented and unrecorded, of black war veterans or emancipated slaves, black experience always had its own venues of remembrance. Black writing also inscribed black memory in the decades after the Civil War. Of course, one cannot be certain of the reading tastes of the black public in Hopkinsville in the late nineteenth and early twentieth centuries. That public would certainly have been much smaller than its white counterpart, owing to wide racial discrepancies in public education and the denial of library access to African Americans. But the existence at that time of a Phillis Wheatley Literary Society, locally published black newspapers such as the *New Age*, regular press dispatches from Hopkinsville to the *Freeman*, and resident writer-journalists, such as the Poston brothers, Horace Slatter, and Claybron Merriweather suggests at the least a modest level of interest and awareness of the black literary and historical voice.[79] Three examples of those voices are apposite, although there are many more. Their authoritative and critical writing about race, even if received through second- or third-hand sources, very likely resonated with the historic memories of the black public in Christian County.

George Washington Williams, author of the groundbreaking two-volume *History of the Negro Race in America* (1883), closely examined Confederate policy toward captured black soldiers and their white officers. The latter would be held guilty of inciting "servile insurrection" against the Confederate states and thus subject to execution. Captured black soldiers, whether freemen or escaped slaves, would be remanded to the states where they were captured. Condemned with their white officers for seeking to "overthrow the institution of African slavery and bring on a servile war in these States," they would more often be condemned to death and summarily executed.[80]

No battle of the war rivals Fort Pillow for the cruel and atrocious actions perpetrated against captured Union troops, particularly black soldiers. A congressional committee in 1864 investigated the battle, relying on interviews with surviving soldiers, black and white. The Joint Congressional Committee on the Conduct of the War found that surrendering black soldiers suffered burning or burial alive and other tortures. Williams, relying heavily on that report and quoting testimony of the survivors, calls Forrest a "cold-blooded murderer." He concludes his review of the congressional investigation by declaring that history has a duty "to record that there is to be found no apologist for cruelties that rebels inflicted upon brave but helpless Black soldiers during the war for the extirpation of slavery. The Confederate conduct at Pillow must remain a foul stain upon the name of the men who fought to perpetuate human slavery in North America, but failed."[81] Williams was one of the first historians to examine the official congressional record of the Ft. Pillow massacre. But his severe conclusions were lost, except to black memory, in the post–Civil War North-South promotion of national reconciliation. Southern views exonerating Forrest at Fort Pillow developed even before Williams published his history.[82]

Williams was much ahead of his time in actively attending to the black experience in the United States, including that of black soldiers. Following his *History of the Negro Race*, he published a history of black troops in the Civil War.[83] For him, race hatred was inseparable from the southern cause. Understanding the capture of Fort Pillow strained Williams's commitment to writing objective history, according to his biographer, John Hope Franklin, as Williams's characterization of events and southern participants utilized highly charged language.[84] Nevertheless, his conclusion that Confederate soldiers waged a war of annihilation against troops attempting to surrender at Fort Pillow has been corroborated in recent scholarship.[85] The contemporary controversy over Forrest Park in Memphis can only be understood in relationship to black historic memory, abetted by historical scholarship.

Like Williams, Joseph T. Wilson was an African American veteran of the Union army who became an historian. His 1890 book, *The Black Phalanx*, documented the actions of black soldiers in defense of the United States from the Revolution through the Civil War. Advertised in black newspapers, Wilson's volume was heralded as "a book for the race" and "bound to be placed in the home of every colored family in the land."[86] *The Black Phalanx* detailed relentless black courage in battle, race consciousness, and patriotism. Wilson also wrote of the black soldier's passion for learning and that he was not content only with winning freedom: "The Phalanx soldiers had a strong sense of race pride, and the idea that ignorance was the cause of their oppression gave zest to their desire to be educated. . . . Every camp had a teacher . . . every company had some one to instruct the soldiers in reading, if nothing more."[87]

Wilson dedicated his book to the white officers who commanded black troops in the Civil War in the face of opprobrium and ridicule from their brother officers and the likelihood of execution if captured. He wrote the book at the request of fellow veterans attending a reunion encampment in 1882. They were black, white, and foreign born—"all American citizens." Both the circumstances motivating Wilson's book and its dedication stand against the racial tribalism of southern memory and embody the universalist meaning of the Civil War that would not be widely embraced for another century.[88]

The outrage about Fort Pillow that risked compromising Williams's objectivity as a historian but not as an exemplar of black historic memory also recurred in Wilson's book. Unrestrained, but using as evidence the same congressional hearings examined by Williams, Wilson called the killing of surrendering troops at Fort Pillow a "massacre," a "shocking crime of wanton indiscriminate murder of some three hundred soldiers [because] they were niggers and fighting with niggers."[89] Williams and Wilson, as well as others chronicling these events, could be assured of a receptive black audience as "blacks all over the South were loath to forget Forrest's massacre of black Union troops garrisoned at Ft. Pillow."[90]

A generation later, Fort Pillow evoked the poetic voice of Paul Laurence Dunbar, whose mother was born into slavery in Kentucky. His father fought in the Civil War. "The Colored Soldiers" is Dunbar's lamentation over the fate of the black troops facing Forrest:

> And at Pillow! God have mercy
> On the deeds committed there,
> And the souls of those poor victims
> Sent to Thee without a prayer.
> Let the fullness of Thy pity
> O'er the hot wrought spirits sway

Of the gallant colored soldiers
Who fell fighting on that day![91]

The full text of Dunbar's poem recalls the scorning of colored soldiers at the outset of the war until they proved their mettle and lifted the fortunes of the Union army.

Dunbar also exposes the "faithful slave" in another poem about black troops. In the vernacular poem, "When Dey 'Listed Colored Soldiers," Dunbar's narrator, a slave woman, thought that she could mourn the loss of her young master until her own husband enlisted in the Union army. Then she knew fully what was at stake when colored soldiers went to war. She could no longer mourn the Confederate dead, although she could feel the sorrow of the white woman, only because it was her own sorrow at the loss of her husband, 'Lias.[92] Dunbar, Williams, Wilson, and other black writers give voice to an historic memory, both tragic and triumphant, that bears little resemblance to black people represented in the mythos of the Old South. The latter, however, remains recalcitrant and unmoved, crystallized in the neo-Confederate resistance to the modern historical understanding of slavery and the Civil War.

Despite his strong race pride and consciousness, Dunbar came to the attention of white critics and audiences—one of the first black writers in the United States to gain a white readership. Valued for his dialect poetry by the early-twentieth-century critic William Dean Howells, as well as other white readers, Dunbar was no mere "plantation" poet. He did not find inspiration in the tradition of Thomas Nelson Page and others who portrayed shuffling stereotypic black people.[93] Quite the contrary. Even in his poems written in black patois, Dunbar does not depict one-dimensional docile slaves so beloved by the Old South, nor compliant freedmen unaware that they "wear the mask." Instead, Dunbar, through varied linguistic registers, portrays black people as thinking and feeling independently of white demand or expectation.

Robert Penn Warren, in his reflections on the centennial of the Civil War, observed that "in the moment of death the Confederacy entered upon its immortality."[94] Over the next century, the United Daughters of the Confederacy, the Sons of Confederate Veterans, and allied custodians of southern memory, including historians, social scientists, writers, and filmmakers, continually vitalized southern heroism and race supremacy. During the last five decades, alternative memories of the black experience have found a wide audience, forcefully challenging a dominant southern narrative and its racial fictions. But long before and without cessation, black historic memory in more restricted precincts challenged the immortality Warren wrote of in 1961.

Riverside Cemetery, Hopkinsville, Confederate Markers at Camp Alcorn, erected 2001.

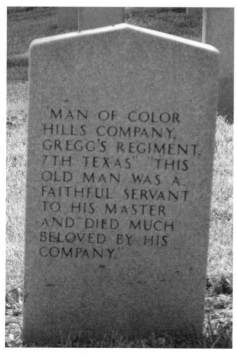

Riverside Cemetery, "grave" of Washington Hall, a black man commemorated at Camp Alcorn.

Riverside Cemetery, grave of Patsy Brent (1841–1921), the only black woman buried at Riverside owing to the influence of her wealthy and influential employers.

Grave of Patsy Brent showing its relationship to burials in the main portion of the cemetery.

Walnut Street Café, Hopkinsville, 2004, Emma Jordan (right), proprietress, with her sister, Thelma Moore.

Paulette Robinson (sister of Emma and Thelma) and grandchildren at the Walnut Street Café, 2004, where the extended family often gathered.

Cousins Tyesha Bailey and Shirley Shelton (sister of Paulette, Emma, and Thelma) at the 2005 Nance extended family Thanksgiving celebration, Walnut Street Café.

The Bingham ancestral tree displayed as a poster at the 2005 family reunion, Trigg County.

Sarah Nance, granddaughter of Ned and Ollie Bingham, at the 2005 Bingham family reunion.

McCray Family Tree

Annie Mae [Willie Warfield]
Eddye Stella
Hallie Rose [Adrian Chambers]
George [Winnie, Maude, Marie, Margaret]
Clinton [Anne Pollard]
Johnnie [Susie Moss]
Arthur [Mary Frances Cattlett]
Laura [George Radford]
Katherine Lena [Thomas Vaughn]
Willie Mae [Sanford Haskins]
Harry Dorothy [John Torian]
Henry [Birdie Mitchell]

Ludd
William
Tommie (Lular Bell)
Charlie
Herbert
Frankie
Ammie

Billie (Patsy Ann Whitlock) McCray

"In The Beginning"

The McCray family tree "In the Beginning," from the booklet at the 2004 reunion.

The McCray brothers—Herbert, Tom, and William—in Hopkinsville, ca. 1937, at the home that Tom and Lular McCray had recently purchased. (Courtesy of Regina Dillard and John Torian.)

McCray family reunion, four generations coming together in Milwaukee, 2004.

Howard and Ammie McCray Weaver on their farm west of Hopkinsville, Newstead Road area, in 2002.

Francis Eugene Whitney (1916–2006) at his real estate office, Hopkinsville, 2002. Whitney was a city councilman, mayor pro-tem, and leader in the African American community for five decades.

6

CIVIL RIGHTS AND BEYOND

The civil rights era created the cultural conditions under which memories divided by race would inevitably collide. As long as those memories had been located in distinct social domains, public conflict over the vernacular meanings of the past, and therefore the present, were largely avoided. Each historic memory simply reiterated the outlook of a distinctive community, secure in its unchallenged values and in the rectitude of its moral vision. But the political movements of the 1960s set out to refashion the future and in the process black historic memory, gaining a new public attention, could be pressed into the service of social change. While changes in the law since the 1960s helped to establish a common ground of shared civic participation and racial understanding, the terrain is hardly smooth. A racial division of historic memory, accordingly, is very much in evidence.

The anxieties, fears, and suspicions attending integration were well placed, because white people and black people began to know each other in new ways, not only in schools but also in factories, businesses, athletics, and other venues. Social contacts unthinkable before the 1960s inevitably produced conflict, which can hardly develop when people remain socially isolated. Hopkinsville has accordingly registered an embarrassment of examples of injured feelings and damaged hopes. Although the new laws rendered discriminatory practices of the Jim Crow era illegal with the speed of a signature, they did not and could not change human attitudes and habits as easily. In other words, legal change, which made possible new and different forms of contact between the races, outpaced changes in customary ways of feeling, thinking, and acting. The sense of disappointment, however, is inevitably greater when expectations of improved race relations are not consistently fulfilled. It could not have been otherwise, since the new social realities of integration confronted majority beliefs rooted in nineteenth-century racial certainties.

Weakened restraints on the black voice in Hopkinsville resulted in public criticism against social interactions that had encoded racial asymmetry since the days of slavery. In 1966, Louis McHenry, representing the NAACP and the Hopkinsville Progressive Citizens Committee, spoke before the Hopkinsville Human Relations Commission. The NAACP attorney and civil rights activist complained of indignity and discrimination in housing, employment, access to credit, and "the inequalities that confront our people daily." Yet less than ten years before, the local newspaper had heralded the "unmarred race relations in the town." That statement, of course, simply indicates that people living in the same town can inhabit very different places.

McHenry condemned racial exclusion, explaining that "the young Negro wants to be heard and made a part of the nation that he is giving his life for in Vietnam." He recounted for his listeners the continuing story of the denial of rights to black people:

> Each day in this community, the Negro is reminded that he is a "Second Class Citizen," and is faced with many denials of the basic right of a citizen, but, yet we are expected to be patient and not speak out, because certain people or groups are not ready for the Negro to have all his rights. Too long have we been denied and deprived of our constitutional rights. We are the last hired, the first fired, bad housing conditions, denied all credit above a few dollars, and we are expected to be submissive and accept any condition that is thrust upon us. . . . before integration, we were told that our education was equal, since the Supreme Court decision, we are told that our children are far behind and can't keep up with white children. . . . a white boy or girl can go on a job without experience and be taught, but our children are expected to know before they can be hired.
>
> The Negroes of Hopkinsville want equal employment opportunities. We are tired of being turned down and told we are not qualified when we readily see it is because of our color. In the field of education, it is pathetic in an "All America [*sic*] City" that after twelve years we have failed to implement the 1954 decision.[1]

McHenry also asserted that the NAACP and Hopkinsville Progressive Citizens wanted the merchants to know that the black community was well aware of its economic impact on the town, from the use of bank accounts, utility purchases, newspaper subscriptions, and the like, but that "we find very few, if any Negroes employed in these areas." He further charged the city with discrimination in housing and public accommodations in spite of a recently passed public accommodations law. In the most personal of their wide-ranging complaints, McHenry on behalf of the two groups asked "that common courtesy be used in public places when addressing the members of our race." "Our mothers, wives and fathers are still being called by their first name, 'Joe,' or 'Aunt Sue,' or 'Uncle Bill' by clerks and other public employees who hate to extend common courtesy to a Negro. The Negro is tired of old traditions which make us feel that we are not a part of the society we help build."[2] The civil rights victories of the 1960s had raised the expectations of many people in Hopkinsville on two fronts. As articulated by McHenry, black people were seeking not only basic rights and access to jobs long closed to them, but also respectful acknowledgment as they too justly claimed the town as their own.

The landmark Supreme Court decision of 1954 ensured that the first major breach of the racial barrier would occur in segregated public schools. Beginning slowly in 1956, the statewide desegregation process in Kentucky was at least outwardly peaceful and remained so. There were no intimations of armed troops, such as those deployed to Little Rock, Arkansas, in 1957, or to Oxford, Mississippi, in 1962, where soldiers and federal marshals fought the governor's minions in "the last battle of the Civil War."[3] Hopkinsville was admired for its racial calm: "For a community which has such a high percentage of Negroes, Hopkinsville's almost unmarred race relations had been a cause of wonder and praise down through the years."[4] A likely explanation for the nearly statewide racial peace was demographic. Kentucky on the eve of integration had the lowest percentage of black people of any state in the Deep or Upper South.[5] Only the small western Kentucky town of Sturgis required a National Guard presence to contain a white mob bent on preventing nine black students from entering the high school.[6]

The seemingly smooth transition to integration in Hopkinsville could not, however, mask the inner disturbances. The Deep South sensibilities of the majority population ensured that any moves toward race mixing would be very unwelcome. This was explicitly stated in a 1958 editorial in the local newspaper, quoted in Chapter 1. Praising the town as "a law abiding, self-respecting American community," the newspaper commended "a history-making step to which a vast majority of its residents were passionately opposed." The editorial speculated that perhaps half the black residents had reservations about school integration. But their hesitation was very different from that of the white citizens. For black people, it was a serious disturbance of the familiar racial accord, and historic memory had bitterly recorded the cost of such disruptions.

The newspaper's laudatory tone might suggest that integration of the city's schools involved more than a few students. But praise for dealing with "what every local citizen considered an almost unsolvable problem" was in fact a response to the integration of three black children in two city schools. That "token desegregation," in the words of the newspaper, could occasion such lavish praise is indicative of the entrenchment of race feeling then pervasive in Hopkinsville. But Hopkinsville was hardly unique in occasioning the deepest concern over the first appearance in a white school of a very small number of black children.

The minority community had every reason for a guarded response to integration, or even outright skepticism, knowing as they did that young black people were not wanted in white institutions. For example, a white history teacher in Hopkinsville confessed that in forty years of teaching his greatest challenge was to accustom himself to the presence of black students entering his classes in the late 1960s. What those same students were experiencing as unwelcome strangers in a hometown classroom is recalled by bell hooks. She explains how she and others felt at the closing of the venerable black high school in Hopkinsville.

> We cannot believe we must leave our beloved Crispus Attucks and go to schools in white neighborhoods. We cannot imagine what it will be like to walk by the principal's office and see a man who will not know our name, who will not care about us. Already the grown-ups are saying it will be nothing but trouble, but they do not protest. . . . We start by leaving behind the pleasure we will feel in going to our all-black school, in seeing friends, in being a part of a school community. Our pleasure is replaced by fear. We no longer like attending school. We are tired of the long hours spent discussing what can be done to make integration work. We discuss with them knowing all the while that they want us to do something, to change, to make ourselves into carbon copies of them so that they can forget we are here, so that they can forget the injustice of their past. They are not prepared to change.[7]

Black students, reluctant integrationists, faced racial hostility, anonymity, and pressures to remake themselves in an image acceptable to white people. No longer part of the exclusively black high school, black students quickly had to assume minority status and the formidable challenge of "fitting in." The same might well be said for black people beginning to take a place in other formerly all-white institutions. The white majority, on the other hand, faced few pressures to alter their identities or their behavior. In her disappointment, hooks surely spoke for many other black Americans, whether newly integrated students or others entering valued jobs in majority offices and business concerns once closed to them, except through the service entrance.

Unknown to their new teachers and administrators, minority students encountered unwarranted and negative assumptions about their abilities and attitudes. While some of the new black students were selected for what hooks calls "the smart classes," many of the boys, known by their peers to be smart, were not. The black students shared an overwhelming feeling that they were under continuing scrutiny and must prove themselves.[8] Integration, moreover, brought to black youth an unwelcome weakening of the primary community that connected home, family, neighborhood, church, and school. Each Attucks student enjoyed a certain fame because he or she was well known within the overlapping primary groups that socially defined their lives. It was not unusual for young people to study with teachers who had taught their parents and other family members. Jessie Quarles, a contemporary of bell hooks's, reflected on the valued continuity between home and school, saying simply that at Attucks, "We were taught the way we were raised."[9]

The instruction at Attucks was generally esteemed. Quality teaching, according to R. B. Atwood, president of the historically black Kentucky State University, was the norm in black communities. On the eve of integration, he observed that black teachers underwent better training on the whole than their white counterparts: "The teaching profession occupies a higher status among Negroes than it does among whites. There are so many other things whites can do to earn money and prestige that are not open to Negroes. As a result, Negroes remain in the profession longer and prepare better."[10] Although they had high regard for the teachers, many Attucks parents felt that the facilities at white schools would be better, and they reluctantly supported integration for that reason. At the same time, they felt the hostility of white people and feared for the safety of their children.

Beyond these concerns, the closing of Crispus Attucks High School abruptly shut down a half-century tradition of independent black secondary education. The high school had been a pillar of Hopkinsville's black community and a symbol of educational achievement. Autonomy and community self-determination are not easily sacrificed. While none would welcome a return to the previous world of legal racial exclusion, many black residents have long identified unforeseen and unwelcome consequences of integration, including its negative impact on black institutional life. Black organizations once enjoyed a monopoly on black membership and of necessity segregation had nurtured black leadership.

DISCUSSION IN GOOD FAITH:
DIVIDED UNDERSTANDINGS

Social contact and shared concerns across racial lines have promoted amicable discussion of common interests such as education. Yet race can still segment perception decades after integration. This was the case in a community forum on the public schools held in August 2005. Sponsored by Focus Twenty-First Century, a black organization encouraging community engagement, the forum assembled at the Virginia Street Baptist Church. A series of speakers including teachers, the superintendent of the county-wide school system, other administrators and educators, and an audience of about equal numbers of black and white citizens discussed how the schools might be improved. Recurrent issues were truancy, discipline, and high rates of minority expulsion. The superintendent made a plea for volunteer mentors and councilors to help students make better decisions instead of succumbing to antisocial behavior. Many of the students in need of this kind of tutoring come from what the superintendent called "dysfunctional homes." A city council member gave a brief lecture on "parental responsibility," while a concerned citizen observed that discipline problems, whatever their source, create retention problems; students with resources transfer to private schools and teachers leave the school system.

Aside from the comment about expulsions reaching high levels among minority students, race for the most part remained in the background. Yet discernible differences separated black and white speakers regarding school discipline and the reason for the overall poor showing of Christian County schools in state assessments. White administrators and teachers tended to lay the blame on negative attitudes among some students and on family problems. The schools, in their view, bore little responsibility for failures that begin at home. Black professionals, on the other hand, spoke of the need for quality teaching at all levels: "If students are challenged, behavior problems will resolve themselves." Or, "All children can learn, and discipline problems ought not to mean that a teacher gives up on children." Another black teacher touched on ambiguities or uncertainties in student understanding of what is expected of them in the classroom. The implication of her remarks is that cultural differences, not social or individual dysfunction, may divide the home from the classroom, and students therefore have a need for "complete structure." They will then always know how to act according to school expectations. Reflecting on the cultural disparities between school and home, a black parent privately went so far as to assert, "integration is the worst thing that ever happened to the black child."

At another community meeting later that month, a local judge remarked that his friend, a second grade teacher, (both white), "predicts without fail" those children who will enter the juvenile justice system. She identifies bad behaviors, inattention, defiant attitudes, and single-parent households as certain determinants of school failure and criminality. The challenge of educating recalcitrant students notwithstanding, the judge's remarks point to the likely damage of a self-fulfilling process, once young children are identified and labeled as delinquents-in-the-making and inevitable failures.

The differing views at the community forum are particularly interesting in light of observations of various educational reformers in Kentucky and nationwide. Reports of the Prichard Committee, an independent non-partisan organization devoted to improving education in Kentucky, lay blame for failing schools on teachers rather than students. The late Robert Sexton, the executive director, pointed out that there are several schools in Kentucky with very large numbers of impoverished students. These schools rank among the poorest in the United States and yet, against conventional expectation, their academic performance is very high, outpacing some of the most affluent schools in the state. Nearby, other poor schools are scoring in the lowest ranks of Kentucky schools. Likewise, in a few Kentucky schools with large numbers of African American students and high poverty levels, young people are performing at academic levels up to or beyond those of white students. In other schools, sometimes in the same districts, with the same demographic profile, African American levels of achievement lag behind those of white students. Robert Sexton asks:

> If children whose parents are undereducated, poor, illiterate, or absent can't learn (as some people, even educators, claim), then why do poor children in some schools do so well?
>
> Good teaching. High performing schools have principals who won't let teachers excuse the poor performance of their students. Everybody in the school believes that every child can learn, and all students are expected to perform. Poverty and race are not accepted as excuses. The adults—not the children—are ultimately responsible. It is teaching that matters.[11]

The Prichard Committee's assessment is consistent with the views of Hopkinsville's black teachers and administrators at the community forum.

THE FIRST AND ONLY BLACK MAYOR: A ONE-WEEK TERM

In 1972, Hopkinsville seemed on the verge of electing a black mayor. The black community generally felt that this outcome would be a bellwether of progress, interrupting the historic memory of racial injustice and exclusion. No one in the town embodied the spirit of amicability between blacks and whites more than F. E. Whitney. It is not unusual to hear white people remark, "F. E. Whitney did more for race relations in Hopkinsville than anyone else." The implication here is that the burden of improving race relations falls primarily to black people. A model of gentlemanly demeanor and personal style, Whitney could count many achievements over his long life, and, like others of his generation, he did so against the great odds set by entrenched racial inequality. A graduate of Kentucky State University in 1937, Whitney had studied mathematics and later entered the Army signal corps during World War II. In themes reiterated countless times by black soldiers of that era, Whitney recounted his experiences with virulent forms of racism.[12] On his return to civilian life, he studied accounting part time on the G.I. Bill at Indiana University while working for a black insurance company in Louisville. Following his studies, he faced the continuing refusal of the accounting board of the state of Kentucky to certify him.

While he did not speak publicly about the other side of "amicable race relations," Whitney was under no illusions about the historic foundations of racial peace in Hopkinsville or the racism prompting his decision to leave politics. "It was just a situation that everybody accepted. They were white, we were black; we were servants, they were the masters. They just operated that way. We never had any vicious clashes. I always said it was just a fact of life."[13]

Black people were afraid that they would lose their jobs if they challenged the status quo, but improvement began slowly after World War II. Whitney eventually started a real estate business in 1948 and also worked as an accountant, gaining federal certification as a tax practitioner. In 1953, he began a long career as a public servant in Hopkinsville, achieving election to the city council. He was returned to office in each election over the next twenty years. During this period, he worked steadily toward opening up to black people possibilities for non-menial employment with the city. A man very much of his generation and locale, his efforts were quiet and conciliatory yet always resolute in trying to improve the lot of African Americans, particularly in employment and in housing.

For example, up to the 1960s, it was very difficult for black people to secure home loans, unless they had the most secure incomes possible. Whitney said doctors, teachers, and undertakers were in the best position to get mortgages. Others, if a bank even agreed to loan them money, found that they could get only a small fraction of the funds needed to purchase a house—so little in most cases that a new home was out of reach. Under terms established by the Veterans Administration, black servicemen began to get home loans. Local banks took notice, once Whitney began calling their attention to the opportunities they were missing. They started to see that their race-based policies were costing them money. In the early 1960s,

Whitney and attorney Louis McHenry were able to secure financing from a local bank to begin a housing development. Besides the investment value, they hoped to make home purchase a possibility for black people who were not professionals. Local banks saw a source of business that they had long rejected, especially in view of the fact that some veterans were securing financing from the FHA. Prior to the efforts of Whitney and McHenry, a black person could only purchase an old property in which white people were no longer interested.

In a pattern repeated throughout the United States, white flight abetted by real estate machinations created a black inner city and a periphery to which black people could not gain access. "We wanted to see to it that the young Negro didn't have to go through that," Whitney explained. After Whitney and McHenry built sixteen homes, white developers saw that money could be made, and they followed the lead of the banks in building homes with black buyers in mind. "That changed the trend," Whitney said.[14] Concurrently, the city improved the streets and sidewalks in the new area.

A pivotal turn of events for Whitney and black people in Hopkinsville occurred during the first two weeks of May 1972. Hopkinsville's mayor, as expected, resigned on May 2 to accept a state appointment. Whitney, as mayor pro tem, immediately became acting mayor. It was the responsibility of the twelve-member city council to name a new mayor, who would serve until the November election. Six news stories appeared over this period, one of which noted that the process of selecting the new mayor "has taken on most of the aspects of a general election." Three candidates emerged—Whitney; a fellow councilman, Al Rutland; and a young businessman and former president of the chamber of commerce, George Atkins. Although the term of office for the appointed mayor would be a scant six months, candidates were making public statements, two were developing what appeared to be platforms, and feelings were intense. Certainly, the newly appointed mayor would have the advantage of incumbency in the fall election.

At the council meeting the night of the mayor's resignation, some members of the council said they regarded the decision on a successor as a contest between Rutland and Atkins, but Whitney asked his fellow councilmen to consider him a candidate.[15] He was particularly disturbed by what he called "the lack of consideration" on the part of his colleagues "in failing to think he might be a candidate before he stated his position."[16] Doubting the necessity of prompt action to name a new mayor, Whitney said, "I do not construe the law to say that council has to act on the matter right now. If it doesn't, then I would simply serve as mayor until November, and then the people can speak on the question . . . I think I am qualified from the standpoint of service and personal ability, and I think I have earned the right to be mayor."[17]

In turning the succession into a political contest, the council, in Whitney's view, also showed its lack of respect for him. As mayor pro tem, and then acting mayor as the succession played out, Whitney believed that he should succeed to the vacated office: "If normal procedure and custom were followed in this case, there would be no need for controversy. If the mayor were absent for any other reason, there would be no question that I would serve." Then, in an unusually candid statement that brought race discrimination to the foreground, Whitney said, "Under the circumstances, I can't help but feel if I had been white, then I would have been assured of being named mayor."[18]

On May 9, a joint statement prepared by thirteen black organizations strongly supported F. E. Whitney for mayor. The organizations included the NAACP, Masonic and Eastern Star Chapters, fraternities and sororities, social clubs, and service organizations. In selecting the next mayor, it seemed to these black organizations that the city council could tangibly address the large issue of exclusion that Louis McHenry and the NAACP complained of several years before and in the intervening period. The joint statement praised Whitney's service as mayor pro tem and cast him as the logical choice for mayor in light of that service. The endorsement stated that Whitney was the only charter member of the modern council system, taking office at its inception in 1953. By virtue of seniority and experience, he was qualified to be mayor. Finally, the statement asserted, "his appointment is the only course the present council can take that will not reflect race prejudice. There is no other option."[19] That evening, the city council met and elected George Atkins as mayor by a vote of nine to two. Councilman Rutland had withdrawn in favor of Atkins. Whitney got the votes of Thomas Hammond, a white councilman, and Rozelle Leavell, the only other black council member. This outcome represented yet another crack, but a particularly jagged one, in Hopkinsville's public façade of racial harmony.

Profoundly disappointed and with a sense of betrayal, Whitney less than two days later submitted to Atkins and the news media "a terse one-sentence statement" resigning his position as mayor pro tem. Atkins was sworn in the next day. Whitney offered no other comment, except to say that he would fill out the remaining eighteen months of his term as city councilman. His distress was very widely shared among the black population of Hopkinsville. After all, he had more experience in city government than the other aspirants, and his relationships with all sectors of the city were positive. He was well educated, a veteran of World War II, and a successful businessman. Black opinion thus continued to come back to the joint endorsement indicating that only his race could prevent Whitney's assuming the post of mayor. In 2002, he explained the response of the black community to the disappointment, saying, "They accepted it because they realized that prejudice was still out there. I think the majority of them felt that we had come a long way since 1953—people on the police force, the fire department, higher jobs, street department, and things like that. They accepted it. But that's when I washed my hands of politics."[20]

Whitney believed that considerable pressure from the outside was exerted on council members to pass over him. He said that one council member, who had promised to support him, said that he had to withdraw that support because he had been threatened. The threat was not physical; instead, he was told that his business would suffer severely if he backed Whitney. Although he might have run in the November election, Whitney did not consider doing so without the support of a majority of the council. He felt that without that support, a mayor's effectiveness would be very limited. Moreover, he wanted to avoid rancor so as not to impede the progress that black people were making.

Nonetheless, because he did not push harder by protesting vigorously and enlisting black community backing, Whitney encountered criticism from younger black people who had come of age in the 1960s. They believed that he had gotten as far as he did because he was, in the eyes of white people, "safe." Well aware of this criticism, Whitney said:

> I think it was [more] for the good of the community than just an individ-
> ual. Some of the younger people didn't understand, because they didn't
> know prejudice like we knew it, like the older persons knew it. They had
> thought it had always been that way, that people had positions. They
> didn't know what a struggle it was to get where we were. Like there was
> the first young man on the fire department, and when he retired he was
> a major or captain. Also positions in the police department as detectives
> and so forth. Young kid seeing it, he thought it had always been there.[21]

But on the matter of race as the prominent factor in Whitney's unsuccessful bid for the mayor's office, there was no generational disagreement within the black community.

Predictably, the two white mayoral contenders in 1972 saw race in terms very different from Whitney's view. Rutland conceded that some people probably thought that it was not time for a black mayor, but he believes that race was secondary. Instead, political ambition and the interests of the chamber of commerce were the driving forces in the election. Atkins had led the organization, and it had influence on the city council, which Whitney also perceived, although in a sinister light.[22] The city continued to enjoy the cachet of a black mayor following in the wake of the 1960s civil rights successes, but the symbolic embrace of F. E. Whitney's achievements speaks falsely and almost cynically of race relations. Along with the photos of all of Hopkinsville's mayors, Whitney's portrait hangs in the city council chambers. His tenure in office is listed as May 3–May 10, 1972.

The unchallenged public representation of race relations as positive, although beginning to weaken in the 1960s, was reiterated by former mayor Atkins. He said that his successful run for the vacated position was "not a political thing, but a community thing." Hopkinsville, he suggested, wanted to be a progressive town, but progress had stalled under his predecessor. Infrastructure had been neglected, and the leadership was more interested in political ambition than in the city's needs. The chamber of commerce and others wanted to get the town moving, and for Atkins that had nothing to do with race. Both in the contest for mayor and even in the 1960s, he said, "It was never a matter of us and them, black and white. It was always a community here. There was no animosity either way. It was always a well-knit community. Despite some separation, there wasn't exclusion, but always inclusion and mixing."[23] The former mayor's characterization of race relations can only be called fanciful.

REMEMBERING MARTIN LUTHER KING JR.

An inclusive, tolerant, multicultural future of narrowed racial division depends on a more committed understanding of the powerful memories and experiences of exclusion marking the African American experience. This can only follow from a broad mutual recognition that grants persons and groups the privilege of telling their stories to an attentive audience on a public stage. Support of public commemoration is no small part of this recognition. Hopkinsville's black population has enjoyed few opportunities to effect a broadly meaningful public memory, as discussed in Chapter 5. The absence of monuments or other markers commemorating black life in the town only compounds feelings of estrangement when the symbols of the Confederacy are abundant.

In the decades following the assassination of Martin Luther King Jr., it has become almost routine for American towns and cities to commemorate the civil rights leader by renaming a city street or a park after him. At the federal level, Ronald Reagan in 1983 signed into law the creation of the Martin Luther King Jr. holiday. In 1996, the black community group Focus 2000 brought a proposal to the Hopkinsville City Council to rename Walnut Street "Martin Luther King Boulevard." Walnut Street is a well-traveled artery through a black neighborhood. It connects two major thoroughfares, East Ninth Street running through the center of downtown and Fort Campbell Boulevard, the traffic-laden strip and commercial hub of the city. Some black residents believed that King's importance justified renaming Ninth Street, since it is a major roadway where signage bearing the King name would be frequent. Recognizing the probable challenge any name change proposal would encounter, it was decided not to suggest Ninth Street for renaming, because its status as a downtown street would likely have provoked intense resistance.

Unlike Civil War remembrance, memories of the life of Martin Luther King Jr. were not distant. On the contrary, those memories took shape for council members as part of their own experience of living through the 1960s. Focus 2000 voiced the sentiments of the widest segment of black opinion that it was time for their town to acknowledge King and his martyrdom to civil rights. Changing the street name would be, in effect, an expression both of respect and of recognition of black Hopkinsville, what had not been forthcoming when F. E. Whitney aspired to the mayor's office. At the same time, the commemorative renaming would demonstrate the town's acknowledgment of King's inclusive, universal message, even if the symbolism of Walnut Street and its contiguous black neighborhoods would seem to "segregate" King's memory.

The Hopkinsville City Council accepted written petitions both pro and con regarding the proposed name change and invited residents to appear before the council to voice their opinions. Those opposing the name change said nothing of King or else expressed admiration for him. The canons of public discourse would admit no airing of overt racial animus, whatever the private feelings of individuals might have been. Those expressing high praise for King neutralized, at least rhetorically, race as a factor in their opposition. Other opponents of the name change explicitly disavowed any racial motives. Arguments against the proposal included an appeal to precedent—that the city had never renamed a street after a famous person, black or white, although many streets bore the names of people. A white business owner on Walnut Street objected to the proposal, arguing that he should not have to incur expenses for new signs and advertising. Another plea against the name change emphasized the nostalgia that people continue to feel for the original Hopkinsville High School, which was built on Walnut Street in the early twentieth century.

The name change proposal enjoyed undisputed support among black people. Those living along Walnut Street were unanimous in their endorsement. Advocates praised King as "one of the greatest humanitarians of the twentieth century, who stood for equality for all men." The name change would be "consistent with the progressive position taken by many cities around this country, regardless of racial composition." Hopkinsville, it was argued, could achieve racial unity only if it embraced respect, honor, and understanding, and this was an opportunity to do so. Reverend C. E. Timberlake, a black minister, said he would feel shame if he were a councilman or a mayor of a city refusing to honor Martin Luther King Jr. in this way. Conceding that he could understand how people can feel nostalgia for the past, he pointed out that the old high school had not stood on Walnut Street for many years and that whites had long ago abandoned the neighborhood. Supporters of the plan, attentive to the claims of emotional attachment to "Walnut Street," proposed a motion to add a subscript ("formerly Walnut Street") to the street signs that would bear the new name.[24] Ultimately, the council, with votes divided by race, defeated the proposal 9–2, while indicating that it would seek a "more appropriate" way to honor King by naming a park after him or perhaps erecting a statue. Neither idea ever materialized. Instead, the council named a portion of the bypass "Martin Luther King Jr. Way." A very small street sign, which easily escapes notice, appears where the pedestrian-free King bypass begins at the Fort Campbell Boulevard intersection. The symbolism was particularly unfortunate and only exacerbated hurt feelings. The new Martin Luther King Jr. Way, difficult to identify by signage, is literally on the margin of the town where black concerns have remained marginal.

Ironically, the new bypass designation had unintended consequences for another naming debate nine years later. How would the school board name the new elementary school built on Martin Luther King Jr. Way? Based on precedent—other schools in town named after the street or area where they are located—it seemed that the new school by default would be called the Martin Luther King Jr. Elementary School. Receiving that designation in 2005, the naming decision did not occur as a matter of course. On the contrary, it followed another rancorous struggle that ended only when the proponents of the King name prevailed by a single vote. School board member Darryl Lynch clearly implied that race was a factor in the debate, given the established relationship between school names and their locations. He argued that if the new school were located anywhere other than on Martin Luther King Jr. Way, there would have been no discussion. Opposition to the name could only spring from racial animus. He said simply, "If there's a problem naming it after the road it's on, then there's a problem in this community."[25] This statement recalled the Whitney imbroglio of more than thirty years before, when black community groups supporting Whitney said that his candidacy would only be a racial issue if the city council appointed someone else as mayor.

Whereas a racially defined memory in some communities resulted in street renaming within the restrictive space of a black community, the Hopkinsville City Council foreclosed even that outcome. The council warranted white people, long absent from the homes and sidewalks along Walnut Street, to reclaim the neighborhood, thus subverting the assertion of a black public memory and voice within a decidedly black urban space. Accordingly, many people interpreted the name change proposal as a racial issue, and the racial division of the vote only reinforced this viewpoint.

In examining the politics of street naming in honor of Martin Luther King, Jr., Derek Alderman posits the "scaling of memory" as a critical factor in the process. Scaling examines the multiple socio-geographic characteristics of the street to be named, including its size, the extent it connects black and white areas, or if it is wholly contained within a black neighborhood. Applied to Hopkinsville, renaming Ninth Street would have expressed a wide scale of memory symbolizing

King's significance for the entire community regardless of race. A narrower scale of memory, however, was reflected in the actual effort to rename Walnut Street, although the same universal meaning was attributed to King's message. The critical factor here was a political reading of the comparative intensity of opposition either proposal might elicit. In proposing to rename Walnut Street, Focus 2000 assumed that the scale of memory, racially restricted geographically to a black neighborhood, would not encounter the resistance that ultimately defeated the plan. Unlike the intra-racial political contest in the case study Alderman discusses, the Hopkinsville renaming effort reflected both a very high level of black racial solidarity and a high level of interracial division.[26]

RACE AND THE JUSTICE SYSTEM: THE BROWN CASE

Hopkinsville is the seventh largest city in Kentucky but has the third highest juvenile crime rate. It also ranks third among Kentucky cities in actual numbers of juveniles entering the justice system. Crime and gang activity out of proportion to its size are extremely sensitive issues in a city eager to maintain the factories and businesses in its industrial park and to promote further economic development and investment. Without irony, some black people in Hopkinsville observe that the Christian County Justice Center constitutes a major industry in the town. Amid the grim figures and personal stories of young black men caught up in the justice system, an intramural basketball team at the Walnut Street Center jokingly called itself "Charges Pending." Racial misunderstandings are possible in police work, as in other domains of social life, but there these misunderstandings are even more consequential. Of the seventy-three officers on the force of a city with the second highest percentage of black people in Kentucky, only five minority officers were in service in 2005.[27]

Lack of preparation for work that can pay a living wage, a school system with high dropout rates and test scores consistently near the bottom of Kentucky districts, truancy, and teenage pregnancy are some of the problems facing Hopkinsville's young people. That drugs are readily available only accelerates a downward spiral.

No case in recent memory did more to arouse the black community and many sympathetic whites than that of Demond Brown. In January 2002, Brown, then nineteen, sped through a red light on the bypass, colliding with a car occupied by a female driver and her daughter. The driver died at the scene and her daughter the next day. Brown was employed, had no criminal record, and was not impaired by alcohol or drugs. The prosecutor charged him with two counts of murder and two counts of wanton endangerment in the first degree because two teenage occupants in his car were injured.

After a trial lasting three days, the jury returned a guilty verdict on each charge, and Brown was sentenced to twenty years in the penitentiary. More than fifty articles referring to the case appeared in the local newspaper over the next six years. The appellate court upheld the decision. Brown's new attorney from the state Department of Public Advocacy appealed to the Supreme Court of Kentucky, which also upheld the verdict. One dissenting justice emphasized that "evidence in this case supports a criminal charge deserving of penitentiary time, but it is simply not sufficient to establish conduct manifesting an 'extreme indifference to the value of human life,' the standard for 20 years to life." He supported reversal of the conviction for lack of evidence of "wanton murder" and recommended a new trial for second-degree manslaughter and reckless homicide, charges calling for a much shorter sentence.[28] Local opinion among those protesting the sentence agreed in large measure with the dissenting Supreme Court justice. Brown was negligent and criminally so in causing two deaths, but the charge of murder was excessive.

Shortly after the verdict, the *Kentucky New Era* published a restrained editorial criticizing the prosecution. It also implicitly questioned the competence of the defense. Murder, it argued, was not an appropriate charge. Rather, a lesser indictment that did not entail premeditation or wantonness, such as manslaughter, would have fit the circumstances more closely. The newspaper rejected race "as a prominent factor in the deliberations," admitting by this particular wording, that race played some role. With more confidence, the editorial observed that "the reality of an all-white jury trying a black defendant who killed two white women will raise subsequent judicial flags," and indeed the racial composition of the jury loomed large before the Supreme Court and in protests within Hopkinsville. Moreover, the newspaper pointed out not only that an all-white jury was assembled without challenge, but also that one member belonged to the same church as the crash victims. The failure to observe "the tenets of basic human decency" transformed a judicial proceeding into "a divisive community issue."[29]

Community protests drawing hundreds of people continued after Brown went to prison. The largest demonstrations probably exceeded in numbers and passion any protests in Hopkinsville during the 1960s. A white woman observed that she could not recall any other instance of white people and black people in joint protest against an injustice toward a black person. John Banks, president of the local NAACP, as well as NAACP activists from Louisville, raised numerous objections to the fairness of the trial, emphasizing particularly the racial composition of the jury. Protesting students from Kentucky State University, a historically black institution in Frankfort, also rallied in Hopkinsville.[30] Black ministers urged parishioners to attend the demonstrations, and some white ministers with their congregants and other citizens of Hopkinsville joined the protests. Lee Huckleberry, a white pastor, said, "There is no question that some of this had to do with prejudice. . . . I saw the racial element from the beginning."[31] Feelings shading into outrage were not unusual, and a black couple was so infuriated by what they regarded as a miscarriage of justice that they pledged their house to cover a $20,000 appeal bond while Brown awaited the Supreme Court's decision.[32] None argued that Brown was innocent of causing the tragedy, but critics argued that his culpability did not constitute murder as defined by Kentucky law.

Walter Shamble, an unsuccessful independent candidate for mayor in 2006, organized a number of protests and continues to criticize what he identifies as racism in the justice system. He asserted that the court and prosecutor had turned a vehicular accident into a homicide, a charge vindicated by Governor Fletcher's general counsel, who was quoted as saying that Brown "should not have been sent to prison for what was essentially a horrible accident."[33] The prosecutor left office after an electoral defeat in the democratic primary in 2006. His electoral opponent reported just before her victory in the primary that many people were supporting her because of the handling of the Brown case.[34] What Shamble and other protesters considered a racially biased prosecution had clearly become a local embarrassment that did not remain local. After serving two and a half years in prison, Brown was released in December 2007, following Governor Fletcher's commutation of his sentence.

CENTRAL CITY REDEVELOPMENT

In 2005, Hopkinsville embarked on a program to revitalize neighborhoods contiguous to the central core of the city. This program came about only after a minority of the city council demanded it as a condition of their supporting an initial project focused on outlying areas and endorsed by the chamber of commerce and real estate developers. Hopkinsville committed two and a half million dollars to the inner city for a five-year period. The program aims to ameliorate the physical condition of the neighborhoods, marked particularly by unkempt properties and unsightly streets and yards, while promoting home ownership or at least affordable, well-maintained rentals.

The revitalization plan springs from a process of neglect long familiar to observers of many American towns and cities. Hopkinsville has witnessed a steady abandonment of the central city. A once flourishing downtown now struggles to staunch further disinvestment of its commercial spaces while trying to tempt new businesses to rent one or another of the empty buildings or storerooms. Neighborhoods in close proximity to downtown are in an equally parlous state. Populated mostly by African Americans, the neighborhoods have a high proportion of properties that are not owner-occupied and "are suffering from extensive blight, deterioration, and disinvestment."[35] Neighborhood decline went unchecked by local government's failure to enforce building codes or to strengthen those that are insufficient. Only absentee landlords benefited. Recreational facilities, originally constructed when the neighborhoods were white, deteriorated after white flight and the new construction of facilities in outlying areas. While inner city neglect was for many years the order of the day, binding together the segregation of race and poverty, commercial and residential growth of the city southward along the Fort Campbell Boulevard corridor proceeded. The process of outer development at the expense of the inner city would have continued unabated without planned intervention.

According to the 2000 census, Hopkinsville is second only to Louisville as the most segregated city in Kentucky, and this alone is cause for concern. A high degree of residential segregation along coincident lines of race and class consigns neighborhoods to the margins of economic growth and opportunity. In Hopkinsville, a history of "redlining," or the conscious delineation of certain urban neighborhoods, defined by race, for discriminatory treatment by banks, insurance companies, or real estate interests is another factor in central city decline. Discrimination usually entailed a denial of service or, in the case of real estate brokers, the targeting of all white neighborhoods for conversion into black zones, where rental units quickly increase and city services diminish. The conversion would also occur through racial scare tactics, particularly by engineering the sale of a home in an all-white neighborhood to a black family, thereby inducing panic among neighbors about declining property values. Sale of other homes and consequent "white flight" would ensue. A case in point for Hopkinsville is the East Eighteenth Street neighborhood, all white in 1971 and by 2000 the most segregated in the city.[36] Difficulty in obtaining credit continues for some of the same reasons identified by Louis McHenry forty-five years ago. Another consequence of redlining is the isolation of black-owned businesses in all black neighborhoods.

Other examples in Hopkinsville that illustrate the structural genesis of neighborhood decline could be easily multiplied. But the important point is that the processes of urban deterioration do not happen according to impersonal, inexorable laws. They occur through collaborative and mutually reinforcing decisions to direct public and private resources away from the central core. Often rationalized as "development," "progress," or "growth," this process leaves behind social and economic casualties in the central city that are usually ignored or justified as a tolerable cost for an essential benefit. Despite the obvious structural foundations of central city decline, some policymakers and urban theorists continue to locate responsibility for neighborhood problems exclusively in the behavioral patterns and values of those living there. That explanation is part of the newly reincarnated "culture of poverty" argument noted in Chapter 3.[37]

Hopkinsville's program of revitalization operates through the Inner City Advisory Committee, appointed by the mayor and city council in June 2005. Acting as an intermediary between citizens of the affected neighborhoods and the city administration, the committee is made up of individuals from the business and commercial sector, local government, and service organizations. But the most important part of the program is the neighborhood network, each composed of a group of residents in one of the targeted areas. In this vein, Jessie Quarles, director of the Christian County Habitat for Humanity and member of the original Inner City Advisory Committee, bluntly told the city council that most of the people in the neighborhoods earmarked for revitalization had little faith in city government.[38] The question of trust was not cast in racial terms. Still, Quarles's observations and those of other proponents of a dedicated effort to ameliorate inner city conditions had as their unmistakable subtext the racial composition both of the inner city and the public and private institutions implementing the revitalization. A recent member of the advisory board emphasized, in a discussion of obstacles facing the program, a high level of alienation in black Hopkinsville, born not only of historical memory but compounded by less education and higher unemployment than in the general population.[39]

The matter of trust was apparent in some of the earliest meetings in August 2005, bringing together neighborhood residents, city officials, and advisory committee members. Several residents were angry about a planned survey to determine community priorities for neighborhood improvement. They felt that city neglect had gotten the neighborhoods to their present state. Jessie Quarles, identifying closely with people in the neighborhoods, said to city officials, "You need to prove to people that you are sincere. 'Sincere' means to come and do the stuff that's obvious—put up street lights, repair the sidewalks, clean up all that trash, tear down those dilapidated houses that drug addicts are selling drugs out of and shooting up in and where women are doing sex to get ten dollars for their next rock of crack. Once you do the obvious, then come to me with a survey asking what we want."[40]

Residents also expressed considerable doubt about the responsiveness of government to their concerns. People on the west side, for example, recalled strong local opposition years before to the building of the county jail in the midst of their neighborhood. Likewise, the residents complained that construction of the massive nearby justice center and parking lot also proceeded independently of neighborhood sentiment. Now asked for their active participation in decisions ostensibly aimed at arresting neighborhood deterioration, it was predictable that skepticism would be pervasive.

More recently, a proposal to direct $100,000 earmarked for the revitalization program toward other purposes aroused anger. The proposed fund diversion reinforced doubts within the affected inner city communities about the good faith of the mayor's office and the city council. The plan was subsequently rescinded, although it chipped away at the accord that was building between the neighborhoods and city government. Even more important than the money set aside for neighborhood revitalization, trust remains the most important asset in this process. It is also the most fragile.

THE MULTICULTURAL IDEAL: DIFFERENCE, COMMON CULTURE, AND THE LIMITATIONS OF CLASS

In its most benign and hopeful expression, the multiculture esteems diversity as a fundamental value. It rejects the pre-1960s restrictions on political and civic participation owing to one's origins, unless a person could make himself over culturally to give the illusion of Anglo descent or at least conformity to what were perceived as Anglo values. Immigrants and their children felt pressure to set aside the culture and language of their nativity if they aspired to something beyond economic marginality and social isolation among co-ethnics. Immigrants did not want to be "hyphenated Americans," because that meant that they were hanging on to old world ways; it also meant that their cultural and political commitments to the United States were suspect. Civic nationalism demanded cultural and linguistic assimilation as a precondition for social assimilation or participation in American institutions. Black people, however, could not exercise these choices. Skin color defined the narrow limits of opportunity regardless of their abilities; it counted for little that black people had internalized the values and beliefs of the only country they had ever known. For a century following the Civil War, color effectively prevented social assimilation and severely limited the economic mobility that acceptance could make possible. It was not without some bitterness that black people observed European immigrants ascending economically, "becoming white," while African Americans remained in place.

Significant cultural changes in the United States since the 1960s have effected a new relationship between racial or ethnic identity, on the one hand, and American citizenship, on the other. That relationship does not entail in law or, to a considerable extent in practice, the zero-sum choice it once did. That is, people may now embrace both the provincialism of their own racial or ethnic origins and the universalism of a democratic civil society. The hyphenation of new Americans or the re-hyphenation of those whose forbears were immigrants is now widely accepted. At the same time, acculturative change—contact and mutual influences across porous ethnic and racial boundaries—is unremarkable. The permeability of those social boundaries is most convincingly indexed by the increasing acceptance of marriages across the lines of race and ethnicity; that acceptance has evolved in tandem with the multicultural envisioning of American society.

In this sense, Henry Louis Gates, Jr., exemplifies the modern multicultural ideal of both/and rather than either/or in his memoir, *Colored People*. He describes the shared significance of being "colored," his preferred term. He not only finds value in the achievements of notable colored people but also in the simple acknowledgment of the common identity that joins him to black strangers casually encountered. Likewise, positive racial meanings as part of self-conception are also nurtured through family, friends, and the memory of the segregated community of his childhood. Gates's description resonates with bell hooks's recall of Crispus Attucks High School and her natal community, or Jessie Quarles's happy reflection on being taught the way she was raised, or Robert Glass's telling of the great care he took as a child in 1940s Hopkinsville in properly greeting the ladies in his neighborhood, lest they complain to his mother. It is also the world of the McCray and Bingham reunions and the reflections on forbears whose lives yield their meaning through the experience of being black.

Yet Gates goes on to qualify his affections for the primary community of color because, as warmly encompassing and meaningful as race is, the human self is constituted of other qualities and identifications: "Even so, I rebel at the notion that I can't be part of other groups, that I can't construct identities through elective affinity, that race must be the most important thing about me. . . . So I'm divided. I want to be black, to know black, to luxuriate in whatever I might be calling blackness at any particular time—but to do so in order to come out the other side, to experience a humanity that is neither colorless nor reducible to color. Bach *and* James Brown. Sushi *and* fried catfish."[41]

We live at a time when Gates and many other Americans of African descent can realistically reach for the resolution of the paradox of "twoness," of race and nationality, so elusive when Du Bois first posed the problem more than a century ago in writing of "two unreconciled strivings, two warring ideals." The United States has thus reached a point where personhood and identity can without apology be constituted of multiple and unrestricted influences, where diversity potentially can bring more and different kinds of people into contact and social exchange within a continually developing common culture. This is surely a cultural change of enormous significance, particularly in regard to racial groups, but to immigrant groups as well. Continuing social exchange and mutual influence are as inevitable as the persistent and often mean-spirited but doomed rearguard actions against them. Some of these countervailing efforts were examined in Chapter 5.

Desegregation in Hopkinsville and elsewhere, it must be said, created conditions of contact unthinkable before the 1960s. The steady interactions of black and white children are, if not certain, at least possible. To be sure, even in integrated settings, self-segregation remains a tempting escape into comfort zones and away from the difficulties of encountering people different from oneself. Nonetheless, sustained contact diminishes the racial and ethnic estrangement that feeds on preformed, negative attitudes and can weaken the hold of the racial certainties of prior generations, as social scientists hypothesized decades ago.[42] Without social contact, individuals different from oneself are easily submerged in the aggregate, typified by old and persistent stereotypes. A recent study of racial contacts after the 1954 Supreme Court decision concludes that increasing tolerance of white people towards blacks and other minorities is linked to school integration.[43]

Many white people after the court decision found various ways, from private schools to suburban migration, to avoid social contact. And it continues. For their part, black people did not see integration as an unmixed blessing, as various Hopkinsville voices explain. Yet opportunities in education and employment that propelled black economic mobility are undeniable.[44] The historic problems of estrangement between blacks and whites have not thereby been "solved;" too many examples of continuing racial animus and polarity come to mind. American society is hardly "post-racial," if that means that color no longer matters in national life. It should matter in the way Gates celebrates blackness, not as a limitation on realizing human possibilities. Still, amid the continuing problems of race in America, it is certain that since the 1960s, increasing contacts among people, particularly the young, set in motion changes leading to greater tolerance on matters of race than at any prior period of history. Otherwise, the first president who is African American could not have been elected.

Cultural shifts, including changes of values and attitudes about race in America, laid the foundation of the multiculture. But they are insufficient. It is essential to recognize a fundamental economic component. One may thus ask of Gates: how does someone accustomed to James Brown and fried catfish encounter Bach and sushi in the first place? In other words, are opportunities to cross the boundaries of the primary community equally available to everyone, or do class factors inhibit the possibility of experiencing and internalizing other ways of being and doing?

An extraordinary expansion of the black middle class has occurred over the last few decades. Black Americans have secured positions in the widest range of American businesses and corporations. At the same time, widespread black poverty continues among people segregated and isolated from whites and from the black middle class. Summarized by the Urban League in its annual report of 2009, two stories define contemporary black America, "accomplishment, prosperity, and increased political power," on the one hand, and, on the other, a black high school graduation rate of less than 50 percent, disproportionate black male incarceration, and an unemployment rate twice that of whites.[45] The Urban League's portrayal vindicates in part William Julius Wilson's argument that "class has become more important than race in determining black access to privilege and power."[46] Yet

Wilson's findings beg the question of why poverty, low income, and underclass standing disproportionately encompass the black population in the early twenty-first century, more than a generation after he set forth his thesis.

The black middle class in well-paid jobs or careers enters a white majority world where, in David Hollinger's words, they can "*test* the social and cultural barriers that have traditionally disadvantaged them."[47] Many have done so successfully. Entering the middle class with others of diverse racial and ethnic backgrounds can establish communities of common interest and ultimately shared memory without sacrificing either participation in one's community of cultural origin or its own vernacular history. People can be bicultural as well as bilingual. On the other hand, social isolation continues to renew and nurture historic memories of racial discrimination and exclusion, further polarizing race relations at a time when new and positive racial accords continue to evolve. The isolation of poverty constrains or blocks altogether social exchange and cultural flows across increasingly porous ethnic and racial boundaries.

Class immobility of the poor is thus a decisive factor inhibiting the realization of a multicultural society. Reaching the middle class is now more difficult than ever for persons of any background, if they lack inherited privilege. Poor whites and poor blacks remain casualties of fundamental changes in the labor market. A restructured American economy has severely reduced factory jobs and led to a split service sector. A sharp decline in manufacturing has been accompanied by a corresponding increase in jobs in the low end of the service economy—poorly paid, unskilled, insecure, high turnover, non-unionized labor. The jobs include hotel and restaurant work, agricultural employment, home health care, and the like. The other end of the service economy belongs to professionals, including doctors, engineers, software designers, specialists in "knowledge and information," and others who have had access to an advanced education. An overall decline in the quality of public education is another factor reducing class mobility. In the heyday of American manufacturing and union membership, a high school diploma could propel a graduate into long-term, well-paid factory employment, but that era has become a distant memory. To all of these factors contributing to middle class shrinkage and even downward mobility, we can add the growing concentration of wealth—not a matter of chance but of legislative design through changes in laws governing taxes, banking, and investment. Wealth can buy a quality private secondary education or can enable a family to settle in an area known for excellent public schools producing graduates who go on to good colleges and universities. Unprecedented concentrations of wealth and inherited privilege now imperil millions of native-born whites, African Americans, and immigrants. Poverty has been thoroughly democratized.

For Americans of African descent who are actors in the second story described by the Urban League, the barriers to middle class attainment are reinforced by the "persistence of the color line."[48] Where residential segregation and unemployment or underemployment are pervasive, the kinds of cross-racial and cross-ethnic contacts that can expand the self to discover new cultural tastes and even ways of looking at the world remain minimal. Exclusion by class restricts human possibilities as much as exclusion by race, and when they coincide, the devastation can be particularly bleak. The result in Hopkinsville and elsewhere can only be a persistent economic bifurcation of black America and the continuing renewal of historic memories insulated from the shifting meanings of race.

The rolling plains along the Newstead Road west of Hopkinsville even now demand little of the observer trying to imagine the physical world inhabited by Ellen McGaughey Wallace and others of the slave owning and enslaved populations of 1860. Not pristine of course, the barrens, as the plains were originally called, still remain relatively undeveloped. Although most of the antebellum country homes and slave quarters are gone, one still sees the small dwellings without plumbing and electricity that not long ago provided shelter for generations of sharecroppers, "slaves by another name," whose enslaved ancestors worked this same land to produce the tobacco and agricultural fortunes of their masters. The white McGaugheys, Wallaces, Torians, Wests, Nances, McCraes, Whitlocks, McReynolds, and other slave-era residents of the Newstead Road and vicinity have left their historic imprint in a variety of public and private documents, as well as in material artifacts, such as cemetery headstones. Not so the anonymous slaves. Nonetheless, culture and genes moved between these proximate yet distant populations.

Since the end of the Civil War, these surnames have also belonged to black people, including slave descendants still living in the area. DNA analysis holds the key to determining with certainty whether a particular individual is descended not only from slaves but also from slaveholders. The relationship between Thomas Jefferson and Sally Hemings is now well known, not because the story is exceptional but because it centers on an American president.

The cultural and biological connections between distinct populations are not a recent development but rather thoroughly embedded in the history of American slavery. It is that recognition of a shared past in black and white that motivates the efforts of two women, one the descendant of slave owners and the other the descendant of slaves of those same masters. Brenda Summers, a former librarian in Stewart County, Tennessee, and Thelma Nance Moore, retired from the Christian County school system, visit two Nance cemeteries in search of their Nance ancestry. They are familiar with the cemetery record of one Nance burial ground, slave schedules, and county censuses. Brenda, particularly, is trying to collate these records with headstone inscriptions and family documents in her possession. Thelma has no relevant personal documents, nor even family lore, since her paternal grandfather was reluctant to speak of Nance family history of the postbellum generations.

Among the largest slave owners living in the area, Joel Nance, friend of Ellen McGaughey Wallace, was Brenda's lineal forbear five generations removed. He was, in other words, her great-great-great-grandfather. She and Thelma together discovered his headstone in the second, previously undocumented Nance cemetery. While Thelma is almost certainly descended from one of his slaves, the possibility must be admitted that he may also be Thelma's lineal ancestor. She and Brenda acknowledge that they are probably distant cousins. As to the black Nances who labored as slaves, then as freedmen, their burial ground remains unknown. Thelma and Brenda continue to look for it, certain that black Nances are buried in the vicinity of the white Nance cemeteries.

More than acknowledging their probable kinship across the line of race, the two women are looking at divided lives paradoxically fashioned by shared ancestry. Their simple but still uncommon gesture is telling, for together they are linking highly segmented historic memories. These excavations of the past in turn can define a present and future neither bereft of color nor obsessed by it.

NOTES

INTRODUCTION

1. James G. Gimpel, *Separate Destinations: Migration, Immigration, and the Politics of Places* (Ann Arbor: Univ. of Michigan Press, 1999), 193, 197–99.

2. A plaque in Stewart County, Tennessee at the remnants of the Great Western Furnace attributes the closure of the forge to the supposed slave uprising of 1856.

3. Ira Berlin, *Slaves Without Masters: The Free Negro in the Antebellum South* (New York: Pantheon Books, 1974).

4. John Hope Franklin, "Slavery and the Martial South," in Franklin, ed., *Race and History: Selected Essays, 1938–1988* (Baton Rouge: Louisiana State Univ. Press, 1989), 96.

5. Albert J. Raboteau, *Slave Religion: The "Invisible Institution" in the Antebellum South* (New York: Oxford Univ. Press, 1978), ix.

6. Morrison's remarks originally appeared in *The World* in 1989. Website of the Toni Morrison Society, http://www.tonimorrisonsociety.org/bench.html.

1. COUNTY AND TOWN: RACE AND A USABLE PAST

1. Tom Capehart, *Trends in Tobacco Farming* (Washington, D.C.: United States Department of Agriculture, 2004), 3.

2. James T. Killebrew provides a finer-grained view of the demography of slavery in his tabulation of the slave population in the southern part of the county lying west of Hopkinsville. Using the slave schedule of 1860, he counted the number of slaves held by friends and neighbors living in the vicinity of Ellen McGaughey Wallace and Albert Wallace. Killebrew listed twenty-seven slave-owners (including three instances of shared ownership by siblings or spouses) holding a total of 663 slaves, yielding a ratio of 24.5 slaves per owner, well above the high county average. *Journal by Ellen Kenton McGaughey Wallace, 1849–1865*, transcribed and edited by

James T. Killebrew, unpublished manuscript, 46 (hereafter cited as Wallace, *Journal*). The actual journal and Killebrew's meticulous transcription and annotation are held at the Kentucky Historical Society in Frankfort, Kentucky. His original transcription appeared in 1988. He appended further annotations in 1991. Discussion of the Wallace journal is taken up in Chapter 2.

3. Calculations based on the data in the 2004 Historical Census Browser, accessed November 9, 2011, University of Virginia, Geospatial and Statistical Data Center, http://fisher.lib.virginia.edu/collections/stats/histcensus/php/county.php.

4. *Statistical View of the United States* (Washington: A. O. P. Nicholson, Public Printer, 1854), 240:

5. W. F. Axton, *Tobacco and Kentucky* (Lexington: The Univ. Press of Kentucky, 1975), 54–55.

6. Carl Ortwin Sauer, *Geography of the Pennyroyal* (Frankfort: The Kentucky Geological Survey, 1927), 241.

7. The "New South," an old designation dating from the nineteenth century, refers to postbellum transformations of the southern economy, including the end of slavery and plantation agriculture and the beginning of industrialization. But in racial terms, the New South for a century was very much like the Old South. Accordingly, the term sometimes refers to changes across the South in the wake of the civil rights movement.

8. Wynn Radford, e-mail message to author, January 2, 2008.

9. Editorial, *Kentucky New Era,* September 6, 1958, 4.

10. U.S. Census Bureau Website, State and County Quick Facts, http://quickfacts.census.gov/qfd/states/21/2137918.html.

11. The McCray family, for example, has held biennial reunions in a variety of places, but in 2006 decided to acknowledge their connection to the "home place" by trying to hold the reunion in Hopkinsville in alternate years.

12. W. Fitzhugh Brundage, *The Southern Past: A Clash of Race and Memory* (Cambridge, Mass.: Harvard Univ. Press, 2005), 136–37.

13. George C. Wright notes a similar obstacle to research in Louisville, where he found only a small number of copies of two black newspapers published between 1890 and 1930, although twelve black newspapers were published during that period. See his article, "Oral History and the Search for the Black Past in Kentucky," *The Oral History Review* 10 (1982): 87.

14. Ibid., 75, 77, 85.

15. E. Merton Coulter, *The South During Reconstruction, 1865–1877* (Baton Rouge: Louisiana State Univ. Press, 1947), 47, 141.

16. E. Merton Coulter, *The Civil War and Readjustment in Kentucky* (Chapel Hill: Univ. of North Carolina Press, 1926), 412. Since the 1960s, the entire history of Reconstruction has undergone a sharp revision, unburdened by the biases of racism and southern partisanship, which had been challenged only by a small number of historians in the early twentieth century. See Eric Foner, *Reconstruction: America's Unfinished Revolution, 1863–1877* (New York: HarperCollins, 1988), and Foner, *Freedom's Lawmakers: A Directory of Black Officeholders during Reconstruction* (Baton Rouge: Louisiana State Univ. Press, 1996). In the latter work, Foner points out that Coulter remained wedded to his original biases, for in 1968 he continued to castigate black officials in Reconstruction governments, attributing whatever good qualities they possessed to their white ancestry (page xii).

17. J. Winston Coleman, Jr., *Slavery Times in Kentucky* (Chapel Hill: Univ. of North Carolina Press, 1940), 249. For a review of various writers supporting this interpretation, see Marion B. Lucas, *A History of Blacks in Kentucky,* vol. 1, *From Slavery to Segregation, 1760–1891* (Frankfort: The Kentucky Historical Society, 1992), 42–43.

18. In 2005, Bill Cunningham, a state supreme court justice, wrote of Kentucky slavery in the benign terms that had expired among historians decades ago. He regards slaves in purely passive terms, describing bondsmen as "a docile mass of involuntary servitude." In accord with Coleman, Cunningham describes slavery in western Kentucky as "a kinder, gentler" variety. Going further, Cunningham expresses a romantic, nostalgic longing for an antebellum social order antithetical to the "cankerous products of modernism," including the "idolatry of tolerance." Resonating with current neo-Confederate views, Cunningham's wistfulness leads to praise for the "redemptive virtues of secession" and the "hidden virtues of the lost cause." See, Bill Cunningham, *A Distant Light: Kentucky's Journey Toward Racial Justice* (Kuttawa, Ky.: McClanahan Publishing House, 2005), 9, 16, 20, 319.

19. Wendell Berry, *The Hidden Wound* (New York: North Point Press, 1989), 7.

20. Ulrich B. Phillips, *American Negro Slavery* (Baton Rouge: Louisiana State Univ. Press, 1918). Phillips regarded the plantation as an agent of civilization for slaves in the same manner as a settlement house in a city provides "models of speech and conduct." See Ulrich B. Phillips, *Life and Labor in the Old South* (Boston: Little, Brown, and Co., 1929), 199.

21. Allan Nevins and Henry Steele Commager, *A Short History of the United States* (New York: Modern Library, 1945), 253–54.

22. Melville J. Herskovits, *The Myth of the Negro Past* (New York: Harper and Brothers, 1941); and W. E. B. Du Bois, *Black Folk, Then and Now* (New York: Henry Holt, 1939).

23. Du Bois, *Black Folk,* vii.

24. W. E. B. Du Bois, *Black Reconstruction in America* (1935; repr., Cleveland: World Publishing Co., 1964), n.p.

25. David Blight, *Race and Reunion: The Civil War in American Memory* (Cambridge, Mass.: The Belknap Press of Harvard Univ. Press, 2001), 313.

26. Marsha Darling, "In the Realm of Responsibility: A Conversation with Toni Morrison," in *Conversations with Toni Morrison,* ed. Danille Taylor-Guthrie (Jackson: Univ. Press of Mississippi, 1994), 247.

27. Ammie Weaver, conversation with author, Hopkinsville, July 31, 2007.

28. Edward Ball, *Slaves in the Family* (New York: Ballantine Books, 1998), 81.

29. David W. Blight, ed., *Narrative of the Life of Frederick Douglass, an American Slave, Written by Himself* (Boston, Bedford Books, 1993).

30. Marion Wilson Starling, *The Slave Narrative: Its Place in American History* (Boston: G. K. Hall and Co., 1981).

31. Phillips, *Life and Labor in the Old South*, 219; Starling, *The Slave Narrative*, 221.

32. August Meier and Elliott Rudwick, *Black History and the Historical Profession, 1915–1980* (Urbana: Univ. of Illinois Press, 1986), xii.

33. Brundage, *The Southern Past*, 145–50.

34. John B. Cade, "Out of the Mouths of Ex-Slaves," *The Journal of Negro History* 20 (July 1935): 294, 337.

35. George P. Rawick, ed., *The American Slave: A Composite Autobiography,* vol. 1. *From Sundown to Sunup: The Making of the Black Community* (Westport: Greenwood Publishing Co., 1972), xiv. Prior to the slave narrative project of the WPA, researchers at Fisk University interviewed former slaves and produced two sets of narratives, *Unwritten History of Slavery* and *God Struck Me Dead*. Rawick included these collections as volumes 18 and 19, respectively, in *The American Slave* series.

36. Donna J. Spindel, "Assessing Memory: Twentieth Century Narratives Reconsidered," *Journal of Interdisciplinary History* 27 (Autumn 1996): 249. The fundamental revision of historical understanding of slavery and indeed the experience of black people written in the active voice, so to speak, is well known and has been effectively summarized by numerous scholars. See, for example, Robert L. Harris, Jr., "Coming of Age: The Transformation of Afro-American Historiography," *Journal of Negro History* 67 (Summer 1982): 107–21, and Peter Novick, *That Noble Dream: The "Objectivity Question" and the American Historical Profession* (New York: Cambridge Univ. Press, 1988), 469–91. Novick's review is particularly insightful in linking the currents of civil rights activity and revisionist scholarship, both forcing recognition of many previously ignored features of black life. While the trends in scholarship usually have little direct bearing on the way ordinary people think about their

world, scholarship and popular conceptions may spring from common roots. Black activism in the civil rights era emphasized a self-determined assertiveness for African Americans, which resonated with new ways of writing black history.

37. Paul Escott, *Slavery Remembered: A Record of Twentieth Century Slave Narratives* (Chapel Hill: Univ. of North Carolina Press, 1979), 188–91.

38. Escott, *Slavery Remembered,* 7–9.

39. F. Kevin Simon, ed. *The WPA Guide to Kentucky*, rev. ed. (Lexington: Univ. Press of Kentucky, 1996), xxiii. Black educators were acutely conscious of the exclusion of black people from state history textbooks. Shortly after the original 1939 publication of the WPA Guide, the *Louisville Defender,* a black newspaper, published a weekly column written by Alice A. Dunnigan entitled "The Achievements of the Kentucky Negro."

40. Of her many books, bell hooks's *Bone Black* (New York: Henry Holt, 1996) expressively portrays the author's experience as a young black woman coming of age in the town on the cusp of desegregation.

41. Ted Poston achieved national prominence in an earlier generation as the first black journalist to write for a mainline white-owned newspaper, the *New York Post,* beginning in the 1930s. See Kathleen A. Hauke, *Ted Poston, Pioneer American Journalist* (Athens: Univ. of Georgia Press, 1998); Kathleen A. Hauke, ed. *The Dark Side of Hopkinsville, Stories by Ted Poston* (Athens: Univ. of Georgia Press, 1991); Kathleen A. Hauke, ed. *Ted Poston: A First Draft of History* (Athens: Univ. Georgia Press, 2000).

42. Harris, "Coming of Age," 115, 118.

43. *Christian County, Its Advantages and Inducements to Immigration*, Publication of Kentucky Geological Survey and Bureau of Immigration (Frankfort: Yeoman Office, S.I.M. Major, 1881).

44. *Hopkinsville Kentuckian,* August 9, 1889, 4.

45. Toni Morrison, "On the Backs of Blacks," in *Arguing Immigration: Are New Immigrants a Wealth of Diversity Or a Crushing Burden?* ed. Nicholas Mills (New York: Touchstone, 1994), 98.

46. W. E. B. Du Bois, *Black Reconstruction in America, 1860–1880* (Cleveland: The World Publishing Co., 1968), 700–701. In more recent years, historian David R. Roediger, in *The Wages of Whiteness: Race and the Making of the American Working Class* (London: Verso, 1991), has stimulated interest in "whiteness studies." On the process of "whitening," see Matthew Fry Jacobson, *Whiteness of a Different Color* (Cambridge: Harvard Univ. Press, 1998) and Karen Brodkin, *How Jews Became White Folks and What that Says about Race in America.* (New Brunswick: Rutgers Univ. Press, 1998).

47. *Kentucky New Era,* January 29, 1934, 2.

48. *Kentucky New Era,* April 21, 1934, 2.

49. *Kentucky New Era,* April 28, 1934, 2.

50. D. D. Cayce, "The Second Promised Land," April 1999. "Jews in Hopkinsville" Folder, Family Files, Drawer I–K, Hopkinsville–Christian County Public Library.

51. *Daily Kentucky New Era,* September 28, 1906, 1.

52. Dorothy Klein, widow of Mose Klein, whose father had constructed the East Sixth Street building, died in 2005 at the age of 100. She lived in a large home on South Main Street in the historic district. Growing up in Hopkinsville, she described the sting of difference and alienation amid her Christian schoolmates in primary and secondary school. Unable to go away to college, she had to settle for two years at the local Bethel Baptist College for Women, where she also experienced isolation based on religion. Asked if those unhappy experiences of marginality made the Jewish relationship to black people any different from the general white-black relationship, she said simply, "I don't think so." Telephone conversation with author, July 8, 2002.

53. *Hopkinsville Kentuckian,* May 1, 1900, 4.

54. John Higham, *Send These to Me* (Baltimore: The Johns Hopkins Univ. Press, 1975), 3.

55. Gary Gerstle, *American Crucible* (Princeton: Princeton Univ. Press, 2001), 3–4.

56. Opposition to the water park among the citizenry, expressed in open city council meetings, remained civil but often impassioned. Objections centered on the estimated two million dollar cost, which opponents felt could be better spent on more immediate public needs, such as flood control. Other objections were racially motivated and privately expressed. Two city council members, white women particularly sensitive to issues of racial justice, reported phone calls from some recalcitrant constituents predicting the rapid deterioration of the park at the hands of black people.

57. John Shelton Reed, *The Enduring South: Subcultural Persistence in Mass Society* (Chapel Hill: Univ. of North Carolina Press, 1972), 57.

58. Robert Martin, Chief Financial Officer, City of Hopkinsville, telephone conversation with author, January 14, 2011.

59. Elward J. Blum, *Reforging the White Republic: Race, Religion, and American Nationalism, 1865–1898* (Baton Rouge: Louisiana State Univ. Press, 2005), 9.

60. Ron Buck, Hopkinsville, conversation with author, November 28, 2005.

61. "Being Hindu In The American 'Bible Belt,'" Hindu Press International, http://www.hinduismtoday.com/blogs-news/hindu-press-international/being-hindu-in-the-american-bible-belt/4623.html.

62. Lawrence W. Levine, *Black Culture and Black Consciousness* (New York: Oxford Univ. Press, 1977), 61–62. See also Edward Ball, *Slaves in the Family* (New York: Ballantine Books, 1998), 103.

63. Charlene Hampton Holloway, *Whitlock's Compositions* (Louisville: Char and Chet's, 2004).

64. *Kentucky New Era,* June 16, 2007, 1.

65. Fawn Brodie, *Thomas Jefferson, An Intimate History* (New York: Norton, 1974), 30.

66. Annette Gordon-Reed, *Thomas Jefferson and Sally Hemings: An American Controversy* (Charlottesville: Univ. of Virginia Press, 1997), 211. Gordon-Reed provides a thorough lawyerly examination of the evidence, pro and con, concluding, prior to the DNA investigation, that Jefferson fathered Hemings's children.

67. Alexander O. Boulton, "The Monticello Mystery—Case Continued," *The William and Mary Quarterly,* 58 (October 2001): 1040.

68. Ibid., 1041.

2. SLAVERY, THE TERROR OF IMAGINATION, AND EXILED FREEDOM IN LIBERIA

1. Erskine Clarke, *Dwelling Place: A Plantation Epic* (New Haven: Yale Univ. Press, 2005), x-xi.

2. Melton A. McLaurin, *Celia, a Slave* (Athens: Univ. of Georgia Press, 1991), x.

3. Wallace, *Journal,* passim. Quotations from the journal faithfully follow Wallace's language as transcribed by James Killebrew, with occasional [*sic*] notations to indicate errors in spelling or usage.

4. Rawick, *The American Slave,* vol. 1, xix.

5. Wallace, *Journal,* 108.

6. Ibid., 111.

7. R. H. McGaughey, ed. *Life with Grandfather* (1981), typescript, Hopkins-ville–Christian County Public Library. John W. McGaughey's complete diary constitutes over six hundred pages of typescript—more than five times longer than the redacted version. The expunged portions of the diary include descriptions of slave beatings and other aspects of the "slave matter." R. H. McGaughey edited the

original diary in order to avoid possible conflicts with descendants of the slaves whom his grandfather owned. (James T. Killebrew, conversation with author.)

8. Wallace, *Journal,* 194.

9. Ibid., 11.

10. Ibid., 12.

11. Ibid., 14.

12. Ibid., 18.

13. See for example, Maia Green, "Witchcraft Suppression Practices and Movements: Public Politics and the Logic of Purification," *Comparative Studies in Society and History* 39 (April 1997): 319–45.

14. Wallace, *Journal,* 32.

15. Herbert Aptheker, *American Negro Slave Revolts* (New York: International Publishers, 1943); Harvey Wish, "The Slave Insurrection Panic of 1856," *The Journal of Southern History* 5 (May 1939): 206–22; Charles B. Dew, "Black Ironworkers and the Slave Insurrection Panic of 1856," *The Journal of Southern History* 41 (August 1975): 321–38; Dan T. Carter, "The Anatomy of Fear: The Christmas Day Insurrection Scare of 1865," *The Journal of Southern History* 42 (August 1976): 345–64.

16. "Slave Insurrections," *New York Times,* December 19, 1856, 4.

17. "The Slave Rebellion," *New York Times,* December 12, 1856, 1.

18. "The Troubles in Tennessee," *Memphis Evening News*, reprinted in the *New York Times,* December 20, 1856, 8.

19. *New York Times,* December 12, 1856, 1.

20. A century later, when black people throughout the South were pressing for their constitutional rights, recalcitrant segregationists attributed their demands to the influence of "outside agitators," the analog to explanations of slave discontent in the 1850s.

21. *New York Times*, December 12, 1856, 1.

22. Ibid.

23. *New York Times,* December 19, 1856, 4.

24. John W. Blassingame, *The Slave Community: Plantation Life in the Antebellum South* (New York: Oxford Univ. Press, 1972).

25. James C. Scott, *Weapons of the Weak: Everyday Forms of Peasant Resistance* (New Haven: Yale Univ. Press, 1985).

26. Lawrence W. Levine, *Black Culture and Black Consciousness: Afro-American Folk Thought From Slavery to Freedom* (New York: Oxford Univ. Press, 1977), 102–33.

27. Paul Laurence Dunbar, "An Ante-Bellum Sermon," in Joan M. Braxton, ed., *The Collected Poetry of Paul Laurence Dunbar* (Charlottesville: Univ. of Virginia Press, 1993), 13–15.

28. *New York Times,* December 25, 1856, 1.

29. A December 21 dispatch from New Orleans reported on "a perfect state of excitement" in Jackson, Mississippi, where slaves were arrested and the mayor called on citizens "to crush the insurrection and rebellion in its bud." Rumors of a slave rebellion were also circulating in northern Alabama. See *New York Times,* December 30, 1856, 1.

30. *New York Times,* December 12, 1856, 1.

31. Ibid.

32. Ibid.

33. W. F. Cooper to M. D. Cooper, December 29, 1856, Cooper Family Papers, Tennessee State Library and Archives, Nashville.

34. J. B. Killebrew, *Recollections of My Life,* vol. 1, typescript, ca. 1898, Franklin, Tenn., 92–93. Personal copy provided by James T. Killebrew.

35. *New York Times,* December 11, 1856, 1.

36. Ibid.

37. Christian County Court Order Book L, December 1, 1856, 532–34, Hopkinsville–Christian County Courthouse.

38. *New York Times,* December 11, 1856, 1.

39. Ibid.

40. *Clarksville Jeffersonian,* December 3, 1856, reprinted in the *New York Times*, December 11, 1856, 1.

41. *The Goodspeed Histories of Montgomery, Robertson, Humphreys, Stewart, Dickson, Cheatham and Houston Counties of Tennessee* (1886; repr., Columbia, Tenn.: Woodward and Stinson Printing Co, 1972), 900–901.

42. Journal, 1862, Eugene Marshall Papers, Rare Book Manuscript and Special Collections Library, Duke University, Durham, N.C. The transcription preserves the errors of the original. Marshall's papers are a primary source for Susan Hawkins's examination of black life in slavery and freedom in the years before and just after the Civil War in the vicinity of Christian and Trigg counties in Kentucky

and Stewart County, Tennessee ("Forts Henry, Heiman, and Donelson: The African American Experience," master's thesis, Murray State University, n.d.).

43. Eugene D. Genovese, *From Rebellion to Revolution: Afro-American Slave Revolts in the Making of the Modern World* (Baton Rouge: Louisiana State Univ. Press, 1979), 106.

44. Rawick, *The American Slave*, vol. 16, 62.

45. Rawick, *The American Slave*, vol. 18, 170.

46. Aptheker, *American Negro Slave Revolts*, 249–50; Daniel Rasmussen, *American Uprising: the Untold Story of America's Largest Slave Revolt* (New York: Harper-Luxe, 2011), 147–63.

47. Richard Hofstadter and Michael Wallace, eds., *American Violence: A Documentary History* (New York: Vintage Books, 1970), 21.

48. George C. Wright, *Racial Violence in Kentucky, 1865–1940* (Baton Rouge: Louisiana State Univ. Press, 1990), 14.

49. See Mary Douglas, *Purity and Danger* (London: Routledge and Kegan Paul, 1966) and her edited volume, *Witchcraft Confessions and Accusations* (London: Tavistock Publications, 1970), xxvi-xxxiv. Corpse mutilation exercised equally grotesque symbolic and functional significance in revolutionary exhumations during the Spanish Civil War. See C. Eric Lincoln, *Discourse and the Construction of Society* (New York: Oxford Univ. Press, 1989), 106–14. Katherine Verdery, in *The Political Lives of Dead Bodies: Reburial and Postsocialist Change* (New York: Columbia Univ. Press, 1999), deals with a contemporary phenomenon vastly different from the postmortem mutilations of slaves in revolt or of dead clerics disfigured by Republican forces during the Spanish Civil War. The extraordinary communicative power of the body in conveying political meanings is the thread running through these cases.

50. Wallace, *Journal*, 29.

51. Ibid., 32.

52. Ibid.

53. Ibid.

54. Ibid., 32–33.

55. Ibid., 33.

56. Ibid.

57. Charles Mayfield Meacham, *A History of Christian County: From Oxcart to Airplane* (Nashville: Marshall and Bruce Co., 1930), 83.

58. Wallace, *Journal*, 34.

59. *New York Times,* September 13, 1868, 5. Exploitation of fears and anxieties about black men consorting with white women still offers some political advantage. In the 2006 senatorial contest in Tennessee, Harold Ford, Jr., the unsuccessful black Democratic candidate, faced an opposition that ran a political ad portraying a white woman claiming to have met Ford at a Playboy club and suggestively inviting him to call her. *New York Times,* "Compounding a Political Outrage," October 27, 2006, A-18. In Hopkinsville, a black sheriff lost his position amid charges of malfeasance in office. Several black people felt strongly that his involvement with a white woman was the real cause of his undoing.

60. Stephen Nissenbaum, *The Battle for Christmas* (New York: Vintage Books, 1996).

61. Ibid., 264–77.

62. Kenneth Stampp, *The Peculiar Institution* (New York: Alfred A. Knopf, 1956), 169.

63. R. H. McGaughey, *Life with Grandfather* [unredacted], 109.

64. Ibid., (Insert October 9, 1858 to December 10, 1859), 11.

65. Ibid., 166.

66. Ibid., 375.

67. Blight, ed., *Narrative of the Life of Frederick Douglass,* 80.

68. Booker T. Washington, *Up from Slavery* (1901; repr., Oxford, Eng.: Oxford Univ. Press, 1995), 79.

69. *New York Times,* December 27, 1856, 1.

70. Carter, "The Anatomy of Fear," 363–64.

71. Wallace, *Journal,* 34.

72. Ibid.

73. Ibid., 35.

74. Ibid.

75. Ibid.

76. Ibid., 125, 154.

77. Ibid., 35.

78. Ibid., 36.

79. *Canton Dispatch,* December 13, 1856, quoted in Coleman, *Slavery Times in Kentucky,* 107–108n.

80. Several informants among the Mbeere people of East Africa often confided to me that the victim of sorcery or poisoning is most likely to suffer his or her fate at the hands of a close kinsman.

81. Wallace, *Journal,* 38.

82. Ibid., 114.

83. Ibid., 121.

84. Ibid., 122–23.

85. Ibid., 128.

86. Ibid., 155.

87. Ibid.

88. Ibid., 144.

89. Ibid., 159.

90. Ibid., 161.

91. Ibid., 165.

92. Ibid., 175.

93. Ibid., 175–76.

94. Ibid., 182–83.

95. Ibid., 190.

96. Ibid., 191.

97. Ibid.

98. Ibid.

99. *Kentucky New Era,* February 3, 2001, 1.

100. *First Annual Report of the Kentucky Colonization Society, Auxiliary to the American Colonization Society for the Colonizing Free People of Colour in the United States,* (Frankfort: J. H. Huleman, 1830), 13.

101. Ibid., 6 (italics original).

102. Juliet E. K. Walker, "The Legal Status of Free Blacks in Early Kentucky, 1792–1825," *The Filson Club History Quarterly* 57 (1983): 383.

103. Christian County Court Order Book L, October 3, 1853, 125, Hopkinsville–Christian County Courthouse.

104. E-mail from D. D. Cayce, First Christian Church (Hopkinsville) Historian to Disciples of Christ Historical Society, July 30, 2002.

105. Christian County Court Order Book L, October 3, 1853, 125, Hopkinsville–Christian County Courthouse.

106. *Christian Standard,* July 3, 1897, 851.

107. Robert T. Brown, *Immigrants to Liberia, 1843–1865: An Alphabetical Listing* (Philadelphia: Institute of Liberia Studies, 1980), 20.

108. *Christian Standard,* July 3, 1897, 851.

109. "Tribute of Respect," Disciples of Christ Historical Society, transcribed copy of original May 18, 1854, document from Ninth Street Christian Church, Hopkinsville, Ky.

110. Ibid.

111. *Annual Report of the Board of Directors to the Kentucky Colonization Society,* (Frankfort, Ky.: Kentucky Colonization Society, 1855), 5.

112. Bell I. Wiley, ed., *Slaves No More: Letters from Liberia 1833–1869* (Lexington: Univ. Press of Kentucky, 1980).

113. Lenora Lindley and Edith L. Bennett, *Spiderwebs, a Steamer-Trunk and Slavery, 1826–1886* (Owensboro: Kentucky Typewriter Corporation, 1964). This collection contains photocopies of the original letters as well as verbatim typed transcripts.

114. Wiley, *Slaves No More,* 8.

115. Lindley and Bennett, *Spiderwebs,* 13. This and the other Eddington letters included here have been abbreviated and substantially edited for readability due to highly irregular spelling and grammar. Rachel Eddington also enlisted the aid of several different scribes in writing them.

116. Lindley and Bennett, *Spiderwebs,* 14–15.

117. Ibid., ii.

118. Washington, *Up From Slavery,* 9.

119. Lindley and Bennett, *Spiderwebs,* 16.

120. Brown, *Immigrants to Liberia,* 15, 23, 32.

121. Lindley and Bennett, *Spiderwebs,* 16.

122. Ibid.,17.

123. Ibid., 18.

124. Ibid., 21.

125. Ibid., 22.

126. Newbell Niles Puckett, *Black Names in America: Origins and Usage*, ed. Murra Heller (Boston: G. K. Hall, 1975).

127. Stanley Lieberson, *A Matter of Taste: How Names, Fashions, and Culture Change* (New Haven, Conn.: Yale Univ. Press, 2000), 203.

128. Wiley, *Slaves No More,* 7–8.

129. Edith Bennett, telephone conversation with author, May 26, 2006.

130. Lindley and Bennett, *Spiderwebs,* unpaginated introduction.

131. Kenneth C. Barnes, *Journey of Hope: The Back-to-Africa Movement in Arkansas in the Late 1800s* (Chapel Hill: Univ. of North Carolina Press, 2004), 8–9.

132. Penny M. Miller, *Kentucky Politics and Government* (Lincoln: Univ. of Nebraska Press, 1994), 80.

3. INSCRIPTIONS OF FREEDOM

1. W. E. B. Du Bois, "The Freedmen's Bureau," *Atlantic Monthly* 87 (1901): 354.

2. Victor Howard, *Black Liberation in Kentucky: Emancipation and Freedom, 1862–1884* (Lexington: Univ. Press of Kentucky, 1983), 12–16.

3. Eric Foner, *Reconstruction, America's Unfinished Revolution: 1863–1877* (1988; repr., New York: Harper Collins, 2005), 8.

4. Marion B. Lucas, *A History of Blacks in Kentucky,* vol. 1. *From Slavery to Segregation, 1760–1891* (Frankfort: Kentucky Historical Society), 155.

5. Victor B. Howard, "The Civil War in Kentucky: The Slave Claims His Freedom," *The Journal of Negro History* 67 (Fall 1982): 251.

6. Lucas, *A History of Blacks in Kentucky,* 160.

7. *New York Times,* July 26, 1865, 4. A portion of Fisk's letter to the Freedmen's Bureau is quoted in the article.

8. Du Bois, "The Freedmen's Bureau," 362.

9. *New York Times,* August 23, 1862, 2.

10. Foner, *Reconstruction,* 6.

11. Christian County, Will Book S, 585–87, Hopkinsville–Christian County Courthouse.

12. Howard, *Black Liberation,* 94.

13. Joab Clark to James Clark, December 9, 1866, reprinted in Christian County Genealogical Society, *Tree Builders* 28 (Summer and Fall 2007): 22–24.

14. *Records of the Field Offices for the State of Kentucky, Bureau of Refugees, Freedmen, and Abandoned Lands, 1865–72* (Washington, D.C.: National Archives and Records Administration, 2003), 1–4.

15. Heather Andrea Williams, *Self-Taught: African American Education in Slavery and Freedom* (Chapel Hill: Univ. of North Carolina Press, 2005), 30–31.

16. Brig. Gen. John Ely to Brig. Gen. Jeff Davis, August 15, 1866, *Records of the Field Offices for the State of Kentucky, Bureau of Refugees, Freedmen, and Abandoned Lands, 1865–1872*, microform edition (Washington, D.C.: National Archives and Records Administration, 2003), Roll 1. All microfilm references in this chapter concern the Kentucky Freedmen's Bureau. Subsequent microfilm citations will specify only the parties concerned, the date, and number of the film roll.

17. Nelson C. Lawrence to Col. Charles F. Johnson, October 12, 1866, Roll 18.

18. William Henry Perrin, *County of Christian, Kentucky* (Chicago: F. A. Battey Publishing Co., 1884), 95.

19. Lawrence to Johnson, October 12, 1866, Roll 18.

20. Daniel L. Hays to John Ely, May 6, 1867, Roll 26.

21. Daniel L. Hays, Notarized Affidavit by Oliver McReynolds, October 12, 1866, Roll 18; *Oliver McReynolds v. Robert Baker*, Christian County Court Filing, October n.d. 1866, Roll 18.

22. Brig. Gen. John Ely to Maj. Gen. Jeff Davis, August 15, 1866, Roll 1.

23. Daniel L. Hays to Gen. Burbank, June 1, 1867, Roll 23.

24. Circular Letter, December 11, 1867, Roll 23.

25. S.F. Johnson to Gen. Davis, July 28, 1866, Roll 16.

26. Nelson C. Lawrence, October 1866 School Report, Roll 90.

27. M. E. Billings to Capt. Brown, Chief Subassistant Commissioner, May 25, 1868, Roll 133.

28. William Killibrew to Daniel L. Hayes, n.d.; Daniel L. Hays to Col. Charles F. Johnson, Chief Sub-Commissioner, Bowling Green, May 25, 1867, Roll 23.

29. W. H. Wilson, Labor Contract, December 30, 1865, Roll 64. The document does not specify the county in which it was drafted.

30. Ross A. Webb, "'The Past Is Never Dead, It's Not Even Past': Benjamin P. Runkle and the Freedmen's Bureau in Kentucky, 1866–1870," in Donald G. Nieman, ed., *The Freedmen's Bureau and Black Freedom* (New York: Garland Publishing, Inc., 1994), 350–53.

31. Hays to Runkle, July 23, 1867, Roll 41.

32. Webb, "'The Past is Never Dead, It's Not Even Past,'" 338–39; *New York Times*, January 25, 1873, 5.

33. B. S. Newton, "Teacher's Monthly School Report," February 1870, Roll 56.

34. D. L. Hays to H. A. Hunter, March 12, 1868, Roll 133.

35. Student file of Lucy Hughes, Alumni and Development Records (Record Group 28), Oberlin College Archives.

36. Lucy R. Hughes to H. A. Hunter, March 18, 1868, Roll 133.

37. James W. Bell, "Teacher's Monthly School Report," February 1868, Roll 51.

38. Christopher Malone to H. A. Hunter, March 17, 1868, Roll 133.

39. Charles Smith, "Teacher's Monthly School Report," April 1870, Roll 57.

40. John Ely to National Freedmen's Relief Association, August 11, 1866, Roll 1.

41. William T. Buckner to H. A. Hunter, March 14, 1868, Roll 133.

42. Buckner to Hunter, March 28, 1868, Roll 133.

43. Hunter to Buckner, March 21, 1868, Roll 133.

44. Eugene Genovese, *Roll, Jordan, Roll: The World the Slaves Made* (New York: Vintage Books, 1976), 91.

45. Escott, *Slavery Remembered,* 189.

46. Rawick, ed., *The American Slave,* vol. 18. See, for example, "Massa's Slave Son," 80–85.

47. Rawick, ed., *The American Slave,* (Indiana and Ohio Narratives), Supplement, Series 1, vol. 5, 193–99.

48. Rawick, ed., *The American Slave,* (Alabama and Indiana Narratives), vol. 6, 151.

49. Christian County Deed Book 44, 518, Hopkinsville–Christian County Courthouse.

50. Buckner to Hunter, March 28, 1868, Roll 133. Now known simply as the Vine Street Cemetery, the burial ground has long since reverted to wilderness, having been reclaimed by trees, scrub, and other flora, as well as wild turkeys, snakes, and the like. The historical importance of the cemetery has long been recognized by a number of people in Hopkinsville, particularly Jessie Quarles. At various times, state and local authorities, including Ben Chandler when he was Kentucky's attorney general, have supported reclamation and encouraged local officials to pursue state funding. No private or public institution has committed itself to the task. *Kentucky New Era,* March 30, 2001, http://www.kentuckynewera.com/article_0828e307–178a-5b3b-81e9–2b493d40d9cd.html (accessed November 9, 2011); and October 17,

2001, http://www.kentuckynewera.com/article_9ab1159a-33ac-5c78-a7b3-17d1457d644f.html (accessed November 9, 2011).

51. Lucas, *A History of Blacks in Kentucky,* 314.

52. Loving Sons of the Union, Articles of Incorporation, Book 1, October 3, 1876, Hopkinsville–Christian County Courthouse.

53. Loving Sons of the Union and Daughters of Liberty, Articles of Incorporation, Book 1, August 9, 1879, Hopkinsville–Christian County Courthouse.

54. Grand Lodge of the Union Benevolent Society, Articles of Incorporation, Book 1, November 28, 1881, Hopkinsville–Christian County Courthouse. The articles of incorporation, filed with the county clerk, represent the sole surviving historical record of these institutional self-help efforts among freedmen. Important questions about the extent of membership, accounts, cases of assistance, including death benefits, remain unanswered.

55. Rawick, ed., *The American Slave,* vol. 16, 104.

56. Birth Records, Todd County, accession no. 994056, Kentucky Department for Libraries and Archives, Frankfort, Ky.

57. Howard, *Black Liberation in Kentucky,* 122–23.

58. Freedmen's Declaration of Marriages, 1866–1887, 3. Hopkinsville–Christian County Courthouse; *Christian County Kentucky 1870 Federal Census* (Russellville, Ky.: A. B. Wilhite, 1995), 86.

59. Freedmen's Declaration of Marriages, 120. This statement has been edited slightly for clarity.

60. Leon F. Litwack, *Been in the Storm So Long* (New York: Alfred A. Knopf, 1979), 240.

61. David W. Blight, *Race and Reunion: The Civil War in American Memory* (Cambridge, Mass.: Harvard Univ. Press, 2001). As Blight points out, the silent film epic *The Birth of a Nation* gave the southern vision added power a half-century after the Civil War by reiterating a view of black people either as once loyal slaves or, in rationalization of white supremacy, rapacious savages threatening white womanhood (Blight, 394–97). Black protests against the film occurred throughout the country, including a small effort in Hopkinsville.

62. Stanley Elkins, *Slavery: A Problem in American Institutional and Intellectual Life* (Chicago: Univ. of Chicago Press, 1959), 53–54. Elkins argues that the legal codes of the South placed no restriction on slave sales, including any consideration of a slave's conjugal relationship. Slave families had no standing in law, and a marital bond between slaves was fundamentally incompatible with the master-slave relationship.

63. Daniel P. Moynihan, *The Negro Family: The Case for National Action* (Washington, D.C.: U.S. Department of Labor, 1965).

64. The phrase, "culture of poverty," was coined by anthropologist Oscar Lewis in *Five Families: Mexican Case Studies in the Culture of Poverty* (New York: Basic Books, 1959). Lewis was interested in how poor people adapt culturally to their dire circumstances. He argued, however, that those adaptations were ultimately the product of structural factors built into societies sharply stratified by class. Still, he came in for the kind of criticism that was also directed at Moynihan. See, for example, Charles Valentine, *Culture and Poverty: Critique and Counter-Proposals* (Chicago: Univ. of Chicago Press, 1968).

65. Carol Stack, *All Our Kin* (New York: Harper and Row, 1974), 44, 50–61, 122

66. Eliot Liebow, *Tally's Corner* (Boston: Little, Brown, 1967), 38, 50–51.

67. Herbert G. Gutman, *The Black Family in Slavery and Freedom, 1750–1925* (New York: Pantheon Book, 1976), 455–56.

68. The original controversy over the Moynihan report is decades old, and its recent revival revisits the large question of cultural versus structural explanations of black family and gender dynamics. The cultural perspective has undergone a revitalization. For a review of the current debate, see William Julius Wilson, "The Moynihan Report and Research on the Black Community," *Annals of the American Academy of Political and Social Science* 621 (January 2009): 34–46.

69. *Freeman*, March 7, 1896, 5.

70. *Freeman*, March 14, 1896, 8.

71. Centennial Volume, General Association of Kentucky Baptists, 1868–1968, 234, author's possession; *Early History of Virginia Street Baptist Church As Compiled by Deacon Louis Berry*, unpublished text, not catalogued. Hopkinsville, Pennyroyal Area Museum. Berry claims that two charter members at the 1818 founding of the New Providence Baptist Church were black.

72. James Melvin Washington, *Frustrated Fellowship: The Black Baptist Quest for Social Power* (Macon: Mercer Univ. Press, 1986), 43, 81.

73. Othal Hawthorne Lakey, *The History of the CME Church* (Memphis: The CME Publishing House, 1985), 102–4.

74. Thomas O. Summers, "Report of the Committee on Expunging the General Rule Forbidding the Buying and Selling of Men, Women, and Children, with an Intention to Enslave Them," *Quarterly Review of the Methodist Episcopal Church, South* XII (New Series) No. 3 (1858): 385.

75. Daniel Stevenson, Journal, 1823–1893, typescript transcription, n.d. Kentucky Wesleyan College, Library Learning Center: Special Methodist/Kentucky/Biography Collection (SMKB S847).

76. *Christian County Kentucky 1870 Federal Census,* 104.

77. Ibid., 100; "History of Freeman Chapel," anonymous typescript, not catalogued, Hopkinsville, Pennyroyal Area Museum.

78. *The Aaron McNeil House Multi-purpose Community Center* (Hopkinsville: Wordcraft Desktop Publishing, 1996), 2–3.

79. *Daily Kentucky New Era,* September 28, 1906, 6.

80. Lakey, *The History of the CME Church,* 121.

81. Carter G. Woodson, *The History of the Negro Church* (Chapel Hill: Academic Affairs Library, Univ. of North Carolina, 2000) 193–94, http://docsouth.unc.edu/church/woodson.html, accessed March 5, 2012.

82. Glenn T. Eskew, "Black Elitism and the Failure of Paternalism in Postbellum Georgia: The Case of Bishop Lucius Henry Holsey," *The Journal of Southern History* 58 (November 1992): 644.

83. Reginald F. Hildebrand, *The Times were Strange and Stirring: Methodist Preachers and the Crisis of Emancipation* (Durham: Duke Univ. Press, 1995), 21–23.

84. Lakey, *The History of the CME Church,* 120–21.

85. Ibid., 96–97.

86. Paul Radin, "Status, Phantasy, and the Christian Dogma," in Rawick, ed., *The American Slave,* vol. 19 (*God Struck Me Dead*), vi.

87. R. E. Park "Principal Washington's Campaign," *Springfield Republican,* 24 (November 1909), reprinted in *Some Reports on a Trip Made by Booker T. Washington of the Tuskegee Institute Through the State of Tennessee November 18–28, 1909,* 27, Robert Ezra Park Collection, box 1, folder 1, Special Collections Research Center, University of Chicago Library.

88. *Christian County Kentucky 1870 Federal Census,* 82.

89. *Hopkinsville Kentuckian,* May 24, 1901, 5; "Profiles in Local Black History," not catalogued, Hopkinsville, Pennyroyal Area Museum.

90. Christian County Will Book Z, 129, Hopkinsville–Christian County Courthouse.

91. Claybron W. Merriweather, *Lights and Shadows* (Peducah: Evening Sun Job Print, 1907).

92. Claybron W. Merriweather, "The Declaration of the Free," in Clayborn W. Merriweather, *The Pleasures of Life: Lyrics of the Lowly, Essays, and Other Poems* (Hopkinsville, Ky.: The New Era Printing Co., 1931), 138.

93. W. E. B. Du Bois, *The Souls of Black Folk* (New York: Penguin Books, 1995), 88.

94. Claybron W. Merriweather, "The Declaration of the Free," 137.

95. James Walter Bass, Death Certificate, Christian County, Ky., March 16, 1925, State Board of Health, Bureau of Vital Statistics, File No. 5760, Register No. 87.

96. Idella Bass Richardson, daughter of James Bass, conversation with author, Indianapolis, October 3, 1971.

97. Lynn Scholes, great-granddaughter of James Bass, telephone conversation with author, July 8, 2002.

98. Margaret Bass Wilkerson, granddaughter of James Bass, conversation with author, Evansville, Indiana, July 2, 2002.

99. Oberlin College Office of the Treasurer, Series 7/1/2 Bookkeeping Records, 1833–1946, Subseries 2. Cash Journals, Journal May 29, 1882–December 31, 1884.

100. George Kinney, Treasurer of Oberlin College, Acknowledgment of Avery Bequest, February 15, 1867, American Missionary Association Archives (H2765), Amistad Research Center, Tulane University, New Orleans, La.

101. R. R. Wright, *Self-Help in Negro Education* (Cheyney, Penn: Committee of Twelve for the Advancement of the Interests of the Negro Race, 1909), 23.

102. *Princeton Clarion,* December 15, 1887, 2.

103. Rebecca Bingham, granddaughter of James Bass, telephone conversation with author, July 18, 2002.

104. Margaret Bass Wilkerson, conversation with author, July 2, 2002.

105. Christian County Will Book S, 31, Hopkinsville–Christian County Courthouse.

106. *Christian County Kentucky 1870 Federal Census,* 27.

107. *The South Kentuckian,* August 26, 1879, reproduced in *Christian County Kentucky Newspaper Abstracts,* Feb. 1879–Oct. 1879 (Russellville, Ky.: A.B. Willhite, 1995), 167.

108. *The South Kentuckian,* January 20, 1880, reproduced in *Christian County Kentucky Newspaper Abstracts,* Oct. 1879–Mar. 1880, (Russellville, Ky.: A.B. Willhite, 1995) 116.

109. *The South Kentuckian,* May 25, 1880, reproduced in *Christian County Kentucky Newspaper Abstracts,* Mar. 1880–Oct. 1880 (Russellville, Ky.: A.B. Willhite, 1996), 53.

110. *Daily Kentucky New Era,* July 11, 1891, 4.

111. William Henry Perrin, ed., *County of Christian, Kentucky, Historical and Biographical* (Chicago and Louisville: F. A. Battey Publishing Co., 1884), 287. Having

purchased Perrin's volume at a used book sale, Thelma Moore read this paragraph aloud, laughing wryly as she did so. She concluded, "All we ever did was work." Conversation with author, August 3, 2007. Louise West Taylor, in another counterpoint to claims of black indolence, spoke of her father having to labor in the 1940s for as little as fifty cents per day. At age 18, she left the rural area to work in Hopkinsville because "our daddy couldn't take care of us the way he wanted to." Then, with calm poignancy, she said, "We worked, and we worked, and we worked and some of us died." Conversation with author, Hopkinsville, August 6, 2007.

112. *Daily Kentucky New Era*, March 15, 1904, 1; and April 18, 1904, 1.

113. *Daily Kentucky New Era*, September 3, 1906, 1.

114. Leon Litwack, *How Free Is Free? The Long Death of Jim Crow* (Cambridge, Mass.: Harvard Univ. Press, 2009), 1–2.

4. FREE BUT NOT EQUAL

1. Elizabeth S. Peck, *Berea's First 125 Years* (Lexington: Univ. Press of Kentucky, 1982), 49–53.

2. *Hopkinsville Kentuckian*, March 3, 1908, 5.

3. *Daily Kentucky New Era*, August 4, 1909, 4.

4. George C. Wright, *Life Behind a Veil: Blacks in Louisville, Kentucky, 1865–1930* (Baton Rouge: Louisiana State Univ. Press, 1985), 4–5.

5. Dunbar, "We Wear the Mask," in *The Collected Poetry of Paul Laurence Dunbar*, 71.

6. 2004 Historical Census Browser, accessed November 9, 2011, University of Virginia, Geospatial and Statistical Data Center, http://fisher.lib.virginia.edu/collections/stats/histcensus/php/county.php.

7. Papers of the Hopkinsville City Council, Records 1906–[1908], June 7, 1907, 281.

8. Meacham, *A History of Christian County Kentucky*, 293–95.

9. George C. Wright, *A History of Blacks in Kentucky*, vol. 2 (Frankfort: Kentucky Historical Society, 1992), 104–5.

10. *New York Times*, July 27, 1869, 2.

11. Louis R. Harlan, ed., *The Booker T. Washington Papers*, vol. 3, 1893–1895 (Urbana: Univ. of Illinois Press, 1974), 583–87.

12. W. E. B. Du Bois, *The Souls of Black Folk* (1903; repr., New York: Penguin, 1995), 88.

13. Ibid.

14. Editorial, *The Crisis*, September 1911, 197.

15. Raymond Wolters, *Du Bois and His Rivals* (Columbia: Univ. of Missouri Press, 2002), 54, 60.

16. Ibid., 66.

17. Ibid., 75–76.

18. "Booker Washington's Greatest Service," *New York Evening Post*, December 2, 1909, reprinted in *Some Reports*, 24–25, Park Collection.

19. "Dr. Washington on Tour," *New York Post*, November 22, 1909, reprinted in *Some Reports*, 6, Park Collection.

20. "A Notable Speech," *Boston Transcript*, December 10, 1909, reprinted in *Some Reports*, 30, Park Collection.

21. *Weekly Kentucky New Era*, November 19, 1909, 5.

22. August Meier, "Booker T. Washington and the Rise of the NAACP," in *Along the Color Line: Explorations in the Black Experience*, August Meier and Elliott Rudwick, eds., (Urbana: Univ. of Illinois Press, 1976), 76–77.

23. *Daily Kentucky New Era*, November 16, 1909, 2.

24. "Special Correspondence of the *New York Evening Post*," November 29, 1909, reprinted in *Some Reports*, 16–17, 27, Park Collection.

25. The city's population in 1910 was 9,419. *Thirteenth Census of the United States*, vol. II (Washington, D.C.: Government Printing Office, 1913), 718.

26. *Daily Kentucky New Era*, November 23, 1909, 4.

27. Harlan, *The Booker T. Washington Papers*, vol. 3, 586.

28. *Kentucky New Era*, November 23, 1909, 4.

29. Harlan, *The Booker T. Washington Papers*, vol. 3, 585.

30. *Daily Kentucky New Era*, November 23, 1909, 4.

31. Du Bois, *The Souls of Black Folk*, 81.

32. "Booker T. Washington," *The Crisis*, December 1915, 82,

33. *The New Age*, April 25, 1924, 1, 3, 4.

34. "Negroes Urged to Farm," *Some Reports*, 16, Park Collection.

35. Park, "Principal Washington's Campaign," in *The Springfield Republican*, November 24, 1909, reprinted in *Some Reports*, 27, Park Collection.

36. 2004 Historical Census Browser, accessed November 9, 2011, University of Virginia, Geospatial and Statistical Data Center, http://fisher.lib.virginia.edu/collections/stats/histcensus/php/county.php.

37. Ibid. The total population of Christian County in 1900 was 37,962, comprised of 21,248 white people and 16,597 black people.

38. Ibid. The census of 1910 provides figures on the number of tenants by race, but it does not breakdown the forms of tenancy.

39. Sarah Wilson Nance, interview with the author, Hopkinsville, December 5, 2005 (emphasis original). The transcription of Mrs. Nance's recorded narration was made by the author. She later read the text and approved it for publication.

40. *Negro Year Book, An Annual Encyclopedia of the Negro, 1916–1917* (Tuskegee Institute: The Negro Year Book Publishing Co., 1916), 379.

41. *Caron's Hopkinsville Kentucky Municipal Directory, 1910* (repr., Russellville, Ky.: A. B. Willhite, n.d.), passim.

42. Ibid., 249.

43. F. E. Whitney, conversation with author, Hopkinsville, October 23, 2001.

44. *Jas. W. Bass and Wife vs. C. N. Campbell and Wife*, Christian County Court, October 22, 1891, A46/K5-A, Box 89, Kentucky Department for Libraries and Archives, Frankfort, Ky.

45. Stephen Steinberg, *The Ethnic Myth: Race, Ethnicity, and Class in America* (1981; repr., Boston: Beacon Press, 2001), 207.

46. E. Franklin Frazier, *Black Bourgeoisie* (New York: Free Press, 1957), 25, 153–57.

47. Today, the east side remains a black neighborhood. Since the 1960s, whites have moved away from the west side as black people moved in. It is important to note, however, that the degree of neighborhood segregation in Hopkinsville and much of the urban South was not nearly as intense as in the North.

48. F. E. Whitney, conversation with author, Hopkinsville, October 23, 2001.

49. Hattie Oldham, conversation with author, Frankfort, Kentucky, June 30, 2003.

50. Ed Owens, telephone conversation with author, April 5, 2008.

51. Ted Poston wrote a series of short stories about black life in the town in the early twentieth century. "The Revolt of the Evil Fairies" is at once a humorous and sad portrayal of the color hierarchy in the black community. See Kathleen A. Hauke, ed., *The Dark Side of Hopkinsville: Stories by Ted Poston* (Athens: Univ. of Georgia Press, 1991), 92–96.

52. *The South Kentuckian,* November 13, 1885, reprinted in *Christian County, Kentucky Miscellaneous Records,* vol. 1, compiled by James T. Killebrew (Christian County Genealogical Society, 1998), 1.

53. Perrin, *Counties of Todd and Christian, Kentucky*, 72.

54. Meacham, *A History of Christian County*, 228.

55. Papers of the Hopkinsville City Council, Record 1900, City of Hopkinsville, January 5, 1900, and March 2, 1900.

56. Commissioner Form Record Book, City of Hopkinsville, January 4, 1916–December 30, 1919, August 29, 1916; *Hopkinsville Kentuckian,* September 16, 1916, 1.

57. *The Crisis,* December 1915, 85.

58. *Hopkinsville Kentuckian,* September 5, 1916, 8.

59. *Hopkinsville Kentuckian,* September 9, 1916, 1. In his charming short story, "Birth of a Notion," Ted Poston tells how a black youth tricks the highly proficient black projectionist into leaving the theater just before the initial showing. In his place, the unskilled theater manager, Stone Wall Jackson Bolton, the grandson of a Klan founder, proceeds to run the film. However, the reels are out of sequence, and the film back to front. The showing is shut down in quick order when "the white lady at the bottom of the quarry" comes on screen because she was seen "leaping up to the top of the quarry so that the colored gentleman . . . could grab her." Poston's story is one of many examples of narratives of resistance, either fictional (in this case) or actual, suffusing the stories black people tell. At the local movie theater, black children always delighted when one of their light complexioned chums, "a high yellow," managed to get admitted to the theater as a white person. Matters of color within the black community nonetheless also caused friction. See, Hauke, *The Dark Side of Hopkinsville*, 72–82.

60. Brundage, *The Southern Past*, 157.

61. Anne E. Marshall, "'A Crisis in Our Lives': Kentucky's Separate Coach Law and the African American Response, 1892–1900," *The Register of the Kentucky Historical Society* Vol. 98 (Summer 2000): 241–43.

62. *Freeman,* April 4, 1891, 4.

63. C. Vann Woodward, *The Strange Career of Jim Crow*, 3rd rev. ed. (New York: Oxford Univ. Press, 1974), 12–13, 25–26.

64. Foner, *Reconstruction*, 593.

65. The Court of Appeals of Kentucky decided *Ohio Valley Railway's Receiver v. Lander, Etc.,* on October 7, 1898. The appellate transcript summarized the lower court trial in Christian County. *Southwestern Reporter,* vol. 47 (August 29–December 19, 1898): 344–50, *http://books.google.com/books?id=YRQ8AAAAIAAJ&pg=PA344&lpg =PA344&dq=Court+of+Appeals+of+Kentucky,+Ohio+Valleys+receiver+vs.+Lander&so urce=bl&ots=J6M36WpNkO&sig=wBNrGYt83MSZKZwiiDILn79mJIQ&hl=en&ei=Yyuo TunlGcrr0gG6* (accessed November 3, 2011).

66. For a more extensive discussion of the Lander case within the larger framework of protest by black Kentuckians against the separate coach law, see George C. Wright, *A History of Blacks in Kentucky*, 69–79.

67. *Freeman*, January 11, 1908, 2.

68. *Freeman*, July 18, 1914, 1.

69. *Freeman*, May 16, 1914, 4.

70. *Freeman*, March 14, 1914, 1. On reading the conclusion of the *Freeman* article, a current white resident remarked, "things really were bad if Hopkinsville represented the epitome of race relations in the South" (Wynn Radford, email to author, September 29, 2009).

71. Wright, *A History of Blacks in Kentucky*, 79.

72. T. Montgomery Gregory, "The Jim Crow Car: An N.A.A.C.P. Investigation," *The Crisis*, December 1915, 88; the other installments of the series appeared as Part II, January 1916, 137–38; and Part III, February 1916, 195–98.

73. Charles Nance, conversation with author, Hopkinsville, August 20, 2005.

74. Alison McGregor, conversation with author, Detroit, June 24, 2006.

75. Kathleen A. Hauke, *The Poston Family of Kentucky*, unpublished manuscript, 104–6, Kathleen Hauke Collection of Poston Family Papers, Box 25, folder 20, Kentucky State University. After an exhaustive search, Hauke concluded that no copies of the *Hopkinsville Contender* survive in any library or archive (Hauke, conversation with author, Washington, D.C., November 30, 2001). This is also noted in her unpublished manuscript.

76. Hauke, *Ted Poston, Pioneer American Journalist*, 18–19.

77. Ulysses S. Poston, "The Negro Awakening," *Current History* (1923): 473, 477.

78. *New York Times*, April 10, 1909, 1.

79. James Jordan, conversation with author, Hopkinsville, September 18, 2005.

80. *Daily Kentucky New Era*, April 9, 1909, 1.

81. *Hopkinsville Kentuckian*, April 10, 1909, 1.

82. *Daily Kentucky New Era*, April 10, 1909, 1.

83. Ibid.; *Hopkinsville Kentuckian*, April 13, 1909, 1.

84. Leon F. Litwack, *Trouble in Mind: Black Southerners in the Age of Jim Crow* (New York: Alfred A. Knopf, 1998), 285.

85. *Hopkinsville Kentuckian*, April 13, 1909, 1.

86. *Freeman*, December 4, 1897, 6.

87. *Hopkinsville Kentuckian,* April 13, 1909, 1.

88. Philip Dray, *At the Hands of Persons Unknown: The Lynching of Black America* (New York: Random House, 2002), ix.

89. James C. Scott, *Weapons of the Weak: Everyday Forms of Peasant Resistance* (New Haven, Conn.: Yale Univ. Press, 1985). See also W. Fitzhugh Brundage, "The Roar on the Other Side of Silence: Black Resistance and White Violence in the American South, 1880–1940," in *Under Sentence of Death: Lynching in the South,* ed. Brundage (Chapel Hill: Univ. of North Carolina Press, 1997).

90. Ibid., 272–73.

91. W. Fitzhugh Brundage, *Lynching in the New South: Georgia and Virginia, 1880–1930* (Urbana: Univ. of Illinois Press, 1993), 39–43.

92. Litwack, *Trouble in Mind,* 284, 286–87.

93. Jonathan Markovitz, *Legacies of Lynching: Racial Violence and Memory* (Minneapolis: Univ. of Minnesota Press, 2004), xvi-xviii.

94. *Daily Kentucky New Era,* April 9, 1909, 1.

95. Both literature and social science provide many examples. Toni Morrison's *The Bluest Eye* (New York: Holt, Rinehart, and Winston, 1970) is a particularly poignant and tragic story of the deformations of racial self-loathing.

96. *Hopkinsville Kentuckian,* August 12, 1909, 1.

97. Ibid.

98. Wright, *Racial Violence in Kentucky, 1865–1940,* 307–23.

99. *Daily Kentucky New Era,* January 25, 1904, 1

100. *Kentucky New Era,* January 26, 1904, 1.

101. E. M. Beck and Stewart E. Tolnay, "When Race Didn't Matter: Black and White Mob Violence against Their Own Color," in *Under Sentence of Death,* ed. Brundage, 138–41.

102. Suzanne Marshall, *Violence in the Black Patch of Kentucky and Tennessee* (Columbia: Univ. of Missouri Press, 1994), xi.

103. Ibid., 41–42; Rick Gregory, "Beliefs of Their Fathers: Violence, Religion, and the Black Patch War, 1904–1914," *Border States: Journal of the Kentucky-Tennessee American Studies Association* 9 (1993): 2.

104. Charles V. Tevis, "A Ku Klux Klan of To-day," *Harper's Weekly,* February 8, 1908, 14.

105. H. A. Vivian, "How Crime is Breeding Crime In Kentucky," *New York Times Magazine,* July 26, 1908, 1.

106. Among the books that have focused on the Black Patch War, three stand out. See Tracy Campbell, *The Politics of Despair: Power and Resistance in the Tobacco Wars* (Lexington: Univ. Press of Kentucky, 1993); Christopher Waldrep, *Night Riders: Defending Community in the Black Patch,* 1890–1915 (Durham: Duke Univ. Press, 1993); and Suzanne Marshall, *Violence in the Black Patch of Kentucky and Tennessee* (Columbia: Univ. of Missouri Press, 1994).

107. *Daily Kentucky New Era,* September 23, 1904, 1.

108. Campbell, *The Politics of Despair*, 3.

109. *Daily Kentucky New Era,* April 2, 1908, 1; Speech of Judge A. J. G. Wells of Murray, Ky., delivered at the courthouse, Hopkinsville, Ky., under the auspices of the Law and Order League of Hopkinsville and Christian County, Hopkinsville, Kentucky, May 28, 1908, Filson Historical Society, Louisville, Ky.

110. *Daily Kentucky New Era,* May 23, 1906, 1.

111. Campbell, *The Politics of Despair,* 91–93.

112. *Daily Kentucky New Era,* January 1, 1908, 1.

113. Ibid., January 16, 1908, 1.

114. Ibid., February 11, 1908, 3.

115. *Hopkinsville Kentuckian,* March 12, 1908, 1.

116. *Daily Kentucky New Era,* April 2, 1908, 1.

117. Ibid., March 10, 1908, 1.

118. Ibid., February 17, 1908, 1; *Hopkinsville Kentuckian,* March 12, 1908, 1; *Daily Kentucky New Era,* March 20, 1908, 1; *Daily Kentucky New Era,* March 24, 1908, 1; *Daily Kentucky New Era,* March 28, 1908, 1.

119. Marvin Dennison, conversation with author, Hopkinsville, November 10, 2005.

120. *Daily Kentucky New Era,* March 24, 1908, 1.

121. *Hopkinsville Kentuckian,* October 8, 1908, 4.

122. J. Milton Henry, *The Land Between the Rivers* (Dallas: Taylor Publishing Co., 1976), 170.

123. Miller, *Kentucky Politics and Government,* 78.

124. *Daily Kentucky New Era,* December 8, 1906, 1.

125. *New York Times,* December 8, 1907, 1.

126. *New York Times,* August 23, 1908, 1.

127. Campbell, *The Politics of Despair*, 7–9, 26–27.

128. Tevis, "A Ku Klux Klan of To-day," 16.

129. *Thirteenth Census of the United States*, vol. II (Washington, D.C.: Government Printing Office, 1913), 718.

130. *Caron's Hopkinsville Kentucky Municipal Directory*, 1.

131. Tevis, "A Ku Klux Klan of To-day," 14.

132. *Hopkinsville Kentuckian*, February 22, 1908, 5.

133. Ibid., February 23, 1908.

134. Dunbar, "To the South, On its New Slavery," in *The Collected Poetry of Paul Laurence Dunbar*, 216.

5. THE ENACTMENT OF MEMORY

1. David Lowenthal, *The Past Is a Foreign Country* (Cambridge, Eng.: Cambridge Univ. Press, 1985), 210.

2. Ira Berlin, "American Slavery in History and Memory and the Search for Social Justice," *The Journal of American History* 90 (March 2004), 1266–68.

3. Derrick Z. Jackson, "Where is the Apology for Slavery?" *Boston Globe*, July 12, 2003, *http://www.learntoquestion.com/resources/database/archives/003371.html* (accessed November 3, 2011).

4. *New York Times*, December 15, 2002, 1.

5. *New York Times*, December 10, 2002, A-28.

6. *New York Times*, December 13, 2002, A-1.

7. *New York Times*, August 4, 1980, A-11.

8. Trent Watts, *One Homogenous People: Narratives of White Southern Identity, 1890–1920* (Knoxville: The Univ. of Tennessee Press, 2010), 140–41.

9. Stuart McConnell, "Epilogue: The Geography of Memory," in *The Memory of the Civil War in American Culture*, ed. Alice Fahs and Joan Waugh (Chapel Hill: Univ. of North Carolina Press, 2004), 258–66.

10. Eric Foner, *Who Owns History?* (New York: Hill and Wang, 2002), xi-xiv.

11. E. J. Hobsbawm, "The New Threat to History," *New York Review of Books*, December 16, 1993, 63. Hobsbawm's concern is with the consequences of postmodernist developments emanating from anthropology and literature, especially as they question objective knowledge and assert instead that facts are only "intellectual constructions."

12. William T. Turner, conversation with author, Hopkinsville, Kentucky, October 28 2005.

13. See Daniel Sutherland, *The Confederate Carpetbaggers* (Baton Rouge: Louisiana State Univ. Press, 1988). Wynn Radford of Hopkinsville engaged in some amateur sleuthing using forensic accounting techniques to investigate the disappearance of the Confederate gold reserve in 1865. Connecting that mystery to Latham, he asked how a man with no prior experience in finance or in the North could establish a successful Wall Street brokerage before he was thirty. Radford has suggested that Latham, as a young Confederate officer, had military connections enabling him to gain access to the Confederate gold reserve, which he then used to establish his New York firm.Wynn Radford, "John Campbell Latham, Jr.: Hopkinsville's Greatest Philanthropist," paper presented to the Athenaeum Society, Hopkinsville, Kentucky, September 6, 2007.

14. David W. Blight, "Decoration Days: The Origins of Memorial Day in North and South," in *The Memory of the Civil War in American Culture,* ed. Fahs and Waugh, 95; Howard L. Sacks and Judith Rose Sacks, *Way Up North in Dixie: A Black Family's Claim to the Confederate Anthem* (Washington, D.C.: Smithsonian Institution Press, 1993). The Jefferson Davis bicentennial at Fairview, Kentucky in June 2008 featured a brass band attired in period Confederate military costume and playing instruments of the time. When I suggested that one of their featured tunes, "Dixie," was probably composed by a black man, a bandsman reacted with an audible gasp.

15. *Hopkinsville Kentuckian,* December 8, 1910, 1.

16. *New York Times,* May 20, 1887, 3.

17. John C. Latham to Hopkinsville Board of Council, May 14, 1887, reprinted in S. C. Mercer, *The Story of a Monument* (New York: Press of Dennison and Brown, 1888), 22.

18. Ibid., 20.

19. Ibid., 23.

20. Ibid., 44.

21. Ibid., 51.

22. Ibid., 58.

23. Charles B. Dew, *Apostles of Disunion* (Charlottesville: Univ. of Virginia Press, 2001), 15.

24. Ibid., 77–79.

25. Jack Glazier, *Dispersing the Ghetto: The Relocation of Jewish Immigrants Across America* (Ithaca: Cornell Univ. Press, 1998), 69–71.

26. Nina Silber, *The Romance of Reunion* (Chapel Hill: Univ. of North Carolina Press, 1993), 142.

27. Mercer, *The Story of a Monument,* 19.

28. Blight, *Race and Reunion,* 191–92.

29. Foner, *Who Owns History?,* 199–202.

30. A resident of Hopkinsville had recorded the name of each soldier and his regiment at the time of death. That list was discovered in 1899. *Kentucky New Era,* March 10, 1899, 1.

31. Larry Walston, conversation with author, November 20, 2005.

32. Tonya Grace, telephone conversation with author, December 1, 2005.

33. Linda Wood, conversation with author, Hopkinsville, December 10, 2005.

34. *Daily Kentucky New Era,* June 20, 1904, 4.

35. Wallace Henderson, "Civil War Days," n.d., 22. Family Files, Drawer B–C, Hopkinsville–Christian County Public Library.

36. *Daily Kentucky New Era,* June 20, 1904, 4.

37. United Daughters of the Confederacy, "Statement of Objectives," http://www.hqudc.org/.

38. W. E. B. Du Bois, "The Freedmen's Bureau," 360.

39. Clifford Geertz, "Thick Description: Toward an Interpretative Theory of Culture," in *The Interpretation of Culture: Selected Essays of Clifford Geertz* (New York: Basic Books, 1973), 5.

40. *Kentucky New Era,* January 22, 1904, 6.

41. William T. Turner, conversation with author, Hopkinsville, October 28, 2005.

42. Linda McHenry, telephone conversation with author, October 15, 2009; Ed Owens, telephone conversation with author, October 15, 2009.

43. Karla F. C. Holloway, *Passed On: African American Mourning Stories* (Durham: Duke Univ. Press, 2003), 184.

44. Thelma Moore, conversation with author, Hopkinsville, August 8, 2004.

45. Emma Jordan, telephone conversation with author, August 10, 2004.

46. Thelma Moore, telephone conversation with author, August 10, 2004.

47. Shirley Shelton, conversation with author, Hopkinsville, September 3, 2005.

48. Robert Penn Warren, *Jefferson Davis Gets His Citizenship Back* (Lexington: Univ. Press of Kentucky, 1980), 95.

49. Ibid., 96.

50. *New York Times,* June 8, 1924, 3-E.

51. Donald E. Collins, *The Death and Resurrection of Jefferson Davis* (Lanham, Md.: Rowman and Littlefield, 2005), 13.

52. H. K. Edgerton, conversation with author, Fairview, KY., June 7, 2008.

53. Kentucky Department of Parks, Davis 200th Commemoration Press Release, March 7, 2008, *http://migration.kentucky.gov/Newsroom/parks/jeffdavis200. htm* (accessed November 5, 2011).

54. Kentucky Department of Parks, *http://www.parks.ky.gov/parks/historic-sites/jefferson-davis/default.aspx/* (accessed November 5, 2011).

55. William C. Davis, *Jefferson Davis: The Man and His Hour* (New York: Harper Collins, 1991), xii-xiii.

56. James Ronald Kennedy and Walter Donald Kennedy, *Was Jefferson Davis Right?* (Gretna, La.: Pelican Publishing Co., 1998).

57. *Todd County Standard,* June 4, 2008, 5.

58. *Kentucky New Era,* June 9, 2008, 1.

59. Raoul Cunningham of Louisville's NAACP stated that, "It's offensive. Even in the days when he was alive, this state did not follow him. So why do we honor him today?" Cunningham carried the protest to the Historical Properties Commission, which took no action. *Kentucky New Era,* May 17, 2006, 1; Raoul Cunningham, telephone conversation with author, April 16, 2010.

60. Allen G. Breed, "Quiet 200th for President of the Confederacy," *San Francisco Chronicle,* February 24, 2008, *http://articles.sfgate.com/2008–02–24/news/17140117_1_davis-family-association-civil-war-cabin* (accessed October 27, 2011).

61. *Todd County News,* May 21, 2010, 1

62. *New York Times,* December 25, 2004, A24.

63. Alan G. Breed, "Some Criticizing Fairview Monument," *Kentucky New Era,* February 19, 2000, 1.

64. *New York Times,* August 5, 2005, A-13.

65. *New York Times,* December 25, 2004, A-24.

66. *Memphis Commercial Appeal,* March 19, 2009, *http://www.commercialappeal.com/news/2009/mar/19/forrest-park-on-historic-register/* (accessed October 27, 2011).

67. Tony Horwitz, "Dying for Dixie," in *Confederates in the Attic* (New York: Pantheon Books, 1998) 89–124.

68. Ibid., 113.

69. Ibid., 112. .

70. Warren, *Jefferson Davis Gets His Citizenship Back,* 20–21.

71. Mary Bess McCain Henderson, et. al., *Dear Eliza . . . The Letters of Mitchell Andrew Thompson* (Ames, Iowa: Carter Press, Inc., n.d.), 76.

72. Bruce Levine, *Half Slave and Half Free: The Roots of the Civil War* (New York: Hill and Wang, 1992), 224.

73. Carl N. Degler, *The Other South: Southern Dissenters in the Nineteenth Century* (New York: Harper and Row, 1974), 158–62.

74. Perrin, *Counties of Todd and Christian, Kentucky,* 74.

75. *Cadiz Record,* August 14, 1947, 8.

76. Bingham Family Reunion Booklet, 2003, in author's possession.

77. "Where It All Began," McCray Reunion Booklet, 2009, in author's possession.

78. Dorothy Quarles, conversation with author, Indianapolis, March 28, 2002.

79. The memory of Phillis Wheatley in all likelihood provided great inspiration for those wanting to "hear" black literary voices. Born in Africa and enslaved in New England, Wheatley quickly achieved literacy and eventual fame as a poet.

80. "Resolution of the Congress of the Confederate States of America," January 1863, cited in George Washington Williams, *History of the Negro Race in America from 1619 to 1880* (New York: G. P. Putnam's Sons, 1883), 350–52.

81. Ibid., 376.

82. See Thomas Jordan and J. P. Pryor, *The Campaigns of Lieut.-Gen. N.B. Forrest, and of Forrest's Cavalry (1868; repr., New York: Da Capo Press, 1996).*

83. George Washington Williams, *A History of Negro Troops in the War of Rebellion, 1861–65* (New York: Harper and Brothers, 1888).

84. John Hope Franklin, *George Washington Williams, a Biography* (Durham: Duke Univ. Press, 1998), 128.

85. Albert Castel, "The Fort Pillow Massacre: An Examination of the Evidence," in *Black Flag Over Dixie: Racial Atrocities and Reprisals in the Civil War,* ed. Gregory J. W. Urwin (Carbondale: Southern Illinois Univ. Press, 2004), 89–103; also, in the same collection, Derek W. Frisby, "'Remember Fort Pillow!': Politics, Atrocity Propaganda, and the Evolution of Hard War," 104–31. This collection does much to

counter "race free" approaches to Civil War history and to expose the brutal facts of race-hatred and murder.

86. *Freeman,* September 3, 1892, 6.

87. Joseph T. Wilson, *The Black Phalanx* (1890; repr., New York: Arno Press, 1968), 503–4.

88. Ibid., unpaginated dedication and preface. The integrated encampment was exceptional as veterans' organizations throughout the North became highly segregated by the 1880s. See Blight, *Race and Reunion,* 195.

89. Wilson, *The Black Phalanx,* 349.

90. Court Carney, "The Contested Image of Nathan Bedford Forrest," *Journal of Southern History* 67 (August 2001): 605.

91. Dunbar, "The Colored Soldiers," in *The Collected Poetry of Paul Laurence Dunbar,* 50–52.

92. Ibid., 182–84.

93. Ibid., xviii–xxiv.

94. Robert Penn Warren, *The Legacy of the Civil War* (1961; repr., Lincoln: Univ. of Nebraska Press, 1998), 15. Anne Elizabeth Marshall examines how the force of that immortality remade Kentucky into a redoubt of Confederate remembrance. Historic memory in effect looked away from the state's unionist past and recalled a Confederate identity undisturbed by post–Civil War racial violence and Jim Crow laws. Of course, Kentucky is highly regionalized, and the postwar embrace of a Confederate past was less of a reinvention in some areas, such as Christian County and the western part of the state, than in others. See Marshall's *Creating a Confederate Kentucky: The Lost Cause and Civil War Memory in a Border State* (Chapel Hill: Univ. of North Carolina Press, 2010).

6. CIVIL RIGHTS AND BEYOND

1. *Kentucky New Era,* June 28, 1966, 1–2.

2. Ibid.

3. William Doyle, *An American Insurrection: The Battle of Oxford, Mississippi* (New York: Doubleday, 2001), 294.

4. *Kentucky New Era,* September 6, 1958, 4.

5. *New York Times,* March 13, 1956, S-2.

6. *New York Times,* September 9, 1956, E-7; Wright, *A History of Blacks in Kentucky,* vol. 2, 202–3.

7. bell hooks, *Bone Black* (New York: Henry Holt, 1996), 154–56.

8. That integration brought new burdens to the black community was not unique to Hopkinsville. Black students, parents, teachers, and administrators throughout the South felt the costs of desegregation. See Brundage, *The Southern Past*, 274–84. Also for a detailed examination of the closing of black schools in one North Carolina county, see David S. Cecelski, *Along Freedom Road* (Chapel Hill: Univ. of North Carolina Press, 1994).

9. Jessie Quarles, conversation with author, Hopkinsville, August 3, 2005.

10. *New York Times,* March 13, 1956, S-2.

11. Robert F. Sexton, "Changes in Our Schools: A Commentary," July 2000, The Prichard Committee for Academic Excellence. Sexton's statement was sent to all weekly and daily newspapers in Kentucky.

12. Always detailed to all-black units in the segregated army, Whitney described units with lawyers, doctors, and engineers whose skills were usually irrelevant to their army assignments. In his experience, particularly in the American South, most of the black soldiers with special training as civilians were assigned to duty far below their level. Racism was pervasive. Particularly memorable was the reaction of a white sergeant to black mechanics who in short order had repaired an aircraft engine. When they started up the engine, the sergeant remarked, "I didn't know niggers had this much sense." Relating the incident, Whitney said, "I'll never forget that as long as I live," and explained that the event was part of what motivated his many efforts on behalf of the race. Some black veterans of his generation whose service included duty in one of the states of the old Confederacy have described their time in the Army as serving on the third front. Francis E. Whitney, conversation with author, Hopkinsville, October 23, 2001. See Litwack, *How Free is Free?* for a discussion of black soldiers in World War II and the racism they encountered both in the military and in southern towns where they were stationed.

13. Ibid.

14. Ibid.

15. *Kentucky New Era,* May 3, 1972, 1.

16. *Kentucky New Era,* May 6, 1972, 1.

17. Ibid.

18. Ibid.

19. *Kentucky New Era,* May 9, 1972, 2.

20. F. E. Whitney, conversation with author, Hopkinsville, July 15, 2002.

21. Ibid.

22. Al C. Rutland, Jr., conversation with author, Hopkinsville, November 14, 2005.

23. George Atkins, telephone conversation with author, November 27, 2005.

24. Discussion of Ordinance 12–96, June 4, 1996; June 18, 1996; January 7, 1997; discussion and vote, February 4, 1997. Minutes, City of Hopkinsville, January 2, 1996–April 15, 1997, Office of the City Clerk.

25. *Kentucky New Era,* September 16, 2005, *http://www.kentuckynewera.com/ article_3f56a7c6–703d-5e4c-a6bc-6750591c5da4.html* (accessed October 28, 2011).

26. Derek H. Alderman, "Street Names and the Scaling of Memory: The Politics of Commemorating Martin Luther King, Jr. within the African American Community," *Area* 35 (June 2003): 164.

27. A new police chief hired in 2005 is reportedly breaking new ground with community policing and positive engagement in the neighborhoods.

28. *Demond T. Brown v. Commonwealth of Kentucky,* 2003 SC 0235 MR (Ky. 2005), 11, 17.

29. *Kentucky New Era,* January 30, 2003, *http://www.kentuckynewera.com/ article_2cf736ab-02cc-5af0–8ed3–20ef49cd0970.html* (accessed October 28, 2011).

30. *Kentucky New Era,* November 30, 2003, *http://www.kentuckynewera.com/ article_cc343467-b13c-5ec6–94cf-43efd0cbff62.html* (accessed October 28, 2011).

31. Lee Huckleberry, phone conversation with author, February 5, 2003.

32. *Kentucky New Era,* December 12, 2007, *http://www.kentuckynewera.com/ web/news/article_2a153a0b-5144–5638-aa14-e28ce9dae556.html* (accessed October 28, 2011).

33. *Kentucky New Era,* December 11, 2007, *http://www.kentuckynewera.com/ web/news/article_671351a2-cd60–5db9-a066- cfc45c0bb84e.html* (accessed October 28, 2011).

34. *Kentucky New Era,* May 8, 2006, *http://www.kentuckynewera.com/web/ news/article_35e64ecf-6df2–5455-b7c7-b75d5eef9cd9.html* (accessed October 28, 2011).

35. *Guide to Implementation of a Neighborhood Revitalization Initiative for the City of Hopkinsville, Kentucky* (Dennison Associates, November 30, 2006), 19.

36. *Kentucky New Era,* April 14, 2001, 1.

37. Paradoxically, two proponents of cultural explanations of poverty concede the primacy of structural factors. Michèle Lamont states that "theoretical shifts," presumably with implications for cultural change, "do not reduce class or racial inequality the way the creation of good, stable jobs would." See Michèle

Lamont, "Introduction: Beyond Taking Culture Seriously," in *The Cultural Territories of Race: Black and White Boundaries,* ed. Michèle Lamont (Chicago: Univ. of Chicago Press, 1999), xi. Likewise, William Julius Wilson without equivocation observes that "in terms of major effects on immediate group social outcomes and racial stratification, structure trumps culture." See William Julius Wilson, *More Than Just Race: Being Black and Poor in the Inner City* (New York: W. W. Norton, 2009), 21.

38. *Kentucky New Era,* June 20, 2007, 1.

39. James Victor, conversation with author, Hopkinsville, August 8, 2007.

40. Jessie Quarles, conversation with author, Hopkinsville, August 17, 2005.

41. Henry Louis Gates, Jr., *Colored People* (New York: Vintage Books, 1995), xv.

42. Gunnar Myrdal, *An American Dilemma* (New York: Harper Bros., 1944); Gordon Allport, *The Nature of Prejudice* (Cambridge: Addison-Wesley, 1954).

43. Charles T. Clotfelter, *After Brown: The Rise and Retreat of School Desegregation* (Princeton: Princeton Univ. Press, 2004), 195.

44. Ibid., 109–10, 182.

45. *The State of Black America 2009,* National Urban League, 11–12.

46. William Julius Wilson, *The Declining Significance of Race: Blacks and Changing American Institutions* (Chicago: Univ. of Chicago Press, 1978), 2.

47. David Hollinger, *Postethnic America: Beyond Multiculturalism* (New York: Basic Books, 1995), 167; italics original.

48. Randall Kennedy, *The Persistence of the Color Line: Racial Politics and the Obama Presidency* (New York: Pantheon Books, 2011).

BIBLIOGRAPHY

ARCHIVES AND RESEARCH LIBRARIES

Amistad Research Center

University of Chicago Library (Special Collections)

Disciples of Christ Historical Society

Duke University Library (Special Collections)

Filson Historical Society

Kentucky Department for Libraries and Archives

Kentucky State University Archives

Kentucky Historical Society

Kentucky Wesleyan College Archives

National Archives

Oberlin College Archives

Tennessee State Library and Archives

Western Kentucky University (Kentucky Library)

GOVERNMENT DOCUMENTS: FEDERAL, STATE, AND LOCAL

Capehart, Tom. *Trends in Tobacco Farming.* Washington, D.C.: United States Department of Agriculture, 2004.

Christian County, Kentucky, 1870 Federal Census. Russellville, Ky.: A.B. Willhite, 1995.

Christian County, Its Advantages and Inducements to Immigration. Publication of Kentucky Geological Survey and Bureau of Immigration. Frankfort, Ky.: Yeoman Office, S.I.M. Major, 1881.

Christian County Will Books and Court Order Books

Gibson County, Indiana, Census of 1880

Moynihan, Daniel P. *The Negro Family: The Case for National Action*. Washington, D.C.: Department of Labor, 1965.

Papers of the Hopkinsville City Council

Papers of the Bureau of Refugees, Freedmen, and Abandoned Lands, Kentucky

Statistical View of the United States. Washington, D.C.: A.O.P. Nicholson, Public Printer, 1854.

Thirteenth Census of the United States, Vol. II. Washington, D.C.: Government Printing Office, 1913.

Todd County, Kentucky, Slave Schedules of 1850 and 1860

CHRISTIAN COUNTY RESOURCES

Pennyroyal Area Museum

Christian County Historical Society

Hopkinsville–Christian County Public Library

NEWSPAPERS AND MAGAZINES

Cadiz Record

Christian Standard

The Crisis

Freeman

Hopkinsville Kentuckian

Kentucky New Era

The New Age (Hopkinsville)

New York Times

Princeton Clarion (Indiana)

Todd County Standard

Todd County News

Tree Builders (Publication of the Christian County Genealogical Society)

NEWSPAPER WEB ARCHIVES

Boston Globe

Kentucky New Era

Memphis Commercial Appeal

San Francisco Chronicle

COURT CASES

Demond T. Brown v. Commonwealth of Kentucky, 2003 SC 0235 MR (Ky. 2005).

"Ohio Valley's Receiver v. Lander, et al. (Court of Appeals of Kentucky, Oct. 7, 1898)," in *Southwestern Reporter* 47 (August 29–December 19, 1898): 344–50, http://books.google.com/books?id=YRQ8AAAAIAAJ&pg=PA344&lpg=PA344&dq=Court+of+Appeals+of+Kentucky,+Ohio+Valleys+receiver+vs.+Lander&source=bl&ots=J6M36WpNkO&sig=wBNrGYt83MSZKZwiiDILn79mJIQ&hl=en&ei=YyuoTunlGcrr0gG6

WEB SOURCES

2004 Historical Census Browser. University of Virginia, Geospatial and Statistical Data Center. http://fisher.lib.virginia.edu/collections/stats/histcensus/php/county.php

Hindu Press International: http://www.hinduismtoday.com/blogs-news/hindu-press-international/being-hindu-in-the-american-bible-belt/4628.html

The Toni Morrison Society. http://www.tonimorrisonsociety.org/bench.html

U.S. Census Bureau, State and County Quick Facts. http://quickfacts.census.gov/qfd/states/21/2137918.html

UNPUBLISHED THESES, MANUSCRIPTS, JOURNALS, FAMILY PAPERS

Cooper Family Papers. Tennessee State Library and Archives, Nashville, Tenn.

Hawkins, Susan. "Forts Henry, Heiman, and Donelson: The African American Experience." Master's Thesis, Murray State University, n.d.

Killebrew, J. B. "Recollections of My Life," vol. 1. Typescript. Franklin, Tenn., 1898. Author's Copy

Journal by Ellen Kenton McGaughey Wallace. Unpublished manuscript. Transcribed and edited by James. T. Killebrew, 1988. Kentucky Historical Society, Frankfort, Ky.

Eugene Marshall Papers. Journal, 1862. Rare Book Manuscript and Special Collections Library, Duke University.

Kathleen A. Hauke Collection of Poston Family Papers, Kentucky State University.

McGaughey, R. H., ed. *Life with Grandfather.* Typescript [redacted], 1981. Hopkinsville–Christian County Public Library. Unredacted version in possession of James T. Killebrew.

Stevenson, Daniel. *Journal, 1823–1893.* Typescript, n.d. Library Learning Center: Special Methodist/Kentucky/Biography Collection (SMKB S847), Kentucky Wesleyan College.

REPORTS

The Aaron McNeil House Multi-purpose Community Center. Hopkinsville: Wordcraft Desktop Publishing, 1996.

Annual Report of the Board of Directors to the Kentucky Colonization Society, 1855.

Caron's Hopkinsville Kentucky Municipal Directory, 1910. Reproduced, Russellville, Ky.: A. B. Willhite, n.d.

Centennial Volume, General Association of Kentucky Baptists, 1868–1968.

Guide to Implementation of a Neighborhood Revitalization Initiative for the City of Hopkinsville, Kentucky. Dennison Associates, November 30, 2006.

Negro Year Book, An Annual Encyclopedia of the Negro, 1916–1917. Tuskegee Institute: The Negro Year Book Publishing Co., 1916.

The State of Black America 2009. National Urban League.

BOOKS AND ARTICLES

Alderman, Derek H. "Street Names and the Scaling of Memory: The Politics Commemorating Martin Luther King, Jr., within the African American Community." *Area* 35 (June 2003): 163–73.

Allport, Gordon. *The Nature of Prejudice.* Cambridge: Addison-Wesley, 1954.

Aptheker, Herbert. *American Negro Slave Revolts.* New York: International Publishers, 1943.

Axton, W. F. *Tobacco and Kentucky.* Lexington: The University Press of Kentucky, 1975.

Ball, Edward. *Slaves in the Family.* New York: Ballantine Books, 1998.

Barnes, Kenneth C. *Journey of Hope: The Back-to-Africa Movement in Arkansas in the Late 1800s.* Chapel Hill: University of North Carolina Press, 2004.

Beck, E. M. and Stewart E. Tolnay. "When Race Didn't Matter: Black and White Mob Violence against Their Own Color." In *Under Sentence of Death: Lynching in the South*, edited by W. Fitzhugh Brundage, 132–54. Chapel Hill: University of North Carolina Press, 1997.

Berlin, Ira. *Slaves Without Masters: The Free Negro in the Antebellum South*. New York: Pantheon Books, 1974.

———. "American Slavery in History and Memory and the Search for Social Justice." *The Journal of American History* 90 (March 2004), 1251–68.

Berry, Wendell. *The Hidden Wound*. New York: North Point Press, 1989.

Blassingame, John W. *The Slave Community: Plantation Life in the Antebellum South*. New York: Oxford University Press, 1972.

Blight, David W. "Decoration Days: The Origins of Memorial Day in North and South." In *The Memory of the Civil War in American Culture*, edited by Alice Fahs and Joan Waugh, 94–129. Chapel Hill: University of North Carolina Press, 2004.

———. *Race and Reunion: the Civil War in American Memory*. Cambridge: Belknap Press of Harvard University Press, 2001.

Blum, Edward J. *Reforging the White Republic: Race, Religion, and American Nationalism, 1865–1898*. Baton Rouge: Louisiana State University Press, 2005.

Boulton, Alexander O. "The Monticello Mystery—Case Continued." *The William and Mary Quarterly*, 58 (October, 2001): 1039–1046.

Braxton, Joan M., ed. *The Collected Poetry of Paul Laurence Dunbar*. Charlottesville: University of Virginia Press, 1993.

Brodie, Fawn. *Thomas Jefferson, An Intimate History*. New York: Norton, 1974.

Brodkin, Karen. *How Jews Became White Folks and What that Says about Race in America*. New Brunswick: Rutgers University Press, 1998.

Brown, Robert T. *Immigrants to Liberia, 1843–1865: An Alphabetical Listing*. Philadelphia: Institute of Liberia Studies, 1980.

Brundage, W. Fitzhugh. *The Southern Past: A Clash of Race and Memory*. Cambridge, Mass.: Harvard University Press, 2005.

———. "The Roar on the Other Side of Silence: Black Resistance and White Violence in the American South, 1880–1940." In *Under Sentence of Death: Lynching in the South*, edited by W. Fitzhugh Brundage, 271–91. Chapel Hill: University of North Carolina Press, 1997.

———. *Lynching in the New South: Georgia and Virginia, 1880–1930*. Urbana: University of Illinois Press, 1993.

Cade, John B. "Out of the Mouths of Ex-Slaves." *The Journal of Negro History* 20 (July 1935): 294–337.

Campbell, Tracy. *The Politics of Despair: Power and Resistance in the Tobacco Wars.* Lexington: University Press of Kentucky, 1993.

Carney, Court. "The Contested Image of Nathan Bedford Forrest." *Journal of Southern History* 67 (August 2001): 601–30.

Carter, Dan T. "The Anatomy of Fear: The Christmas Day Insurrection Scare of 1865." *The Journal of Southern History* 42 (August 1976): 345–64.

Castel, Albert. "The Fort Pillow Massacre: An Examination of the Evidence." In *Black Flag Over Dixie: Racial Atrocities and Reprisals in the Civil War*, edited by Gregory J. W. Urwin, 89–103. Carbondale: Southern Illinois University Press, 2004.

Cecelski, David S. *Along Freedom Road: Hyde County, North Carolina and the Fate of Black Schools in the South.* Chapel Hill: University of North Carolina Press, 1994.

Clarke, Erskine. *Dwelling Place: A Plantation Epic.* New Haven, Conn.: Yale University Press, 2005.

Clotfelter, Charles T. *After Brown: the Rise and Retreat of School Desegregation.* Princeton: Princeton University Press, 2004.

Collins, Donald E. *The Death and Resurrection of Jefferson Davis.* Lanham, Md.: Rowman and Littlefield, 2005.

Coleman, J. Winston, Jr. *Slavery Times in Kentucky.* Chapel Hill: University of North Carolina Press, 1940.

Coulter, E. Merton. *The Civil War and Readjustment in Kentucky.* Chapel Hill: University of North Carolina Press, 1926.

———. *The South During Reconstruction, 1865–1877.* Baton Rouge: Louisiana State University Press, 1947.

Cunningham, Bill. *A Distant Light: Kentucky's Journey Toward Racial Justice.* Kuttawa, Ky.: McClanahan Publishing House, 2005.

Darling, Marsha. "In the Realm of Responsibility: A Conversation with Toni Morrison." In *Conversations with Toni Morrison*, edited by Danille Taylor-Guthrie, 246–54. Jackson: University Press of Mississippi, 1994.

Davis, William C. *Jefferson Davis: The Man and His Hour.* New York: HarperCollins, 1991.

Degler, Carl N. *The Other South: Southern Dissenters in the Nineteenth Century.* New York: Harper and Row, 1974.

Dew, Charles B. "Black Ironworkers and the Slave Insurrection Panic of 1856." *The Journal of Southern History* 41 (August, 1975): 321–38.

———. *Apostles of Disunion.* Charlottesville: University of Virginia Press, 2001.

Douglas, Mary. *Purity and Danger.* London: Routledge and Kegan Paul, 1966.

———, ed. *Witchcraft Confessions and Accusations.* London: Tavistock Publications, 1970.

Douglass, Frederick. *Narrative of the Life of Frederick Douglass, An American Slave, Written by Himself.* Edited by David W. Blight. Boston: Bedford Books, 1993.

Doyle, William. *An American Insurrection: The Battle of Oxford, Mississippi.* New York: Doubleday, 2001.

Dray, Philip. *At the Hands of Persons Unknown: The Lynching of Black America.* New York: Random House, 2002.

Du Bois, W. E. B. *Black Folk, Then and Now.* New York: Henry Holt, 1939.

———. "The Freedmen's Bureau." *Atlantic Monthly* 87 (1901): 354–65.

———. *Black Reconstruction in America, 1860–1880.* Cleveland: The World Publishing Co., 1964. First published 1935.

———. *The Souls of Black Folk.* New York: Penguin Books, 1995. First published 1903.

Elkins, Stanley. *Slavery: A Problem in American Institutional and Intellectual Life.* Chicago: University of Chicago Press, 1959.

Escott, Paul. *Slavery Remembered: A Record of Twentieth Century Slave Narratives.* Chapel Hill: University of North Carolina Press, 1979.

Eskew, Glenn T. "Black Elitism and the Failure of Paternalism in Postbellum Georgia: The Case of Bishop Lucius Henry Holsey." *The Journal of Southern History* 58 (November 1992): 637–66.

Foner, Eric. *Reconstruction, America's Unfinished Revolution: 1863–1877.* New York: Harper Collins, 2005.

———. *Freedom's Lawmakers: A Directory of Black Officeholders during Reconstruction.* Baton Rouge: Louisiana State University Press, 1996.

———. *Who Owns History?* New York: Hill and Wang, 2002.

Franklin, John Hope. *George Washington Williams, a Biography.* Durham: Duke University Press, 1998.

———. "Slavery and the Martial South." In *Race and History: Selected Essays, 1938–1988.* Baton Rouge: Louisiana State University Press, 1989.

Frazier, E. Franklin. *Black Bourgeoisie.* New York: Free Press, 1957.

Frisby, Derek W. "'Remember Fort Pillow!': Politics, Atrocity Propaganda, and the Evolution of Hard War." In *Black Flag Over Dixie: Racial Atrocities and Reprisals in the Civil War*, edited by Gregory J. W. Urwin, 104–31. Carbondale: Southern Illinois University Press, 2004.

Gates, Henry Louis Jr. *Colored People*. New York: Vintage Books, 1995.

Geertz, Clifford. "Thick Description: Toward an Interpretative Theory of Culture." In *The Interpretation of Culture: Selected Essays of Clifford Geertz*. New York: Basic Books, 1973.

Genovese, Eugene D. *From Rebellion to Revolution: Afro-American Slave Revolts in the Making of the Modern World*. Baton Rouge: Louisiana State University Press, 1979.

———. *Roll, Jordan, Roll: The World the Slaves Made*. New York: Vintage Books, 1976.

Gerstle, Gary. *American Crucible*. Princeton: Princeton University Press, 2001.

Gimpel, James G. *Separate Destinations: Migration, Immigration, and the Politics of Places*. Ann Arbor: University of Michigan Press, 1999.

Glazier, Jack. *Dispersing the Ghetto: The Relocation of Jewish Immigrants across America*. Ithaca: Cornell University Press, 1998.

Gordon-Reed, Annette. *Thomas Jefferson and Sally Hemings: An American Controversy*. Charlottesville: University of Virginia Press, 1997.

Gregory, Rick. "Beliefs of Their Fathers: Violence, Religion, and the Black Patch War, 1904–1914." *Border States On-Line: Journal of the Kentucky-Tennessee American Studies Association* 9 (1993): n.p. http://spider.georgetowncollege.edu/htallant/border/bs9/gregory.htm

Green, Maia. "Witchcraft Suppression Practices and Movements: Public Politics and the Logic of Purification." *Comparative Studies in Society and History* 39 (April 1997): 319–45.

Gutman, Herbert G. *The Black Family in Slavery and Freedom, 1750–1925*. New York: Pantheon Book, 1976.

Harlan, Louis R., ed. *The Booker T. Washington Papers*. Vol. 3, 1893–1895. Urbana: University of Illinois Press, 1974. www.historycooperative.org/btw/vol.3/html

Harris, Robert L., Jr. "Coming of Age: the Transformation of Afro-American Historiography." *Journal of Negro History* 67 (Summer 1982): 107–21.

Hauke, Kathleen A. *Ted Poston, Pioneer American Journalist*. Athens: University of Georgia Press, 1998.

———, ed. *Ted Poston: A First Draft of History*. Athens: University of Georgia Press. 2000.

————, ed. *The Dark Side of Hopkinsville, Stories by Ted Poston.* Athens: University of Georgia Press, 1991.

Herskovits, Melville J. *The Myth of the Negro Past.* New York: Harper and Brothers, 1941.

Henderson, Mary Bess McCain, et al. *Dear Eliza . . . The Letters of Mitchell Andrew Thompson.* Ames, Iowa: Carter Press, Inc., n.d.

Henry, J. Milton. *The Land Between the Rivers.* Dallas: Taylor Publishing Co., 1976.

Higham, John. *Send These to Me.* Baltimore: The Johns Hopkins University Press, 1975.

Hildebrand, Reginald F. *The Times Were Strange and Stirring: Methodist Preachers and the Crisis of Emancipation.* Durham: Duke University Press, 1995.

Hobsbawm, Eric. "The New Threat to History." *New York Review of Books,* 16 December 1993, 62–64.

Hofstadter, Richard and Michael Wallace, eds. *American Violence: A Documentary History.* New York: Vintage Books, 1970.

Hollinger, David. *Postethnic America: Beyond Multiculturalism.* New York: Basic Books, 1995.

Holloway, Charlene Hampton. *Whitlock's Compositions.* Louisville, Ky.: Char and Chet's, 2004.

Holloway, Karla F. C. *Passed On: African American Mourning Stories.* Durham: Duke University Press, 2003.

hooks , bell. *Bone Black.* New York: Henry Holt, 1996.

Horwitz, Tony. *Confederates in the Attic.* New York: Pantheon Books, 1998.

Howard, Victor B. "The Civil War in Kentucky: The Slave Claims His Freedom." *The Journal of Negro History* 67 (Fall 1982): 245–56.

————. *Black Liberation in Kentucky: Emancipation and Freedom, 1862–1884.* Lexington: University Press of Kentucky, 1983.

Jacobson, Matthew Fry. *Whiteness of a Different Color.* Cambridge, Mass.: Harvard University Press, 1998.

Jordan, Thomas and J. P. Pryor. *The Campaigns of Lieut.-Gen. N. B. Forrest, and of Forrest's Cavalry.* New York: Da Capo Press, 1996. First published 1868.

Kennedy, James and Ronald Kennedy. *Was Jefferson Davis Right?* Gretna, La: Pelican Publishing Co., 1998.

Kennedy, Randall. *The Persistence of the Color Line: Racial Politics and the Obama Presidency.* New York: Pantheon Books, 2011.

Lakey, Othal Hawthorne. *The History of the CME Church*. Memphis: The CME Publishing House, 1985.

Lamont, Michèle. "Introduction: Beyond Taking Culture Seriously." In *The Cultural Territories of Race: Black and White Boundaries*, edited by Michèle Lamont, ix–xx. Chicago: University of Chicago Press, 1999.

Levine, Bruce. *Half Slave and Half Free: The Roots of the Civil War*. New York: Hill and Wang, 1992.

Levine, Lawrence W. *Black Culture and Black Consciousness: Afro-American Folk Thought From Slavery to Freedom*. New York: Oxford University Press, 1977.

Lewis, Oscar. *Five Families: Mexican Case Studies in the Culture of Poverty*. New York: Basic Books, 1959.

Lieberson, Stanley. *A Matter of Taste: How Names, Fashions, and Culture Change*. New Haven: Yale University Press, 2000.

Liebow, Eliot. *Tally's Corner*. Boston: Little, Brown, 1967.

Lincoln, C. Eric. *Discourse and the Construction of Society*. New York: Oxford University Press, 1989.

Lindley, Lenora and Edith L. Bennett. *Spiderwebs, a Steamer-Trunk and Slavery, 1826–1886*. Owensboro, Ky.: Kentucky Typewriter Corp., 1964.

Litwack, Leon F. *Been in the Storm So Long*. New York: Alfred A. Knopf, 1979.

———. *Trouble in Mind: Black Southerners in the Age of Jim Crow*. New York: Alfred A. Knopf, 1998.

———. *How Free Is Free? The Long Death of Jim Crow*. Cambridge, Mass.: Harvard University Press, 2009.

Lowenthal, David. *The Past Is a Foreign Country*. Cambridge, Eng.: Cambridge University Press, 1985.

Lucas, Marion B. *A History of Blacks in Kentucky*. Vol. 1, *From Slavery to Segregation, 1760–1891*. Frankfort: The Kentucky Historical Society, 1992.

Markovitz, Jonathan. *Legacies of Lynching: Racial Violence and Memory*. Minneapolis: University of Minnesota Press, 2004.

Marshall, Anne Elizabeth. "'A Crisis in Our Lives': Kentucky's Separate Coach Law and the African American Response, 1892–1900." *The Register of the Kentucky Historical Society* 98 (Summer 2000): 241–43.

———. *Creating a Confederate Kentucky: The Lost Cause and Civil War Memory in a Border State*. Chapel Hill: University of North Carolina Press, 2010.

Marshall, Suzanne. *Violence in the Black Patch of Kentucky and Tennessee*. Columbia: University of Missouri Press, 1994.

McConnell, Stuart. "Epilogue: The Geography of Memory." In *The Memory of the Civil War in American Culture*, edited by Alice Fahs and Joan Waugh, 258–66. Chapel Hill: University of North Carolina Press, 2004.

McLaurin, Melton A. *Celia, a Slave*. Athens: University of Georgia Press, 1991.

Meacham, Charles M. *A History of Christian County Kentucky: From Oxcart to Airplane*. Nashville: Marshall and Bruce Co., 1930.

Meier, August. "Booker T. Washington and the Rise of the NAACP." In *Along the Color Line: Explorations in the Black Experience*, edited by August Meier and Elliott Rudwick, 75–93. Urbana: University of Illinois Press, 1976.

———, and Elliott Rudwick. *Black History and the Historical Profession, 1915–1980*. Urbana: University of Illinois Press, 1986.

Mercer, S. C. *The Story of a Monument*. New York: Press of Dennison and Brown, 1888.

Merriweather, Claybron W. *Lights and Shadows*. Peducah, Ky.: Evening Sun Job Print, 1907.

———. *The Pleasures of Life: Lyrics of the Lowly, Essays, and Other Poems*. Hopkinsville, Ky.: The New Era Printing Company, 1931.

Miller, Penny M. *Kentucky Politics and Government*. Lincoln: University of Nebraska Press, 1994.

Morrison, Toni. "On the Backs of Blacks." In *Arguing Immigration: Are New Immigrants a Wealth of Diversity Or a Crushing Burden?* edited by Nicholas Mills, 97–100. New York: Touchstone, 1994.

Myrdal, Gunnar. *An American Dilemma*. New York: Harper Bros., 1944.

Nevins, Allan, and Henry Steele Commager. *A Short History of the United States*. New York: Modern Library, 1945.

Nissenbaum, Stephen. *The Battle for Christmas*. New York: Vintage Books, 1996.

Novick, Peter. *That Noble Dream: The "Objectivity Question" and the American Historical Profession*. New York: Cambridge University Press, 1988.

Peck, Elizabeth S. *Berea's First 125 Years*. Lexington: University Press of Kentucky, 1982.

Perrin, William H. *Counties of Todd and Christian, Kentucky: Historical and Biographical*. Chicago: F. A. Battey Publishing Co, 1884.

———. *County of Christian, Kentucky*. Chicago: F. A. Battey Publishing Co., 1884.

Phillips, Ulrich B. *American Negro Slavery*. Baton Rouge: Louisiana State University Press, 1918.

———. *Life and Labor in the Old South*. Boston: Little, Brown, and Co., 1929.

Poston, Ulysses S. "The Negro Awakening." *Current History* 19 (December 1923): 473–80.

Puckett, Newbell Niles. *Black Names in America: Origins and Usage.* Edited by Murray Heller. Boston: G. K. Hall, 1975.

Raboteau, Albert J. *Slave Religion: The "Invisible Institution" in the Antebellum South.* New York: Oxford University Press, 1978.

Radin, Paul. "Status, Phantasy, and the Christian Dogma." In *The American Slave: A Composite Autobiography*, Vol. 19, *God Struck Me Dead*, edited by George P. Rawick, iv–xi. Westport, Conn: Greenwood Publishing Co., 1972. First published 1941.

Rasmussen, Daniel. *American Uprising: the Untold Story of America's Largest Slave Revolt.* New York: HarperLuxe, 2011.

Rawick, George P., ed. *The American Slave: A Composite Autobiography*. Vol. 1, *From Sundown to Sunup: The Making of the Black Community.* Westport: Greenwood Publishing Co., 1972.

Reed, John Shelton. *The Enduring South: Subcultural Persistence in Mass Society.* Chapel Hill: University of North Carolina Press, 1972.

Roediger, David R. *The Wages of Whiteness: Race and the Making of the American Working Class.* London: Verso, 1991.

Sacks, Howard L., and Judith Rose Sacks. *Way Up North in Dixie: A Black Family's Claim to the Confederate Anthem.* Washington, D.C.: Smithsonian Institution Press, 1993.

Sauer, Carl Ortwin. *Geography of the Pennyroyal.* Frankfort: The Kentucky Geological Survey, 1927.

Scott, James C. *Weapons of the Weak: Everyday Forms of Peasant Resistance.* New Haven, Conn.: Yale University Press, 1985.

Sexton, Robert F. "Changes in Our Schools: A Commentary." The Prichard Committee for Academic Excellence, July 2000.

Silber, Nina. *The Romance of Reunion.* Chapel Hill: University of North Carolina Press, 1993.

Simon, F. Kevin, ed. *The WPA Guide to Kentucky.* Lexington: University Press of Kentucky, 1996. First published 1939.

Smith, Lenora Lindley, and Edith L. Bennett. *Spiderwebs, a Steamer-Trunk and Slavery, 1826–1886.* Owensboro, Ky.: Kentucky Typewriter Corporation, 1964.

Spindel, Donna J. "Assessing Memory: Twentieth Century Slave Narratives Reconsidered." *Journal of Interdisciplinary History* 27 (Autumn 1996): 247–61.

Stack, Carol. *All Our Kin.* New York: Harper and Row, 1974.

Stampp, Kenneth. *The Peculiar Institution.* New York: Alfred A. Knopf, 1956.

Starling, Marion Wilson. *The Slave Narrative: Its Place in American History.* Boston: G. K. Hall and Co., 1981.

Steinberg, Stephen. *The Ethnic Myth: Race, Ethnicity, and Class in America.* Boston: Beacon Press, 2001. First published 1981.

Summers, Thomas O., Ed. "The Fourth General Conference of the Methodist Episcopal Church, South." *Quarterly Review of the Methodist Episcopal Church, South,* Vol. XII, New Series, Article V, (1858): 383–92.

Sutherland, Daniel. *The Confederate Carpetbaggers.* Baton Rouge: Louisiana State University Press, 1988.

The Goodspeed Histories of Montgomery, Robertson, Humphreys, Stewart, Dickson, Cheatham and Houston Counties of Tennessee. Columbia, Tenn.: Woodward and Stinson Printing Co, 1972. First published 1886.

Valentine, Charles A. *Culture and Poverty: Critique and Counter-Proposals.* Chicago: University of Chicago Press, 1968.

Verdery, Katherine. *The Political Lives of Dead Bodies: Reburial and Postsocialist Change.* New York: Columbia University Press, 1999.

Waldrep, Christopher. *Night Riders: Defending Community in the Black Patch, 1890–1915.* Durham: Duke University Press, 1993.

Walker, Juliet E. K. "The Legal Status of Free Blacks in Early Kentucky, 1792–1825." *The Filson Club History Quarterly* 57 (1983): 383–95.

Warren, Robert Penn. *Jefferson Davis Gets His Citizenship Back.* Lexington: University Press of Kentucky, 1980.

———. *The Legacy of the Civil War.* Lincoln: University of Nebraska Press, 1998. First published 1961.

Washington, Booker T. *Up from Slavery.* Oxford: Oxford University Press, 1995. First published 1901.

Washington, James Melvin. *Frustrated Fellowship: The Black Baptist Quest for Social Power.* Macon: Mercer University Press, 1986.

Watts, Trent. *One Homogenous People: Narratives of White Southern Identity, 1890–1920.* Knoxville: University of Tennessee Press, 2010.

Webb, Ross A. "'The Past Is Never Dead, It's Not Even Past': Benjamin P. Runkle and the Freedmen's Bureau in Kentucky, 1866–1870." In *The Freedmen's Bureau and Black Freedom*, edited by Donald G. Nieman, 325–42. New York: Garland Publishing, Inc., 1994.

Wiley, Bell I., ed. *Slaves No More: Letters from Liberia 1833–1869.* Lexington: University Press of Kentucky, 1980.

Williams, George Washington. *History of the Negro Race in America from 1619 to 1880.* New York, G. P. Putnam's Sons, 1883.

———. *A History of Negro Troops in the War of Rebellion, 1861–65.* New York: Harper and Brothers, 1888.

Williams, Heather Andrea. *Self-Taught: African American Education in Slavery and Freedom.* Chapel Hill: University of North Carolina Press, 2005.

Wilson, Joseph T. *The Black Phalanx.* New York: Arno Press, 1968. First published 1890.

Wilson, William Julius. *The Declining Significance of Race: Blacks and Changing American Institutions.* Chicago: University of Chicago Press, 1978.

———. "The Moynihan Report and Research on the Black Community." *Annals of the American Academy of Political and Social Science* 621 (January 2009): 34–46.

———. *More Than Just Race: Being Black and Poor in the Inner City.* New York: W. W. Norton, 2009.

Wish, Harvey. "The Slave Insurrection Panic of 1856." *The Journal of Southern History* 5 (May 1939): 206–22.

Wolters, Raymond. *Du Bois and His Rivals.* Columbia: University of Missouri Press, 2002.

Woodson, Carter G. *The History of the Negro Church.* Chapel Hill: Academic Affairs Library, University of North Carolina, 2000. docsouth.unc.edu/church/woodson/woodson.html

Woodward, C. Vann. *The Strange Career of Jim Crow.* 3rd ed. New York: Oxford University Press, 1974.

Wright, George C. "Oral History and the Search for the Black Past in Kentucky." *The Oral History Review,* 10 (1982): 73–91.

———. *Life Behind a Veil: Blacks in Louisville, Kentucky, 1865–1930.* Baton Rouge: Louisiana State University Press, 1985.

———. *Racial Violence in Kentucky, 1865–1940.* Baton Rouge: Louisiana State University Press, 1990.

———. *A History of Blacks in Kentucky,* Vol. 2. Frankfort: Kentucky Historical Society, 1992.

Wright, R. R. *Self-Help in Negro Education.* Cheyney, Pa.: Committee of Twelve for the Advancement of the Interests of the Negro Race, 1909.

INDEX

All geographic entries are located in Kentucky unless otherwise indicated. Page numbers in boldface with the designation "(following)" refer to photograph sections located after pages 71 and 187.

Wheatley, Phillis, 246n79

Whig Party, in 1860 presidential election, 179

White Americans, 6, 12, 22, 29, 102, 147, 206; assistance to freedmen from, 78, 81; Booker T. Washington's popularity among, 119, 120, 122, 126–27; class divisions among, 23, 150–51; economic dependence of blacks on, 73, 111; involvement in 1856 rumored slave rebellion, 41, 49–50; patronage of black institutions, 97–98, 99–102, 106–7; shared past with blacks, 213–14; southern heritage of, 160, 175; violence among, 6–7, 42, 75–80, 82–83, 88, 149; worldview of, 33–34, 38–39. *See also* Black Americans, white stereotypes regarding; black-white racial divide; paternalism, white; paternity, white; slave owners

whiteness: privilege of, 23, 24, 25, 114, 116, 131; studies of, 219n46

white supremacy, 47, 50, 90, 100–102, 161–62; apologists for, 16, 162, 231n61; black conciliation toward, 118, 144; in Hopkinsville, 5–6, 27, 102, 114–18, 170. *See also* domination, racial

Whitlock, Charles, 31

Whitlock, John C., 31

Whitney, Francis Eugene, 131, 133, **187** (following), 248n12; failure to receive mayoral appointment, 196–99, 201, 202

Whitney, James T., 131, 132, 133

Wiley, Bell I., 64, 65, 70

Williams, George Washington, *History of the Negro Race in America from 1619 to 1880*, 185, 186, 187

Williams, Parmelia, 24

Wilson, Joseph T., *The Black Phalanx*, 185–86, 187

Wilson, W. H., labor contract involving, 83–84

Wilson, William Julius, 211, 249–50n37

Wish, Harvey, 39

witch-finding movements, 38

women, black: opposition to KY separate railroad coach law, 137-38. *See also* domestic workers; slaves, sexual exploitation of female; *and individual black women*

women, white, 142–43, 144, 145, 146. *See also* slave owners; *and individual white women*

Wood, Hunter, Sr., 99

Woodson, Carter G., 19, 21, 99–100, 136

Woodward, C. Vann, 136

Works Progress Administration (WPA): *The American Slave: A Composite Autobiography*, 19–20; slave narrative project, 92, 218–19n35

World War II, black soldiers in, 196, 248n12

Wright, George C., 16, 47, 116, 140, 146, 216n13

Wright, Mary, 46

Wright, R. R., Jr., 107

Wright, Tom, 127

Young, Sol, 42